Option Pricing

Mathematical models and computation

Paul Wilmott Oxford University and Imperial College, London

Jeff Dewynne Southampton University

Sam Howison Oxford University

**OXFORD
FINANCIAL
— PRESS —**

Option Pricing: Mathematical Models and Computation

Paul Wilmott	Mathematical Institute 24–29 St. Giles' Oxford OX1 3LB, UK and Department of Mathematics Imperial College London SW7 2BZ, UK
Jeff Dewynne	Department of Mathematics University of Southampton Southampton SO9 5NH, UK
Sam Howison	Mathematical Institute 24–29 St. Giles' Oxford OX1 3LB, UK

Published by Oxford Financial Press, PO Box 348, Oxford OX4 1DR, UK
First edition September 1993; reprinted with corrections May 1994
Typeset in LaTeX
Cover design by Gabrielle Dexter
Printed by Information Press, Southfield Rd, Eynsham, Oxford OX8 1JJ

ISBN 0 9522082 0 2

Preface

This book is based on the lecture notes for a professional development course 'Mathematics Applied to Finance' given at Oxford University. This course is organized by the Department for Continuing Education and the Oxford Centre for Industrial and Applied Mathematics (OCIAM). The delegates on this course have been traders, market makers and researchers from the City of London. We are grateful for the valuable insight into the workings of the financial markets which they have given us. Many of them have made suggestions for the content of the book.

In what follows we describe the modelling of financial derivative products from an applied mathematician's viewpoint. Our intended audience is twofold. Firstly, practitioners with a background in finance will find the mathematical basis of option pricing explained clearly, explicitly and comprehensively, from modelling through analysis to computation. Some mathematics is assumed, but we explain everything that is not contained in the basic calculus, probability and algebra courses of a degree or equivalent in mathematics, physics, chemistry, engineering or similar subjects. Secondly, we give enough detail of the finance that the book can be read by mathematicians whose knowledge of financial markets is only sketchy. It is sufficiently self-contained that it could be used for a course on the subject, on its own or in conjunction either with a more probability-based text such as Duffie (1992) or with a more practically-oriented book such as Hull (1993) or Gemmill (1992).

Our philosophy may be described briefly as follows:

- We present a unified approach to modelling many derivative products as partial differential equations. We make no more fuss over valuing an average strike option (a particularly exotic product) than over valuing the simplest option. There is a minimal use of fudges or approximations.

- We describe the theory of partial differential equations. We explain why they are one of the best approaches to modelling in many physical or financial subjects.

- We do not fear numerical solutions. We would rather have an accurate numerical solution of the correct model than an explicit solution of the wrong model. Explicit solutions are so rare that fast accurate numerical analysis is essential.

The authors of any book on financial models must decide at the outset what will be the mathematical basis of their approach. Essentially, this entails a decision on the amount of more or less rigorous analysis to incorporate, along with a choice whether or not to couch the discussion largely in terms of the language of stochastic processes. We feel that the interests of communication with our readers, especially those at the practical end of the subject, are best served by a relatively informal approach. We have therefore tried to stress the intuitive aspects of the subject, and this has led us naturally to emphasise the derivation and use of differential equations and associated numerical techniques. We hope that the rigour thereby forgone is compensated for by improved directness. We emphasise that there are excellent texts that fully cover more theoretical aspects of the subject.

The first chapter is an introduction to the subject of option pricing and markets. It is aimed at the reader who is new to the financial side of the subject and it contains no technical mathematical material.

Chapter 2 opens with a description of the movement of asset prices as a random walk. The underlying basis for the models used thereafter is that the future value of asset prices cannot be predicted with certainty. This does not mean that the movements cannot be modelled, only that any such model must incorporate a degree of randomness. We see that, despite the random nature of asset prices, there are many problems for which we can make deterministic (that is, not probabilistic) statements. It is fortunate that such problems also happen to be the most interesting and important financially. Later in this chapter we describe the methods of stochastic calculus, building intuitively on the ideas of ordinary calculus.

In Chapter 3 the mathematical modelling becomes more explicitly related to option pricing. This chapter is perhaps the most important in the book. In it we present the cornerstone of the subject of option pricing: the derivation of the original Black–Scholes partial differential equation for the value of an option. After deriving this equation we discuss the boundary conditions for different types of option, including options on dividend paying assets and American options.

The fact that partial differential equations prove to be central to our approach to financial modelling provides the motivation for the next four chapters. The type of partial differential equation that occurs most often in financial theory is the parabolic partial differential equation, the canonical example of which is the heat or diffusion equation. Posing the problems in the form of a parabolic partial differential equation means that we have more than a century's worth of theory on which to call. Once the problem has been presented in such a form we may consider ourselves to be on well-known territory.

In Chapter 4 we discuss two types of linear partial differential equation: the first order and the parabolic second order. We describe the boundary conditions needed to give unique solutions. In Chapter 5 the diffusion equation is dealt with in some detail. The general solution of the initial value problem on the whole line is derived and used to deduce the Black–Scholes formulæ for European call and put options. In Chapter 6 we then consider free boundary problems, in particular those arising from models of American options where the possibility of early exercise gives rise to a free boundary. An asymptotic description of the behaviour of the optimal exercise boundary for times immediately before expiry is derived. The American option problem is formulated as a variational inequality in Chapter 7. The theory of this chapter sets the scene for the numerical solution of free boundary problems. In Chapter 8 we discuss modifications necessary to account for the payment of dividends and then derive explicit formulæ for option prices when parameters are time-dependent.

Having dealt with the necessary basic theory, we come to some more advanced subjects in mathematical finance in Chapters 9–15. These chapters deal with path-dependent options, options in the presence of transaction costs, stochastic interest rates and bond pricing. In Chapter 9 we derive a general theory for options depending on history functionals of asset prices and give several examples in detail. Three exotic options have individual chapters to themselves: barrier options in Chapter 10, Asian options in Chapter 11 and lookback options in Chapter 12. In Chapter 13 we consider a simple model for options in the presence of transaction costs. These can affect option prices quite significantly, and the model we discuss is of both practical importance and mathematical interest.

In the first thirteen chapters the only random variable in our problems is the asset price. In Chapter 14 we consider the pricing of bonds; this entails the introduction of a simple stochastic model for the short-term interest rate. We also mention the pricing of bond options. In Chapter 15 we briefly show how to value convertible bonds; these bonds can have a value that depends on *two* random variables, an underlying asset and an interest rate.

Many of the models we derive do not admit closed form solutions. While it might be possible to modify them so that they can be solved in closed form, such modifications would probably have no basis in financial reality. We prefer, therefore, to accept that, for many practical problems, numerical methods of solution are necessary. The final chapters of the book are devoted to this topic.

Numerical methods are introduced and discussed generally in Chapter 16. In Chapter 17, we introduce finite differences for continuous models. In Chapter 18 we demonstrate the explicit finite-difference method in some detail, discussing the important questions of stability and convergence. The various forms of implicit finite-difference methods are described in Chapter 19: they include the fully implicit, Crank–Nicolson and θ-methods.

In Chapter 20 we discuss the numerical solution of free boundary problems, again with particular emphasis on finite-difference methods. This leads on, in Chapter 21, to the numerical solution of American option problems. The final chapter on numerical methods, Chapter 22, gives details of how to solve exotic option problems. The average strike option is discussed in detail.

At the end of the book are five appendices covering related but slightly tangential topics and one appendix containing a summary of many of our models. In Appendix A we show how to find probability density functions for random variables and derive the Kolmogorov and Fokker–Planck equations. In Appendix B we consider first exit time problems, which are important in American and barrier options. In Appendix C we discuss the application of binomial and trinomial models to the valuation of a variety of options, including path-dependent options. In Appendix D we describe the numerical method of finite elements. Finally, in Appendix E we bring together many of the partial differential equation models for option prices in an accessible form. This reference guide contains a list of equations and boundary conditions.

We would like to thank the following for their advice and encouragement: Stuart Wheeler and Robert Sheehan of IG Index Ltd, Michael Adam, Brian Draper, David Harding, Martin Lueck, David Huyton and Tim Hoggard of Adam Harding & Lueck Ltd, Mark Blundell of Oxford Trading & Research Ltd, Simon Babbs of Midland Montagu, Robert Campbell of Salomon Brothers, Arjan Shahani of the University of Southampton, Mohammed Apabhai, Man-Wai Chiu, Miguel Hidalgo, Fouad Khennach, Robert Klugman, Lothar Lemp, Immo Rupf and Elizabeth Whalley, graduate students at Oxford, Chris Harris, Adam Hartley, Rob Hutchings, Steve Miller, John Ockendon and Alan Tayler of Oxford University, Colin Atkinson, John Barrett and Gerald Moore of Imperial College, Karen Mason of the Prudential Assurance Company Ltd, Maureen Doherty, Laura Duffy and Gaynor Evans of Rewley House, Oxford, Gil Strang of MIT and Cambridge-Wellesley Press, and especially Alistair Fitt of the University of Southampton.

Technical Point

Throughout the book, at the end of many sections and subsections, are scattered 'Technical Points'. As the name suggests, these items describe some of the more technical matters in our subject, matters which would disrupt the flow if contained in the main body of the text, yet which are too large to appear as footnotes. These items may be ignored on a first reading.

Occasionally, some words or phrases appear in **bold face**. *This means that such a word or phrase is being defined. In some cases this definition is technical and in others simply descriptive.*

Contents

Chapter 1

An Introduction to Options and Markets

1.1 What is an option?

The simplest financial option, a **European call option**, is a contract with the following conditions:

- At a prescribed time in the future, known as the **expiry date**, the owner of the option *may*
- purchase a prescribed asset, known as the **underlying asset** or, briefly, the **underlying**, for a
- prescribed amount, known as the **exercise price** or **strike price**.

The word 'may' in this description implies that for the holder of the option, this contract is a *right* and not an *obligation*. (The other party to the contract, who is known as the **writer**, *does* have a potential obligation: he must sell the asset if the holder chooses to buy it.) Since the option confers on its holder a right with no obligation it has some value. Moreover, it must be paid for at the time of opening the contract. (Conversely, the writer of the option must be compensated for the obligation he has assumed.) One of our main concerns throughout this book is to find this value:

- How much would one pay for this right?

A simple example

How much is the following option now worth? Today's date is 22nd August 1993.

- On 14th April 1994 the owner of the option may
- purchase one XYZ share for 250p.

In order to gain an intuitive feel for the price of this option let us imagine two possible situations that might occur on the expiry date, 14th April 1994, nearly eight months in the future.

If the XYZ share price is 270p on 14th April 1994 then the owner of the option would be able to purchase the asset for only 250p. This action, which is called **exercising** the option, yields an immediate profit of 20p. That is, he can buy the share for 250p and immediately sell it for 270p:

$$270\text{p} - 250\text{p} = 20\text{p} \ \text{ profit.}$$

On the other hand, if the XYZ share price is only 230p on 14th April 1994 then it would not be sensible to exercise the option. Why buy something for 250p when it can be bought for 230p elsewhere?

If the XYZ share only takes the values 230p or 270p on 14th April 1994, with equal probability, then the expected profit to be made is

$$\tfrac{1}{2} \times 0 \ + \ \tfrac{1}{2} \times 20 = 10\text{p}.$$

Ignoring interest rates for the moment, it seems reasonable that the order of magnitude for the value of the option is 10p.

Of course, valuing an option is not as simple as this, but let us suppose that the owner did indeed pay 10p for this option. Now if the share price rises to 270p at expiry he has made a net profit calculated as follows:

profit on exercise	=	20p
cost of option	=	-10p
net profit	=	10p

This net profit of 10p is 100% of the up-front premium. The downside of this speculation is that if the share price is less than 250p at expiry he has lost all of the 10p invested in the option, giving a loss of 100%.

Option prices thus respond in an exaggerated way to changes in the underlying asset price. This effect is called **gearing**.

We can see from this simple example that the greater the share price on 14th April 1994, the greater the profit. Unfortunately, we do not know this share price in advance. However, it seems reasonable that the higher the share price is now (and this is something we *do* know) then the higher the price is likely to be in the future. Thus the value of a call option *today* depends on today's share price. Similarly, the dependence of the call option value on the exercise price is obvious: the lower the exercise price, the less that has to be paid on exercise, and so the higher the option value.

Implicit in this is that the option is to expire a significant time in the future. Just before the option is about to expire, there is little time for the asset price to change. In that case the price at expiry is known with a fair degree of certainty. We can conclude that the call option price must also be a function of the time to expiry.

Later we also see how the option price depends on a property of the 'randomness' of the asset price, the volatility. The larger the volatility, the more jagged is the graph of asset price against time and the more probable a profitable outcome at expiry. The value of a call option should increase with increasing volatility. Finally, the option price must depend on prevailing bank interest rates; the option is usually paid for up-front at the opening of the contract whereas the payoff, if any, does not come until later. The option price should reflect the income that would otherwise have been earned by investing the premium in the bank.

The option to *buy* an asset discussed above is known as a **call** option. The right to *sell* an asset is known as a **put** option and has payoff properties which are opposite to those of a call. A put option allows its owner to sell the asset on a certain date for a prescribed amount. Whereas the owner of a call option wants the asset price to rise—the higher the asset price at expiry the greater the profit—the owner of a put option wants the asset price to fall as low as possible.

1.2 Arbitrage

One of the fundamental concepts underlying the theory of option pricing is that of **arbitrage**. This can be loosely stated as 'there's no such thing as a free lunch'. More formally, in financial terms, there are never any opportunities to make an instantaneous risk-free profit. (More correctly, such opportunities cannot exist for a significant length of time before prices move to eliminate them.) The financial application of this principle leads to some elegant modelling.

Almost all finance theory, this book included, assumes the existence of **risk-free** investments that give a guaranteed return[1] with no chance of default. A good approximation to such an investment is a government bond or a deposit in a sound bank. The greatest risk-free return that one can make on a portfolio of assets is the same as the return if the equivalent amount of cash were placed in a bank.

The key words in the definition of arbitrage are 'instantaneous' and 'risk-free'; by investing in equities, say, one can *probably* beat the bank, but this cannot be *certain*. If one wants a greater return then one must accept a greater risk. Why should this be so? Suppose that an opportunity did exist to make a guaranteed return of greater magnitude than from a bank deposit. Suppose also that most investors behave sensibly. Would any sensible investor put money in the bank when putting it in the alternative investment yields a greater return? Obviously not. Moreover, if he could also borrow money at less than the return on the alternative investment then he should borrow as much as possible from the bank to invest in the higher-yielding opportunity. In response to the pressure of supply and demand we would expect the bank to raise its interest rates to attract money and/or the yield from the other investment to drop. There is some elasticity in this argument because of the presence of 'friction' factors such as transaction costs, differences in borrowing and lending rates, problems with liquidity, tax laws, etc., but on the whole the principle is sound since the market place *is* inhabited by **arbitragers** whose (highly paid) job it is to seek out and exploit irregularities or mispricings such as the one we have just illustrated.

---

[1]As explained in Chapter 14, the return available may depend on the time for which the deposit is made; the different rates available for different periods reflect the possibility that interest rates may change in the future. We assume that a known guaranteed return is always available for a period equal to the lifetime of our option.

Technical Point: risk.

Risk *is commonly described as being of two types: specific and non-specific. (The latter is also called market or systematic risk.) Specific risk is the component of risk associated with a single asset (or a sector of the market, for example chemicals), whereas non-specific risk is associated with factors affecting the whole market. An unstable management would affect an individual company but not the market; this company would show signs of specific risk, a highly volatile share price perhaps. On the other hand the possibility of a change in interest rates would be a non-specific risk, as such a change would affect the market as a whole.*

It is often important to distinguish between these two types of risk because of their behaviour within a large portfolio. Provided one has a sensible definition of risk, it is possible to diversify away specific risk by having a portfolio with a large number of assets from different sectors of the market; however, it is not possible to diversify away non-specific risk[2]*. It is commonly said that specific risk is not rewarded, and that only the taking of greater non-specific risk should be rewarded by a greater return.*

A popular definition of the risk of a portfolio is the variance of the return. A bank account which has a guaranteed return, at least in the short term, has no variance and is thus termed riskless or risk-free. On the other hand, a highly volatile stock with a very uncertain return and thus a large variance is a risky asset. This is the simplest and commonest definition of risk, but it does not take into account the distribution of the return, but rather only one of its properties, the variance. Thus as much weight is attached to the possibility of a greater than expected return as to the possibility of a less than expected return. Other, more sophisticated, definitions of risk avoid this property and attach different weights to different returns.

---

[2] Market risk can be eliminated from a portfolio by taking opposite positions in two assets which are highly negatively correlated—as one increases in value the other decreases. This is not diversification but 'hedging' which, as we see below, is of the utmost importance in option pricing.

1.3 Reading the financial press

Armed with the jargon of calls, puts, expiry dates etc., we are in a position to read the options pages in the financial press. Our examples are taken from the *Financial Times* of Thursday 4th February 1993.

In Figure 1.1 is shown the options section of the *Financial Times*. This table shows the prices of some of the options traded on the London International Financial Futures and Options Exchange (LIFFE). The table lists the last quoted prices on the previous day for a large number of options, both calls and puts, with a variety of exercise prices and expiry dates. Most of these examples are options on individual equities, but at the bottom of the third column we see options on the *FT-SE* index, which is a weighted arithmetic average of 100 equity shares quoted on the London Stock Exchange.

First, let us concentrate on the prices quoted for Rolls-Royce options, to be found in the third column labelled 'R. Royce'. Immediately beneath R. Royce is the number 134 in parentheses. This is the closing price, in pence, of Rolls-Royce shares on the previous day. To the right of R. Royce/(134) are the two numbers 130 and 140: these are two exercise prices, again in pence. Note that for equity options the *Financial Times* only prints the exercise price each side of the closing price. Many other exercise prices exist (at intervals of 10p in this case) but are not printed in the *Financial Times* for want of space.

Examine the six numbers to the right of the 130. The first three (11, 15, 19) are the prices of call options with different expiry dates and the next three (9, 14, 17) are the prices of put options. The expiry date of each of these options can be found by looking at the top of each column. There we see that Rolls-Royce has options expiring in March, June and September. Option prices are only quoted on an exchange for a small number of expiry dates and only for exercise prices at discrete intervals (here ..., 130, 140, ...). For LIFFE-traded options on equities the expiry dates come in intervals of three months. When it is created, the longest dated option has a lifespan of nine months. Later in the year the December series of Rolls-Royce options will come into being.

Since a call option permits the owner to pay the exercise price

LIFFE EQUITY OPTIONS

Option		CALLS Apr	CALLS Jul	CALLS Oct	PUTS Apr	PUTS Jul	PUTS Oct
Alld Lyons	550	48	60	68	10	24	30
(°585)	600	22	34	44	34	50	55
ASDA	57	9	12½	14	4	7	9
(°61)	67	4	8	9	8½	11½	14
Brit. Airways	280	27	33	39	9½	20	24
(°296)	300	17	24	29	18	30	34
SmKl Bchm A	460	30	47	53	17	26	52
(°470)	500	13	27	36	42	48	54
Boots	500	23	32	43	21	33	37
(°501)	550	6½	15	23	56	67	70
B.P.	260	16½	23	29	11	17	21
(°265)	280	8	15	19	22	28	34
British Steel	70	13	16½	19	3½	6½	8½
(°79)	80	8	12	14	7½	11½	13
Bass	600	31	48	61	24	38	45
(°604)	650	12	27	39	58	70	73
C & Wire	700	40	60	70	25	43	50
(°710)	750	18	35	46	56	73	80
Courtaulds	550	40	52	61	17	30	37
(°568)	600	16	29	38	45	60	64
Com. Union	600	35	49	57	21	32	40
(°623)	650	11	26	34	53	61	70
Fisons	220	22	31	39	18	30	35
(°222)	240	14	22	31	31	43	48
GKN	460	27	36	45	21	28	34
(°472)	500	8½	20	28	48	53	57
Grand Met.	420	38	53	59	11	21	27
(°439)	460	16	31	36	30	41	47
I.C.I.	1100	53	82	92	50	68	88
(°1132)	1150	31	62	72	80	100	117
Kingfisher	550	34	48	53	21	38	45
(°559)	600	12	25	33	52	68	73
Ladbroke	200	16	25	29	18	26	32
(°202)	220	8	16	22	32	38	44
Land Secur	460	45	49	53	5	17	21
(°493)	500	17	25	31	20	38	41
M & S	330	18	25	34	12	20	24
(°333)	360	6	12	20	32	38	41
Sainsbury	550	43	54	63	12	24	29
(°577)	600	16	28	38	38	50	56
Shell Trans.	550	32	44	50	12	19	26
(°576)	600	6	19	25	44	47	53
Storehouse	200	18	26	34	8	17	18
(°204)	220	11	17	22	21	25	28
Trafalgar	90	11	14	18	8	9	13
(°93)	100	6½	11	14	12	17	18
Utd. Biscuits	360	18	25	33	19	25	29
(°366)	390	6	14	20	41	45	49
Unilever	1100	72	90	110	16	35	42
(°1149)	1150	39	60	82	42	56	63

Option		Feb	May	Aug	Feb	May	Aug
Brit Aero	280	23	40	53	16	34	46
(°287)	300	14	33	47	27	49	60

Option		CALLS Feb	CALLS May	CALLS Aug	PUTS Feb	PUTS May	PUTS Aug
BAA	750	41	61	71	6	16	31
(°786)	800	11	33	45	29	41	55
BAT Inds	950	45	58	74	8	37	46
(°982)	1000	16	33	50	30	64	73
BTR	550	22	30	38	5½	20	28
(°565)	600	3	10	19	38	53	55
Brit. Telecom	420	10	23	29	7	15	24
(°420)	460	1	8	12½	40	41	50
Cadbury Sch	460	15	25	35	8	24	30
(°465)	500	3½	10	19	37	51	55
Eastern Elec	400	18	32	-	6	15	-
(°411)	430	5	-	-	24	-	-
Guinness	460	24	36	46	8	25	30
(°473)	500	6	19	28	33	48	56
GEC	300	9	19	23	7	13	21
(°301)	330	1	7	11	30	32	41
Hanson	260	7½	14½	18	5½	12	16½
(°262)	280	1	5½	9½	20	25	28
LASMO	160	8	18	22	9	18	23
(°161)	180	3	8½	15	24	33	36
Lucas Inds	140	15	23	26	4	11	16
(°151)	160	4	13	17	14	24	28
P. & O.	550	24	42	52	15	40	52
(°564)	600	5½	21	33	45	72	82
Pilkington	100	7	15	18	6	12	16
(°102)	110	4	10	14	12	17	22
Prudential	300	24	30	34	2½	11	15
(°321)	330	6	13	19	14	26	31
R.T.Z.	650	34	47	60	9	30	40
(°672)	700	10	25	39	36	59	69
Scot. & New	420	23	38	45	5	13	24
(°343)	460	4½	17	24	26	35	48
Tesco	240	22	27	30	2	8	12
(°257)	260	7	14	21	9	19	22
Thames Wtr	460	24	37	42	3½	12	22
(°479)	500	3½	16	20	25	32	45
Vodafone	390	18	34	43	8	21	28
(°398)	420	5½	19	29	27	36	45

Option		Mar	Jun	Sep	Mar	Jun	Sep
Abbey Nat.	360	28	34	42	11	17	23
(°379)	390	11	19	27	27	33	38
Amstrad	20	5½	6½	7½	1½	1½	2½
(°24)	25	2½	3½	4½	3½	4	4½
Barclays	420	45	54	59	11	21	30
(°458)	460	20	33	38	33	41	51
Blue Circle	220	22	30	35	10	21	27
(°230)	240	12	19	27	22	33	39
British Gas	280	15½	19	23	6½	15	18
(°287)	300	6½	9½	14	18	27	30
Dixons	220	15	25	28	13	19	25
(°221)	240	8	17	21	26	31	38
Eurotunnel	420	38	55	70	20	35	45
(°435)	460	18	37	50	45	57	67

Option		CALLS Mar	CALLS Jun	CALLS Sep	PUTS Mar	PUTS Jun	PUTS Sep
Glaxo	650	38	60	82	29	42	52
(°664)	700	17	38	58	60	72	80
Hillsdown	140	17	22	24	6	15	20
(°147)	160	6	12	16	18	27	31
Lonrho	70	9	12	15	5	8½	11
(°75)	80	4½	8	11½	11	14	17
HSBC 75p shs	550	45	57	70	17	34	46
(°576)	600	18	32	48	44	60	70
Natl Power	280	24	32	36	6	11	18
(°294)	300	11	21	25	15	20	27
Reuters	1400	69	108	135	47	78	100
(°1426)	1450	40	82	113	78	103	122
R. Royce	130	11	15	19	9	14	17
(°134)	140	6	11	16	16	20	23
Scot Power	200	20	25	28	2	5	10½
(°216)	220	6	13	17	9	13½	22
Sears	100	9	11	15	5	8½	11
(°104)	110	4	7	9½	10	14	16
Forte	180	15	20	25	10	19	24
(°186)	200	7	13	17	21	32	36
Thorn EMI	800	61	81	90	10	22	39
(°843)	850	28	50	60	29	43	66
TSB	160	19	23	27	5	8½	12
(°176)	180	6½	13	17	15	18	22
Vaal Reefs	30	6	6	6½	3	4	4½
(°$34)	35	2	4	5½	5½	6	8
Wellcome	850	50	75	100	28	48	63
(°866)	900	26	52	75	57	77	92

EURO FT-SE INDEX (°2872)

	2675	2725	2775	2825	2875	2925	2975	3025
CALLS								
Feb	205	155	108	68	36	16	5	2
Mar	215	170	129	92	61	38	22	11
Apr	-	188	-	115	-	61	-	28
Jun	-	217	-	152	-	100	-	60
Sep	-	252	-	188	-	129	-	-
PUTS								
Feb	1½	3½	7	15	34	65	104	151
Mar	9	12	21	34	53	81	114	153
Apr	-	26	-	51	-	97	-	163
Jun	-	50	-	80	-	125	-	185
Sep	-	-	-	120	-	-	-	-

FT-SE INDEX (°2872)

	2650	2700	2750	2800	2850	2900	2950	3000
CALLS								
Feb	233	183	135	89	50	24	9	3
Mar	243	197	153	113	79	51	31	17
Apr	254	210	170	131	99	73	51	36
May	266	226	186	151	121	93	72	52
Jun	-	235	-	164	-	107	-	67
Dec †	-	-	-	235	-	187	-	130
PUTS								
Feb	1½	2½	4½	10	23	47	85	131
Mar	8	12	17	29	46	69	100	138
Apr	16	22	31	44	63	86	116	151
May	26	35	45	61	80	105	133	166
Jun	-	40	-	70	-	113	-	175
Dec †	-	90	-	125	-	185	-	-

February 3 Total Contracts 31,257
Calls 21,861 Puts 9,396
FT-SE Index Calls 7,946 Puts 4,410
Euro FT-SE Calls 816 Puts 278
°Underlying security price. † Long dated expiry mths
Premiums shown are based on closing offer prices.

Figure 1.1: The options section of the *Financial Times* of 4th February 1993.

to obtain the asset, we can see that call options with exercise price 140p are cheaper than those with exercise price 130p. This is because more must be paid for the share at exercise. The converse is true for puts: the owner of a 140p put can realise more by selling the share at exercise than the owner of a 130p put, and so the former is worth more.

Now let us look at the options on the *FT-SE* index. Towards the bottom of the third column we see prices for the *FT-SE* index call options with exercise prices at 50p intervals from 2650 to 3000 and expiry dates at monthly intervals. (Although the index is just a number it is given a nominal price in pence equal to its numerical value.) Since options typically expire around the middle of the month the February options have only about 10 days left. In Figure 1.2 we plot the value of the February call options against exercise price.

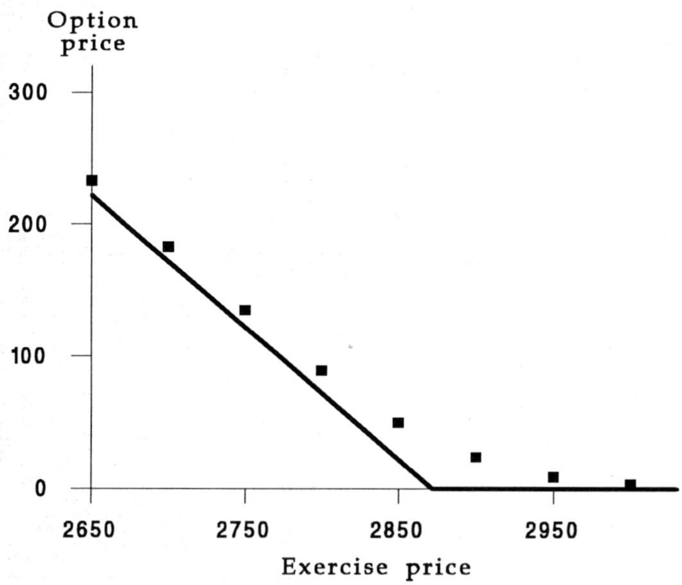

Figure 1.2: The *FT-SE* index call option values versus exercise price and the option values at expiry assuming that the index value is then 2872.

The closing value of the *FT-SE* index on 3rd February 1993 was 2872. Suppose that the *FT-SE* index did not change between 4th February and expiry. Then the value of each call option at expiry would be the 'ramp function'

$$\begin{array}{ll} 2872 - \text{exercise price} & \text{for exercise price} \leq 2872 \\ 0 & \text{for exercise price} \geq 2872. \end{array}$$

In Figure 1.2 we also plot this ramp function. Notice that the data points are close to but above the ramp function. The difference between the two is due to the indeterminacy in the future index value: the index is unlikely to be at 2872 at the time of expiry of the February options. We return to the example of the *FT-SE* index call options in Chapter 3.

Finally, note that for each option type there is only one quoted price in this table. In reality the option could not be bought and sold for the same price since the market maker has to make a living. Thus there are *two* prices for the option. The difference between the two prices is known as the bid-ask or bid-offer spread; the investor pays the ask (or offer) price and sells for the bid price, which is less than the ask price. The price quoted in the newspapers is usually a mid-price, the average of the bid and ask prices.

Technical Point: the trading of options.

Before 1973 all option contracts were what is now called 'over-the-counter' (OTC). That is, they were individually negotiated by a broker on behalf of two clients, one being the buyer and the other the seller. Trading on an official exchange began in 1973 on the Chicago Board Options Exchange (CBOE), with trading initially only in call options on some of the most heavily traded stocks. With the listing of options on an exchange the cost of setting up an option contract decreased significantly due to the increased competition.

Options are now traded on all of the world's major exchanges. They are no longer restricted to equity options but include options on indices, futures, government-bonds, commodities, currencies etc. The OTC market still exists and options are written by institutions to meet a client's needs. This is where exotic options contracts are created; they are very rarely quoted on an exchange.

When an option contract is first initiated there must be two sides to the agreement. Consider a call option. On one side of the contract is the buyer, the party who has the right to exercise the option. On the other side is the party who must, if required, deliver the underlying asset. The latter is called the **writer** *of the option.*

Many options are registered and settled via a **clearing house**. *This central body is also responsible for the collection of* **margin** *from the writers of options. This margin is a sum of money (or equivalent) which is held by the clearing house on behalf of the writer. It is a guarantee that he is able to meet his obligations should the asset price move against him.*

The trade in the simplest call and put options (colloquially called **vanilla** *options, because they are ubiquitous) is now so great that it can, in some markets, have a value in excess of that of the trade in the underlying. In some cases too the exchange-traded options are more liquid than the underlying asset. To give an idea of the size*[3] *of the derivatives (including futures) markets, there is an estimated $10,000* billion *in derivatives investments worldwide in total (this is a gross figure; the net figure is much smaller). Citicorp alone has an estimated exposure equivalent to a notional contract value of $1,426bn. As the number and type of derivative products have increased so there has been a corresponding growth in option pricing as a subject for academic and corporate research. This is especially true today as increasingly exotic types of option are created.*

1.4 What are options for?

Options have two primary uses: speculation and hedging. An investor who believes that a particular stock, XYZ again, say, is going to rise can purchase some shares in that company. If he is correct, he makes money, if he is wrong he loses money. This investor is speculating. If the share price rises from 250p to 270p he makes a profit of 20p or 8%. If it falls to 230p he makes a loss of 20p or 8%. Alternatively, suppose that he thinks that the share price is going to rise within the next couple of months and that he buys a call with

[3]These values are taken from a review of the derivatives market in the *Financial Times* of 8th December 1992.

exercise price 250p and expiry date in three months' time. We have seen in the earlier example that if such an option costs 10p then the profit or loss is magnified to 100%. Options can be a cheap way of exposing a portfolio to a large amount of risk.

If, on the other hand, the investor thinks that XYZ shares are going to fall he can do one of two things: sell shares or buy puts. If he speculates by selling shares that he does not own (which in certain circumstances is perfectly legal in many markets) he is selling **short** and will profit from a fall in XYZ shares. (The opposite of a short position is a **long** position.) The same argument concerning the exaggerated movement of option prices applies to puts as well as calls and he may decide to buy puts instead of selling the asset. However, the investor may own XYZ shares as a long-term investment. In this case he might wish to insure against a temporary fall in the share price, while being reluctant to liquidate his XYZ holdings only to buy them back again later, possibly at a higher price if his view of the share price is wrong, and certainly having incurred some transaction costs on the two deals.

The discussion so far has been from the point of view of the holder of an option. Let us now consider the position of the other party to the contract, the writer. While the holder of a call option has the possibility of an arbitrarily large payoff, with the loss limited to the initial premium, the writer has the possibility of an arbitrarily large *loss*, with the profit limited to the initial premium. Similarly, but to a lesser extent, writing a put option exposes the writer to large potential losses for a profit limited to the initial premium. One could therefore ask

- Why would anyone write an option?

The first likely answer is that the writer of an option expects to make a profit by taking a view on the market. Writers of calls are, in effect, taking a short position in the underlying; they expect its value to fall. It is usually argued that such people must be present in the market, for if everyone expected the value of a particular asset to rise its market price would be higher than, in fact, it is. (Such people are also potential customers for put options on the underlying.) Similarly, there must also be people who believe that the value of the underlying will rise (or the price would be lower than, in fact, it is). These latter people are potential writers of put options and buyers of call options. An extension of this argument is that writers of options are using them as insurance against adverse movements in the underlying, in the same way as holders do.

Although this motivation is plausible, it is not the whole story. Market makers have to make a living, and in doing so they cannot necessarily afford to bear the risk of taking exposed positions. Instead, their profit comes from selling at slightly above the 'true value' and buying at slightly below; the less risk associated with this policy, the better. This idea of reducing risk brings us to the subject of hedging. We introduce it by a simple example.

Since the value of a put option rises when an asset price falls, what happens to the value of a portfolio containing both assets and puts? The answer depends on the ratio of assets and options in the portfolio. A portfolio that only contains assets falls when the asset price falls, while one that is all put options rises. Somewhere in between these two extremes is a ratio at which a small movement in the asset does not result in any movement in the value of the portfolio. This ratio is instantaneously risk-free. The reduction of risk by taking advantage of such correlations between the asset and option price movements is called **hedging**. *If a market maker can sell an option for more than it is worth and then hedge away all the risk for the rest of the option's life, he has locked in a guaranteed, risk-free profit.* This idea, which will be recognised as a kind of arbitrage, is central to the theory and practice of option pricing.

Beyond the primary roles just discussed, many more general problems can be cast in terms of options. This is an increasingly important way of analysing decision-making. A simple example is that of a company which owns a mine, from which gold can be produced at a known cost. The mine can be started up and closed down, depending on current gold prices. How much does this flexibility add to the value of the company in the eyes of a predator, or of its shareholders? The answer can be arrived at by modelling the mine as an option, in this case on gold. We do not pursue this topic here; see Copeland, Koller & Murrin (1990) for an introduction.

Technical Point: MPT and the CAPM.

The **Modern Portfolio Theory** *of Markowitz and Tobin (see Markowitz 1991) and the* **Capital Asset Pricing Model** *of Mossin, Lintner and Sharpe (see Sharpe 1985) describe the relationship between risk and reward under an assumption of 'efficient markets'(see Section 2.2 for a discussion of this term). All assets, including options, are classified according to their expected return, their standard deviation of return (the risk), and the correlation between the changes in their return and the changes in the return of the* **market portfolio**. *This correlation is called the* **beta** *of the asset and the market portfolio is the portfolio that contains all securities, each in proportion to its market value.*

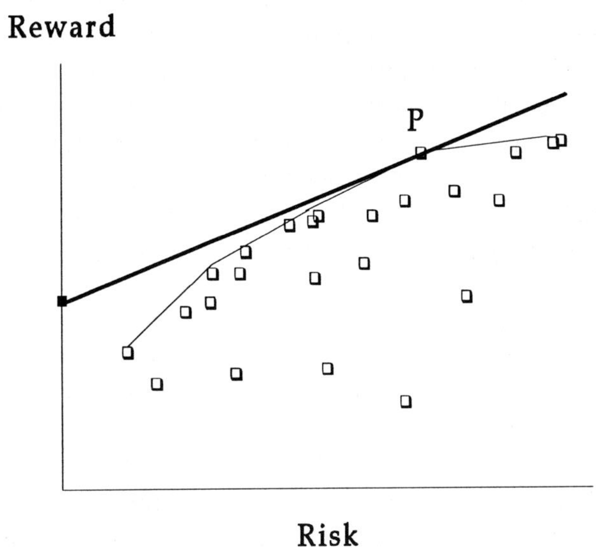

Figure 1.3: Reward versus risk, the efficient frontier and the capital market line.

These theories are concerned with finding portfolios with the minimum level of risk consistent with a given return; such portfolios are called efficient. A rational investor should, in theory, choose to in-

vest in a portfolio that is efficient. It is common to plot risk/reward diagrams such in Figure 1.3. In this figure the squares are the possible investments in a portfolio and the curved line is the **efficient frontier**, *containing all the efficient portfolios. Furthermore, since there exist risk-free investments, represented by the square on the vertical axis in Figure 1.3, it is possible to realise any point on the bold line in the figure by combining in one portfolio the risk-free investment with the portfolio at point P. Thus the bold line, which is termed the* **capital market line**, *is everywhere above the efficient frontier and the portfolios which it represents are in this sense optimal. The particular position on the line that an investor should choose depends on the amount of risk and level of return, or reward, that the investor will accept. The slope of the capital market line can be thought of as the excess return expected for each unit of risk taken.*

In an ideal world where every investor chooses portfolios lying on the capital market line, those assets whose risk/return profiles are inefficient will find that their price falls until they become a sound investment. At this point they will lie on this capital market line.

We do not need any of the theory behind MPT and the CAPM in this book but the whole subject of option pricing can be related to these theories, and the interested reader can refer to Sharpe (1985) for further details.

1.5 Other types of option

Call and put options form a small section of the available derivative products. The earlier description of an option contract concentrated on a European option but nowadays most options are American. The European/American classification has nothing to do with the continent of origin but refers to a technicality in the option contract. An **American option** is one that may be exercised at *any time* prior to expiry. The options described above, which may only be exercised *at* expiry, are called **European**. To the mathematician, American options are more interesting since they can be interpreted as free boundary problems—we see this in Chapter 3 and again in Chapters 6, 7 and 21. Not only must a *value* be assigned to the option but, and this is a feature of American options only, we must determine *when it is best to exercise the option.* We see that the 'best' time to exercise is not subjective but that arbitrage arguments lead to a natural determination of when to exercise.

Other types of option which we describe in this book include the so-called 'exotic' or 'path-dependent' options. These options have values which depend on the history of an asset price, not just on its value on exercise. An example would be an option to purchase an asset for the arithmetic average value of that asset over the month before expiry. An investor might want such an option in order to hedge sales of a commodity, say, which occur continually throughout this month. Once the idea of history dependence is accepted it is a very small step to imagining options which depend on the geometric average of the asset price, the maximum or the minimum of the asset price etc. This then brings us to the question of how to calculate the arithmetic average, say, of an asset price which may be quoted every 30 seconds or so; for a very liquid stock this would give 200,000 prices per year. In practice the option contract might specify that the arithmetic average is the mean of the closing price every business day, of which there are only 250 every year. Does this 'discrete sampling' give different option values if the sampling takes place at different times?

We show how to put the following options into a unifying framework:

- barrier options (the option can either come into existence or become worthless if the underlying asset reaches some prescribed value before expiry);
- Asian options (the price depends on some form of average);
- lookback options (the price depends on asset price maximum or minimum).

We discuss European and American versions of these as well as both continuous and discrete sampling of the history-dependent factor.

1.6 Interest rates and present value

For almost the whole of this book we assume that the interest rate is a known function of time, not necessarily constant. This is not an unreasonable assumption when valuing options, since a typical equity option has a total lifespan of about nine months. During such a relatively short time interest rates may change but not sufficiently to affect the prices of options significantly. (An interest rate change from 10% *p.a.* to 12% *p.a.* typically decreases a nine-month option value by about 2%.) However, towards the end of the book, in Chapters 14 and 15 on bond pricing, we relax the assumption of known interest rates and present a model where the short term rate is a random variable. This is important in valuing interest rate dependent products, such as bonds, since they have a much longer lifespan, typically 10 or 20 years; the assumption of known or constant interest rates is not a good one over such a long period.

For valuing options the most important concept concerning interest rates is that of **present value** or **discounting**. Ask the question

- How much would I pay *now* to receive a guaranteed amount E at the future time T?

If we assume that interest rates are constant, the answer to this question is found by discounting the future value, E, using continuously compounded interest. With a constant interest rate r, money in the bank $M(t)$ grows exponentially according to

$$\frac{dM}{dt} = rM. \tag{1.1}$$

The solution of this is simply

$$M = ce^{rt},$$

where c is the constant of integration. Since $M = E$ at $t = T$, the value at time t of the certain payoff is

$$M = Ee^{-r(T-t)}.$$

If interest rates are a known function of time $r(t)$, then (1.1) can be modified trivially and results in

$$M = Ee^{-\int_t^T r(s)ds}.$$

Further reading

- Sharpe (1985) describes the workings of financial markets in general. It is a very good broad introduction to investment theory and practice.

- Blank, Carter & Schmiesing (1991) discuss the uses of options and other products by different sorts of finance practitioners. Copeland, Koller & Murrin (1990) discuss the use of options in valuing companies.

- Good descriptions of options and trading strategies can be found in MacMillan (1980) and the opening chapters of Cox & Rubinstein (1985).

- For a more mathematical treatment of many aspects of finance see Merton (1990).

Chapter 2

The Random Nature of the Stock Market

2.1 Introduction

Since the mid 1980s it has been impossible for newspaper readers or television viewers to be unaware of the nature of financial time series. The values of the major indices (*Financial Times Stock Exchange* 100, or *FT-SE*, in the UK, the *Dow Jones* in the US and the *Nikkei Dow* in Japan) are quoted frequently. Graphs of these indices appear on television news bulletins throughout the day. As an extreme example of a financial time series, Figure 2.1 shows the *FT-SE* daily closing prices for the six months each side of the October 1987 stock market crash. To many people these 'mountain ranges' showing the variation of the value of an asset[1] or index with time are an excellent example of the 'random walk'.

It must be emphasised that this book is *not* about the prediction of asset prices. Indeed, our basic assumption, common to most of option pricing theory, is that we *do not know* and *cannot predict* tomorrow's values of asset prices. The past history of the asset value is there as a financial time series for us to examine as much as we want—but we cannot use it to forecast the next move that the asset will make. This does not mean that it tells us nothing. We know

[1]We use the word **asset** for any financial product whose value is quoted or can, in principle, be measured. Examples include equities, indices, currencies and commodities.

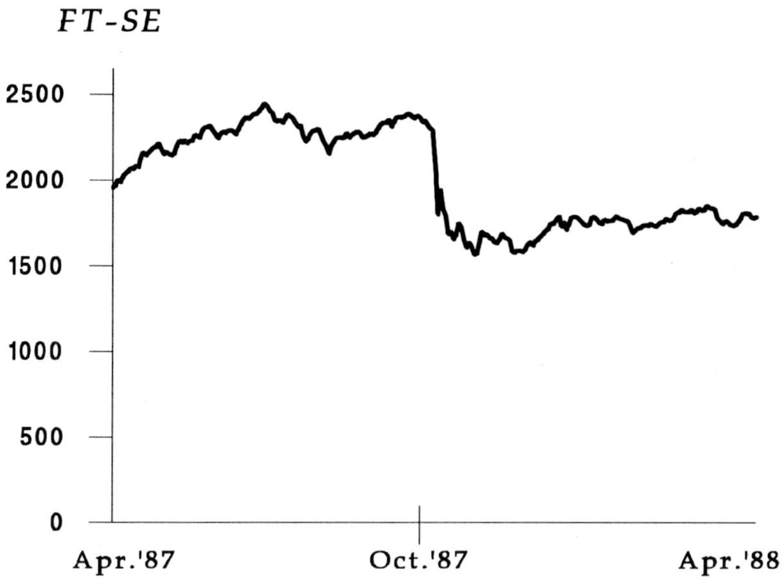

Figure 2.1: *FT-SE* closing prices from April 1987 to April 1988.

from our examination of the past what are the likely jumps in asset price, what are their mean and variance and, generally, what is the likely distribution of future asset prices. These qualities must be determined by a statistical analysis of historical data. Since this is not a statistical text, we assume that we know them, although a brief discussion is given in the Technical Point at the end of the next section.

Almost all models of option pricing are founded on one simple model for asset price movements, involving parameters derived, for example, from historical data. This chapter is devoted to a discussion of this model.

2.2 A simple model for asset prices

It is often stated that asset prices must move randomly because of the **Efficient Market Hypothesis**. There are several different forms of this hypothesis with different restrictive assumptions, but they all basically say two things:

- The past history is fully reflected in the present price, which does not hold any further information;

- Markets respond immediately to any new information about an asset price.

Thus the modelling of asset prices is really about modelling the arrival of new information which affects the price. With the two assumptions above, changes in the asset price are a **Markov process**.

Firstly, we note that the *absolute* change in the asset price is not by itself a useful quantity: a change of 1p is much more significant when the asset price is 20p than when it is 200p. Instead, with each change in asset price, we associate a **return**, defined to be the change in the price divided by the original value. This relative measure of the change is clearly a better indicator of its size than any absolute measure.

Now suppose that at time t the asset price is S. Let us consider a small subsequent time interval dt, during which S changes to $S + dS$, as sketched in Figure 2.2. (We use the notation $d\cdot$ for the small change in any quantity over this time interval.) How might we model the corresponding return on the asset, dS/S? The commonest model decomposes this return into two parts. One is a predictable, deterministic return akin to the return on money invested in a risk-free bank. It gives a contribution

$$\mu\, dt$$

to the return dS/S, where μ is a measure of the average rate of growth of the asset price, also known as the drift. In simple models μ is taken to be a constant[2]. In more complicated models, for exchange rates, for example, μ can be a function of S and t.

The second contribution to dS/S models the random change in the asset price in response to external effects, such as unexpected

[2] Actually, as far as determining the value of an option it does not matter what μ is as long as it is known.

news. It is represented by a random sample drawn from a normal distribution with mean zero and adds a term

$$\sigma\, dX$$

to dS/S. Here σ is a number called the **volatility**, which measures the standard deviation of the returns. The quantity dX is the sample from a normal distribution, which is discussed further below.

Putting these contributions together, we obtain the **stochastic differential equation**

$$\frac{dS}{S} = \sigma\, dX + \mu\, dt, \tag{2.1}$$

which is the mathematical representation of our simple recipe for generating asset prices.

The only symbol in (2.1) whose role is not yet entirely clear is dX. If we were to cross out the term involving dX, by taking $\sigma = 0$, we would be left with the ordinary differential equation

$$\frac{dS}{S} = \mu\, dt$$

or

$$\frac{dS}{dt} = \mu S.$$

When μ is constant this can be solved exactly to give exponential growth in the value of the asset, i.e.

$$S = S_0 e^{\mu(t-t_0)},$$

where S_0 is the value of the asset at $t = t_0$. Thus if $\sigma = 0$ the asset price is totally deterministic and we can predict the future price of the asset with certainty.

The term dX, which contains the randomness that is certainly a feature of asset prices, is known as a **Wiener process**. It has the following properties:

- dX is a random variable, drawn from a normal distribution;
- the mean of dX is zero;

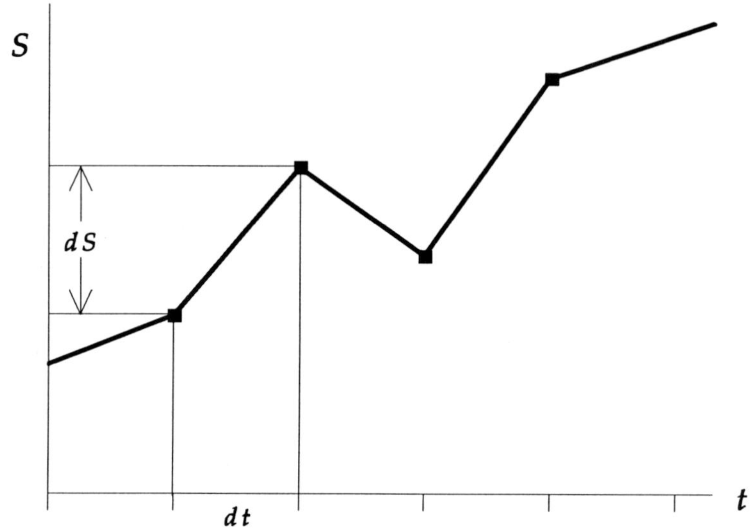

Figure 2.2: Detail of a discrete random walk.

- the variance of dX is dt.

One way of writing this is

$$dX = \phi\sqrt{dt},$$

where ϕ is a random variable drawn from a standardized normal distribution. The standardized normal distribution has zero mean, unit variance and a probability density function given by

$$\frac{1}{\sqrt{2\pi}}e^{-\frac{1}{2}\phi^2}$$

for $-\infty < \phi < \infty$. If we define the expectation operator $\mathcal{E}$ by

$$\mathcal{E}[F(\cdot)] = \frac{1}{\sqrt{2\pi}}\int_{-\infty}^{\infty} F(\phi)e^{-\frac{1}{2}\phi^2}\,d\phi, \tag{2.2}$$

for any function F, then

$$\mathcal{E}[\phi] = 0$$

and

$$\mathcal{E}[\phi^2] = 1.$$

The reason for dX being scaled with $\sqrt{dt}$ is that any other choice for the magnitude of dX would lead to a problem that is either meaningless or trivial when we finally consider what happens as $dt \to 0$, a limit in which we are particularly interested. We shall consider this matter in more detail later (see also Appendix A).

We have given some economically reasonable justification for the model (2.1). A more practical justification for it is that it fits real time series data very well, at least for equities and indices. (The agreement with currencies is less good, especially in the long term.) There are some discrepancies; for instance, real data appears to have a greater probability of large rises or falls than the model predicts. But, on the whole, it has stood the test of time remarkably well and can be the starting point for more sophisticated models. As an example of such generalization, the coefficients of dX and dt in (2.1) could be any function of S and/or t. The particular choice of functions is a matter for the mathematical modeller and statistician, and different assets may be best represented by other stochastic differential equations.

Equation (2.1) is a particular example of a **random walk**. It cannot be solved to give a deterministic path for the share price, but it can give interesting and important information concerning the behaviour of S in a probabilistic sense. Suppose that today's date is t and today's asset price is S. If the price at a later date t', in six months' time, say, is S', then S' will be distributed about S with a probability density function of the form shown in Figure 2.3. The future asset price, S', is thus most likely to be close to S and less likely to be far away. The further that t' is from t the more spread out this distribution is. If S follows the random walk given by (2.1) then the probability density function represented by this skewed bell-shaped curve is the lognormal distribution (this is shown in Appendix A) and the random walk (2.1) is therefore known as a lognormal random walk.

We can think of (2.1) as a recipe for generating a time series—each time the series is restarted a different path results. Each path is called a **realisation** of the random walk. This recipe works as follows. Suppose, as an example, that today's price is \$1, and we have $\mu = 1$, $\sigma = 0.2$ with $dt = 1/250$ (one day as a proportion of 250

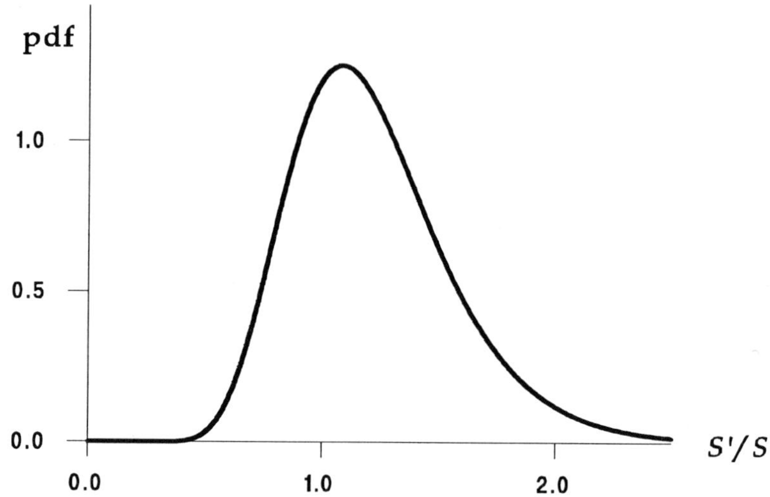

Figure 2.3: The probability density function (pdf) for S'/S.

business days per year). We now draw a number at random from a normal distribution with mean zero and variance 1/250; this is dX. Suppose that we draw the number $dX = 0.08352\ldots$. Now perform the calculation in (2.1) to find dS:

$$dS = 1.0 \times \$1.0 \times \frac{1}{250} + 0.2 \times \$1.0 \times 0.08352\ldots = \$0.020704\ldots.$$

Add this value for dS to the original value for S to arrive at the new value for S after one time-step: $S + dS = \$1.020704\ldots$ Repeat the above steps, using the new value for S and drawing a new random number. If this sequence is repeated it generates a time series of random numbers which appears similar to genuine series from the stock market, such as that in Figure 2.1.

Firstly, let us now briefly consider some of the properties of (2.1). Equation (2.1) does not refer to the past history of the asset price; the next asset price $(S + dS)$ depends solely on today's price. This independence from the past is called the **Markov property**. Secondly, we consider the mean of dS:

$$\mathcal{E}[dS] = \mathcal{E}[\sigma S\, dX + \mu S\, dt] = \mu S\, dt,$$

since $\mathcal{E}[dX] = 0$. On average, the next value for S is higher than the old by an amount $\mu S\,dt$.

Thirdly, we consider the variance of dS:

$$\mathrm{Var}[dS] = \mathcal{E}[dS^2] - \mathcal{E}[dS]^2 = \mathcal{E}[\sigma^2 S^2 dX^2] = \sigma^2 S^2 dt.$$

The square root of the variance is the standard deviation and is thus proportional to σ.

If we were to compare two random walks with different values for the parameters μ and σ we would see that the one with the larger value for μ rises more steeply and the one with the larger value of σ would appear more jagged. Typically, for stocks and indices the value of σ is in the range 0.05 to 0.4. Government bonds are examples of assets with low volatility, while 'penny shares' and shares in high-tech companies generally have high volatility. The volatility is often quoted as a percentage, so that $\sigma = 0.2$ would be called a 20% volatility.

In the next section we learn how to manipulate functions of random variables.

Technical Point: parameter estimation.
None of the analysis that we have presented so far is of much use unless we can estimate the parameters in our random walk. In particular, we find later that only the volatility parameter, σ, in the random walk (2.1) appears in the value of an option. How can we estimate σ, for example from historic data?

This is not a statistics text book and the reader is referred to Spiegel (1980) for general details of parameter estimation. However, a simple approach is as follows. Suppose that we have the values of the asset price S consisting of $n + 1$ values at equal time steps; closing prices, say. Call these values $S_1, \ldots, S_{n+1}$ in chronological order with S_1 the first value.

Since we are assuming that changes in the logarithm of the asset price, $\log S$, are normally distributed we can use the usual unbiased variance estimate $\bar{\sigma}^2$ for σ^2. Let

$$\bar{m} = \frac{1}{n\,dt} \sum_{i=1}^{n} \log(S_{i+1}/S_i);$$

then

$$\bar{\sigma}^2 = \frac{1}{(n-1)\,dt}\sum_{i=1}^{n}\left(\log(S_{i+1}/S_i) - \bar{m}\right)^2.$$

The time-step between data points, dt, is assumed to be constant and if measured as a fraction of a year the resulting parameters are annualised.

There is a great deal more to the subject of parameter estimation, for example sizes of data sets or time dependence, but this book is not the place to discuss them. For further information specific to option pricing see Leong (1993).

2.3 Itô's lemma

In real life asset prices are quoted at discrete intervals of time. There is thus a practical lower bound for the basic time-step dt of our random walk (2.1). If we used this time-step in practice to value options, though, we would find that we had to deal with unmanageably large amounts of data. Instead, we set up our mathematical models in the **continuous time** limit $dt \to 0$; it is much more efficient to solve the resulting differential equations than it is to value options by direct simulation of the random walk on a practical timescale. In order to do this, we need some technical machinery that enables us to handle the random term dX as $dt \to 0$, and this is the content of this section.

Itô's lemma is the most important result about the manipulation of random variables that we require. It is to functions of random variables what Taylor's theorem is to functions of deterministic variables. It relates the small change in a function of a random variable to the small change in the random variable itself. Our heuristic approach to Itô's lemma is based on the Taylor series expansion; for a more rigorous yet still readable analysis, see Schuss (1980).

Before coming to Itô's lemma we need one result, which we do not prove rigorously (see Technical Point 1 below). This result is that, with probability one,

$$dX^2 \to dt \quad \text{as} \quad dt \to 0. \tag{2.3}$$

Thus, the smaller dt becomes, the closer dX^2 comes to being equal to dt.

Suppose that $f(S)$ is a smooth function of S and forget for the moment that S is stochastic. If we vary S by a small amount dS then clearly f also varies by a small amount provided we are not close to singularities of f. From the Taylor series expansion we can write

$$df = \frac{df}{dS}dS + \frac{1}{2}\frac{d^2 f}{dS^2}dS^2 + \cdots, \tag{2.4}$$

where the dots denote a remainder which is smaller than any of the terms we have retained. Now recall that dS is given by (2.1). Here dS is simply a number, albeit random, and so squaring it we find that

$$\begin{aligned} dS^2 &= (\sigma S\, dX + \mu S\, dt)^2 \\ &= \sigma^2 S^2 dX^2 + 2\sigma\mu S^2 dt\, dX + \mu^2 S^2 dt^2. \end{aligned} \tag{2.5}$$

We now examine the order of magnitude of each of the terms in (2.5). (See Technical Point 2 below for the symbol $O(\cdot)$.) Since

$$dX = O(\sqrt{dt}),$$

the first term is the largest for small dt and dominates the other two terms. Thus, to leading order,

$$dS^2 = \sigma^2 S^2 dX^2 + \cdots.$$

Since $dX^2 \to dt$, to leading order

$$dS^2 \to \sigma^2 S^2 dt.$$

We substitute this into (2.4) and retain only those terms which are at least as large as $O(dt)$. Using also the definition of dS from (2.1), we find that

$$\begin{aligned} df &= \frac{df}{dS}(\sigma S\, dX + \mu S\, dt) + \tfrac{1}{2}\sigma^2 S^2 \frac{d^2 f}{dS^2} dt \\ &= \sigma S \frac{df}{dS} dX + \left(\mu S \frac{df}{dS} + \tfrac{1}{2}\sigma^2 S^2 \frac{d^2 f}{dS^2}\right) dt. \end{aligned} \tag{2.6}$$

This is Itô's lemma[3] relating the small change in a function of a random variable to the small change in the variable itself.

Because the order of magnitude of dX is $O(\sqrt{dt})$, we see that the second derivative of f with respect to S appears in the expression for df at order dt. The order dt terms play a significant part in our later analyses, and any other choice for the order of dX would not lead to the interesting results we discover. It can be shown that any other order of magnitude for dX leads to unrealistic properties for the random walk in the limit $dt \to 0$; if $dX \gg \sqrt{dt}$ the random variable goes immediately to zero or infinity, and if $dX \ll \sqrt{dt}$ the random component of the walk vanishes in the limit $dt \to 0$.

Observe that (2.6) is made up of a random component proportional to dX and a deterministic component proportional to dt. In this respect it bears a resemblance to equation (2.1). Equation (2.6) is also a recipe, this time for determining the behaviour of f, and f itself follows a random walk.

As a simple example, consider the function $f(S) = \log S$. Differentiation of this function gives

$$\frac{df}{dS} = \frac{1}{S} \quad \text{and} \quad \frac{d^2 f}{dS^2} = -\frac{1}{S^2}.$$

Thus, using (2.6), we arrive at

$$df = \sigma\, dX + \left(\mu - \tfrac{1}{2}\sigma^2\right) dt.$$

This is a constant coefficient stochastic differential equation. The jump df is normally distributed and this explains why (2.1) is sometimes called a lognormal random walk.

---

[3]We have here applied Itô's lemma to functions of the random variable S which is defined by (2.1). The lemma is, of course, more general than this and can be applied to functions of any random variable, G, say, described by a stochastic differential equation of the form

$$dG = A(G,t)\, dX + B(G,t)\, dt.$$

Thus given $f(G)$, Itô's lemma says that

$$df = A\frac{df}{dG} dX + \left(B\frac{df}{dG} + \tfrac{1}{2}A^2\frac{d^2 f}{dG^2}\right) dt.$$

The result (2.6) can be further generalized by considering a function of the random variable S and of time, $f(S,t)$. This entails the use of partial derivatives since there are now *two* independent variables, S and t. We can expand $f(S+dS,t+dt)$ in a Taylor series about (S,t) to get

$$df = \frac{\partial f}{\partial S}dS + \frac{\partial f}{\partial t}dt + \frac{1}{2}\frac{\partial^2 f}{\partial S^2}dS^2 + \cdots.$$

Using our expressions (2.1) for dS and (2.3) for dX^2 we find that the new expression for df is

$$df = \sigma S\frac{\partial f}{\partial S}dX + \left(\mu S\frac{\partial f}{\partial S} + \tfrac{1}{2}\sigma^2 S^2\frac{\partial^2 f}{\partial S^2} + \frac{\partial f}{\partial t}\right)dt. \tag{2.7}$$

Technical Point 1: the limit of dX^2 as $dt \to 0$.
To be technically correct we should write the stochastic differential equation (2.1) in the integrated form

$$S(t) = S(t_0) + \sigma\int_{t_0}^{t} S\,dX + \mu\int_{t_0}^{t} S\,dt.$$

All the theory for stochastic calculus is based on this representation of a random walk and, strictly speaking, (2.1) is only short-hand notation.

We do not yet have a definition for the term involving the integration with respect to the Wiener process. One definition of such integrals, due to Itô, is that, for any function h,

$$\mathrm{Int} = \int_{t_0}^{t} h(\tau)\,dX(\tau) = \lim_{m\to\infty}\mathrm{Int}_m$$

where

$$\mathrm{Int}_m = \sum_{k=0}^{m-1} h(t_k)(X(t_{k+1}) - X(t_k)). \tag{2.8}$$

Here $t_0 < t_1 \ldots < t_m = t$ is any partition (or division) of the range $[t_0,t]$ into m smaller regions and X is the running sum of the random variables dX. The important point to note about (2.8) is that the *value of the function h inside the summation is taken at the left-hand end of the small regions, i.e. at $t = t_k$ and not at t_{k+1}.*

If $h(t)$ were a smooth function the integral would be the usual Stieltjes integral and it would not matter that h was evaluated at the left-hand end. However, because of the randomness, which does not go away as $dt \to 0$, the fact that the summation depends on the left-hand value of h in each partition becomes important. For example,

$$\int_{t_0}^{t} X(\tau)\, dX(\tau) = \tfrac{1}{2}(X(t)^2 - X(t_0)^2) - \tfrac{1}{2}(t - t_0).$$

The last term would not be present if X were smooth.

Using the formal definition of stochastic integration it can be shown that

$$f(S(t)) = f(S(t_0)) + \int_{t_0}^{t} \sigma S \frac{df}{dS}\, dX + \int_{t_0}^{t} \mu S \frac{df}{dS} + \tfrac{1}{2}\sigma^2 S^2 \frac{d^2 f}{dS^2}\, dt,$$

which when written in the short-hand notation becomes (2.6) as 'derived' above. We can conclude that the rules for differentiation and integration are different from those of classical calculus, but can generally be derived heuristically by remembering the simple rule of thumb

$$dX^2 = dt.$$

Technical Point 2: order notation.

Order notation *is a convenient shorthand representation of the idea that some complicated quantity, such as a term in an equation, is 'about the same size as' some other, usually simpler, quantity. Suppose that $F(t)$ and $G(t)$ are two functions of t and that, as $t \to 0$,*

$$F(t) \le CG(t)$$

for some constant C (equivalently, $\lim_{t\to 0} F(t)/G(t)$ is bounded by C). Then we write

$$F(t) = O(G(t)) \qquad \text{as} \quad t \to 0.$$

There is nothing special about $t = 0$ in this definition; we could have been concerned with any value of t (including infinity). If the limit of $F(t)/G(t)$ is actually 1, it is usual to write

$$F(t) \sim G(t) \qquad \text{as} \quad t \to 0,$$

although conventions differ on the exact interpretation of the symbol $\sim$ ('twiddles'); it is sometimes taken to be equivalent to $O(\cdot)$. If $F(t)/G(t) \to 0$ as $t \to 0$, we write

$$F(t) = o(G(t)) \qquad \text{as} \quad t \to 0;$$

this is sometimes abbreviated to

$$F(t) \ll G(t).$$

In the discussion of Itô's Lemma above, we have both $dX = O(\sqrt{dt})$ as $dt \to 0$ and $dX \sim \sqrt{dt}$ as $dt \to 0$. We see also that $dX\,dt = o(dt)$ as $dt \to 0$ (or $dX\,dt \ll dt$), and this is why we are able to ignore terms of this size in Itô's lemma.

2.4 The elimination of randomness

The two random walks in S (equation (2.1)) and f (equation (2.7)) are both driven by the single random variable dX. We can exploit this fact to construct a third variable g whose variation dg is wholly deterministic during the small time period dt. For the moment this appears to be merely a clever trick but it takes on major importance when we come to value options.

Let Δ be a number at our disposal and let

$$g = f - \Delta S$$

where Δ is held constant during the timestep dt. We can write

$$\begin{aligned}
dg &= df - \Delta\, dS \\
&= \sigma S \frac{\partial f}{\partial S} dX + \left(\mu S \frac{\partial f}{\partial S} + \tfrac{1}{2}\sigma^2 S^2 \frac{\partial^2 f}{\partial S^2} + \frac{\partial f}{\partial t} \right) dt \\
&\quad - \Delta(\sigma S\, dX + \mu S\, dt) \\
&= \sigma S \left(\frac{\partial f}{\partial S} - \Delta \right) dX \\
&\quad + \left(\mu S \left(\frac{\partial f}{\partial S} - \Delta \right) + \tfrac{1}{2}\sigma^2 S^2 \frac{\partial^2 f}{\partial S^2} + \frac{\partial f}{\partial t} \right) dt.
\end{aligned}$$

(If Δ were allowed to vary during the time-step then in evaluating dg we would need to include terms in $d\Delta$.) Now, by choosing $\Delta = \partial f/\partial S$ (evaluated before the jumps, i.e. at time t) we can make the coefficient of dX vanish. This leaves a value for dg which is known: the random walk for g is purely deterministic. Essentially, this 'trick' used the fact that the two random walks, for S and for f, are correlated and so not independent. Since their random components are proportional, by taking the correct linear combination of f and S it can be eliminated altogether. This is just the argument we used informally in Section 1.3, and in the next chapter it turns out to be crucial in the discussion of option pricing.

Further reading

- Cox & Rubinstein (1985) gives a good description of the **binomial model** in which asset prices do not change continuously in time but rather jump at discrete intervals to one of two new values. Such discrete models, although not necessarily accurate models of the real world, can often give insight into financial problems.

- Jump-diffusion models are discussed by Jarrow & Rudd (1983) and Merton (1976). In these models asset prices behave as we have described with one additional property: they can occasionally undergo random jumps of a substantial fraction of their value.

- For a further and more detailed description of the movement of equity prices see Brealey (1983), Fama (1965) and Mandelbrot (1963).

Exercises

1. If $dS = \sigma S\,dX + \mu S\,dt$, and A and n are constants, find the stochastic differential equations satisfied by

   (a) $f(S) = AS$,
   (b) $f(S) = AS^n$.

2. Consider the general stochastic differential equation

$$dG = A(G,t)\,dX + B(G,t)\,dt.$$

Use Itô's lemma to show that it is theoretically possible to find a function $f(G)$ which itself follows a random walk but with zero drift.

3. There are n assets satisfying the following stochastic differential equations:

$$dS_i = \sigma_i S_i \, dX_i + \mu_i S_i \, dt \quad \text{for} \quad i = 1, \ldots, n.$$

The Wiener processes dX_i satisfy

$$\mathcal{E}[dX_i] = 0, \quad \mathcal{E}[dX_i^2] = dt$$

as usual, but the asset price changes are correlated with

$$\mathcal{E}[dX_i \, dX_j] = \rho_{ij} \, dt$$

where $-1 \le \rho_{ij} = \rho_{ji} \le 1$.

Derive Itô's lemma for a function $f(S_1, \ldots, S_n)$ of the n assets $S_1, \ldots, S_n$. [Hint: As with a function of a single variable, use Taylor's theorem with the additional 'rules'

$$dX_i^2 \to dt \quad \text{and} \quad dX_i \, dX_j \to \rho_{ij} \, dt.]$$

Chapter 3

Basic Option Theory

3.1 The value of an option

In this chapter we discuss option strategies in general and derive the original Black–Scholes differential equation for the price of the simplest options, the so-called vanilla options. We then discuss the boundary conditions to be satisfied by different types of option including the American option. *This chapter is fundamental to the whole subject of option pricing and should be read with care.*

Let us introduce some simple notation. It is used consistently throughout the book.

- We denote by V the value of an option[1]; V is a function of the current value of the underlying asset, S, and time, t: $V = V(S,t)$. The value of the option also depends on the following parameters:

- σ, the volatility of the underlying asset;

- E, the exercise price;

- T, the expiry;

- r, the interest rate.

[1]When the distinction is important we use $C(S,t)$ and $P(S,t)$ to denote a call and a put respectively.

We now consider what happens just at the moment of expiry of a call option, that is, at time $t = T$. A simple arbitrage argument tells us its value at this special time.

If $S > E$ at expiry, it makes financial sense to exercise the call option, handing over an amount E, to obtain an asset worth S. The profit from such a transaction is then $S - E$. On the other hand, if $S < E$ at expiry, we should not exercise the option because we would make a loss of $E - S$. In this case, the option expires valueless. Thus, the value of the call option at expiry can be written as

$$C(S,T) = \max(S - E, 0). \tag{3.1}$$

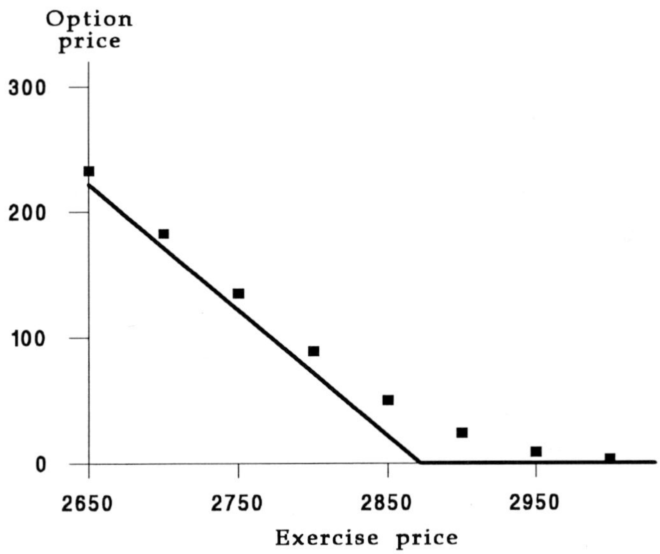

Figure 3.1: The value of a call option at and before expiry against exercise price; option values from *FT-SE* index option data.

As we get nearer to the expiry date we can expect the value of our call option to approach (3.1). To confirm this we reproduce in Figure 3.1 the figure from Chapter 1 which compares real *FT-SE* index call option data with the value of the option at expiry for fixed S. In this figure we show $\max(S-E,0)$ as a function of E for fixed S (=2872) and superimpose the real data for V taken from the February call option series. Observe that the real data is always just above the predicted line. This reflects the fact that there is still some time remaining before the option expires—there is potential left for the asset price to rise further, giving the option even greater value. This difference between the option value before and at expiry is called the **time value** and the value at expiry the **intrinsic value**[2].

If one owns an option with a given exercise price, then one is less interested in how the option value varies with exercise price than with how it varies with asset price, S. In Figure 3.2 we plot

$$\max(S-E,0)$$

as a function of S (the bold line) and also the value of an option at some time before expiry. The latter curve is just a sketch of a plausible form for the option value. For the moment the reader must trust that the value of the option before expiry is of this form. Later in this chapter we see how to derive equations and sometimes formulæ for such curves.

The bold line, being the payoff for the option at expiry, is called a **payoff diagram**. The reader should be aware that some authors use the term 'payoff diagram' to mean the difference between the terminal value of the contract (*our* payoff) and the original premium. We choose not to use this definition for two reasons. Firstly, the premium is paid at the start of the option contract and the return, if any, only comes at expiry. Secondly, the payoff diagram has a natural interpretation, as we see, as the final condition for a diffusion equation.

3.2 Strategies and payoff diagrams

Each option and portfolio of options has its own payoff at expiry. An argument similar to that given above for the value of a call at

[2]Other important jargon is **at-the-money**, which refers to that option whose exercise price is closest to the current value of the underlying asset, **in-the-money**, which is a call (put) whose exercise price is less (greater) than the current asset price—so that the option value has a significant intrinsic component—and **out-of-the-money**, which is a call or put with no intrinsic value.

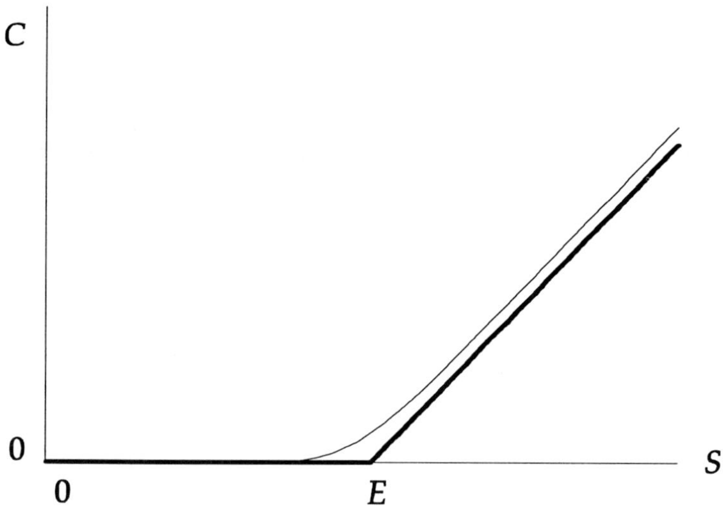

Figure 3.2: The payoff diagram for a call, $C(S,T)$, and the option value $C(S,t)$ prior to expiry, as functions of S.

expiry leads to the payoff for a put option. At expiry the put option is worthless if $S > E$ but has the value $E - S$ for $S < E$. Thus the payoff at expiry for a put option is

$$\max(E - S, 0).$$

The payoff diagram for a European put is shown in Figure 3.3, where the bold line shows the payoff function $\max(E - S, 0)$. The other curve is again a sketch of the option value prior to expiry. Although the time value of the call option of Figure 3.2 is everywhere positive, for the put the time value is negative for sufficiently small S, where the option value falls below the payoff. We return to this point later.

Although the two most basic structures for the payoff are the call and the put, in principle there is no reason why an option contract cannot be written with a more general payoff. An example of another payoff is shown in Figure 3.4. This payoff can be written as

$$B\mathcal{H}(S - E),$$

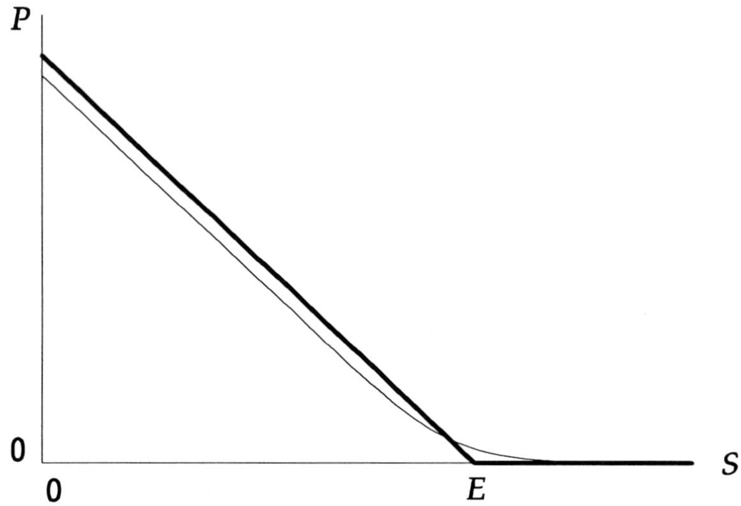

Figure 3.3: The payoff diagram for a put, $P(S,T)$, and the option value $P(S,t)$ prior to expiry, as functions of S.

where $\mathcal{H}(\cdot)$ is the **Heaviside function**, which has value 1 when its argument is positive but is zero otherwise. This option may be interpreted as a straight bet on the asset price; it is called a **cash-or-nothing call**. Options with general payoffs are usually called **binaries** or **digitals**.

By combining calls and puts with various exercise prices one can construct portfolios with a great variety of payoffs at expiry. For example, we show in Figure 3.5 the payoff for a 'bullish vertical spread' which is constructed by buying one call option and writing one call option with the same expiry date but a larger exercise price. This portfolio is called 'bullish' because the investor profits from a rise in the asset price, 'vertical' because there are two different exercise prices involved, and 'spread' because it is made up of the same type of option, here calls. The payoff function for this portfolio can be written as

$$\max(S - E_1, 0) - \max(S - E_2, 0)$$

with $E_2 > E_1$.

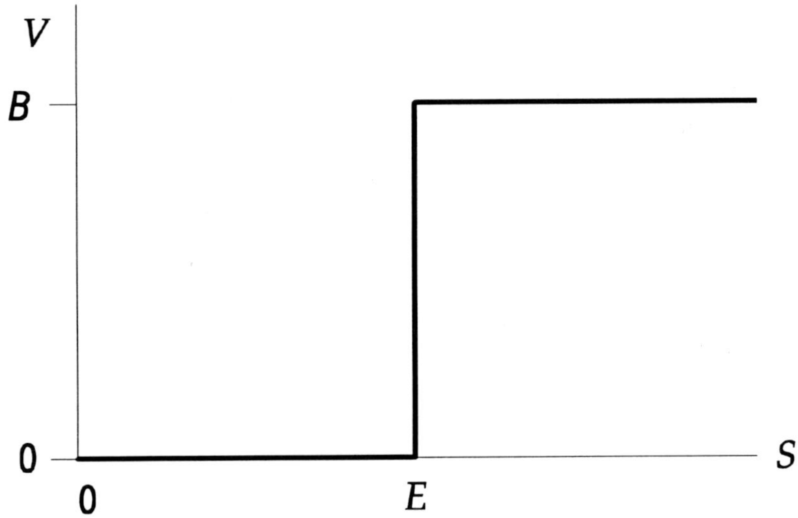

Figure 3.4: The payoff diagram for a cash-or-nothing call, equivalent to a bet on the asset price.

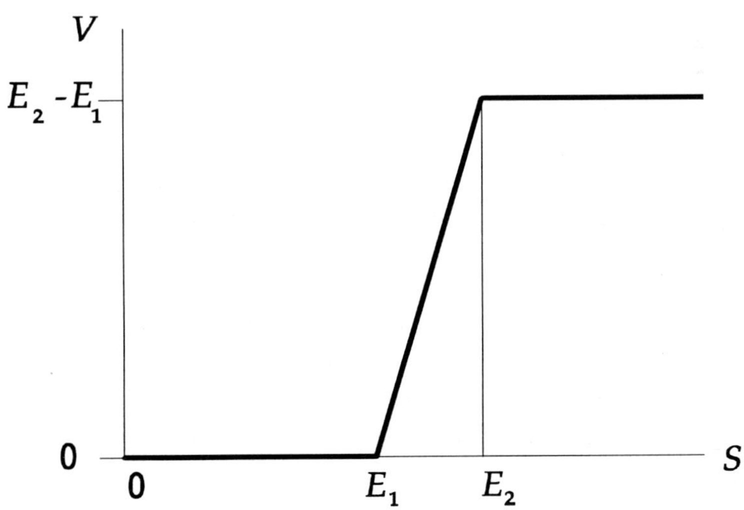

Figure 3.5: The payoff diagram for a bullish vertical spread.

Many other portfolios can be constructed. Some examples are 'combinations', containing both calls and puts, and 'horizontal' or 'calendar spreads', containing options with different expiry dates. Others are given in the exercises at the end of this chapter.

The appeal of such strategies is in their ability to redirect risk. In exchange for the premium—which is the maximum possible loss and known from the start—one can construct portfolios to benefit from virtually any move in the underlying asset. If one has a view on the market and this turns out to be correct then, as we have seen, one can make large profits from relatively small movements in the underlying asset.

3.3 Put-call parity

Although call and put options are superficially different, in fact they can be combined in such a way that they are perfectly correlated. This is demonstrated by the following argument.

Suppose that we are long one asset, long one put and short one call. The call and the put both have the same expiry date, T, and the same exercise price, E. Denote by Π the value of this portfolio. We thus have

$$\Pi = S + P - C,$$

where P and C are the values of the put and the call respectively. The payoff for this portfolio at expiry is

$$S + \max(E - S, 0) - \max(S - E, 0).$$

This can be rewritten as

$$S + (E - S) - 0 = E \quad \text{if} \quad S \leq E,$$

or

$$S + 0 - (S - E) = E \quad \text{if} \quad S \geq E.$$

Whether S is greater or less than E at expiry the payoff is always the same, namely E.

Now ask the question

- How much would I pay for a portfolio that gives a guaranteed E at $t = T$?

This is, of course, the same question that we asked in Chapter 1 and the answer is arrived at by discounting the final value of the portfolio. Thus this portfolio is now worth $Ee^{-r(T-t)}$. This equates the return from the portfolio with the return from a bank deposit. If this were not the case then arbitragers could (and would) make an instantaneous riskless profit: by buying and selling options and shares and at the same time borrowing or lending money in the correct proportions, they could lock in a profit today with zero payoff in the future. Thus we conclude that

$$S + P - C = Ee^{-r(T-t)}. \tag{3.2}$$

This relationship between the underlying asset and its options is called **put-call parity**. It is an example of risk elimination, achieved by carrying out one transaction in the asset and each of the options. In the next section, we see that a more sophisticated version of this idea, involving a continuous rebalancing, rather than the one-off transactions above, allows us to value call and put options independently.

3.4 The Black–Scholes analysis

Before describing the Black–Scholes analysis (Black & Scholes 1973) which leads to the value of an option we list the assumptions that we make for most of the book.

- The asset price follows the lognormal random walk (2.1).

  Other models do exist[3], and in many cases it is possible to perform the Black–Scholes analysis to derive a differential equation for the value of an option. Explicit formulæ rarely exist for such models. However, this should not discourage their use, since an accurate numerical solution is usually quite straightforward.

- The risk-free interest rate r and the asset volatility σ are known functions of time over the life of the option.

[3]See, for example, Jarrow & Rudd (1983) and Cox & Rubinstein (1985) for jump-diffusion models and constant elasticity of variance models. In the former model the asset price random walk need not be continuous but can have random discontinuous jumps; in the latter the volatility can be a function of S.

Only in Chapters 14 and 15 do we drop the assumption of deterministic behaviour of r; there we model interest rates by a stochastic differential equation.

- There are no transaction costs associated with hedging a portfolio.

  In Chapter 13 we describe a model which allows for transaction costs.

- The underlying asset pays no dividends during the life of the option.

  This assumption can be dropped if the dividends are known beforehand. They can be paid either at discrete intervals or continuously over the life of the option. We discuss this point later in this chapter and further in Chapter 8.

- There are no arbitrage possibilities. The absence of arbitrage opportunities means that all risk-free portfolios must earn the same return.

- Trading of the underlying asset can take place continuously. This is clearly an idealization and becomes important in the chapter on transaction costs, Chapter 13.

- Short selling is permitted and the assets are divisible.

  We assume that we can buy and sell any number (not necessarily an integer) of the underlying asset, and that we may sell assets that we do not own.

Suppose that we have an option whose value $V(S,t)$ depends only on S and t. It is not necessary at this stage to specify whether V is a call or a put; indeed, V can be the value of a whole portfolio of different options although for simplicity the reader can think of a simple call or put. Using Itô's lemma, equation (2.7), we can write

$$dV = \sigma S \frac{\partial V}{\partial S} dX + \left(\mu S \frac{\partial V}{\partial S} + \tfrac{1}{2}\sigma^2 S^2 \frac{\partial^2 V}{\partial S^2} + \frac{\partial V}{\partial t} \right) dt. \qquad (3.3)$$

This gives the random walk followed by V. Note that we require V to have at least one t derivative and two S derivatives.

Now construct a portfolio consisting of one option and a number $-\Delta$ of the underlying asset. This number is as yet unspecified. The value of this portfolio is

$$\Pi = V - \Delta S. \tag{3.4}$$

The jump in the value of this portfolio in one time-step is

$$d\Pi = dV - \Delta\, dS.$$

Here Δ is held fixed during the time-step; if it were not then $d\Pi$ would contain terms in $d\Delta$. Putting (2.1), (3.3) and (3.4) together, we find that Π follows the random walk

$$d\Pi = \sigma S\left(\frac{\partial V}{\partial S} - \Delta\right) dX + \left(\mu S\frac{\partial V}{\partial S} + \tfrac{1}{2}\sigma^2 S^2\frac{\partial^2 V}{\partial S^2} + \frac{\partial V}{\partial t} - \mu\Delta S\right) dt. \tag{3.5}$$

As we demonstrated in Section 2.4, we can eliminate the random component in this random walk by choosing

$$\Delta = \frac{\partial V}{\partial S}. \tag{3.6}$$

Note that Δ is the value of $\partial V/\partial S$ at the *start* of the time-step dt.

This results in a portfolio whose increment is wholly deterministic:

$$d\Pi = \left(\frac{\partial V}{\partial t} + \tfrac{1}{2}\sigma^2 S^2\frac{\partial^2 V}{\partial S^2}\right) dt. \tag{3.7}$$

We now appeal to the concepts of arbitrage and supply and demand, with the assumption of no transaction costs. The return on an amount Π invested in riskless assets would see a growth of $r\Pi\, dt$ in a time dt. If the right-hand side of (3.7) were greater than this amount, an arbitrager could make a guaranteed riskless profit by borrowing an amount Π to invest in the portfolio. The return for this strategy would be greater than the cost of borrowing. Conversely, if the right-hand side of (3.7) were less than $r\Pi\, dt$ then the arbitrager would short the portfolio and invest Π in the bank. Either way the arbitrager would make a riskless, no cost, instantaneous profit. The existence of such arbitragers with the ability to trade at low cost ensures that the return on the portfolio and on the riskless account are more or less equal. Thus, we have

$$r\Pi\, dt = \left(\frac{\partial V}{\partial t} + \tfrac{1}{2}\sigma^2 S^2 \frac{\partial^2 V}{\partial S^2} \right) dt. \tag{3.8}$$

Substituting (3.4) and (3.6) into (3.8) and dividing throughout by dt we arrive at

$$\frac{\partial V}{\partial t} + \tfrac{1}{2}\sigma^2 S^2 \frac{\partial^2 V}{\partial S^2} + rS\frac{\partial V}{\partial S} - rV = 0. \tag{3.9}$$

This is the **Black–Scholes partial differential equation**. With its extensions and variants, it plays the major role in the rest of the book.

It is hard to overemphasise the fact that, under the assumptions stated earlier, *any* derivative security whose price depends *only* on the current value of S and on t, and which is paid for up front, must satisfy the Black–Scholes equation (or a variant incorporating dividends or time-dependent parameters). Many seemingly complicated option valuation problems, such as exotic options, become simple when looked at in this way. It is also important to note, though, that many options, for example American options, have values that depend on the history of the asset price as well as its present value. We see later how they fit into the Black–Scholes framework.

Before moving on, we make three remarks about the derivation we have just seen. Firstly, the **delta**, given by

$$\Delta = \frac{\partial V}{\partial S},$$

is the rate of change of the value of our option or portfolio of options with respect to S. It is of fundamental importance in both theory and practice, and we return to it repeatedly. It is a measure of the correlation between the movements of the option or options and those of the underlying asset.

Secondly, the linear differential operator $\mathcal{L}_{BS}$ given by

$$\mathcal{L}_{BS} = \frac{\partial}{\partial t} + \tfrac{1}{2}\sigma^2 S^2 \frac{\partial^2}{\partial S^2} + rS\frac{\partial}{\partial S} - r$$

has a financial interpretation as a measure of the difference between the return on a hedged option portfolio (the first two terms) and the return on a bank deposit (the last two terms). Although this return is identically zero for a European option we see later that this need not be so for an American option.

Thirdly, we note that the Black–Scholes equation (3.9) does not contain the growth parameter μ. In other words, the value of an option is independent of how rapidly or slowly an asset grows. The only parameter from the stochastic differential equation (2.1) for the asset price that affects the option price is the volatility, σ. A consequence of this is that two people may differ in their estimates for μ yet still agree on the value of an option.

3.5 The Black–Scholes equation

Equation (3.9) is the first partial differential equation that we have derived in this book. As we have said, the theory and solution methods for partial differential equations are discussed in depth in Chapters 4–7. Nevertheless, we now introduce a few basic points in the theory so that the reader is aware of what we are trying to achieve.

By deriving the partial differential equation for a quantity, such as an option price, we have made an enormous step towards finding its value. We hope to be able to find an expression for this value by solving the equation. Sometimes this involves solution by numerical means if exact formulæ cannot be found. However, a partial differential equation on its own generally has many solutions. The value of an option should be unique (otherwise, arbitrage possibilities would arise) and so, to pin down the solution, we must also impose boundary conditions. A boundary condition specifies the behaviour of the required solution at some part of the solution domain.

The commonest type of partial differential equation in financial problems is the parabolic equation. In its simplest form a parabolic equation relates the partial derivatives of a function, $V(S,t)$, say, of two variables, S and t, say. The highest derivative with respect to S must be a second derivative and the highest derivative with respect to t must only be a first derivative. Thus (3.9) comes into this category. If the signs of these particular derivatives are the same, when they appear on the same side of the equation, then the equation is called backward parabolic; otherwise it is called forward parabolic. Equation (3.9) is backward parabolic.

Once we have decided that our partial differential equation is of this parabolic type we can make general statements about the sort of boundary conditions that lead to a unique solution. Typically, we must pose two conditions in S, which has the second derivative associated with it, but only one in t. For example we could specify that

$$V(S,t) = V_a(t) \quad \text{on} \quad S = a$$

and

$$V(S,t) = V_b(t) \quad \text{on} \quad S = b$$

where V_a and V_b are given functions of t.

If the equation is of backward type we must also impose a 'final' condition such as

$$V(S,t) = V_T(S) \quad \text{on} \quad t = T$$

where V_T is a known function. We then solve for V in the region $t < T$. That is, we solve 'backwards in time', hence the name. If the equation is of forward type we impose an 'initial' condition on $t = 0$, say, and solve in $t > 0$, in the forward direction. Of course, we can change from backward to forward by the simple change of variables $t' = -t$. This is why both types of equation are mathematically the same and it is common to transform backward equations into forward equations before any analysis. It is important to remember, however, that the parabolic equation cannot be solved in the wrong direction; that is, we should not impose initial conditions on a backward equation.

3.6 Boundary and final conditions

3.6.1 European options

Having derived the Black–Scholes equation for the value of an option, we must next consider final and boundary conditions, for otherwise the partial differential equation does not have a unique solution. For the moment we restrict our attention to a European call, with value now denoted by $C(S,t)$, with exercise price E and expiry date T.

The final condition, to be applied at $t = T$, comes from the arbitrage argument described in Section 3.1. At $t = T$, the value of a call is known with certainty to be the payoff:

$$C(S, T) = \max(S - E, 0). \tag{3.10}$$

This is the final condition for our partial differential equation.

Our 'spatial' or asset-price boundary conditions are applied at zero asset price, $S = 0$, and as $S \to \infty$. We can see from (2.1) that if S is ever zero then dS is also zero and therefore S can never change. This is the only deterministic case of the stochastic differential equation (2.1). If $S = 0$ at expiry the payoff is zero. Thus the call option is worthless on $S = 0$ even if there is a long time to expiry. Hence on $S = 0$ we have

$$C(0, t) = 0. \tag{3.11}$$

As the asset price increases without bound it becomes ever more likely that the option will be exercised and the magnitude of the exercise price becomes less and less important. Thus as $S \to \infty$ the value of the option becomes that of the asset and we write

$$C(S, t) \sim S \quad \text{as} \quad S \to \infty. \tag{3.12}$$

For a European call option, without the possibility of early exercise, (3.9)-(3.12) can be solved exactly to give the Black–Scholes value of a call option. We show how to do this in Chapter 5, and at the end of this section we quote the results for a European call and put.

For a put option, with value $P(S, t)$, the final condition is the payoff

$$P(S, T) = \max(E - S, 0). \tag{3.13}$$

We have already mentioned that if S is ever zero then it must remain zero. In this case the final payoff for a put is known with certainty to be E. To determine $P(0, t)$ we simply have to calculate the present value of an amount E received at time T. Assuming that interest rates are constant we find the boundary condition at $S = 0$ to be

$$P(0, t) = Ee^{-r(T-t)}. \tag{3.14}$$

More generally, for a time-dependent interest rate we have

$$P(0,t) = Ee^{-\int_t^T r(\tau)d\tau}.$$

As $S \to \infty$ the option is unlikely to be exercised and so

$$P(S,t) \to 0 \quad \text{as} \quad S \to \infty. \tag{3.15}$$

Technical Point: boundary conditions at infinity.
We see later that we can transform (3.9) into an equation with constant coefficients by the change of variable $S = Ee^x$. The point $S = 0$ becomes $x = -\infty$ and $S = \infty$ becomes $x = \infty$. As we also see, a physical analogy to the financial problem would be the flow of heat in an infinite bar. Clearly, prescribing boundary conditions for the temperature of the bar at $x = \pm\infty$ has no effect whatsoever unless that temperature is highly singular there. If the temperature at infinity is well behaved then the temperature in any finite region of the bar is governed wholly by the initial data: it cannot be influenced by the ends at infinity. Since most option problems can be transformed into the diffusion equation it is also not strictly necessary to prescribe the boundary conditions at $S = 0$ and $S = \infty$. We only need to insist that the value of the option is not too singular. We can distinguish between

- *prescribing a boundary condition in order to make the solution unique, and*
- *determining the solution in the neighbourhood of the boundary, perhaps to assist or check the numerical solution.*

The boundary conditions (3.11) and (3.12) contain more information than is strictly mathematically necessary *(see Section 4.6). Nevertheless, they are financially* useful*: they tell us more information about the behaviour of the option at certain special parts of the S-axis and can be used to improve the accuracy of any numerical method. It can actually be shown that an even more accurate expression for the behaviour of C as $S \to \infty$ is*

$$C(S,t) \sim S - Ee^{-r(T-t)}.$$

This is a simple correction to (3.12) which accounts for the discounted exercise price.

Throughout the book we give boundary conditions to show the local behaviour of the option price.

3.6.2 The Black–Scholes formulæ: European options

Here we quote the exact solution of the European call option problem (3.9)–(3.12) when the interest rate and volatility are constant; in Chapter 5 we show how to derive it systematically. In Chapter 8 we drop the constraint that r and σ are constant and find more general formulæ.

When r and σ are constant the exact, explicit solution for the European call is

$$C(S,t) = SN(d_1) - Ee^{-r(T-t)}N(d_2), \tag{3.16}$$

where $N(\cdot)$ is the cumulative distribution function for a standardised normal random variable, given by

$$N(x) = \frac{1}{\sqrt{2\pi}} \int_{-\infty}^{x} e^{-\frac{1}{2}y^2}\,dy.$$

Here also,

$$d_1 = \frac{\log(S/E) + (r + \frac{1}{2}\sigma^2)(T-t)}{\sigma\sqrt{T-t}}.$$

and

$$d_2 = \frac{\log(S/E) + (r - \frac{1}{2}\sigma^2)(T-t)}{\sigma\sqrt{T-t}}.$$

For a put, i.e. (3.9), (3.13), (3.14) and (3.15), the solution is

$$P(S,t) = Ee^{-r(T-t)}N(-d_2) - SN(-d_1). \tag{3.17}$$

It is easy to show that these satisfy put-call parity (3.2).

The delta for a European call is

$$\Delta = \frac{\partial C}{\partial S} = N(d_1), \tag{3.18}$$

and for a put it is

$$\Delta = \frac{\partial P}{\partial S} = N(d_1) - 1.$$

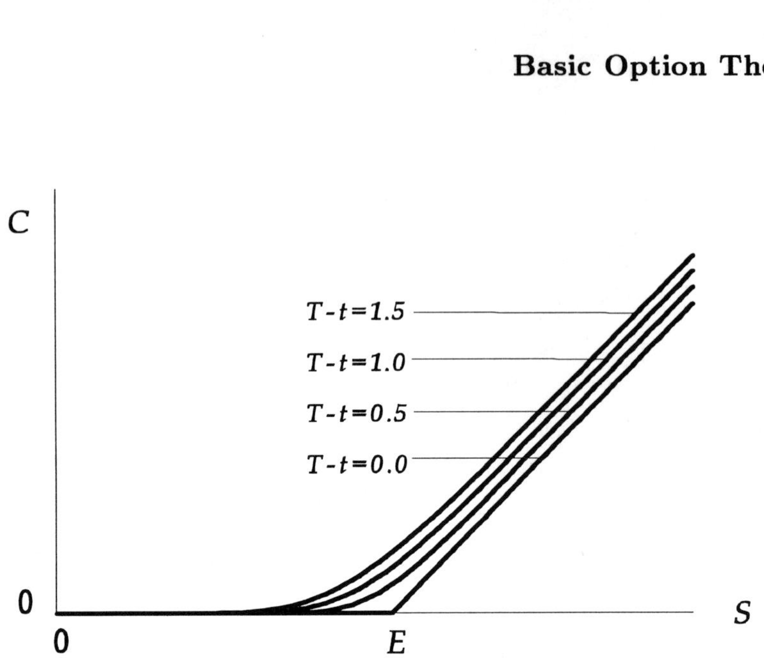

Figure 3.6: The European call value $C(S,t)$ as a function of S for several values of time to expiry; $r = 0.1$, $\sigma = 0.2$, $E = 1$ and $T - t = 0$, 0.5, 1.0 and 1.5.

The latter follows from the former by put-call parity.

Other derivatives of the option value (with respect to S, t, r and σ) can play important roles in hedging and are discussed briefly at the end of this chapter.

In Figures 3.6 and 3.7 we show plots of the European call and put values for several times up to expiry. Note how the curves approach the payoff functions as $t \to T$. In Figure 3.8 we show the European call delta as a function of S, again for several times up to expiry. The delta is always between zero and one, and approaches a step function as $t \to T$.

Equations (3.16) and (3.17) for the values of European call and put options are interesting in that they contain the function for the cumulative normal distribution $N(x)$. Thus the value of an option is related to the probability density function for the random variable S. It can be shown, and we discuss this in Appendix A, that the value of an option has a natural interpretation as the discounted expected value of the payoff at expiry. This leads on to the subject

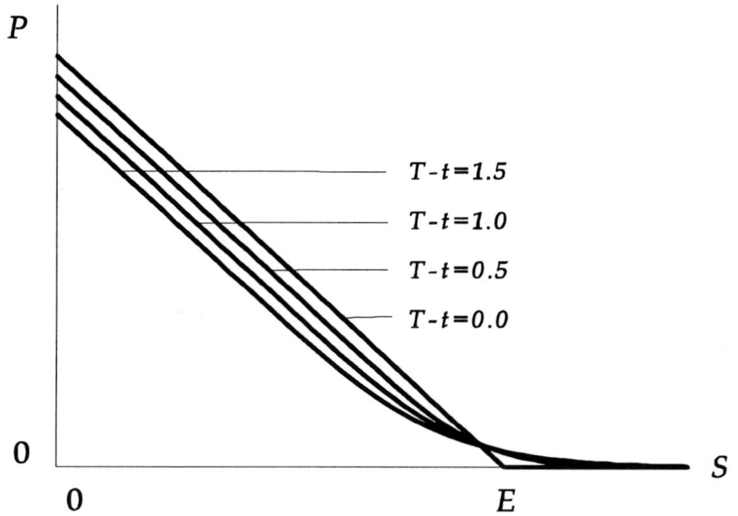

Figure 3.7: The European put value $P(S,t)$ as a function of S for several values of time to expiry; $r = 0.1$, $\sigma = 0.2$, $E = 1$ and $T - t = 0$, 0.5 1.0 and 1.5.

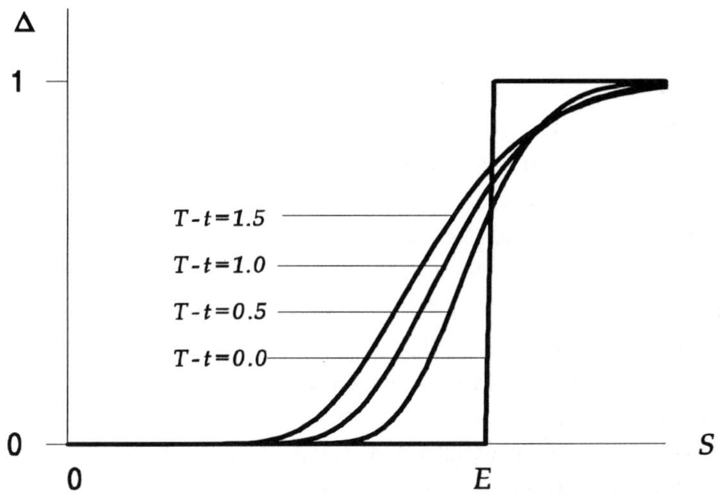

Figure 3.8: The European call delta as a function of S for several values of time to expiry; $r = 0.1$, $\sigma = 0.2$, $E = 1$ and $T - t = 0$, 0.5, 1.0 and 1.5.

of the 'risk-neutral valuation' of contingent claims, a phrase which is explained in that Appendix.

3.7 Options on dividend-paying assets

Many assets, such as equities, pay out dividends. The price of an option on such an underlying is affected by these payments and we must therefore modify the Black–Scholes analysis. In this section we show how this is done for the very simplest dividend payment: a continuous and constant dividend yield. We need this model for the later discussion of the American call option. In Chapter 8 the subject of dividend payments is discussed in more detail.

Several different structures are possible for the dividend payments. From the modelling point of view, the following points are important:

- payments may be deterministic or stochastic;
- payments may be made continuously or at discrete times.

In this book we only consider deterministic dividends, whose amount and timing are known at the start of an option's life. This is a reasonable assumption since many companies endeavour to maintain a similar payment from year to year.

Let us consider the very simplest type of payment. Suppose that in a time dt the underlying asset pays out a dividend $D_0 S\,dt$ where D_0 is a constant. This payment is independent of time except through the dependence on S. The **dividend yield** is defined as the ratio of the dividend payment to the asset price. Thus the dividend $D_0 S\,dt$ represents a constant and continuous dividend yield. This dividend structure is a good model for index options; the many discrete dividend payments on a large index can be approximated by a continuous yield without serious error.

Arbitrage considerations show that the asset price must fall by the amount of the dividend payment, that is, the random walk for the asset price (2.1) is modified to

$$dS = \sigma S\,dX + (\mu - D_0)S\,dt. \tag{3.19}$$

We have seen that the Black–Scholes equation is unaffected by the coefficient of dt in the stochastic differential equation for S and so one might expect the dividend to have no effect on the option price. This is not the case. We have allowed for the effect of the dividend payment on the asset price but not its effect on the value of our hedged portfolio. Since we receive $D_0 S\,dt$ for every asset held and since we hold $-\Delta$ of the underlying, our portfolio changes by an amount

$$-\,D_0 S \Delta\, dt, \tag{3.20}$$

i.e. the dividend our assets receive. Thus, we must add (3.20) to our earlier $d\Pi$ to arrive at

$$d\Pi = dV - \Delta\, dS - D_0 S \Delta\, dt.$$

The analysis proceeds exactly as before but with the addition of this new term. We find that

$$\frac{\partial V}{\partial t} + \tfrac{1}{2}\sigma^2 S^2 \frac{\partial^2 V}{\partial S^2} + (r - D_0) S \frac{\partial V}{\partial S} - rV = 0. \tag{3.21}$$

This model is also applicable to options on foreign currencies, though only for short dated options as it is debatable whether (2.1) is a good model for currencies over long timescales. Since holding an amount of foreign currency yields interest at the foreign rate r_f, in this case $D_0 = r_f$.

We now consider the effect that a nonzero dividend yield has on the boundary and final conditions. The Black–Scholes equation is modified to (3.21) and it can easily be seen that for a call option the final condition is still (3.10), and that the boundary condition at $S = 0$ remains as (3.11). The only change to the boundary conditions is that

$$C(S,t) \sim S e^{-D_0(T-t)}, \quad \text{as} \quad S \to \infty. \tag{3.22}$$

This is because in the limit $S \to \infty$, the option becomes equivalent to the asset *but without its dividend income.*

With the addition of a constant dividend yield D_0 we may show that the value of the European call option is

$$C(S,t) = e^{-D_0(T-t)} S N(d_{10}) - E e^{-r(T-t)} N(d_{20}),$$

where

$$d_{10} = \frac{\log(S/E) + (r - D_0 + \tfrac{1}{2}\sigma^2)(T-t)}{\sigma\sqrt{T-t}}, \quad d_{20} = d_1 - \sigma\sqrt{T-t}.$$

These results are discussed further in Chapter 6.

3.8 American options

We recall from Section 1.4 that an American option has the additional feature that exercise is permitted at any time during the life of the option. The explicit formulæ quoted above, which are valid for European options where early exercise is not permitted, do not necessarily give the value for American options. In fact, since the American option gives its holder greater rights than the European option via the right of early exercise, potentially it has a higher value. The following arbitrage argument shows how this can happen.

Figure 3.7 shows that before expiry there is a large range of asset values S for which the value of a European put option is less than its intrinsic value (the payoff function). Suppose that S lies in this range, so that $P(S,t) < \max(E-S,0)$. Now imagine that the option can be exercised at this time. An obvious arbitrage opportunity arises: by purchasing the option for P, exercising it by selling the asset for E, and repurchasing the asset in the market for S, a risk-free profit of $E - P - S$ is made. Of course, such an opportunity would not last long before the value of the option was pushed up by the demand of arbitragers. We conclude that when early exercise is permitted we must impose the constraint

$$V(S,t) \geq \max(S-E,0). \tag{3.23}$$

It follows that the value of an American put option must be different from the corresponding European put. As Figure 3.7 shows, the range of values for which the latter lies below the payoff is significant.

A second example of an American option whose value differs from that of a European equivalent is a call option on a dividend-paying asset. Recall from equation (3.22) that for large values of S, the dominant behaviour of the European option is

$$C(S,t) \sim Se^{-D_0(T-t)}.$$

If $D_0 > 0$, this certainly lies below the payoff $\max(S-E,0)$ for large S, and an arbitrage argument as above shows that the American version of this option must also be more valuable than the European version since it must satisfy the constraint

$$C(S,t) \geq \max(S-E,0).$$

The valuation of American options is what is known as a **free boundary problem**. Typically at each time t there is a value of S which marks the boundary between two regions: to one side one should hold the option and to the other side one should exercise it. We denote this boundary by $S_f(t)$ (in general this critical asset value varies with time). Since we do not know S_f *a priori* we are lacking one piece of information compared with the corresponding European valuation problem. With the European option we know which boundary conditions to apply and, equally importantly, *where* to apply them. With the American problem we do not know *a priori* where to apply boundary conditions. This situation is common to many physical problems and as a canonical example we mention the **obstacle problem**.

At its simplest, an obstacle problem arises when an elastic string is held fixed at two ends, A and B, and passes over a smooth object which protrudes between the two ends (see Figure 3.9). Again, we do not know *a priori* the region of contact between the string and the obstacle, only that the string is either in contact with the obstacle, in which case its position is known, or it must satisfy an equation of motion, which, in this case, says that it must be straight. Beyond this, the string must satisfy two constraints. The first simply says that the string must lie above or on the obstacle; combined with the equation of motion, the curvature of the string must be negative or zero. Another interpretation of this is that the obstacle can never exert a negative force on the string: it can push but not pull. The second constraint on the string is that its slope must be continuous. This is obvious except at points where the string first loses contact with the obstacle, and there it is justified by a local force balance: a lateral force is needed to create a kink in the string. In summary,

- the string must be above or on the obstacle;
- the string must have negative or zero curvature;
- the string must be continuous;
- the string slope must be continuous.

Under these constraints, the solution to the obstacle problem can be shown to be unique. The string and its slope are continuous, but

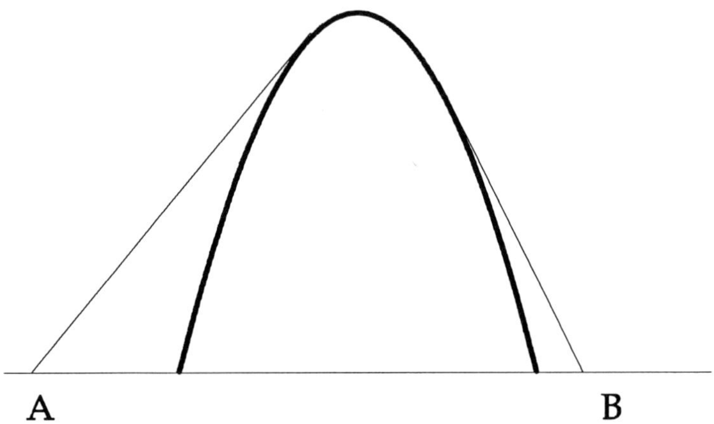

Figure 3.9: The classical obstacle problem: the string is held fixed at A and B and must pass smoothly over the obstacle in between.

in general the curvature of the string, and hence its second derivative, has discontinuities.

An American option valuation problem can also be shown to be uniquely specified by a set of constraints, similar to those just given for the obstacle problem. They are:

- the option value must be greater than or equal to the payoff function;
- the Black–Scholes equality is replaced by an inequality (this is made precise shortly);
- the option value must be a continuous function of S;
- the option delta (its slope) must be continuous.

The first of these constraints says that the arbitrage profit obtainable from early exercise must be less than or equal to zero. It does not mean that early exercise should never occur, merely that arbitrage opportunities should not. Thus, either the option value is the same as the payoff function, and the option should be exercised, or, where it exceeds the payoff, it satisfies the appropriate Black–Scholes equation. It turns out that these two statements can be combined into one inequality for the Black–Scholes equation, which is our second constraint above. There are some interesting features to this inequality, and we return to it briefly below.

The third constraint, that the option value is continuous, follows from simple arbitrage. If there were a discontinuity in the option value as a function of S, and if this discontinuity persisted for more than an infinitesimal time, a portfolio of options only would make a risk-free profit with probability one should the asset price ever reach the value at which the discontinuity occurred[4].

Just as in the obstacle problem, we do not know the position of S_f, and we must impose *two* conditions at S_f if the option value is to be uniquely determined. This is one more than if S_f were specified. The second condition at S_f, our fourth constraint above, is that the option delta must also be continuous there. Its derivation is rather more delicate, and we only give two informal financially-based arguments. Readers who prefer a more formal approach will find it in the books by Merton (1990) and Duffie (1992).

Consider the American put option, with value $P(S,t)$. We have already argued that this option has an exercise boundary $S = S_f(t)$, where the option should be exercised if $S < S_f(t)$ and held otherwise. Assuming that $S_f(t) < E$, the slope of the payoff function $\max(E - S, 0)$ at the contact point is -1. There are three possibilities[5] for the slope (delta) of the option, $\partial P/\partial S$, at $S = S_f(t)$:

- $\partial P/\partial S < -1$;
- $\partial P/\partial S > -1$;
- $\partial P/\partial S = -1$.

We show that the first two are incorrect.

[4]This result does *not* prohibit discontinuous option prices, caused for example by an instantaneous change in the terms of the contract such as the imposition of a constraint by a change from European to American. Indeed, such discontinuities, or jumps, play an important part in later chapters.

[5]A fourth is that $\partial P/\partial S$ does not exist at $S = S_f(t)$. We assume, as can be shown to be the case, that it does.

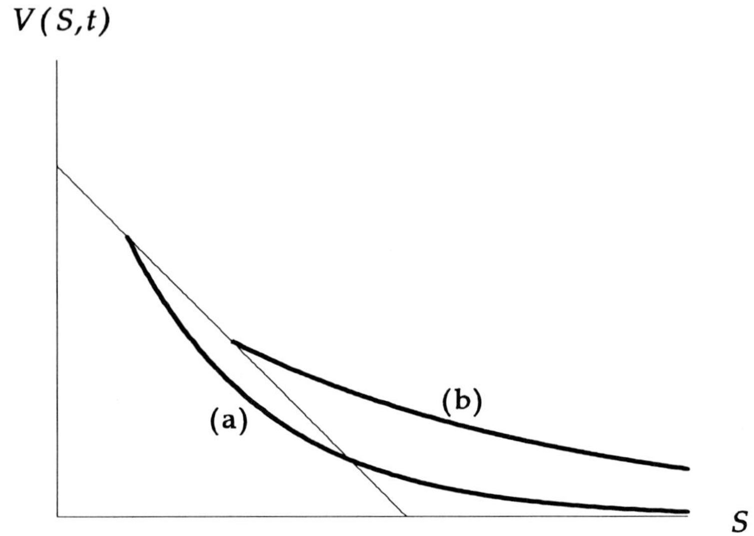

Figure 3.10: Exercise price (a) too low (b) too high.

Suppose first that $\partial P/\partial S < -1$. Then as S increases from $S_f(t)$, $P(S,t)$ drops below the payoff $\max(E-S,0)$, since its slope is more negative; see Figure 3.10(a). This contradicts our earlier arbitrage bound $P(S,t) \geq \max(E-S,0)$, and so is impossible.

Now suppose that $\partial P/\partial S > -1$, as in Figure 3.10(b). In this case, we argue that an option value with this slope would be sub-optimal for the holder, in the sense that it does not give the option its maximum value consistent with the Black–Scholes risk-free hedging strategy and the arbitrage constraint $P(S,t) \geq \max(E-S,0)$. In order to see this, we must discuss the strategy adopted by the holder. There are two aspects to consider. One is the day-to-day arbitrage-based hedging strategy which, as above, leads to the Black–Scholes equation. The other is the **exercise strategy**: the holder must decide, in principle, how far S should fall before he would exercise the option. The basis of this decision is, naturally enough, that the chosen strategy should maximise an appropriate measure of the value of the option to its holder[6]. Because the option satisfies a partial differ-

[6]This choice also minimises the benefit to the writer, but since the holder can

ential equation with $P(S_f(t),t) = E - S_f(t)$ as one of the boundary conditions, the choice of $S_f(t)$ affects the value of $P(S,t)$ for *all* larger values of S. Clearly the case of Figure 3.10(a) corresponds to too low a value of $S_f(t)$, and an arbitrage profit is possible for S just above $S_f(t)$. Conversely, if $\partial P/\partial S > -1$ at $S = S_f(t)$, the value of the option near $S = S_f(t)$ can be increased by choosing a smaller value for S_f: the exercise value then moves up the payoff curve and $\partial P/\partial S$ decreases. The option is thus again misvalued. In fact, the increase in P is passed on by the partial differential equation to all values of S greater than S_f, and by decreasing S_f we arrive at the crossover point between our two incorrect possibilities, which simultaneously maximises the benefit to the holder and avoids arbitrage. This yields the correct free boundary condition $\partial P/\partial S = -1$ at $S = S_f(t)$.

We must stress that the argument just given is not a rigorous formal derivation of the second free boundary condition. Such a derivation might be couched in the language of stochastic control and optimal stopping problems, or of game theory; both are beyond the scope of this book. Suffice it to say that the correct formulation of a rational operator's strategy when holding an American option can be shown to lead to the condition that the option value meets the payoff function smoothly, as long as the latter is smooth too.

A second, more heuristic, derivation of the smoothness condition, again based on an arbitrage argument, is as follows. Let us again consider the American put option with price $P(S,t)$, although the argument can easily be generalised. Let us suppose that S is near S_f. We consider a simple portfolio, long one of the asset and one put option:

$$\Pi = P + S.$$

The jump in the value of this portfolio over a small time dt is

$$d\Pi = dP + dS.$$

Since $P = E - S$ for $S < S_f$, for a downward move in S we have

$$d\Pi = 0 \quad \text{for} \quad S < S_f.$$

---

close the contract by exercising and the writer cannot, the latter's point of view is not relevant to this argument. Of course, the writer requires a greater premium in recompense for the one-sided nature of the contract.

On the other hand, if the next move in S is upwards, then

$$d\Pi = \left(\sigma S\frac{\partial P}{\partial S} + \sigma S\right) dX + O(dt),$$

where the $O(dt)$ remainder contains the drift term from dS and the remaining terms due to Itô's lemma applied to P.

Thus,

$$\mathcal{E}[d\Pi] = \tfrac{1}{2}\sigma S\left(\frac{\partial P}{\partial S} + 1\right)\mathcal{E}[|dX|] = \sqrt{\frac{2\,dt}{\pi}}\sigma S\left(\frac{\partial P}{\partial S} + 1\right) + O(dt).$$

This portfolio has an expected return of order $\sqrt{dt}$ over a time dt. Since this is $O(1/\sqrt{dt})$ greater in magnitude than the return on a riskless portfolio, $r\Pi\,dt$, it could not be sustained in the presence of arbitragers. We conclude that

$$\frac{\partial P}{\partial S} = -1,$$

i.e. that the gradient $\partial P/\partial S$ must be continuous at $S = S_f$.

Finally, we return to the second of constraint above, the 'inequality' satisfied by the Black–Scholes operator. Recall that the Black–Scholes partial differential equation follows from an arbitrage argument. This argument is only partially valid for American options, but the intimate relationship between arbitrage and the Black–Scholes operator persists; the former now yields an inequality (rather than an equation) for the latter.

We set up the delta-hedged portfolio as before, with exactly the same choice for the delta. However, in the American case it is not necessarily possible for the option to be held both long and short since there are times when it is optimal to exercise the option. Thus, the writer of an option may be exercised against. Arbitrage no longer leads to a unique value for the return on the portfolio, only to an inequality. We can only say that the return from the portfolio cannot be greater than the return from a bank deposit. For an American put, this gives

$$\frac{\partial P}{\partial t} + \tfrac{1}{2}\sigma^2 S^2\frac{\partial^2 P}{\partial S^2} + rS\frac{\partial P}{\partial S} - rP \le 0. \tag{3.24}$$

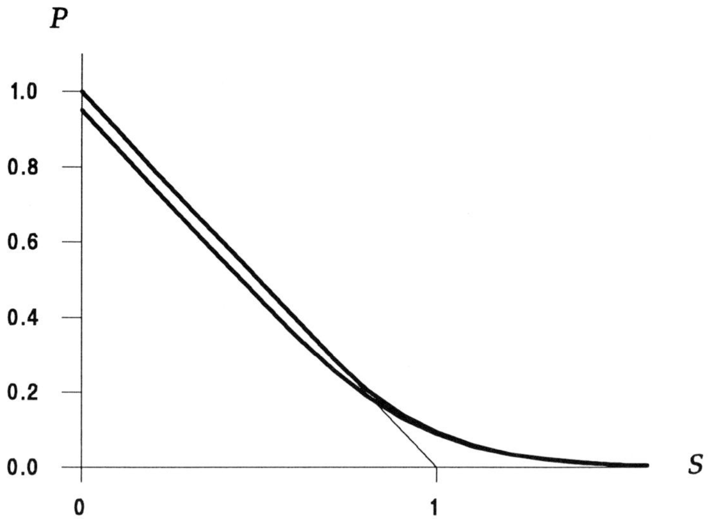

Figure 3.11: The values of European and American put options as functions of S; $r = 0.1$, $\sigma = 0.4$, $E = 1$, six months to expiry.

The *inequality* here would be an *equality* for a European option. When it is optimal to hold the option the equality, i.e. the Black–Scholes equation, is valid and the constraint (3.23) must be satisfied. Otherwise, it is optimal to exercise the option, and only the inequality in (3.24) holds and the equality in (3.23) is satisfied—the obstacle is the solution.

More generally, for other vanilla options (and including a dividend yield) we have

$$\frac{\partial V}{\partial t} + \tfrac{1}{2}\sigma^2 S^2 \frac{\partial^2 V}{\partial S^2} + (r - D_0)S\frac{\partial V}{\partial S} - rV \leq 0.$$

We see other examples of such partial differential inequalities in later chapters on exotic options.

In Figure 3.11 we compare the values of European and American put options at six months before expiry with $\sigma = 0.4$ and $r = 0.1$. The former is given by the explicit formula (3.17) and the latter has been calculated numerically by the methods of Chapter 21.

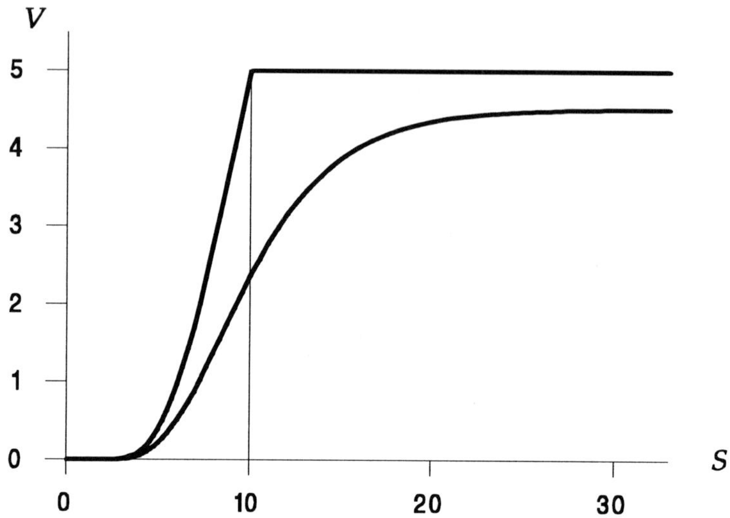

Figure 3.12: European and American values of a cash-or-nothing call with $E = 10$, $B = 5$, $r = 0.1$, $\sigma = 0.4$, $D = 0.02$ and one year to expiry.

Technical Point: options with discontinuous payoffs.
The condition that the Δ for an American option must be continuous assumes that the payoff function is itself continuous. That is, it is only possible for the option value to meet the payoff tangentially if the payoff has a well-defined tangent at the point of contact.

As an example, consider an American cash-or-nothing call option with payoff given by

$$V(S,T) = \begin{cases} 0 & S < E \\ B & S \geq E \end{cases}$$

The payoff is discontinuous. The option value is continuous, but the Δ is discontinuous at $S = E$. It is clear that the optimal exercise boundary is always *at $S = E$; there is no gain to be made from holding such an option once S has reached the exercise price. Indeed,* *potential interest on the payoff is lost if it is held after* S *has reached* E*. Thus, there is no point in hedging for* $S > E$*; looked at another way,* $\Delta = 0$ *for* $S > E$*. Clearly* $\Delta > 0$ *for* $S < E$*.*

Mathematically, we find that we have two boundary conditions, namely $V(0,t) = 0$, $V(E,t) = B$ *and a payoff condition* $V(S,T) = 0$ *for* $0 \leq S \leq E$*. There is no point in considering values of* $S > E$*, since the option would have been exercised. Unlike the usual American option, where 'spatial' boundary conditions are applied at an unknown value of* S*, and so an extra condition is needed, both the spatial conditions here are at known values of* S*. These three conditions therefore give a unique solution of the Black–Scholes equation; the* Δ *is determined by this solution. Note that it is impossible for the* Δ *to be continuous at* $S = E$ *(even though* V *is) because the payoff function is discontinuous.*

This option also illustrates very well the idea that the exercise strategy for an American option should maximise its value to the holder. It is particularly clear here that the choice $S_f(t) = E$ *gives the largest values of* $V(S,t)$ *for all* $S < E$*, as illustrated in Figure 3.12.*

3.9 Hedging in practice

Hedging is the reduction of the sensitivity of a portfolio to the movement of an underlying asset by taking opposite positions in different financial instruments. Two extreme cases have been introduced above; in both cases the sensitivity of the portfolio was reduced to zero. The first example was in the demonstration of put-call parity for European options and the second was in the Black–Scholes analysis with delta-hedging. These are, however, fundamentally different hedging strategies. The former involves a one-off purchase of three products (a call, a put and the underlying); the resulting portfolio can then be left unattended with the riskless return locked in. The latter is a dynamic strategy; the delta hedge requires a continuous rebalancing of the portfolio and the ratio of the holdings in the asset and the derivative product. The delta-hedge position must be monitored continually, and in practice it can suffer from losses due to the costs of transacting in the underlying.

One use for delta-hedging is for the writer of an option who also wishes to cover his position. If the writer can get a premium slightly above the fair value for the option then he can trade in the underlying (or the futures contract, since this is usually cheaper to trade in because the transaction costs are lower) to maintain a delta-neutral position until expiry. Since he charges more for the option than it was theoretically worth he makes a net profit without any risk—in theory. This is only a practical policy for those with access to the markets at low dealing costs, such as market makers. If the transaction costs are significant then the frequent rehedging necessary to maintain a delta-neutral position renders the policy impractical. We discuss this point further in Chapter 13, and Gemmill (1992) gives a practical example illustrating the shortcomings of the purely theoretical approach.

The delta for a whole portfolio is the rate of change of the value of the portfolio with respect to changes in the underlying asset. Thus, when delta hedging between an option and an asset, the position taken is called 'delta-neutral' since the sensitivity to these changes is zero. For a general portfolio the maintenance of a delta-neutral position requires a short position in the underlying asset. This entails the selling of assets which are not owned—so-called short selling. A broker may require a margin to cover any movements against the short seller but this margin usually receives interest at the bank rate.

There are more sophisticated trading strategies than simple delta-hedging, and the reader should consult Cox & Rubinstein (1985) for details. Here we mention only the basics.

With Π denoting the value of any portfolio, the **delta** of a portfolio has been defined as

$$\Delta = \frac{\partial \Pi}{\partial S}.$$

In delta-hedging the largest random component of the portfolio is eliminated. One can be more subtle and hedge away smaller order effects due, for instance, to the curvature (the second derivative) of the portfolio value with respect to the underlying asset. This entails knowledge of the **gamma** of a portfolio, defined by

$$\Gamma = \frac{\partial^2 \Pi}{\partial S^2}.$$

(Remember that this is not always continuous for American options.) The decay of time value in a portfolio is represented by the **theta**, given by

$$\Theta = -\frac{\partial \Pi}{\partial t}.$$

Finally, sensitivity to volatility is usually called the **vega** and is given by

$$\frac{\partial \Pi}{\partial \sigma},$$

and sensitivity to interest rate is called **rho**, where

$$\rho = \frac{\partial \Pi}{\partial r}.$$

By balancing their portfolio with the correct number of the underlying asset, hedgers can eliminate the short-term dependence of the portfolio on movements in time, asset price, volatility or interest rate.

3.10 Implied volatility

We have suggested in the above modelling and analysis that the way to use the Black–Scholes and other models is to take parameter values estimated from historic data, substitute them into a formula (or perhaps solve an equation numerically), and so derive the value for a derivative product. This is no longer the commonest use of option models, at least not for the simplest options. This is partly because of difficulty in measuring the value of the volatility of the underlying asset. Despite our assumption to the contrary, it does not appear to be the case that volatility is constant for long periods of time (see Hull & White 1987). Nor is it obvious that the historic volatility is independent of the time series from which it is calculated.

A direct measurement of volatility is therefore difficult in practice. However, despite these difficulties it is plainly true that option prices are quoted in the market. This suggests that, even if we do not know the volatility, the market 'knows' it. Take the Black–Scholes formulæ, for example, and substitute in the interest rate, the price of the underlying, the exercise price and the time to expiry. All of these are very simple to measure and are either quoted constantly or are defined as part of the option contract. All that remains is to specify the volatility and the option price follows. Since the option price increases monotonically with volatility (this is easy to show from the explicit formulæ and, as we have already mentioned, is clear financially) there is a one-to-one correspondence between the volatility and the option price. Thus we could take the option price quoted in the market and, working backwards, deduce the market's opinion of the value for the volatility. This volatility, derived from the quoted price for a single option, is called the **implied volatility**.

There are more advanced ways of calculating the market view of volatility using more than one option price. In particular, using option prices for a variety of expiry dates one can, in principle, deduce the market's opinion of the future values for the volatility of the underlying (the **term structure of volatility**).

One unusual feature of implied volatility is that the implied volatility does not appear to be constant across exercise prices. That is, if the value of the underlying, the interest rate and the time to expiry are fixed, the prices of options across exercise prices should reflect a uniform value for the volatility. In practice this is not the case and this highlights a flaw in some part of the model. Which part of the model is incorrect is the subject of a great deal of academic research. We illustrate this effect in Figure 3.13, which shows the implied volatilities as a function of exercise price using the *FT-SE* index option data in Figure 1.1. Observe how the volatility of the options deeply in-the-money is greater than for those at-the-money. This curve is traditionally called the 'smile', although depending on market conditions it may be lopsided as in Figure 3.13, or even a 'frown'.

3.11 Forward and futures contracts

Options are not the only contingent claims in existence. In this section we briefly describe two other types of contract, forward contracts and futures contracts. Neither contains the element of choice (to exercise or not to exercise) that is inherent in an option, and hence they are easier to value.

A **forward contract** is an agreement between two parties whereby one contracts to buy a specified asset from the other for a specified price, known as the **forward price**, on a specified date in the future,

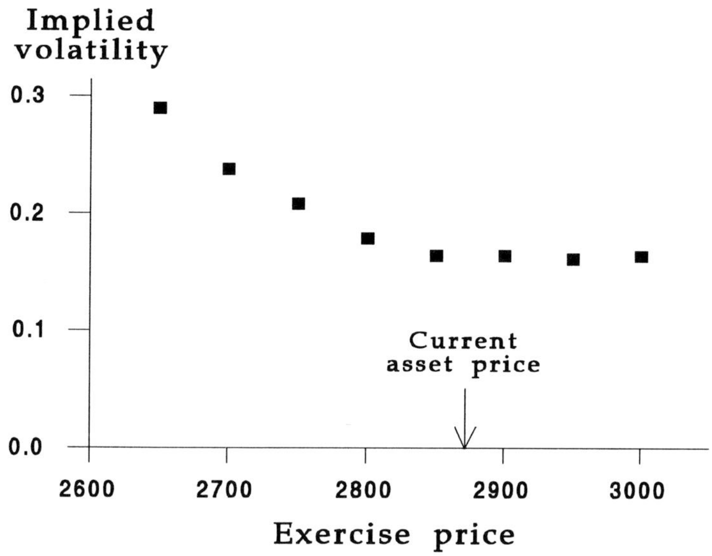

Figure 3.13: Implied volatilities as a function of exercise price. Data is taken from *FT-SE* index option prices.

the delivery date or maturity date. This contract has similarities to an option contract if we think of the forward price as equivalent to the exercise price. However, as well as the absence of choice, the forward contract is different from the option contract in that no money changes hands until delivery.

Unlike an option, the forward price is not set at one of a number of fixed values for all contracts on the same asset with the same expiry. Instead, it is determined at the outset, individually for each contract. Suppose that the time at which the contract is agreed is t_0, and that the asset price at that time is $S(t_0)$. Denoting the forward price by F, we must find a relationship between $S(t_0)$ and F that will ensure fair value for both parties to the contract.

Arbitrage provides the fair value, at least when interest rates are known. Consider first the party who is short the contract, and so must deliver the asset at time T. Although he does not know at time

t_0 what the asset price will be at time T, this does not matter. He can satisfy his part of the contract by borrowing an amount $S(t_0)$ now, buying the asset, and using the money received at exercise, F, to pay off the loan. Assuming that the risk-free interest rate r is constant, the loan will cost $S(t_0)e^{r(T-t_0)}$. The forward price must therefore be given by

$$F = S(t_0)e^{r(T-t_0)}. \tag{3.25}$$

If this were not so, there would be a risk-free profit or loss on the transaction, in contradiction to the existence of arbitrage. A similar argument applies to the party who is long the contract, and yields the same price.

We can put the forward contract into the option framework by noting that the payoff of the forward contract at time T is $S - F$. The solution of the Black–Scholes equation with this final data is simply

$$S - Fe^{-r(T-t)},$$

at any earlier time t. However, the value of this contract is zero at initiation of the contract, time $t = t_0$, since no money changes hands until expiry. Thus we arrive at (3.25).

Another way of looking at this result is to notice that a long position in the forward contract is equivalent to a long position in a European call option and a short position in a put option, both with the same expiry and exercise price as the forward contract. For earlier times, formula (3.25) is just a restatement of the put-call parity result (3.2).

We also note that the value of a forward contract changes with time, because S changes. At any time t between t_0 and T, a party to a forward contract can lock in a profit (or loss) by entering into the equal and opposite contract. The argument above shows that the value then is

$$V(S,t) = S(t) - Fe^{r(T-t)}; \tag{3.26}$$

when $t = t_0$ the value is zero, and when $t = T$ it is the payoff, $S(T) - F$.

We have so far assumed that the asset in question pays no dividend. If it pays a constant dividend yield D_0, a simple modification to the argument above shows that the forward price is related to the current price by

$$F = S(t_0)e^{(r-D_0)(T-t_0)}. \tag{3.27}$$

In some cases D_0 may be negative, an example being the cost of holding an asset such as gold, which has to be stored and insured.

A **futures contract** is in essence a forward contract, but with some technical modifications. Whereas a forward contract may be set up between any two parties, futures are usually traded on an exchange which will specify certain standard features of the contract such as delivery date and contract size. A further complication is the margin requirement, a system designed to protect both parties to a futures contract against default. Whereas the profit or loss from a forward contract is only realised at the expiry date, the value of a futures contract is evaluated every day, and the change in value is paid to one party by the other, so that the net profit or loss is paid across gradually over the lifetime of the contract. Despite these differences, it can be shown that under some not too restrictive assumptions the futures price is almost the same as the forward price, and so it is given by (3.25). When interest rates are predictable, the two coincide exactly.

3.12 Warrants

Warrants are derivative securities related to options. They are usually call options on shares in a company, but with the difference that if they are exercised, the company issues new shares to complete the contract; an ordinary option refers to shares that already exist. There is thus a dilution of asset value on exercise, since the assets of the company are divided among more shares. From the company's point of view, warrants function as a deferred rights issue, thereby acting as a means of raising capital different from conventional rights issues and issue of debt. (The convertible bond, which combines features of debt with warrants, is discussed in Chapter 15.) A further difference between options and warrants lies in the lifespan: some warrants have 10 or more years to expiry. A final complication is that many warrants can be exercised intermittently at times before their expiry; a typical contract allows exercise for a short period in each of the five years prior to the final expiry date.

The question of asset dilution is complex. The central issue is to determine the behaviour of the share price at the expiry date, and this depends on the rights of the warrant-holders. A simple example illustrates this point. Suppose that a company issued one warrant per share entitling the holder (who is not the shareholder) to subscribe for one more share at 10p. Suppose too that the asset value per share of the company just before exercise is 100p. Then, if the warrant is exercised, the share price after exercise of the warrant must be $(100+10)/2 = 55$p, since the shareholders can, in principle, then wind up the company and distribute the assets. Now consider two extreme cases. In the first, the warrant-holders have no rights before exercise. The share price before exercise would then be 100p, which is the value that would be realised by the shareholders on winding up the company before exercise. Thus, the share price would suffer a drop across the exercise time. Conversely, if the company is illiquid, or rules protect the warrant-holders' rights, an arbitrage argument shows that the share price must be continuous across the exercise time. In practice, the latter case is nearer the truth than the former, and the share price incorporates the dilution in the run-up to exercise dates for warrants. (If the warrants expire at the money, even more complicated strategic decisions must be made.) Thus, we assume that the payoff at expiry of a warrant is

$$\max(S - E, 0)$$

as for a call option, where S is continuous across the exercise date.

Assuming that the share price behaviour at expiry is understood, warrants with just one expiry date can be priced as call options. Suppose, though, that there are two or more exercise dates, $t = T$ and $t = T_1 < T$. If the asset pays no dividend, then the straightforward European value (3.16) applies, since it is not optimal to exercise before $t = T$. Now suppose that a constant dividend yield D_0 is paid on the asset. Working backwards from $t = T$, we can still use the formula (3.16) until $t = T_1^+$; let us call this value $V_{BS}(S, T_1^+)$. As we noted for an American call option on a dividend-paying asset, for some values of S, $V_{BS}(S, T_1^+)$ is below the payoff $\max(S-E, 0)$. Just before T_1, on the other hand, the warrant must have a value greater than or equal to the payoff. We conclude that the warrant price must jump as a function of time across the exercise date $t = T_1$; for times before T_1, we solve the Black–Scholes equation for the warrant value $V(S,t)$ with final data

$$V(S,T_1) = \max(S - E, V_{BS}(S,T_1^+)).$$

This procedure can be extended in an obvious way to allow for further exercise dates.

Note that the jump in the warrant value as a function of time does not contradict the arbitrage argument we used earlier to show that option values must be continuous. Because the nature of the warrant changes instantaneously from exercisable to non-exercisable, it is a different product before and after time T_1. From the point of view of the warrant holder, if he exercises the warrant he ceases to hold a warrant but instead holds shares with the value that the warrant had just before exercise. The theoretical value of the warrant drops across T_1 but if the warrant-holder acts optimally, he does not experience this.

Further reading

- Carefully read the original papers of Black & Scholes (1973) and Merton (1973).

- Compare the binomial method for valuing options with the differential equation approach. The binomial method can be found in, for example, Cox & Rubinstein (1985). We discuss it in Appendix C.

- Jarrow & Rudd (1983) contains another derivation of the Black–Scholes formulæ using the 'risk-neutral' valuation method.

- Hull (1993) discusses the estimation of volatility using the implied volatilities of several options.

- There has been a great deal of work done on testing the validity of the Black–Scholes formulæ in practice. For details of how the call option formula stands up in practice see MacBeth & Merville (1979) and for a test of put-call parity see Klemkosky & Resnick (1979).

- Hull (1993) describes the workings of futures markets in some detail.
- Cox, Ingersoll & Ross (1981) establish the equivalence of forward and futures prices using an arbitrage argument.
- Several authors treat warrant pricing. Cox & Rubinstein (1985) in particular treat the complexities of exercise and the strategies involved. McHattie (1992) describes the UK warrant market in some detail.

Exercises

1. Today's date is 9th January 2000 and XYZ's share price stands at \$10. On 8th November 2000 there is to be a Presidential election and you believe that, depending on which party is elected, XYZ's share price will either rise or fall by approximately 10%. Construct a portfolio of options which will do well if you are correct. Calls and puts are available with expiry dates in March, June, September, December and with strike prices of \$10 plus or minus 50c. Draw the payoff diagram and describe the payoff mathematically.

2. Draw the expiry payoff diagrams for each of the following portfolios:

   (a) Short one share, long two calls with exercise price E.
   (b) Long one call and one put, both with exercise price E.
   (c) Long one call with exercise price E_1 and one put with exercise price E_2. Compare the three cases $E_1 > E_2$, $E_1 = E_2$ and $E_1 < E_2$.
   (d) As (c) but also short two calls with exercise price E.

   ((a) and (b) are different ways of creating a **straddle**. When $E_1 < E < E_2$, (d) is called a **butterfly spread**.) Use the market data of Figure 1.1 to calculate the cost of an example of each portfolio. What view about the market does each strategy express?

3. Show by substitution that two exact solutions of the Black–Scholes equation (3.9) are

(a) $V(S,t) = AS$,
(b) $V(S,t) = Ae^{rt}$,

where A is an arbitrary constant. What do these solutions represent and what is the Δ in each case?

Show that the formulæ (3.16) for a call and (3.17) for a put also satisfy (3.9) with the relevant boundary conditions (one at each of $S = 0$ and $S = \infty$) and final conditions at $t = T$.

4. Find the most general solution of the Black–Scholes equation that has the special form

   (a) $V = V(S)$, i.e. independent of time;
   (b) $V = A(t)B(S)$.

   These are examples of 'similarity solutions' which are discussed further in Chapter 5.

5. The **instalment option** has the same payoff as a vanilla call or put option; it may be European or American. Its unusual feature is that, as well as paying the initial premium, the holder must pay 'instalments' during the life of the option. The instalments may be paid either continuously or discretely. The holder can choose at any time to stop paying the instalments, at which point the contract is cancelled and the option ceases to exist. When instalments are paid continuously at a rate $L(t)$ per unit time, derive the differential equation satisfied by the option price. What new constraint must it satisfy?

   (Hint: The value of the standard portfolio decreases by an amount $L\,dt$ in time dt; this decrease may make the option value negative.)

6. Use arbitrage arguments to prove the following simple bounds on European call options on an asset that pays no dividends:

   (a) $C < S$;
   (b) if two otherwise identical calls have exercise prices E_1 and E_2 with $E_1 < E_2$, then

$$0 \leq C(S,t;E_1) - C(S,t;E_2) \leq E_2 - E_1;$$

(c) if two otherwise identical call options have expiry times T_1 and T_2 with $T_1 < T_2$, then

$$C(S, t; T_1) \leq C(S, t; T_2).$$

Derive similar restrictions for put options.

7. Derive the put-call parity result for American options in the form

$$C - P \leq S - Ee^{-r(T-t)}.$$

8. Calculate the exercise price for a forward contract when the interest rate $r(t)$ is a known function of time.

Chapter 4

Partial Differential Equations

4.1 Introduction

The modelling of Chapter 3 culminates in the formulation of the pricing problem for a derivative product as a partial differential equation. We now take a break from the financial modelling to discuss some of the theory behind such differential equations. This theory is covered in the next four chapters. In Chapter 4 we describe the elementary theory and the nature of boundary and initial conditions. In Chapter 5 we derive some explicit solutions, including the original Black–Scholes formulæ. In Chapters 6 and 7 we describe in detail the special problems arising when there are free boundaries. These two chapters are of particular importance when considering the valuation of American options.

The study of partial differential equations in complete generality is a vast undertaking. Fortunately, however, almost all the partial differential equations encountered in financial applications belong to a much more manageable subset of the whole: first order linear equations and second order linear parabolic equations. These technical terms are discussed below; more detailed treatments of the areas beyond the scope of this text are given by, for example, Williams (1980), Strang (1986), Keener (1988) and Kevorkian (1990).

We begin this chapter with a review of these equations: their physical interpretation, mathematical properties of their solutions, and techniques for obtaining explicit solutions to specific problems. Then, we exploit this knowledge in the context of financial models, and we set the scene for the numerical methods of Chapters 16–19.

Before doing this, though, it is helpful to step back and consider in general terms the questions we should ask when considering a partial differential equation. Such questions usually include any or all of the following:

- Does the equation make sense mathematically? If it is to be solved in a region, what must we say about the solution on the boundary of that region in order to obtain a **well-posed problem**, i.e. one whose solution exists, is unique, and is, in some sense, 'well behaved'? Such specifications of the solution on the boundary are called **boundary conditions** or, if applied at a particular value of time t, **initial conditions** or **final conditions**. The term 'well behaved' used here is usually taken to imply that the solution depends continuously on the initial and boundary conditions, so that small changes in these conditions cannot induce large changes in the solution itself. Beyond this, we also want to know what mathematical properties the solution must or can have. For example, is it guaranteed to be smooth or can it have discontinuities?

- Can we develop analytical tools to solve the equation? Explicit solutions are useful both to illustrate the general behaviour of the equation and for their application in practice. We note, though, that many explicit solutions may be so cumbersome as to be of less practical use than a well-designed numerical approximation.

- How should we solve the equation numerically, if this should be necessary? What implications do the mathematical properties of the solution have for the numerical method we choose? Are there alternative formulations, such as a change of variable or a weak statement of the problem (see Chapter 6), that lead to a better (simpler, more adaptable, more accurate, more robust, faster) numerical scheme?

These aims guide us in the sections to follow.

4.2 First order linear equations

Although partial differential equations are in general intrinsically more complicated than ordinary differential equations, there is one kind that can be reduced to a one-parameter system of ordinary differential equations. If the latter can be solved explicitly, then the complete solution to the original partial differential equation is known.

Suppose that $u(S,t)$ satisfies

$$\alpha(S,t)\frac{\partial u}{\partial S} + \beta(S,t)\frac{\partial u}{\partial t} = \gamma(S,t)u \tag{4.1}$$

for some known functions $\alpha(S,t)$, $\beta(S,t)$ and $\gamma(S,t)$. This equation is first order, because it contains no derivatives of higher order than the first. It is also linear, because if $u_1(S,t)$ and $u_2(S,t)$ are any two solutions, so is $c_1u_1(S,t) + c_2u_2(S,t)$ for any constants c_1 and c_2.

Suppose for the moment that $\alpha(S,t)$ and $\beta(S,t)$ are constants, α_0 and β_0, and that $\gamma(S,t) = 0$. Thus, equation (4.1) is

$$\alpha_0\frac{\partial u}{\partial S} + \beta_0\frac{\partial u}{\partial t} = 0. \tag{4.2}$$

This equation has a simple interpretation. The left-hand side of this equation is the **directional derivative** of u along the vector (α_0, β_0) in the (S,t) plane. In this direction, i.e. along any line with equation $\beta_0 S - \alpha_0 t =$ constant, the partial differential equation (4.2) reduces to an *ordinary* differential equation. To see this let us change to new coordinates

$$\xi = \beta_0 S + \alpha_0 t,$$

$$\zeta = \beta_0 S - \alpha_0 t;$$

this is just a rotation and uniform scaling of the old (S,t) plane to the new (ξ,ζ) plane. In these new variables (4.2) becomes

$$\frac{\partial u}{\partial \xi} = 0.$$

The solution of this ordinary differential equation is just $u = F(\zeta)$, for some function F, i.e. u is independent of ξ and is constant along the lines $\zeta =$ constant. Once we know u at one point on one of these

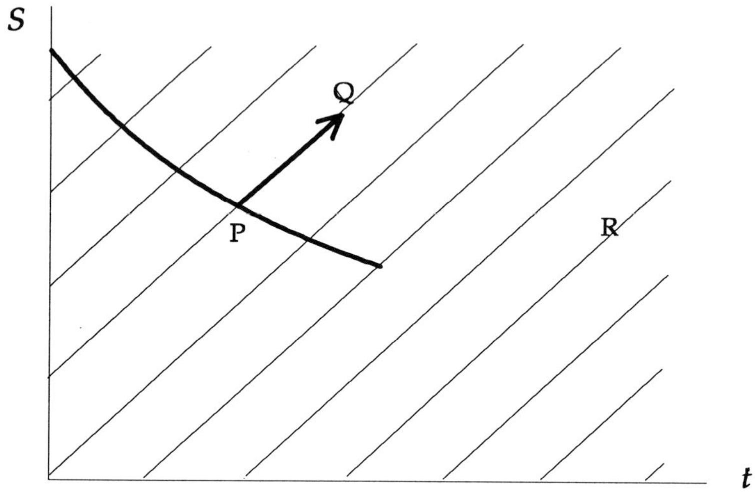

Figure 4.1: Characteristics and boundary data for a constant-coefficient linear equation.

lines, we also know it everywhere else on the same line. The only variation in u is from line to line.

The lines $\beta_0 S - \alpha_0 t =$ constant, along which u is determined by solving an ordinary differential equation, are known as **characteristics**. We can think of them as representing directions in which information propagates via an ordinary differential equation rather than via the full partial differential equation.

Without further information, we cannot determine F, which remains arbitrary. It is the analogue for a partial differential equation of the arbitrary constant that arises in the general solution of a first order ordinary differential equation. If, though, we are given the value of u on some curve in the (S, t) plane, we can find F in the region covered by all the characteristics drawn through that curve, provided that the given curve is not itself a characteristic. This point is illustrated in Figure 4.1, which shows a family of characteristics. Suppose that we are given the value of u all along the bold curve. This data can be used to find the function F and hence the value of u at any point such as Q on any characteristic passing through this curve. However, since the bold curve does not reach some of the characteristics, it is not possible to determine u at any point such as R which is not on a characteristic through the bold curve. The intimate nature of the relationship between the solution of a first order partial differential equation and its characteristics makes the specification of boundary data very important.

The theory of linear first order partial differential equations can be discussed in greater generality than we have space for here. However, whenever we need to solve such an equation in this book we find that our examples always permit a simple explicit solution. These simple solutions enable us to describe the sort of boundary data that we need without obscuring the point with complicated algebra.

4.3 The diffusion equation

The **heat** or **diffusion** equation[1]

$$\frac{\partial u}{\partial t} = \frac{\partial^2 u}{\partial x^2} \tag{4.3}$$

has been studied for nearly two centuries as a model of the flow (or diffusion) of heat in a continuous medium. It is one of the most successful and widely used models of applied mathematics, and a considerable body of theory on its properties and solution is available. It is often helpful as a guide to intuition to bear in mind the physical situations that lead to the heat equation, and we mention them wherever it is appropriate. Thus, we recall that the basic equation (4.3) models the diffusion of heat in one space dimension. Here $u(x, t)$ represents the temperature in a long thin uniform bar of material whose sides are perfectly insulated so that its temperature varies only with distance x along the bar and, of course, with time t. Fourier's Law of heat conduction provides a model for, or mathematical description of, the local heat flux; it states that the flux is proportional to the temperature gradient $-\partial u/\partial x$. Furthermore, the local energy density in the form of heat can be assumed to be proportional to u. Overall conservation of energy, written in

[1] We use x rather than S as the spatial independent variable because all our applications of the diffusion equation occur after a change of variable of the form $S = Ee^x$.

the form

$$\frac{\partial(\text{energy density})}{\partial t} + \frac{\partial(\text{energy flux})}{\partial x} = 0,$$

then shows that $\partial u/\partial t$ is proportional to $\partial^2 u/\partial x^2$; a suitable scaling of x and t allows the constant of proportionality to be taken equal to 1. (This kind of scaling is discussed in the Technical Point on dimensionless variables in Section 5.4.) Equation (4.3) is also widely used as a model for molecular diffusion of a substance through a substrate, in which case $u(x,t)$ models the concentration of the diffusant, and Fick's Law gives the flux by diffusion as proportional to $-\partial u/\partial x$. Again a conservation argument followed by a scaling of x and t leads to (4.3), which in this context is usually referred to as the diffusion equation.

4.4 Basic properties of the diffusion equation

We begin with a list of some of the elementary properties of the diffusion equation.

- It is a linear equation. That is, if u_1 and u_2 are solutions, then so is $c_1u_1 + c_2u_2$ for any constants c_1 and c_2.

- It is a **second order** equation, since the highest order derivative occurring is the second, in the term $\partial^2 u/\partial x^2$.

- It is a **parabolic** equation (the term parabolic is discussed further in the Technical Point at the end of this section). Its characteristics are given by t = constant. Thus, information propagates along these lines in (x,t) space, and if a change is made to u at a particular point, for example on the boundary of the solution region, its effect is felt instantaneously everywhere else.

- Generally speaking, its solutions are **analytic** functions of x. This means that for each value of t greater than the initial time, $u(x,t)$ regarded as a function of x has a convergent power series in terms of $x - x_0$ for each x_0 away from spatial boundaries. For practical purposes, we can think of a solution of the diffusion equation as being as smooth a function of x as we could ever need, but discontinuities in time may be induced by the boundary conditions; this is again a consequence of the fact that information propagates along the characteristics $t =$ constant.

From the physical point of view, diffusion is a smoothing-out process: heat flows from hot to cold and so evens out temperature differences. The properties above go some way towards showing that solutions of the diffusion equation, which is a mathematical model of the physical process, have the same tendency. Anticipating some results from Section 4.4, it can be shown further that even though the initial values of u may be rather irregular or jagged, for any $t > 0$ the solution of the **initial value problem**

$$\frac{\partial u}{\partial t} = \frac{\partial^2 u}{\partial x^2}, \qquad -\infty < x < \infty,$$

with initial data

$$u(x, 0) = u_0(x)$$

and

$$u \to 0 \text{ as } x \to \pm\infty$$

is analytic for all $t > 0$. This smoothness, which is characteristic of all linear parabolic equations, is very helpful when it comes to numerical solution. An illustration is the following special solution, which is derived in Section 5.2:

$$u_\delta(x, t) = \frac{1}{2\sqrt{\pi t}} e^{-x^2/4t} \qquad -\infty < x < \infty, \quad t > 0. \tag{4.4}$$

For $t > 0$ this is a smooth Gaussian curve, but at $t = 0$ it is 'equal' to the delta-function described in Section 5.2. It vanishes for $x \neq 0$, at $x = 0$ it is 'infinite', but its integral is still 1, and all the heat is initially concentrated at $x = 0$. This function is shown in Figure 4.2 for several values of t; note how the curve becomes taller and narrower as t gets smaller. The function u_δ represents the evolution of an idealised 'hotspot', a unit amount of heat initially concentrated into a single point, and it is called the **fundamental solution** of the diffusion equation. It also illustrates the infinite propagation speed mentioned above. At $t = 0$, the solution (4.4) is zero for all $x \neq 0$, but for any $t > 0$, however small, and any x, however large,

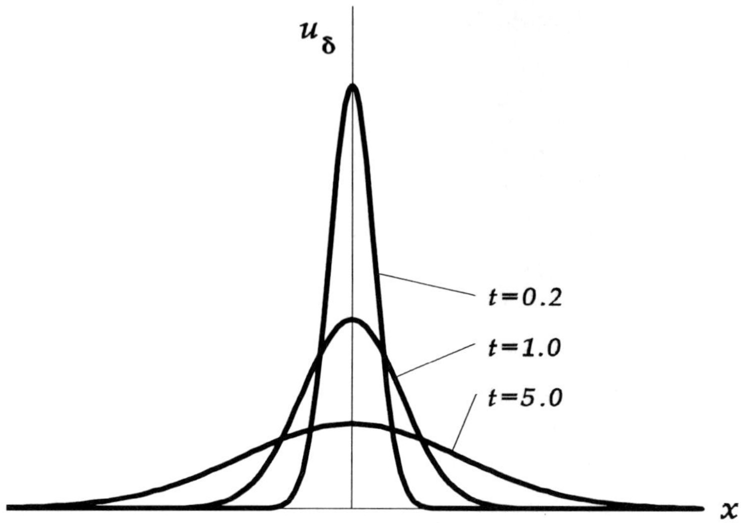

Figure 4.2: The fundamental solution of the diffusion equation.

$u_\delta(x,t) > 0$: the heat initially concentrated at $x = 0$ immediately diffuses out to all values of x. Note, though, that u_δ falls off very rapidly as $|x| \to \infty$.

Technical Point: characteristics of second order linear partial differential equations.
The notion of characteristics as curves along which information can propagate is also applicable to second order equations, although the details are rather more complicated. Suppose that $u(x,t)$ satisfies the general second order linear equation

$$a(x,t)\frac{\partial^2 u}{\partial x^2} + b(x,t)\frac{\partial^2 u}{\partial x \partial t} + c(x,t)\frac{\partial^2 u}{\partial t^2} + d(x,t)\frac{\partial u}{\partial x} + e(x,t)\frac{\partial u}{\partial t} + f(x,t)u + g(x,t) = 0.$$

The idea is still to see whether there are directions in which the derivative terms can be written as directional derivatives, so that the equation is partly like an ordinary differential equation along curves *with these vectors as tangents. Once again, these curves are called characteristics. If we write them as $x = x(\xi)$, $t = t(\xi)$, where as before ξ is a parameter along the curves, then $x(\xi)$ and $t(\xi)$ satisfy*

$$a(x,t)\left(\frac{dt}{d\xi}\right)^2 - b(x,t)\frac{dt}{d\xi}\frac{dx}{d\xi} + c(x,t)\left(\frac{dx}{d\xi}\right)^2 = 0.$$

There now arises the question whether this equation, regarded as a quadratic in $(dx/d\xi)/(dt/d\xi)$, has two distinct real roots, two equal real roots, or no real roots at all. These cases correspond to the discriminant $b^2 - 4ac$ being greater than zero, zero, or less than zero. The first case, two real families of characteristics, is called **hyperbolic***; it is the analogue for second order equations of the first order linear equations discussed in Section 4.2. The second case, an exact square, is called* **parabolic***; the diffusion equation, which has $b = c = 0$, is the simplest example. All the second order equations in this book are parabolic. The final case, with no real characteristics, is called* **elliptic***, but it is not relevant to our discussions.*

Note that the definitions given here are pointwise: the hyperbolic/parabolic/elliptic distinction is specified at each point. It is possible for an equation to change type as $a(x,t)$, $b(x,t)$ and $c(x,t)$ vary, if the discriminant changes sign. In particular, the Black–Scholes equation

$$\frac{\partial V}{\partial t} + \tfrac{1}{2}\sigma^2 S^2 \frac{\partial^2 V}{\partial S^2} + rS\frac{\partial V}{\partial S} - rV = 0$$

is parabolic for $S > 0$ but hyperbolic at $S = 0$, where it reduces to an ordinary differential equation with characteristic $S = 0$. This fact has important financial implications: the line $S = 0$ is a barrier across which information cannot cross.

4.5 Initial and boundary conditions

We now consider what initial and boundary conditions are appropriate for solutions of the diffusion equation, first in a finite region, then in an infinite one.

4.5.1 The initial value problem in a finite interval

Suppose we wish to solve $\partial u/\partial t = \partial^2 u/\partial x^2$ in the finite interval $-L < x < L$ and for $t > 0$, representing heat flow in a bar of finite length $2L$.

Obviously we should specify the initial temperature $u(x,0) = u_0(x)$ for $-L < x < L$. With the heat flow analogy in mind, it seems reasonable on physical grounds that we have enough information to determine $u(x,t)$ uniquely if we specify either the temperatures at the ends of the bar or the heat fluxes at both ends but not both. This turns out to be the case; in fact both the following statements of the problem can be shown to be well-posed:

$$\text{(i)} \quad \frac{\partial u}{\partial t} = \frac{\partial^2 u}{\partial x^2}, \qquad \begin{array}{l} -L < x < L, \text{ with } u(x,0) = u_0(x), \\ u(-L,t) = g_-(t),\ u(L,t) = g_+(t); \end{array}$$

$$\text{(ii)} \quad \frac{\partial u}{\partial t} = \frac{\partial^2 u}{\partial x^2}, \qquad \begin{array}{l} -L < x < L, \text{ with } u(x,0) = u_0(x), \\ -\dfrac{\partial u}{\partial x}(-L,t) = h_-(x),\ \dfrac{\partial u}{\partial x}(L,t) = h_+(t). \end{array}$$

In the first case it is the temperature and in the second case the heat fluxes that are specified at $x = -L$ and $x = L$.

4.5.2 The initial value problem on an infinite interval

Suppose now that we consider heat flow in a very long bar, by taking the limit $L \to \infty$ in the example above. When the bar is infinitely long, it is still important to say how u behaves at large distances, but we do not have to be as precise in our specification of u at the 'boundaries' $x = \pm\infty$ as we were in the finite case. There are some technical difficulties here, associated with the notion of infinity; but roughly speaking as long as u is not allowed to grow too fast, the solution exists, is unique, and depends continuously on the initial data $u_0(x)$. To be specific, the solution to the initial value problem

$$\frac{\partial u}{\partial t} = \frac{\partial^2 u}{\partial x^2} \qquad -\infty < x < \infty, \quad t > 0, \tag{4.5}$$

with

$$u(x,0) = u_0(x), \tag{4.6}$$

where

$$\text{(i)} \qquad u_0(x) \text{ is sufficiently well behaved,} \tag{4.7}$$

$$\text{(ii)} \qquad \lim_{|x|\to\infty} u_0(x)e^{-ax^2} = 0 \quad \text{for any } a > 0, \tag{4.8}$$

and lastly where

$$\lim_{|x|\to\infty} u(x,t)e^{-ax^2} = 0 \qquad \text{for any } a > 0,\ t > 0, \tag{4.9}$$

is well-posed. The precise definition of the phrase 'sufficiently well behaved' here is beyond the scope of this book, but certainly any function that has no worse than a finite number of jump discontinuities is acceptable. We also note that although it is necessary to prescribe the behaviour at infinity, in practice the limitations above are not too severe. All the initial value problems in this book satisfy the growth conditions quite comfortably.

We sometimes need to consider initial value problems defined on a semi-infinite interval, and in this case we require a combination of the two sets of conditions above. If, for example, we need to solve (4.5) for $0 < x < \infty$, $t > 0$, then given sufficiently smooth initial data $u_0(x)$ for $0 < x < \infty$, a sufficiently smooth boundary value at $x = 0$, $u(0,t) = g_0(t)$, and the growth conditions (4.8), (4.9) as $x \to \infty$, the problem is well-posed.

4.6 Forward versus backward

In all the above we have discussed the **forward** equation

$$\partial u/\partial t = \partial^2 u/\partial x^2,$$

with conditions given at $t = 0$. The reader may ask, what is wrong with the equation

$$\frac{\partial u}{\partial t} = -\frac{\partial^2 u}{\partial x^2} \tag{4.10}$$

(with the same initial and boundary conditions)? This equation might, for example, arise if in a forward problem we had replaced t by $T - \tau$ for some constant T, whereupon $\partial u/\partial t$ becomes $-\partial u/\partial \tau$.

It turns out that this backward problem is **ill-posed**: for most initial and boundary data the solution does not exist at all, and even if it does exist, it is likely to blow up (for example, u may tend to ∞) within a finite time. A good example is the fundamental solution of the diffusion equation (4.4). At time T this solution is equal to

$$\frac{1}{2\sqrt{\pi T}} e^{-x^2/4T},$$

which is as smooth and well-behaved as we could wish. If we use this function as our initial data $u_0(x)$ for equation (4.10), then the solution is

$$u(x,t) = \frac{1}{2\sqrt{\pi(T-t)}} e^{-x^2/4(T-t)},$$

and this becomes singular (blows up) at $t = T$, when it is equal to the delta function $\delta(x)$. Moreover, it cannot be continued beyond this time (at least, not as a 'normal' function).

Physically this distinction makes good sense. If the forward diffusion equation models the evolution of the temperature from its initial values, the backward equation poses the question of determining the temperature from which the initial distribution could have evolved; this is clear from the time-reversal argument above. Since forward diffusion smooths out jagged temperature distributions, backward diffusion makes smooth initial data become more jagged. Another way of seeing this is to note that under forward diffusion heat flows from hot to cold, whereas under backward diffusion it flows from cold to hot, and so the hot places become ever hotter, leading to blow-up.

There are, however, some well-posed problems for equation (4.10); in particular the **final value problem** for the backward diffusion equation is well-posed. Thus, we can solve (4.10) for $0 < t < T$ with $u(x,T) = u_T(x)$ given. This is easily shown by converting (4.10) to a forward problem by replacing t by $T - t$.

Further reading

- For further information about first order partial differential equations and their solution see Williams (1980), Strang (1986), Keener (1988) and Kevorkian (1990).

- Three books devoted wholly to the diffusion equation are those by Crank (1989), Hill & Dewynne (1990) and Carslaw & Jaeger (1989).

Exercises

1. Show that the solution to the initial value problem is unique provided that it is sufficiently smooth and decays sufficiently fast at infinity, as follows:

   Suppose that $u_1(x,t)$ and $u_2(x,t)$ are both solutions to the initial value problem (4.5)–(4.9). Show that $v(x,t) = u_1 - u_2$ is also a solution of (4.5) with $v(x,0) = 0$.

   Show that if
   $$E(t) = \int_{-\infty}^{\infty} v^2 \, dx,$$
   then
   $$E(t) \geq 0, \qquad E(0) = 0,$$
   and, by integrating by parts, that
   $$\frac{dE}{dt} \leq 0;$$
   thus $E(t) \equiv 0$, hence $v(x,t) \equiv 0$.

   Note, though, that as yet we have no guarantee that $u(x,t)$ exists, nor that the above manipulations can be justified.

2. Show that $\sin nx \; e^{-n^2 t}$ is a solution of the forward diffusion equation, and that $\sin nx \; e^{n^2 t}$ is a solution of the backward diffusion equation. Now try to solve the initial value problem for the forward and backward equations in the interval $-\pi < x < \pi$ by expanding the solution in a Fourier series in x with coefficients depending on t. What difference do you see between the two problems? Which is well-posed?

Chapter 5

Explicit Solutions of the Diffusion Equation in Fixed Domains

5.1 Introduction

In this chapter we describe some techniques for obtaining analytical solutions to diffusion equations in fixed domains, where the spatial boundaries are known in advance. Free boundary problems, in which the spatial boundaries vary with time in an unknown manner, are discussed in Chapter 6. We highlight in particular one method: we discuss similarity solutions in some detail. This method can yield important information about particular problems with special initial and boundary values, and it is especially useful for determining local behaviour in space or in time. It is also useful in the context of free boundary problems, and in Chapter 6 we see an application to the local behaviour of the free boundary for an American call option near expiry. Beyond this, though, we can also use similarity techniques to derive the fundamental solution of the diffusion equation, and from this we can deduce the general solution for the initial-value problem on an infinite interval. This in turn leads immediately to the Black–Scholes formulæ for the values of European call and put options.

5.2 Similarity solutions

It may sometimes happen that the solution $u(x,t)$ of a partial differential equation, together with its initial and boundary conditions, depends only on one special combination of the two independent variables. In such cases, the problem can be reduced to an ordinary differential equation in which this combination is the independent variable. The solution to this ordinary differential equation is called a **similarity solution** to the original partial differential equation. The mathematical reasons for the existence of this reduction are subtle and beyond the scope of this book, although the Technical Point at the end of this section, which deals with the mechanics of finding similarity solutions, does hint at them. We simply give two examples here.

Example 1. Suppose that $u(x,t)$ satisfies the following problem on the semi-infinite interval $x > 0$:

$$\frac{\partial u}{\partial t} = \frac{\partial^2 u}{\partial x^2}, \qquad x, t > 0, \tag{5.1}$$

with the initial condition

$$u(x, 0) = 0, \tag{5.2}$$

and a boundary condition at $x = 0$,

$$u(0, t) = 1; \tag{5.3}$$

we also require that

$$u \to 0 \text{ as } x \to \infty. \tag{5.4}$$

These equations model the evolution of temperature in a long bar, initially at zero temperature, after the temperature at one end is suddenly raised to 1 and held there.

Following the arguments suggested in the Technical Point below, we look for a solution in which $u(x,t)$ depends only on x and t through the combination $\xi = x/\sqrt{t}$, so that $u(x,t) = U(\xi)$. Differentiation shows that

$$\frac{\partial u}{\partial t} = -\frac{1}{2t}\xi U'(\xi)$$

and

$$\frac{\partial^2 u}{\partial x^2} = \frac{1}{t} U''(\xi),$$

where $' = d/d\xi$. Substitution into equation (5.1) shows that all the terms involving t on its own may be cancelled, and $U(\xi)$ satisfies the second order *ordinary* differential equation

$$U'' + \tfrac{1}{2}\xi U' = 0. \tag{5.5}$$

From the initial and boundary conditions (5.2)–(5.4),

$$U(0) = 1, \quad U(\infty) = 0. \tag{5.6}$$

(The second of these incorporates both (5.2) and (5.4), since as $t \to 0$ from above, $\xi \to \infty$.)

Multiplying both sides of (5.5) by the integrating factor $e^{\xi^2/4}$ yields an exact derivative, and so

$$U'(\xi) = Ce^{-\xi^2/4}$$

for some constant C. Integrating, we find that

$$U(\xi) = C \int_0^{\xi} e^{-s^2/4} ds + D$$

where D is a further constant. Applying the boundary conditions (5.6), writing $\int_0^{\xi} = \int_0^{\infty} - \int_{\xi}^{\infty}$, and using the standard result

$$\int_0^{\infty} e^{-s^2/4} ds = \sqrt{\pi},$$

we find that

$$U(\xi) = \frac{1}{\sqrt{\pi}} \int_{\xi}^{\infty} e^{-s^2/4} ds;$$

that is,

$$u(x,t) = \frac{1}{\sqrt{\pi}} \int_{x/\sqrt{t}}^{\infty} e^{-s^2/4} ds.$$

It is easy to verify that this function does satisfy the problem statement (5.1)–(5.4), so that the solution does indeed depend only on $x/\sqrt{t}$.

Example 2. For our second example we derive the fundamental solution $u_\delta(x,t)$, which we introduced in Chapter 4. We again look for a solution of the diffusion equation that depends on x only through the combination $\xi = x/\sqrt{t}$, but now we try the form

$$u_\delta(x,t) = t^{-1/2}\, U_\delta(\xi).$$

The $t^{-1/2}$ term multiplying $U_\delta(\xi)$ is there to ensure that $\int_{-\infty}^{\infty} u(x,t)\,dx$ is constant for all t, which can be shown by direct calculation. A similar computation to the example above shows that $U_\delta(\xi)$ satisfies the ordinary differential equation

$$U_\delta'' + (\tfrac{1}{2}\xi U_\delta)' = 0.$$

The general solution of this, obtained by integrating twice, the second time with the help of the integrating factor $e^{\xi^2/4}$, is

$$U_\delta(\xi) = Ce^{-\xi^2/4} + D$$

for constant C and D. Choosing $D = 0$ and normalising the solution by setting $C = 1/(2\sqrt{\pi})$, so that $\int_{-\infty}^{\infty} u\,dx = 1$, yields the fundamental solution

$$u_\delta(x,t) = \frac{1}{2\sqrt{\pi t}} e^{-x^2/4t}$$

as required.

The similarity solution technique is rarely successful in solving a complete boundary value problem, because it requires such special symmetries in the equation and initial and boundary conditions. On the other hand, it comes into its own in local analyses in space or in time, for example the initial motion of a free boundary in an American option problem or the value of an at-the-money option shortly before exercise, which are hard to resolve numerically.

Technical Point: group invariances and similarity solutions.

The key to the similarity solutions above is that both the equations and the initial and boundary conditions are invariant under the scalings $x \mapsto \lambda x$, $t \mapsto \lambda^2 t$ for any real number λ. Such a scaling is called *a* **one-parameter group** *of transformations. This invariance is readily verified using the new variables* $X = \lambda x$, $T = \lambda^2 t$, *whereupon* u *is easily seen to satisfy* $\partial u/\partial T = \partial^2 u/\partial X^2$. *Furthermore, in Example 1, the initial and boundary conditions become* $u(X, 0) = 0$, $u(0, T) = 1$ *for any* λ. *Now* $x/\sqrt{t} = X/\sqrt{T}$ *is the only combination of* X *and* T *which is independent of* λ, *and so the solution must be a function of* $x/\sqrt{t}$ *only. It is essential that the equation, the boundary conditions and the initial conditions should* all *be invariant under the scaling transformation for the method to work. In Example 2, the function of* t, *in this case* $t^{-1/2}$, *multiplying* $U_\delta(\xi)$ *is present because the diffusion equation, being linear, is also invariant under the one parameter group* $u \mapsto \mu u$. *A good practical test for similarity solutions is to try* $u = t^\alpha f(x/t^\beta)$ *in the hope that* x *and* t *will remain in the equations only in the combination* $\xi = x/t^\beta$. *In Example 1 above, the result of doing this is* $\alpha = 0$ *from the boundary condition at* $x = 0$ *and* $\beta = \frac{1}{2}$ *from the diffusion equation, while in Example 2,* $\alpha = -\frac{1}{2}$ *because we want the integral of* $u(x, t)$ *over* x *to be independent of* t, *and again* $\beta = \frac{1}{2}$.

5.3 An initial value problem

The fundamental solution of the diffusion equation can be used to derive an explicit solution to the initial value problem (4.5)–(4.9), in which we have to solve the diffusion equation for $-\infty < x < \infty$ and $t > 0$, with arbitrary initial data $u(x, 0) = u_0(x)$ and suitable growth conditions at $x = \pm\infty$. The key to the solution is the fact that we can write the initial data as

$$u_0(x) = \int_{-\infty}^{\infty} u_0(\xi)\delta(\xi - x)\, d\xi$$

where $\delta(\cdot)$ is the Dirac delta function. (Properties of the delta function are discussed in the Technical Point below.) We recall that the fundamental solution of the diffusion equation ,

$$u_\delta(\xi, t) = \frac{1}{2\sqrt{\pi t}} e^{-\xi^2/4t},$$

has initial value

$$u_\delta(\xi, 0) = \delta(\xi).$$

Now note that because $u_\delta(\xi - x, t) = u_\delta(x - \xi, t)$,

$$u_\delta(\xi - x, t) = \frac{1}{2\sqrt{\pi t}} e^{-(\xi - x)^2/4t}$$

is a solution of the diffusion equation using either ξ or x as the spatial independent variable, and its initial value is

$$u_\delta(\xi - x, 0) = \delta(\xi - x).$$

Thus, for each ξ, the function

$$u_0(\xi) u_\delta(\xi - x, t),$$

regarded as a function of x and t with ξ held fixed, satisfies the diffusion equation $\partial u / \partial t = \partial^2 u / \partial x^2$, and has initial data $u_0(\xi)\delta(\xi - x)$. Because the diffusion equation is linear, we can superpose solutions of this form. Doing so for all ξ by integrating from $\xi = -\infty$ to $\xi = \infty$, we obtain a further solution of the diffusion equation,

$$u(x, t) = \frac{1}{2\sqrt{\pi t}} \int_{-\infty}^{\infty} u_0(\xi) e^{-(x - \xi)^2/4t} d\xi, \tag{5.7}$$

which has initial data

$$u(x, 0) = \int_{-\infty}^{\infty} u_0(\xi)\delta(\xi - x)\, d\xi = u_0(x).$$

This, therefore, is the explicit solution of the initial value problem (4.5)–(4.9). It can be shown (Exercise 1 of Chapter 4) that this solution is unique. The derivation above is not the only way of finding it: the Fourier Transform is an alternative, but we do not describe it here (see any of the books referred to in Chapter 4 for treatments).

The solution (5.7) can be interpreted physically as follows. Recall that the Fundamental Solution of the diffusion equation describes the spreading out of a unit 'packet' of heat which, at $t = 0$, is all concentrated at the origin. Mathematically, this 'packet' is represented by a delta function. Now imagine the initial temperature distribution $u_0(x)$ as being made up of many small packets, the packet at $x = \xi$ having magnitude $u_0(\xi)$. Each of these evolves to give a temperature distribution equal to the Fundamental Solution, multiplied by

$u_0(\xi)$ and with x replaced by $x-\xi$. Because the diffusion equation is linear, we obtain the whole temperature distribution by superposing (adding) the evolutions of these individual packets; in the limit, this sum is replaced by the integral (5.7).

Technical Point: the delta function and the Heaviside function.

The Dirac delta function, written $\delta(x)$, is not in fact a function in the normal sense of the word, but is rather a 'generalised function'. For technical reasons, its definition is as a linear map, but it is really motivated by the need for a mathematical description of the limit of a function whose effect is confined to a smaller and smaller interval, but yet remains finite.

Suppose, for example, that I receive money at the rate $f(t)\,dt$ in a time dt where f is equal to the following function:

$$f(t) = \begin{cases} 1/2\epsilon, & -\epsilon \le t \le \epsilon \\ 0, & |t| > \epsilon. \end{cases}$$

This function is drawn in Figure 5.1 for several values of ϵ. As ϵ gets smaller the graph becomes taller and narrower. It is clear that the total payment is

$$\int_{-\infty}^{\infty} f(t)\,dt$$

and is equal to 1 independently of ϵ, but that for all $t \ne 0$, $f(t) \to 0$ as $\epsilon \to 0$. The limiting 'function' is zero for all nonzero t, yet its integral is still 1! This is an informal way of defining the **delta function,** *$\delta(t)$: it is the 'limit' as $\epsilon \to 0$ of any one-parameter family of functions $\delta_\epsilon(t)$ with the following properties:*

- *for each ϵ, $\delta_\epsilon(t)$ is piecewise smooth;*
- $\displaystyle\int_{-\infty}^{\infty} \delta_\epsilon(t)\,dt = 1;$
- *for each $t \ne 0$,* $\displaystyle\lim_{\epsilon\to 0} \delta_\epsilon(t) = 0.$

Such a sequence of functions is called a delta-sequence. The function $f(t)$ above is one such; another, which uses x as the independent

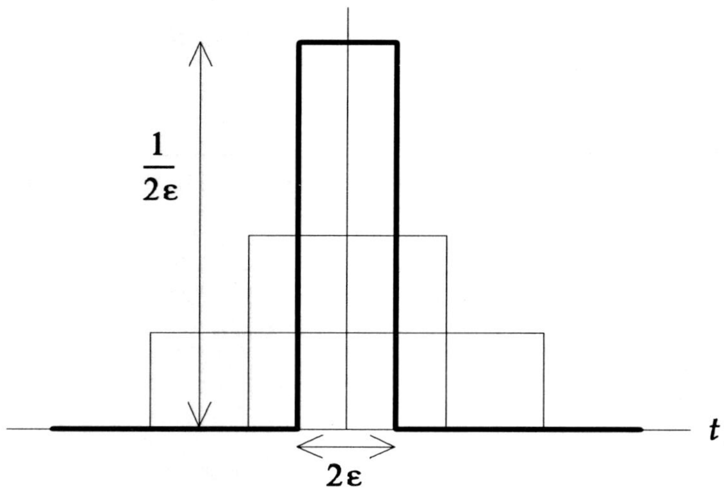

Figure 5.1: Three members of a limiting sequence for the delta function.

variable[1] *instead of* t, *is*

$$\delta_\epsilon(x) = \frac{1}{2\sqrt{\pi\epsilon}} e^{-x^2/4\epsilon}.$$

With ϵ *replaced by* t, *this is the fundamental solution of the diffusion equation discussed in Chapter 4. It is easily confirmed that the latter function has integral* 1, *and that, like* $f(t)$, *for* $x \neq 0$ *it tends to zero as* $\epsilon \to 0$, *while for* $x = 0$ *its value increases without limit.*

This 'pointwise' view of the delta function is rather hard to work with, since the functions δ_ϵ *become increasingly badly-behaved near the origin as* $\epsilon \to 0$. *Indeed the limiting 'function' is not a normal function at all (this is why the term 'generalised function' is used). Instead, we use the fact that integration smooths out the bad behaviour; the integral of* any *member of a delta-sequence* is *well-behaved, being equal to 1. This idea motivates the definition of the delta function via its integral action: for any smooth function* $\phi(x)$,

[1]Whether we use x or t as the argument for the delta function depends on the application we have in mind.

called a **test function**,

$$\int_{-\infty}^{\infty} \delta(x)\phi(x)\,dx = \lim_{\epsilon\to 0}\int_{-\infty}^{\infty} \delta_\epsilon(x)\phi(x)\,dx = \phi(0).$$

(In fact, this defines the delta function as the continuous linear map from smooth functions $\phi(x)$ to real numbers that has the value $\phi(0)$, usually written as $<\delta,\phi>=\phi(0)$.)

It is apparent that for any $a, b > 0$,

$$\int_{-a}^{b} \delta(x)\phi(x)\,dx = \phi(0),$$

and that for any x_0,

$$\int_{-\infty}^{\infty} \delta(x-x_0)\phi(x)\,dx = \phi(x_0),$$

so multiplying by $\delta(x-x_0)$ and integrating 'picks out' the value of ϕ at x_0. We also have

$$\int_{-\infty}^{x} \delta(\xi)\,d\xi = \mathcal{H}(x),$$

where $\mathcal{H}(x)$ is the **Heaviside function**, *defined by*

$$\mathcal{H}(x) = \begin{cases} 0 & \text{for } x<0 \\ 1 & \text{for } x\geq 0. \end{cases}$$

Conversely,

$$\mathcal{H}'(x) = \delta(x).$$

The last pair of relations shows that the derivative of a function that has a jump discontinuity has a delta function component at the same point, multiplied by the magnitude of the jump. This fact is often useful in the analysis of differential equations with discontinuous functions or coefficients. We give a simple example.

Suppose that $M(t)$ represents the amount of money owned by a person who is initially penniless, but at time $t = t_0 > 0$ receives an amount D_δ. Then, clearly,

$$M(t) = \begin{cases} 0 & \text{for } 0<t<t_0 \\ 0+D_\delta & \text{for } t\geq t_0, \end{cases}$$

and so $M(t)$ satisfies the differential equation

$$\frac{dM}{dt} = D_\delta \delta(t - t_0).$$

The discontinuity in $M(t)$ gives a delta function at $t = t_0$. Conversely, when we see a differential equation with a delta function on the right-hand side, there must be a corresponding delta function in the highest order derivative on the left-hand side in order to maintain a balance. This in turn means that the next highest order derivative has a jump discontinuity of magnitude equal to the coefficient of the delta function. These jump conditions can be used to join together smooth segments of the solution across discontinuities. The delta function in examples like this can be multiplied by a smooth function of x or t, but care must be taken to avoid products like $\delta(x)\mathcal{H}(x)$ or $\delta^2(x)$, for which no sensible definition can be given.

More details about delta functions, and about other generalised functions (or 'distributions') are given by Richards & Youn (1990).

5.4 The Black–Scholes equation: explicit solutions

The Black–Scholes equation and boundary conditions for a European call with value $C(S,t)$ are, as described in Sections 3.5 and 3.7,

$$\frac{\partial C}{\partial t} + \tfrac{1}{2}\sigma^2 S^2 \frac{\partial^2 C}{\partial S^2} + rS\frac{\partial C}{\partial S} - rC = 0, \tag{5.8}$$

with

$$C(0,t) = 0, \qquad C(S,t) \sim S \quad \text{as } S \to \infty,$$

and

$$C(S,T) = \max(S - E, 0).$$

Equation (5.8) looks a little like the diffusion equation, but it has more terms, and each time C is differentiated with respect to S it is multiplied by S, giving nonconstant coefficients. Also the equation is clearly in backward form, with final data given at $t = T$.

The first thing to do is to get rid of the awkward S and S^2 terms multiplying $\partial C/\partial S$ and $\partial^2 C/\partial S^2$. At the same time we take the opportunity of making the equation **dimensionless**, as defined in the Technical Point below, and we turn it into a forward equation. We set

$$S = Ee^x, \quad t = T - \tau/\tfrac{1}{2}\sigma^2, \quad C = Ev(x, \tau).$$

This results in the equation

$$\frac{\partial v}{\partial \tau} = \frac{\partial^2 v}{\partial x^2} + (k_1 - 1)\frac{\partial v}{\partial x} - k_1 v \tag{5.9}$$

where $k_1 = r/\tfrac{1}{2}\sigma^2$. The initial condition becomes

$$v(x, 0) = \max(e^x - 1, 0).$$

Notice in particular that this equation contains only *one* parameter, k_1, instead of the *four* parameters E, T, σ^2 and r in the original statement of the problem. The only essential factor controlling the option value is $r/\tfrac{1}{2}\sigma^2$, which is the only dimensionless parameter in the problem; the effect of all other factors is simply brought in by inverting the above transformations, i.e. by a straightforward arithmetical calculation.

Equation (5.9) now looks much more like a diffusion equation, and we can turn it into one by a simple change of variable. If we try putting

$$v = e^{\alpha x + \beta \tau} u(x, \tau),$$

for some constants α and β to be found, then differentiation gives

$$\beta u + \frac{\partial u}{\partial \tau} = \alpha^2 u + 2\alpha \frac{\partial u}{\partial x} + \frac{\partial^2 u}{\partial x^2} + (k_1 - 1)\left(\alpha u + \frac{\partial u}{\partial x}\right) - k_1 u.$$

We can obtain an equation with no u term by choosing

$$\beta = \alpha^2 + (k_1 - 1)\alpha - k_1,$$

while the choice

$$0 = 2\alpha + (k_1 - 1)$$

eliminates the $\partial u/\partial x$ term as well. These equations for α and β give

$$\alpha = -\tfrac{1}{2}(k_1 - 1), \quad \beta = -\tfrac{1}{4}(k_1 + 1)^2.$$

We then have

$$v = e^{-\frac{1}{2}(k_1 - 1)x - \frac{1}{4}(k_1 + 1)^2 \tau} u(x, \tau),$$

where

$$\frac{\partial u}{\partial \tau} = \frac{\partial^2 u}{\partial x^2} \quad \text{for } -\infty < x < \infty,\ \tau > 0,$$

with

$$u(x,0) = u_0(x) = \max(e^{\frac{1}{2}(k_1+1)x} - e^{\frac{1}{2}(k_1-1)x}, 0). \tag{5.10}$$

This may seem like a long way to travel from the original formulation, but we have reached the payoff. The solution to the diffusion equation problem is just that given in equation (5.7):

$$u(x,\tau) = \frac{1}{2\sqrt{\pi\tau}} \int_{-\infty}^{\infty} u_0(s) e^{-(x-s)^2/4\tau} ds \tag{5.11}$$

where $u_0(x)$ is given by (5.10).

It remains to evaluate the integral in (5.11). It is convenient to make the change of variable $x' = (x-s)/\sqrt{2\tau}$, so that

$$\begin{aligned} u(x,\tau) &= \frac{1}{\sqrt{2\pi}} \int_{-\infty}^{\infty} u_0(x'\sqrt{2\tau}+x) e^{-\frac{1}{2}x'^2} dx' \\ &= \frac{1}{\sqrt{2\pi}} \int_{-x/\sqrt{2\tau}}^{\infty} e^{\frac{1}{2}(k_1+1)(x+x'\sqrt{2\tau})} e^{-\frac{1}{2}x'^2} dx' \\ &\qquad - \frac{1}{\sqrt{2\pi}} \int_{-x/\sqrt{2\tau}}^{\infty} e^{\frac{1}{2}(k_1-1)(x+x'\sqrt{2\tau})} e^{-\frac{1}{2}x'^2} dx' \\ &= I_1 - I_2, \end{aligned}$$

say.

Here

$$\begin{aligned} I_1 &= \frac{1}{\sqrt{2\pi}} \int_{-x/\sqrt{2\tau}}^{\infty} e^{\frac{1}{2}(k_1+1)(x+x'\sqrt{2\tau})-\frac{1}{2}x'^2} dx' \\ &= \frac{e^{\frac{1}{2}(k_1+1)x}}{\sqrt{2\pi}} \int_{-x/\sqrt{2\tau}}^{\infty} e^{\frac{1}{4}(k_1+1)^2\tau} e^{-\frac{1}{2}(x'-\frac{1}{2}(k_1+1)\sqrt{2\tau})^2} dx' \\ &= \frac{e^{\frac{1}{2}(k_1+1)x+\frac{1}{4}(k_1+1)^2\tau}}{\sqrt{2\pi}} \int_{-x/\sqrt{2\tau}-\frac{1}{2}(k_1+1)\sqrt{2\tau}}^{\infty} e^{-\frac{1}{2}\rho^2} d\rho \\ &= e^{\frac{1}{2}(k_1+1)x+\frac{1}{4}(k_1+1)^2\tau} N(d_1), \end{aligned}$$

where

$$d_1 = \frac{x}{\sqrt{2\tau}} + \tfrac{1}{2}(k_1 + 1)\sqrt{2\tau},$$

and

$$N(d_1) = \frac{1}{\sqrt{2\pi}} \int_{-\infty}^{d_1} e^{-\frac{1}{2}s^2}\, ds$$

is the cumulative distribution function for the normal distribution.

The calculation of I_2 is identical to that of I_1, except that (k_1+1) is replaced by $(k_1 - 1)$ throughout.

Lastly, we retrace our steps, writing

$$v(x,\tau) = e^{-\frac{1}{2}(k_1-1)x-\frac{1}{4}(k_1+1)^2\tau}u(x,\tau)$$

and then putting $x = \log(S/E)$, $\tau = \frac{1}{2}\sigma^2(T-t)$, and $C = Ev(x,\tau)$, to recover

$$C(S,t) = SN(d_1) - Ee^{-r(T-t)}N(d_2),$$

where

$$\begin{aligned} d_1 &= \frac{\log(S/E) + (r+\frac{1}{2}\sigma^2)(T-t)}{\sigma\sqrt{(T-t)}}, \\ d_2 &= \frac{\log(S/E) + (r-\frac{1}{2}\sigma^2)(T-t)}{\sigma\sqrt{(T-t)}}. \end{aligned}$$

The corresponding calculation for a European put option follows similar lines, but having evaluated the call, a simpler way is to use the put-call parity formula

$$C - P = S - Ee^{-r(T-t)}$$

for the value P of a put given the value of the call.

Technical Point: dimensionless variables.
The differential equations used to model physical and financial processes often contain many **parameters***; these might be material properties of the substances involved, for example thermal conductivity, or constants of the underlying stochastic processes, such as their rate of return or volatility. An early step in most solutions is*

to scale the dependent and independent variables with 'typical values' in order to collect these parameters together as far as possible. Thus above we scaled S and V with E, the only a priori *typical value available. Although S might be measured in £ (or \$, or DM, or any other units), x has no units, and nor does v. This is important, since an expansion of the form $e^S = 1 + S + \frac{1}{2}S^2 + \ldots$ is meaningless if S is a dimensional quantity. (Note that an absolute change in an asset value, dS, is dimensional, but that the relative change, dS/S, is not.)*

Having carried out this scaling, we can collect the remaining parameters into **dimensionless groups**, *also called* **dimensionless parameters**. *This scaling then tells us the true number of independent constants in the solution. If one of the resulting dimensionless parameters is very large or very small, we may subsequently be able to exploit this fact to construct a useful approximation to the solution. Such an approximation is called an* **asymptotic expansion**, *and the theory of* **asymptotic analysis** *aims to devise techniques for this kind of approximation. It also aims to analyse the techniques in order to make sure that we can be confident that the effects we have neglected in making the approximation are genuinely unimportant.*

In the Black–Scholes equation, both r and σ^2 have units $(\text{time})^{-1}$; $(\text{years})^{-1}$ or $(\text{days})^{-1}$, for example. The quantity $k_1 = r/\frac{1}{2}\sigma^2$ is dimensionless; it is the only dimensionless parameter in the basic problem for a European call or put.

Further reading

- For a discussion of similarity solutions of the diffusion equation see Hill & Dewynne (1990).

Exercises

1. Find a similarity solution to the problem

$$\frac{\partial u}{\partial t} = \frac{\partial^2 u}{\partial x^2}, \quad -\infty < x < \infty, \quad t > 0,$$

with

$$u(x,0) = \mathcal{H}(x).$$

Show that $\partial u/\partial x$ is the fundamental solution $u_\delta(x,t)$, either by direct differentiation or by constructing the initial value problem that it satisfies.

2. Suppose that $u(x,t)$ satisfies the following initial value problem on a semi-infinite interval:

$$\frac{\partial u}{\partial t} = \frac{\partial^2 u}{\partial x^2}, \quad x > 0,\ t > 0,$$

with

$$u(x,0) = u_0(x),\ x > 0, \quad u(0,t) = 0,\ t > 0.$$

Define a new function $v(x,t)$ by reflection in the line $x = 0$, so that

$$v(x,t) = u(x,t) \quad \text{if } x > 0,$$
$$v(x,t) = -u(-x,t) \quad \text{if } x < 0.$$

Show that $v(0,t) = 0$, and use (5.7) to show that

$$u(x,t) = \frac{1}{2\sqrt{\pi t}} \int_0^\infty u_0(s) \left(e^{-(x-s)^2/4t} - e^{-(x+s)^2/4t} \right) ds.$$

The function multiplying $u_0(s)$ here is called the **Green's function** for this initial-boundary value problem. This solution is applicable to barrier options.

3. Find similarity solutions to

$$\frac{\partial u}{\partial t} = \frac{\partial^2 u}{\partial x^2} + F(x), \quad x > 0,\ t > 0,$$

with

$$u(x,0) = 0,\ x > 0, \quad u(0,t) = 0,\ t > 0.$$

in the two cases

(a) $F(x) = x$;
(b) $F(x) = 1$.

Extend case (b) by letting $u(0,t) = t$. A related similarity solution plays an important role in the free boundary problems studied in the next chapter.

4. Suppose that a and b are constants. Show that the parabolic equation
$$\frac{\partial u}{\partial t} = \frac{\partial^2 u}{\partial x^2} + a\frac{\partial u}{\partial x} + bu$$
can always be reduced to the diffusion equation. Use a change of time variable to show that the same is true for the equation
$$c(t)\frac{\partial u}{\partial t} = \frac{\partial^2 u}{\partial x^2}$$
where $c(t) > 0$. Suppose that σ^2 and r in the Black–Scholes equation are both functions of t, but that r/σ^2 is constant. Derive the Black–Scholes formulæ in this case.

5. Suppose that in the Black–Scholes equation, $r(t)$ and $\sigma^2(t)$ are both non-constant but known functions of t. Show that the following procedure reduces the Black–Scholes equation to the diffusion equation.
   (a) Set $S = Ee^x$, $C = Ev$ as before, and put $t = T - \tau$ to get the equation
   $$\frac{\partial v}{\partial \tau} = \tfrac{1}{2}\sigma^2(\tau)\frac{\partial^2 v}{\partial x^2} + \left(r(\tau) - \tfrac{1}{2}\sigma^2(\tau)\right)\frac{\partial v}{\partial x} - r(\tau)v.$$
   Note that we have not yet scaled time, merely changed its origin.
   (b) Now introduce a new time variable $\hat{\tau}$ such that $\frac{1}{2}\sigma^2(\tau)d\tau = d\hat{\tau}$, i.e.
   $$\hat{\tau}(\tau) = \int_0^\tau \tfrac{1}{2}\sigma^2(s)\,ds.$$
   (See the previous question where this calculation is requested.) This change of time variable amounts to measuring time weighted by volatility, so that the new 'time' passes more slowly when the volatility is high. The resulting equation is
   $$\frac{\partial v}{\partial \hat{\tau}} = \frac{\partial^2 v}{\partial x^2} + a(\hat{\tau})\frac{\partial v}{\partial x} - b(\hat{\tau})v,$$
   where $a(\hat{\tau}) = r/\frac{1}{2}\sigma^2 - 1$, $b(\hat{\tau}) = r/\frac{1}{2}\sigma^2$ (note that the dependence of r and σ^2 on $\hat{\tau}$ is obtained by substituting

for τ in terms of $\hat{\tau}$ by inverting the change of variable above).

(c) Show (or verify) that the general solution of the *first* order partial differential equation obtained from the equation for v by omitting the term $\partial^2 v/\partial x^2$, namely

$$\frac{\partial v}{\partial \hat{\tau}} = a(\hat{\tau})\frac{\partial v}{\partial x} - b(\hat{\tau})v,$$

is

$$v(x, \hat{\tau}) = F(x + A(\hat{\tau}))e^{-B(\hat{\tau})},$$

where $dA/d\hat{\tau} = a(\hat{\tau})$, $dB/d\hat{\tau} = b(\hat{\tau})$ and $F(\cdot)$ is an arbitrary function.

(d) Now seek a solution to the full equation for v in the form

$$v(\hat{x}, \hat{\tau}) = e^{-B(\hat{\tau})}V(x, \hat{\tau}),$$

where $\hat{x} = x + A(\hat{\tau})$ is as above. Choose $B(\hat{\tau})$ so that V satisfies the diffusion equation

$$\frac{\partial V}{\partial \hat{\tau}} = \frac{\partial^2 V}{\partial x^2}.$$

(e) What happens to the initial data under this series of transformations?

See Harper (1993) for further examples of this ingenious procedure applied to other equations.

6. Show that equation (5.9) can also be reduced to the diffusion equation by writing

$$v(x, \tau) = e^{-k_1 \tau}V(\xi, \tau),$$

where

$$\xi = x + (k_1 - 1)\tau.$$

What disadvantages might there be to this change of variables?

7. If $C(S,t)$ and $P(S,t)$ are the values of a European call and put with the same exercise and expiry, show that $C - P$ also satisfies the Black–Scholes equation (5.8), with the particularly simple final data $C - P = S - E$ at $t = T$. Deduce from the put-call parity theorem that $S - Ee^{-r(T-t)}$ is also a solution; interpret these results financially.

8. Use the explicit solution of the diffusion equation to derive the Black–Scholes value for a European put option without using put-call parity.

9. In dimensional variables, heat conduction in a bar of length L is modelled by
$$\rho c \frac{\partial U}{\partial T} = k \frac{\partial^2 U}{\partial X^2}$$
for $0 < X < L$, where $U(X,T)$ is the dimensional temperature, ρ is the density, c is the specific heat, and k is the thermal conductivity. Suppose that U_0 is a typical value for temperature variations, either of the initial temperature $U_0(X)$, or of the boundary values at $X = 0, L$; make the equation dimensionless.

10. Suppose that the underlying asset pays a continuous dividend yield at a rate D_0 (see Chapter 3), so that the modified Black–Scholes equation is
$$\frac{\partial V}{\partial t} + \tfrac{1}{2}\sigma^2 S^2 \frac{\partial^2 V}{\partial S^2} + (r - D_0)S\frac{\partial V}{\partial S} - rV = 0.$$
How many dimensionless parameters are there in this problem? Calculate the value of a European call and put. What is the statement of the put-call parity theorem in this case?

Chapter 6

American Options as Free Boundary Problems

6.1 Free boundary problems

In this chapter, we consider two valuation problems for American type options as free boundary problems. The first, and probably the better-known, is the American put problem: it is easy to show that the Black–Scholes formula for a European put cannot give the correct price for an American put, since it predicts values below the payoff. Here, we discuss some aspects of its correct formulation as a free boundary problem and give an analysis of the free boundary near to expiry. Secondly, we discuss an American call option on an asset which pays dividends at a continuous rate.

The discussion of Chapter 3 shows that the possibility of early exercise sometimes leads to a free boundary problem for the price of an American option. As the option can be exercised at any time, its value up to and including expiry must always be greater than or equal to its intrinsic value, which for a call is $\max(S - E, 0)$, and for a put is $\max(E - S, 0)$. Without this restriction, in some cases the Black–Scholes value drops below the intrinsic value; we conclude that there is a range of prices within which it is better to exercise the option than to hold it to expiry. The dividing price between exercise and non-exercise is called the **optimal exercise price** $S_f(t)$. It depends on the time remaining to expiry as well as the other parameters of the problem such as the volatility. Because the optimal exercise price is not known *a priori* as a function of time, it is called a **free boundary** for the associated Black–Scholes partial differential equation. The problem of determining the option price is then a **free boundary problem.** We see below that there is just one free boundary $S = S_f(t)$ for the American put option. For S less than $S_f(t)$ the option should be exercised, while for S greater than $S_f(t)$ the option can be held. However, we may consider American options or portfolios of options with a more general payoff function, and in this case there may not be just one free boundary. Instead, there may be several optimal exercise prices separating ranges where the option should be exercised from ranges where the option should be held.

In this chapter we consider some analytic aspects of the free boundary problems for American puts and calls. In particular, we discuss carefully the movement of the free boundary (the optimal exercise price) for an American call on a dividend-paying asset at times near expiry. Close to expiry the option price changes very rapidly as a function of time. This rapid movement in the option price also gives rise to rapid changes in the optimal exercise price, and this makes the numerical solution of an American option problem difficult at these times. For this reason the analysis of this section is useful as it gives an analytic approximation for times close to expiry which can be used to check or improve the accuracy of a numerical scheme.

6.2 The American put

Consider the Black–Scholes partial differential equation for the valuation of a European put, given in Chapter 3:

$$\frac{\partial P}{\partial t} + \tfrac{1}{2}\sigma^2 S^2 \frac{\partial^2 P}{\partial S^2} + rS\frac{\partial P}{\partial S} - rP = 0, \tag{6.1}$$

with payoff

$$P(S,T) = \max(E - S, 0) \tag{6.2}$$

and boundary conditions

$$P(0,t) = Ee^{-r(T-t)}, \quad P(S,t) \to 0 \text{ as } S \to \infty. \tag{6.3}$$

As is well-known, the value of the European put falls below its intrinsic value for some values of S. This is easily seen by considering the value of the put option at $S = 0$. Here the intrinsic value of the option is E but, from the boundary condition (6.3) $P(0,t) = Ee^{-r(T-t)} \leq E$. Thus the value of the option is less than its intrinsic value for $t < T$. If the American put option were valued according to the European put option formula then there would be arbitrage possibilities. The absence of these means that we must impose the condition

$$P(S,t) \geq \max(E - S, 0). \tag{6.4}$$

for the American put.

Now recall the discussion in Chapter 3 in which we demonstrated that an American option does not satisfy an equality but an *inequality*. For an American option, instead of (6.1), we have

$$\frac{\partial P}{\partial t} + \tfrac{1}{2}\sigma^2 S^2 \frac{\partial^2 P}{\partial S^2} + rS\frac{\partial P}{\partial S} - rP \leq 0.$$

We have just shown that a free boundary must exist since the European put option formula does not satisfy the constraint (6.4). Suppose further that $P = E - S$ for some $S < E$. If this is the case then P most certainly does not satisfy the Black–Scholes *equation* (unless $r = 0$) since

$$\begin{aligned}\frac{\partial}{\partial t}(E-S) + \tfrac{1}{2}\sigma^2 S^2 \frac{\partial^2}{\partial S^2}(E-S) + rS\frac{\partial}{\partial S}(E-S) - r(E-S) &= -rE \\ &< 0.\end{aligned}$$

But P *does* satisfy the *inequality*. When $P = E - S$ the return from the portfolio is less than the return from an equivalent bank deposit, and hence it is optimal to exercise the option. At any given time t, we must divide the S axis into two distinct regions, one where early exercise is optimal and

$$P = E - S, \quad \frac{\partial P}{\partial t} + \tfrac{1}{2}\sigma^2 S^2 \frac{\partial^2 P}{\partial S^2} + rS\frac{\partial P}{\partial S} - rP < 0,$$

and the other where early exercise is not optimal and

$$P > E - S, \quad \frac{\partial P}{\partial t} + \tfrac{1}{2}\sigma^2 S^2 \frac{\partial^2 P}{\partial S^2} + rS\frac{\partial P}{\partial S} - rP = 0.$$

Let $S_f(t)$ be defined to be the largest value of S, at time t, for which we have $P(S,t) = \max(E - S, 0)$. Then

$$P(S_f(t), t) = \max(E - S_f(t), 0),$$

but

$$P(S,t) > \max(E - S, 0) \quad \text{if } S > S_f(t).$$

This defines the free boundary $S_f(t)$, shown in Figure 6.1.

A local analysis near the free boundary, discussed in more detail from the point of view of modelling in Chapter 3, shows that

$$\frac{\partial P}{\partial S}(S_f(t), t) = -1.$$

This gives us two boundary conditions at the free boundary, namely

$$P(S_f(t), t) = \max(E - S_f(t), 0), \quad \frac{\partial P}{\partial S}(S_f(t), t) = -1. \tag{6.5}$$

We can think of these as being one boundary condition to determine the option value on the free boundary, and the other boundary condition to determine the location of the free boundary.

It is very important to realise that the condition

$$\frac{\partial P}{\partial S}(S_f(t), t) = -1 \quad \text{if } P(S_f(t), t) = E - S_f(t)$$

is *not* implied by the fact that $P(S_f(t), t) = E - S_f(t)$. Since we do not know *a priori* where $S_f(t)$ is, we need an extra condition to determine it. Arbitrage arguments show that the gradient of P should be continuous, and this gives us the extra condition we require.

Technical Point: free boundary conditions.
We emphasise also that both the boundary conditions for the American put are based on financial reasoning, namely arbitrage. Many other candidates are equally possible from the purely mathematical point of view; although it would not be a model for option pricing, we would also get a well-posed free boundary problem if we imposed a condition such as

$$\frac{\partial P}{\partial S}(S_f(t), t) = 0 \quad \textit{if} \quad P(S_f(t), t) = E - S_f(t),$$

or one such as

$$\frac{\partial P}{\partial S}(S_f(t), t) = -\frac{dS_f}{dt}.$$

This latter condition is, in fact, the proper free boundary condition for the Stefan model of melting ice. It is, of course, a totally inappropriate condition for American puts.

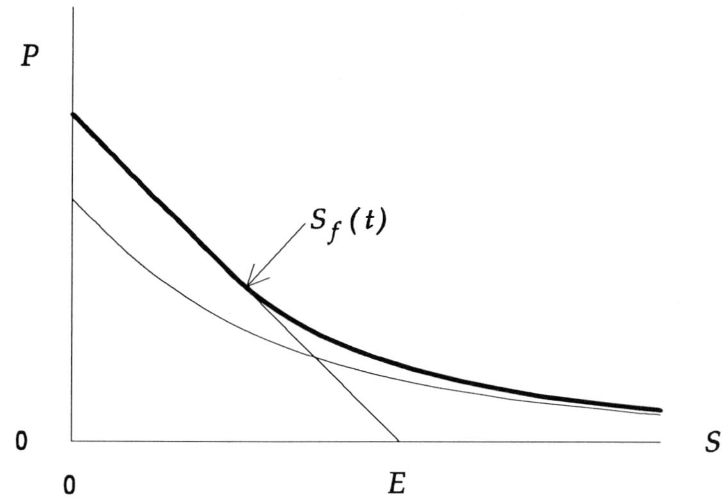

Figure 6.1: European and American put values before expiry. The upper curve is the value of the American put, which joins smoothly onto the payoff function (also shown).

6.3 The American call with dividends

We now consider some analytical aspects of the model for an American call option on a dividend-paying asset, introduced in Chapter 3. Recall that the value $C(S,t)$ of the call satisfies

$$\frac{\partial C}{\partial t} + \tfrac{1}{2}\sigma^2 S^2 \frac{\partial^2 C}{\partial S^2} + (r - D_0)S\frac{\partial C}{\partial S} - rC = 0 \qquad (6.6)$$

so long as exercise is not optimal. The payoff condition is

$$C(S,T) = \max(S - E, 0), \qquad (6.7)$$

and because the option can be exercised at any time, we always have

$$C(S,t) \geq \max(S-E,0). \tag{6.8}$$

If there is an optimal exercise boundary $S = S_f(t)$ (and we shortly see that there is), then at $S = S_f(t)$,

$$C(S_f(t),t) = S_f(t) - E, \quad \frac{\partial C}{\partial S}(S_f(t),t) = 1. \tag{6.9}$$

If an optimal exercise boundary does exist, then (6.6) is only valid while $C(S,t) > \max(S-E,0)$, since a direct calculation shows that $\max(S-E,0)$ is not a solution of the Black–Scholes equation (6.6). Again, (6.6) can be replaced by the inequality

$$\frac{\partial C}{\partial t} + \tfrac{1}{2}\sigma^2 S^2 \frac{\partial^2 C}{\partial S^2} + (r - D_0)S\frac{\partial C}{\partial S} - rC \leq 0,$$

in which equality only holds when $C(S,t) > \max(S-E,0)$. As in the case of the American put, the financial reason for this is that, if early exercise is optimal, then it is so because the option would be less valuable if it were held than if it were exercised immediately and the funds deposited in a bank.

6.4 Analysis of the American call option

In what follows we shall assume that the interest rate and dividend yield satisfy $r > D_0 > 0$. As for the European call, it is convenient to make (6.6)–(6.9) dimensionless and to reduce (6.6) to a constant coefficient and forward equation. It also happens to be helpful here to subtract off the payoff $S - E$ from the call value $C(S,t)$. We therefore put

$$S = Ee^x, \quad t = T - \tau/\tfrac{1}{2}\sigma^2, \quad C(S,t) = S - E + Ec(x,\tau),$$

and the result is

$$\frac{\partial c}{\partial \tau} = \frac{\partial^2 c}{\partial x^2} + (k_2 - 1)\frac{\partial c}{\partial x} - k_1 c + f(x) \tag{6.10}$$

for $-\infty < x < \infty$, $\tau > 0$, with

$$c(x,0) = \max(1-e^x,0) = \begin{cases} 1 - e^x & x < 0 \\ 0 & x \geq 0; \end{cases}$$

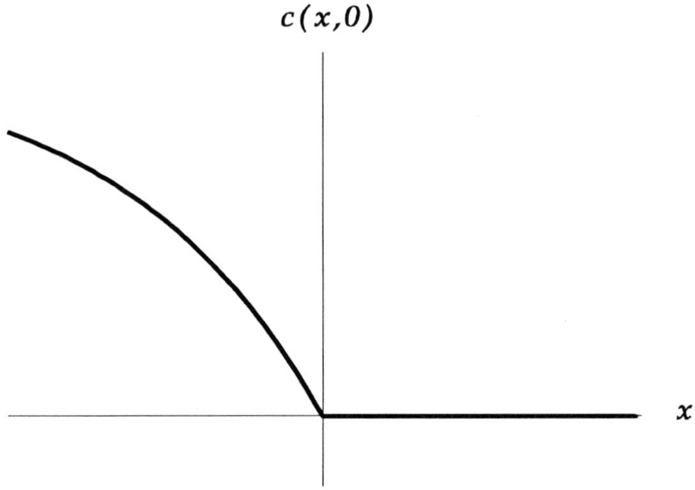

Figure 6.2: $c(x,0)$ for the American call problem.

$f(x)$ is defined in (6.12). The graph of the function $c(x,0)$ is sketched in Figure 6.2. The two dimensionless parameters k_1 (which also appeared in the European call solution earlier) and k_2 are given by

$$k_1 = r/\tfrac{1}{2}\sigma^2, \quad k_2 = (r - D_0)/\tfrac{1}{2}\sigma^2. \tag{6.11}$$

The function f is given by

$$f(x) = (k_2 - k_1)e^x + k_1. \tag{6.12}$$

Since $r > D_0 > 0$, it follows that $k_1 > k_2 > 0$.

Assume for the moment that a free boundary does exist, and call it $x = x_f(t)$ (in original variables, $S = S_f(t)$). Then at this boundary we have

$$c(x_f(\tau),\tau) = \frac{\partial c}{\partial x}(x_f(\tau),\tau) = 0.$$

Note that the boundary conditions on the free boundary have been simplified; this is the reason for subtracting the payoff function from the call value. The constraint $C \geq \max(S - E, 0)$ becomes

$$c \geq \max(1 - e^x, 0).$$

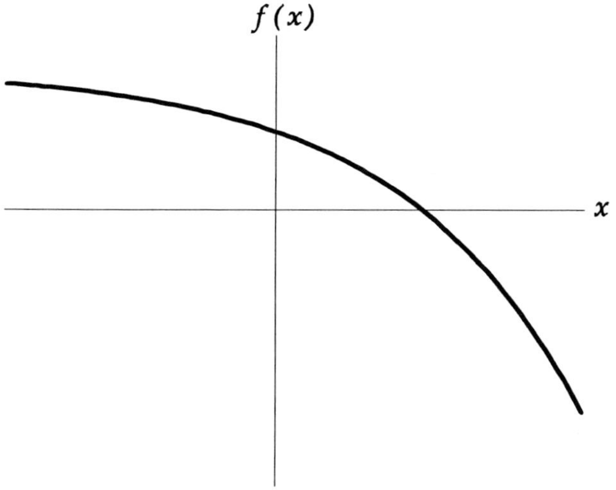

Figure 6.3: The consumption/replenishment term $f(x)$.

The behaviour of $f(x)$ is crucial to the behaviour of the free boundary. Indeed, when $f(x)$ is given by (6.12) the existence of this term implies the existence of the optimal exercise boundary. To see this, let us consider further its graph, sketched in Figure 6.3. We see that $f(x)$ is positive for $x < x_0$ where

$$x_0 = \log(k_1/(k_1 - k_2)) = \log(r/D_0) > 0,$$

and negative for $x \geq x_0$.

We now look at what would happen if there were no constraint and thus no free boundary. Consider the initial data $c(x, 0)$ for $x > 0$. For $x > 0$, $c(x, 0) = \partial c(x, 0)/\partial x = \partial^2 c(x, 0)/\partial x^2 = 0$. Thus, from (6.10) at expiry we have

$$\frac{\partial c}{\partial \tau} = f(x).$$

For $0 < x < x_0$, $f(x) > 0$ and c immediately becomes positive. For $x > x_0$, $f(x) < 0$ and c immediately becomes negative. Unfortunately, the latter does not satisfy the constraint, which for $x > 0$

requires that c remain positive. If we hold the option in $x > x_0$ the constraint is violated and the option value has fallen below its intrinsic value. This is impossible for an American style option, and hence we deduce that there must be an optimal exercise boundary.

Moreover, it is clear from this argument where the optimal exercise boundary $x_f(\tau)$ must start from. We must have $x_f(0^+) = x_0$, since this is the only point that is consistent with $c(x_f(0^+), 0^+) = 0$. Financially, this corresponds to

$$S_f(T) = \frac{rE}{D_0},$$

and is independent of σ. Thus, immediately before expiry, the option should be exercised at asset values such that the return on the asset, $D_0 S$, exceeds the interest rate return on the exercise price, rE. Note also that if $D_0 = 0$, $x_f = \infty$ ($S_f(T) = \infty$) and there is no free boundary: without dividends we recover the well-known result that it is always optimal to hold an American call to expiry.

We also point out that the point $S = rE/D$ is the value of S at which

$$\mathcal{L}_{BS}(\max(S - E, 0)) = 0.$$

Technical Point: physical interpretation.

Equation (6.10) is a little more complicated than the diffusion equation; there are three extra terms, $(k_2 - 1)\partial c/\partial x$, $-k_1 c$ and $f(x)$. The first of these can be interpreted as a **convection** *term, the second as a* **reaction** *term and the third, $f(x)$, can be interpreted as a* **consumption** *term where $f(x) < 0$ or a* **replenishment** *term where $f(x) > 0$. In order to understand the meaning of these terms and their effect on $c(x, t)$, let us consider combinations of these with other terms in (6.10).*

Consider the term $(k_1 - 1)\partial c/\partial x$. Physically, this represents convection (financially, drift). This may be seen by balancing it against the $\partial c/\partial \tau$ on the left-hand side of the partial differential equation and, for the moment, dropping all the other terms. This balance gives the first order hyperbolic equation $\partial c/\partial \tau = (k_2 - 1)\partial c/\partial x$. This equation may be solved by the method of characteristics (see Chapter

4) to yield $c(x,\tau) = F(x+(k_2-1)\tau)$ *for some function* F*. Since* c *is constant along the lines* $x+(k_2-1)\tau$ = *constant, this represents a wave travelling with constant speed* $1-k_2$*—hence the use of the word convection. This analysis suggests that by changing to the moving frame of reference* $\xi = x+(k_2-1)\tau$*, the* k_2-1 *term could be eliminated from the problem. This is indeed the case; the equation becomes*

$$\frac{\partial c}{\partial \tau} = \frac{\partial^2 c}{\partial \xi^2} - k_1 c - f(\xi-(k_2-1)\tau),$$

in the variables ξ *and* τ*.*

The second term in (6.10) new to the diffusion equation, $-k_1 c$*, represents reaction (or discounting) at a rate proportional to* c*. If we balance this term against the* $\partial c/\partial\tau$ *we find that this balance gives* $c = c_0 e^{-k_1 t}$*. This suggests this term could be eliminated by writing* $c(x,\tau) = e^{-k_1\tau} w(x,\tau)$*, to account for the exponential decay implied by it. This is the case, and the problem in the new dependent variable* w *is*

$$\frac{\partial w}{\partial \tau} = \frac{\partial^2 w}{\partial \xi^2} - e^{k_1\tau} f(\xi-(k_2-1)\tau).$$

Finally, and most importantly, the third new term in (6.10), $f(x)$*, represents a consumption term if* $f(x) < 0$ *and a replenishment term if* $f(x) > 0$*. We may see this by balancing this term against the* $\partial c/\partial\tau$ *term. If* $f(x) < 0$*, then* $\partial c/\partial\tau < 0$ *in this balance and* $c(x,\tau)$ *decreases with* τ*, while if* $f(x) > 0$*,* $c(x,\tau)$ *increases.*

6.5 A local analysis of the free boundary

We now ask how the free boundary $x = x_f(\tau)$ moves away from $x_f(0) = x_0$. We cannot solve the problem for the free boundary exactly, but we can find an asymptotic solution which is valid close to expiry.

In order to perform this analysis, which is local in both time and asset price, we look at equation (6.10) only near $x = x_0$, and for small values of τ. We approximate $f(x)$ by a Taylor series about x_0 (which corresponds to the final position of the optimal exercise boundary), namely

$$\begin{aligned} f(x) &= f(x_0) + f'(x_0)(x - x_0) + O((x - x_0)^2) \\ &\sim (x - x_0)f'(x_0) \\ &= -k_1(x - x_0). \end{aligned}$$

We need only keep the highest spatial derivative of c, i.e. $\partial^2 c/\partial x^2$, since this will be the larger than c or $\partial c/\partial x$ in a region where c is changing rapidly. The upshot is an approximate local problem for c. Call this local solution $\hat{c}(x, \tau)$; it satisfies

$$\frac{\partial \hat{c}}{\partial \tau} = \frac{\partial^2 \hat{c}}{\partial x^2} - k_1(x - x_0)$$

with

$$\hat{c} = \frac{\partial \hat{c}}{\partial x} = 0 \quad \text{on} \quad x = x_f(\tau), \quad x_f(0) = x_0.$$

It is fortunate that we can solve this local problem exactly. In fact, it has a similarity solution in terms of the variable

$$\xi = (x - x_0)/\sqrt{\tau},$$

of the form

$$\hat{c} = \tau^{3/2} c^*(\xi),$$

where c^* satisfies some yet to be determined ordinary differential equation. At the same time we try a free boundary of the form

$$x_f(\tau) = x_0 + \xi_0 \sqrt{\tau},$$

where ξ_0 is also yet to be determined. Although the free boundary is still unknown, we now have to only to find the constant ξ_0 rather than a fully τ-dependent function $x_f(\tau)$.

Substituting the expression $\hat{c} = \tau^{3/2} c^*(\xi)$ into the partial differential equation for $\hat{c}$ gives

$$\sqrt{\tau}\left(\tfrac{3}{2}c^* - \tfrac{1}{2}\xi \frac{dc^*}{d\xi}\right) = \sqrt{\tau}\,\frac{d^2 c^*}{d\xi^2} - k_1(x - x_0),$$

and dividing through by $\sqrt{\tau}$ gives, as intended, an ordinary differential equation. We have

$$\frac{d^2 c^*}{d\xi^2} + \tfrac{1}{2}\xi \frac{dc^*}{d\xi} - \tfrac{3}{2}c^* = k_1 \xi, \tag{6.13}$$

while the free boundary conditions

$$\hat{c} = \frac{\partial \hat{c}}{\partial x} = 0 \quad \text{on} \quad x = x_f(\tau)$$

reduce to

$$c^*(\xi_0) = \frac{dc^*}{d\xi}(\xi_0) = 0.$$

We also need to know how $\hat{c}(x,\tau)$ behaves for $\xi \to -\infty$. This follows from the behaviour of $\hat{c}(x,\tau)$ for large negative x: as $x \to -\infty$, $\partial^2\hat{c}/\partial x^2 \to 0$ and so $\hat{c}(x,\tau)$ looks like $-k_1 xt$. Thus

$$c^*(\xi) \sim -k_1\xi \quad \text{as} \quad \xi \to -\infty$$

(implying also that $\hat{c} = t^{3/2}c^* \sim t^{3/2}(x - x_0)/t^{1/2} \sim xt$ + smaller terms).

The first step in solving this two point boundary value problem for $c^*(\xi)$ is to find the general solution of the homogeneous ordinary differential equation

$$\frac{d^2c^*}{d\xi^2} + \tfrac{1}{2}\xi\frac{dc^*}{d\xi} - \tfrac{3}{2}c^* = 0.$$

Fortunately one solution, $c_1^*(\xi)$ say, is easy to find. Trying simple low order polynomial solutions shows that

$$c_1^*(\xi) = \xi^3 + 6\xi$$

is an exact solution of the homogeneous equation. A second independent solution may be found by the method of reduction of order: we set $c_2^*(\xi) = c_1^*(\xi)a(\xi)$ and we find a *first* order ordinary differential equation for $a(\xi)$. The arithmetic is straightforward but tedious, and the result is that $c_2^*(\xi)$ is found to be

$$c_2^*(\xi) = (\xi^2 + 4)e^{-\frac{1}{4}\xi^2} + \tfrac{1}{2}(\xi^2 + 6\xi)\int_{-\infty}^{\xi} e^{-\frac{1}{4}s^2}\,ds.$$

Thus the general solution of the homogeneous equation is

$$c^*(\xi) = Ac_1^*(\xi) + Bc_2^*(\xi).$$

The second step in solving the original ordinary differential equation (6.13) is to observe that $c_p^*(\xi) = -k_1\xi$ is an exact solution. Thus the general solution is given by the sum of c_p^* and the general solution of the homogeneous equation, i.e.

$$c^*(\xi) = -k_1\xi + Ac_1^*(\xi) + Bc_2^*(\xi).$$

As $\xi \to -\infty$, $c_2^*(\xi) \to 0$, while $c_1^*(\xi)$ tends to ∞ like ξ^3. We know $c^*(\xi) \sim -k_1\xi$ as $\xi \to -\infty$ and therefore $A = 0$. Thus

$$c^*(\xi) = -k_1\xi + Bc_2^*(\xi).$$

The free boundary conditions $c^*(\xi_0) = 0$ and $dc^*(\xi_0)/d\xi = 0$ give us two equations for B and ξ_0. These are

$$Bc_2^*(\xi_0) = \xi_0, \quad \text{and} \quad B\frac{dc_2^*}{d\xi}(\xi_0) = 1.$$

Dividing these equations gives

$$\xi_0 \frac{dc_2^*}{d\xi}(\xi_0) = c_2^*(\xi_0)$$

which, after some rearrangement, leads to the transcendental equation

$$\xi_0^3 e^{\frac{1}{4}\xi_0^2} \int_{-\infty}^{\xi_0} e^{-s^2/4} ds = 2(2 - \xi_0^2). \tag{6.14}$$

The constant B is then given by $B = \xi_0/c_2^*(\xi_0)$.

Transcendental equations of the form (6.14) are characteristic features of similarity solutions of free boundary problems. It can be shown, for example by graphical methods, that this equation has just one root, and this can be found (by a numerical method such as the bisection algorithm or Newton iteration) to be

$$\xi_0 = 0.9034\ldots\ .$$

We have found a local solution $\hat{c}(x, \tau)$ which is a valid approximation to the American call problem for τ near to zero and x near to x_0.

Reverting to financial variables, we have shown that at expiry the optimal exercise price of an American call on a dividend-paying

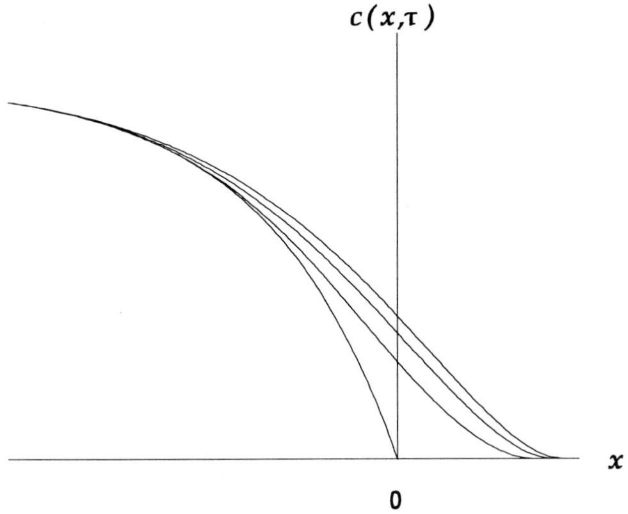

Figure 6.4: The function $c(x, \tau)$ at three different times.

asset tends to the value rE/D_0. Also, from the local analysis, we know that as $t \to T$

$$S_f(t) \sim \frac{rE}{D}\left(1 + \xi_0\sqrt{\tfrac{1}{2}\sigma^2(T-t)} + \cdots\right)$$

where ξ_0 is a 'universal constant' of option pricing. Beyond this interesting fact, the local analysis is also important for the early stages of a numerical calculation where prices change rapidly: the effect of the rapid changes in $S_f(t)$ is felt throughout the solution region, not just near $S = S_f(T)$. In Figures 6.4 and 6.5 we show the values of $c(x, \tau)$ in dimensionless variables, and the original $C(S, t)$, prior to expiry.

Further reading

- Hill & Dewynne (1990) and Crank (1984) discuss similarity solutions to free boundary problems for the diffusion equation.

Exercises

1. Find the explicit solution to the obstacle problem (7.1) when

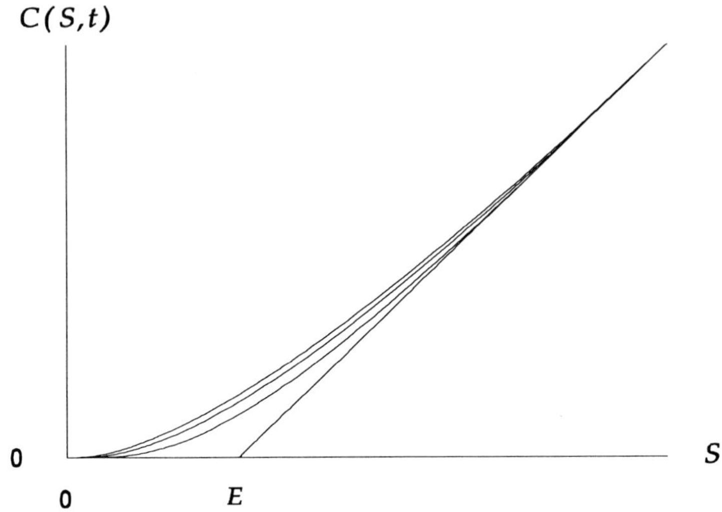

Figure 6.5: The option value $C(S,t)$ at the same three times.

the obstacle is $f(x) = \frac{1}{2} - x^2$. Try to find the solution when $f(x) = \frac{1}{2} - \sin^2(\pi x/2)$; the free boundaries now have to be found numerically.

2. The function $u(x,t)$ satisfies the following free boundary problem with free boundary $x = x_f(t)$, where $x_f(0) = 0$:

$$\frac{\partial u}{\partial t} = \frac{\partial^2 u}{\partial x^2}, \qquad 0 < x < x_f(t),$$

$$u(x_f(t),t) = 0, \qquad \frac{\partial u}{\partial x}\,(x_f(t),t) = -\frac{dx_f}{dt},$$

$$u(0,t) = 1, \qquad t > 0.$$

Show that there is a similarity solution $u(x,t) = u^*(x/\sqrt{t})$, $x_f(t) = \xi_0\sqrt{t}$, where ξ_0 satisfies the transcendental equation

$$\tfrac{1}{2}\xi_0 e^{\frac{1}{4}\xi_0^2} \int_0^{\xi_0} e^{-s^2/4}\,ds = 1.$$

(This is a solution to the Stefan problem, in which $u(x,t)$ models the temperature in a pure material that melts at temperature $u = 0$; here a semi-infinite bar of the material is initially solid at the melting temperature, and melting is initiated by raising the temperature at $x = 0$ to 1 and holding it there, so that the region $0 < x < x_f(t)$ is liquid. The conditions at the free boundary express the facts that melting takes place at $u = 0$, and that the heat flux into the free boundary is balanced by the rate at which latent heat is taken up during the change of phase from solid to liquid.)

3. The function $c(x,t)$ satisfies the following problem in the region $0 < x < x_f(t)$, where $x_f(0) = 0$:

$$\frac{\partial c}{\partial t} = \frac{\partial^2 c}{\partial x^2} - 1, \qquad 0 < x < x_f(t),$$

$$c(x_f(t),t) = 0, \qquad \frac{\partial c}{\partial x}(x_f(t),t) = 0,$$

$$c(0,t) = t, \qquad t > 0.$$

Show that there is a similarity solution $c(x,t) = c^*(x/\sqrt{t})$, $x_f(t) = \xi_0\sqrt{t}$, where ξ_0 satisfies the transcendental equation

$$\tfrac{1}{2}\xi_0 e^{\frac{1}{4}\xi_0^2} \int_0^{\xi_0} e^{-s^2/4}\, ds = 1.$$

4. Show that $u(x,t)$ of exercise 1 and $c(x,t)$ of exercise 2 are related by

$$u = \frac{\partial c}{\partial t}.$$

This requires you to show that the equations and boundary conditions all correspond. The only tricky case is the free boundary condition for $c(x,t)$: differentiating the condition $c(x_f(t),t) = 0$ with respect to t yields

$$\begin{aligned}\frac{\partial c}{\partial x}(x_f(t),t)\frac{dx_f}{dt} + \frac{\partial c}{\partial t} &= \frac{\partial c}{\partial x}(x_f(t),t)\frac{dx_f}{dt} + u(x_f(t),t) \\ &= 0 + u(x_f(t)),\end{aligned}$$

which demonstrates that condition $u(x_f(t),t) = 0$ holds; the second free boundary condition for u is obtained by differentiating $\partial c(x_f(t),t)/\partial x$ with respect to t and using the partial differential equation for $c(x,t)$.

Chapter 7

American Options as Variational Inequalities

7.1 Variational inequalities and the obstacle problem

From the previous chapter, it is clear that the mathematical analysis of American options is more complicated than that of European options. We mention at the outset that it is almost always impossible to find a useful explicit solution to any given free boundary problem, and so a primary aim is to construct efficient and robust numerical methods for their computation. This means that we need a theoretical framework within which to analyse free boundary problems in fairly general terms.

This chapter begins with a discussion of the canonical free boundary problem, the obstacle problem. It is not directly interpretable in financial terms, but in addition to its mathematical simplicity, its physical interpretations are of considerable use as a complement to financial intuition. It is one of the simplest of all free boundary problems to analyse, because it has straightforward equations with straightforward physical interpretations, and because it is not time-dependent. Nevertheless, it can be used to introduce linear complementarity problems and variational inequalities, which are crucial to a successful numerical attack on American options and more complicated problems. It is also a good framework within which to discuss such mathematical questions as the existence and uniqueness of solutions.

The philosophy behind variational inequalities is that, as it is difficult to deal with free boundaries, it is worth the effort of attempting to reformulate the problem in such a way as to eliminate any explicit dependence on the free boundary. The free boundary does not then interfere with the solution process, and it can be recovered from the solution *after* the latter has been found. We start by considering a simple example of such a reformulation, in the context of the obstacle problem. We then apply the lessons learnt from the obstacle problem to more complicated American options. These problems too have linear complementarity and variational inequality formulations which lead to efficient and accurate numerical solution schemes with the desirable property of not requiring explicit tracking of the free boundary. These methods are discussed in detail in Chapters 20 and 21.

7.1.1 The obstacle problem

Consider an elastic string held fixed at two ends and constrained to lie above a fixed obstacle of height $f(x)$, as in Figure 3.9. Let the ends of the string be at $x = \pm 1$, and call the displacement of the string $u(x)$. We assume that $f(\pm 1) < 0$, and that $f(x) > 0$ at some points $-1 < x < 1$, so that there definitely is a contact region. We also assume, at least initially, that $f'' < 0$, where $' = d/dx$, thereby guaranteeing that there is only one contact region. The free boundary is then the set of points, marked as A and B in Figure 3.9, where the string first meets the obstacle. These are *a priori* unknown, and have to be determined as part of the solution.

In the contact region, $u = f$, while where the string is not in contact with the obstacle it is straight, so $u'' = 0$. Normally, one would need just two boundary conditions to determine the straight portions of the string uniquely, and the values of u at the two ends of each straight portion would certainly do; indeed, we do have $u(-1) = 0$, $u(A) = f(A)$ and similar conditions for the other straight portion. However, because A and B are unknown, we need two more boundary conditions than usual in order to determine these points, and here a physical argument based on a force balance shows that at points such as A and B, u' must be continuous as well as u. As a free boundary problem we can write the particular example given in Figure 3.9 as the problem of finding $u(x)$ *and* the points A, B such that

$$
\begin{array}{ccc}
 & u(-1)=0, & \\
u''=0, & & -1<x<A, \\
u(A)=f(A), & & u'(A)=f'(A), \\
u(x)=f(x), & & A<x<B, \\
u(B)=f(B), & & u'(B)=f'(B), \\
u''=0, & & B<x<1, \\
 & u(1)=0. &
\end{array}
\tag{7.1}
$$

Given any particular $f(x)$ with the same general shape as in Figure 3.9 it is straightforward in principle to show that $u(x)$, A and B are uniquely determined by this problem, and to find them. The procedure is tedious, and for all but specially simple f, A and B must be determined numerically as solutions of an algebraic or transcendental equation. The details are even more complicated when f'' is not always less than or equal to zero, because then multiple contact regions can occur, but again, in principle, it can be done.

7.1.2 The linear complementarity formulation

An alternative approach to the problem is to note that either the string lies above the obstacle, $u > f$, in which case it is straight, $u'' = 0$, or that the string is in contact with the obstacle, $u = f$, in which case $u'' = f'' < 0$. This means that we can write the problem as what is called a **linear complementarity problem**[1],

$$u''(u-f)=0, \quad -u''\geq 0, \quad (u-f)\geq 0, \tag{7.2}$$

subject to the conditions that

$$u(-1)=u(1)=0, \quad u, u' \text{ are continuous.} \tag{7.3}$$

[1]In general, a problem of the form

$$\mathcal{AB}=0, \quad \mathcal{A}\geq 0, \quad \mathcal{B}\geq 0,$$

is called a complementarity problem, and in this example the factors $\mathcal{A}=u''$ and $\mathcal{B}=u-f$ are both linear in u and f.

7.1.3 The variational inequality formulation

The third formulation of the problem, as a **variational inequality**, is motivated by the following calculation. Let $\mathcal{K}$ denote the set of all functions $v(x)$ such that

- $v(-1) = 0$ and $v(1) = 0$;
- $v(x) \geq f(x)$ for $-1 \leq x \leq 1$;
- $v(x)$ is continuous;
- $v'(x)$ is piecewise continuous.

We call any function $v(x) \in \mathcal{K}$ a **test function** and the set $\mathcal{K}$ is called a space of test functions. Note that $u(x) \in \mathcal{K}$, and that although we expect u itself to have a continuous derivative for *all* x, the test functions need only be piecewise continuous. (This fact proves useful when we contemplate a finite-element solution; see Appendix D.)

For any $v \in \mathcal{K}$ we have $(v - f) \geq 0$, and, because $-u'' \geq 0$,

$$-u''(v - f) \geq 0,$$

which gives

$$\int_{-1}^{1} -u''(v - f)\, dx \geq 0.$$

We also have

$$\int_{-1}^{1} -u''(u - f)\, dx = 0,$$

and subtracting we find that

$$\int_{-1}^{1} -u''(v - u)\, dx \geq 0. \tag{7.4}$$

Note that (7.4) does not involve $f(x)$ explicitly; $f(x)$ only occurs implicitly through the fact that v and u are members of $\mathcal{K}$.

Integrating (7.4) by parts shows that

$$\left[-u'(v - u)\right]_{-1}^{1} + \int_{-1}^{1} u'(v - u)'\, dx \geq 0,$$

and since $u = v$ at $x = \pm 1$ we find that

$$\int_{-1}^{1} u'(v-u)'\,dx \geq 0.$$

This is true for *every* $v \in \mathcal{K}$ if u is a solution of the original problem (7.1). This motivates the **variational inequality formulation** of the free boundary problem, namely:

- Find $u \in \mathcal{K}$ such that $\int_{-1}^{1} u'(v-u)'\,dx \geq 0$ for every $v \in \mathcal{K}$. (7.5)

Obviously the minimum value of this integral, zero, is obtained when $v = u$.

Using techniques of functional analysis, it can be shown that any solution of the variational inequality problem (7.5) is a solution of the linear complementarity problem (7.2), (7.3) and of the original problem (7.1), and *vice versa*. Moreover, it can be shown that the variational inequality has one and only one solution. While this may seem trivial here, since after all we are able to deduce that the free boundary problem has one and only one solution by elementary curve sketching, it is quite important in more complicated situations. Because it is relatively easy to prove in general that a variational inequality has one and only one solution, this can then be used to infer the existence and uniqueness of solutions of free boundary problems in much more complicated situations. Consequently, it is a considerable step forward if a free boundary problem can be recast as a variational inequality. Although this is quite uncommon, several problems of practical importance are equivalent to variational inequalities, and in the following section we show that American options are among these.

Reformulation as a variational inequality is also a step forward from the numerical point of view, for two important reasons. Firstly, the free boundary or boundaries do not appear explicitly; they can be found quite simply *a posteriori* as the set of points where the equations switch over. Secondly, it is in general only necessary to approximate the first derivatives of the unknown function rather than the second derivatives, with consequent gains in speed and accuracy. We return to the numerical analysis of variational inequalities in Chapter 20.

The proofs of the statements in this section require some knowledge of abstract functional analysis, although the basic idea is simply the minimisation of an appropriate energy functional over convex sets of functions (the space of test functions $\mathcal{K}$ is convex in the sense that if $u, v \in \mathcal{K}$ then so too is $\lambda u+(1-\lambda)v$ for any $0 \leq \lambda \leq 1$). The details can be found in the books by Elliott & Ockendon (1982), Friedman (1988) or Kinderlehrer & Stampacchia (1980).

7.2 A variational inequality for the American put

In Chapter 3, we gave an informal discussion of both obstacle problems and American options, hinting that they were mathematically very similar. Here, we strengthen the analogy by showing that the Black–Scholes formulation of the free boundary problem for an American put can be reduced to a linear complementarity problem and a **parabolic variational inequality**.

We recall from Section 5.4 that the Black–Scholes partial differential equation (6.1) can be transformed into the diffusion equation by a series of changes of variable. Specifically, setting

$$S = Ee^{x}, \quad t = T - \tau/\tfrac{1}{2}\sigma^2, \quad P(S,t) = Ee^{-\frac{1}{2}(k_1-1)x-\frac{1}{4}(k_1+1)^2\tau}u(x,\tau),$$

where $k_1 = r/\frac{1}{2}\sigma^2$, yields the diffusion equation

$$\frac{\partial u}{\partial \tau} = \frac{\partial^2 u}{\partial x^2} \tag{7.6}$$

wherever $P(S,t)$ lies above the payoff $\max(E-S,0)$. Let us also define

$$g(x,\tau) = e^{\frac{1}{4}(k_1+1)^2\tau}\max(e^{\frac{1}{2}(k_1-1)x} - e^{\frac{1}{2}(k_1+1)x}, 0). \tag{7.7}$$

Then the initial condition for (7.6) is

$$u(x,0) = g(x,0), \tag{7.8}$$

while the constraint that $P(S,t) \geq \max(E-S,0)$ becomes

$$u(x,\tau) \geq g(x,\tau). \tag{7.9}$$

Finally, we have the conditions that

$$u(x,\tau) \to 0 \text{ as } x \to \infty, \quad u \text{ and } \frac{\partial u}{\partial x} \text{ are continuous everywhere.} \tag{7.10}$$

We note that, by direct calculation,

$$\frac{\partial g}{\partial \tau} - \frac{\partial^2 g}{\partial x^2} \geq 0 \qquad \text{for } x \neq 0, \tag{7.11}$$

which means financially that the return from the riskless delta-hedged portfolio is less than the riskless interest rate r.

In order to avoid technical complications, let us accept that, since we are going to have to restrict any numerical scheme to a finite mesh, we may as well restrict the problem to a finite interval. That is we consider the problem (7.6)–(7.9) only for x in the interval $-x^- < x < x^+$, where x^+ and x^- are large. This means that we impose the boundary conditions

$$u(x^+, \tau) = 0, \quad u(-x^-, \tau) = g(-x^-, \tau). \tag{7.12}$$

In financial terms, we assume that we can replace the exact boundary conditions by the approximations that for small values of S, $P = E - S$, while for large values, $P = 0$.

The fact that both the obstacle problem and the American put problem satisfy constraints suggests that the latter might also have linear complementarity and variational inequality formulations, and this is indeed the case. The option problem is very similar to the obstacle problem, but with an obstacle which is time-dependent, i.e. the transformed payoff function $g(x, \tau)$. Since the partial differential equation is parabolic, the variational inequality that arises from this problem is called a **parabolic variational inequality**.

We first remark that we can write (7.6)–(7.9) in the linear complementarity form

$$\begin{gathered} \left(\frac{\partial u}{\partial \tau} - \frac{\partial^2 u}{\partial x^2}\right)(u(x,\tau) - g(x,\tau)) = 0, \\ \left(\frac{\partial u}{\partial \tau} - \frac{\partial^2 u}{\partial x^2}\right) \geq 0, \qquad (u(x,\tau) - g(x,\tau)) \geq 0, \end{gathered} \tag{7.13}$$

with the initial and boundary conditions (7.8) and (7.12), namely

$$u(x, 0) = g(x, 0),$$

$$u(-x^-, \tau) = g(-x^-, \tau), \quad u(x^+, \tau) = g(x^+, \tau) = 0,$$

and the conditions that

$$u(x,\tau) \text{ and } \frac{\partial u}{\partial x}(x,\tau) \text{ are continuous.} \tag{7.14}$$

The two possibilities in this formulation correspond to situations in which it is optimal to exercise the option ($u = g$) and those in which it is not ($u > g$).

Following the pattern for the obstacle problem, we introduce a space of test functions $\mathcal{K}$, and convert the linear complementarity formulation of the American put problem into a (parabolic) variational inequality. The space of test functions, $\mathcal{K}$, consists of functions $\phi(x,\tau)$ that satisfy

- $\phi(x,\tau)$ and $\partial\phi/\partial\tau$ are both continuous and $\partial\phi/\partial x$ is piecewise continuous;
- $\phi(x,\tau) \geq g(x,\tau)$ for all x and τ;
- $\phi(x^+,\tau) = g(x^+,\tau) = 0$ and $\phi(-x^-,\tau) = g(-x^-,\tau)$;
- $\phi(x,0) = g(x,0)$.

As before, $u(x,\tau)$ is itself an element of $\mathcal{K}$. Proceeding as we did for the obstacle problem, we note that for any $\phi \in \mathcal{K}$ we have $\phi \geq g$, and hence

$$\left(\frac{\partial u}{\partial \tau} - \frac{\partial^2 u}{\partial x^2}\right)(\phi(x,\tau) - g(x,\tau)) \geq 0.$$

Consequently, for any $0 \leq \tau \leq \frac{1}{2}\sigma^2 T$,

$$\int_{-x^-}^{x^+} \left(\frac{\partial u}{\partial \tau} - \frac{\partial^2 u}{\partial x^2}\right)(\phi(x,\tau) - g(x,\tau))\, dx \geq 0.$$

We also have

$$\int_{-x^-}^{x^+} \left(\frac{\partial u}{\partial \tau} - \frac{\partial^2 u}{\partial x^2}\right)(u(x,\tau) - g(x,\tau))\, dx = 0,$$

since the integrand vanishes identically. Subtracting, we find that

$$\int_{-x^-}^{x^+} \left(\frac{\partial u}{\partial \tau} - \frac{\partial^2 u}{\partial x^2}\right)(\phi(x,\tau) - u(x,\tau))\, dx \geq 0,$$

and this inequality is true for every $\phi \in \mathcal{K}$. It contains no explicit reference to the obstacle $g(x,\tau)$; the constraint only enters into the formulation via the space of test functions $\mathcal{K}$.

Integrating by parts, we find that

$$\int_{-x^-}^{x^+} \frac{\partial u}{\partial \tau}(\phi - u) + \frac{\partial u}{\partial x}\left(\frac{\partial \phi}{\partial x} - \frac{\partial u}{\partial x}\right) dx - \left[\frac{\partial u}{\partial x}(\phi - u)\right]_{-x^-}^{x^+} \geq 0.$$

Since all test functions, including $u(x,\tau)$, satisfy the same conditions at x^+ and $-x^-$, we are left with the following (parabolic) variational inequality for $u(x,\tau)$:

- Find $u(x,t) \in \mathcal{K}$ such that, for all $\phi(x,t) \in \mathcal{K}$, and for all $0 \leq t \leq \frac{1}{2}\sigma^2 T$,

$$\int_{-x^-}^{x^+} \frac{\partial u}{\partial \tau}(\phi - u) + \frac{\partial u}{\partial x}\left(\frac{\partial \phi}{\partial x} - \frac{\partial u}{\partial x}\right) dx \geq 0. \qquad (7.15)$$

Alternatively, there is a global formulation:

- Find $u(x,t) \in \mathcal{K}$ such that, for all $\phi \in \mathcal{K}$,

$$\int_0^{\frac{1}{2}\sigma^2 T} \int_{-x^-}^{x^+} \frac{\partial u}{\partial \tau}(\phi - u) + \frac{\partial u}{\partial x}\left(\frac{\partial \phi}{\partial x} - \frac{\partial u}{\partial x}\right) dx\, d\tau \geq 0. \quad (7.16)$$

It turns out that these are two equivalent ways of stating the problem as a variational inequality. Just as the term **parabolic variational inequality** is sometimes used to indicate that the problem arises from a parabolic partial differential equation, so the obstacle problem is sometimes called an **elliptic variational inequality** because the underlying partial differential equation is elliptic. Note also that neither variational inequality (7.15) or (7.16) assumes the existence of a second partial derivative with respect to x for $u(x,t)$. For this reason (7.15) and (7.16) are also called **weak formulations** of the original partial differential equation problem, since they assume weaker conditions about the existence of derivatives.

It can be shown that any solution $u(x,t) \in \mathcal{K}$ of the variational inequalities (7.15) or (7.16) is a solution of the linear complementarity problem (7.6)–(7.9), and hence of the free boundary problem

(6.1)–(6.5). This result is slightly surprising, because it means that satisfying either of (7.15) or (7.16) implies the existence of a well-defined second derivative. The details can be found in, for example, Elliott & Ockendon (1982), or Friedman (1988).

As with the obstacle problem the advantage of the variational inequality formulations (7.15), (7.16), and indeed of the linear complementarity formulation (7.6)–(7.9), is that there is no explicit mention of the free boundary. If we can solve either of the variational inequalities, or the linear complementarity problem, then we find the optimal exercise boundary by the condition that defines it, namely that it divides the region where $u(x,\tau) > g(x,\tau)$ from the region where $u(x,\tau) = g(x,\tau)$.

Technical Point: existence and uniqueness.
It can also be shown that there is one, and only one, solution of (7.15) and (7.16), and hence of the American put problem. This is important because it is not at all obvious from the differential equations and boundary conditions that the American put problem does have a solution at all, unlike the European put problem, where we can write down the exact solution explicitly. Moreover, it is not obvious from the equations that the free boundary problem has only one solution; these questions are in general much more difficult to answer for free boundary problems than for fixed boundary problems. Thus a great advantage of the theory of variational inequalities is that we can use it to show that the American put problem is well posed, namely that it has a solution and that solution is unique.

The proofs can be found in Elliott & Ockendon (1982), Friedman (1988) and Kinderlehrer & Stampacchia (1980). Again some knowledge of abstract functional analysis is necessary in order to understand the details, but as with the obstacle problem the central idea is minimisation over convex sets of functions.

7.3 A variational inequality for the American call

Finally, we briefly show how the Black–Scholes formulation of the free boundary problem for an American call on an underlying paying a continuous constant dividend yield can be reduced to a linear complementarity problem and a parabolic variational inequality. Since the details are almost identical to those given in the previous section for an American put, we state only the main results.

Using the change of variables

$$S = Ee^x, \quad t = T - \tau/\tfrac{1}{2}\sigma^2,$$

$$C(S,t) = Ee^{-\frac{1}{2}(k_1-1)x-\frac{1}{4}((k_2-1)^2+4k_1)\tau}u(x,\tau),$$

in equation (3.21), where $k_1 = r/\frac{1}{2}\sigma^2$ and $k_2 = (r - D_0)/\frac{1}{2}\sigma^2$, yields the diffusion equation

$$\frac{\partial u}{\partial \tau} = \frac{\partial^2 u}{\partial x^2} \tag{7.17}$$

wherever $C(S,t)$ lies above the payoff $\max(S - E, 0)$.

Let us define

$$g(x,\tau) = e^{\frac{1}{4}((k_2-1)^2+4k_1)\tau} \max(e^{\frac{1}{2}(k_2+1)x} - e^{\frac{1}{2}(k_2-1)x}, 0); \tag{7.18}$$

then the initial condition for (7.17) is

$$u(x,0) = g(x,0), \tag{7.19}$$

while the constraint that $C(S,t) \geq \max(S - E, 0)$ becomes

$$u(x,\tau) \geq g(x,\tau). \tag{7.20}$$

Finally, we have the conditions that

$$u(x,\tau) \to 0 \text{ as } x \to -\infty, \quad u \text{ and } \frac{\partial u}{\partial x} \text{ are continuous.} \tag{7.21}$$

We note that, for $k_2 < k_1$ and $x \neq 0$, we have by direct calculation

$$\frac{\partial g}{\partial \tau} - \frac{\partial^2 g}{\partial x^2} \geq 0.$$

Again, we only solve the problem on the interval $-x^- < x < x^+$, where x^+ and x^- are large. This means that we impose the approximate boundary conditions

$$u(x^+,\tau) = g(x^+,\tau), \quad u(-x^-,\tau) = g(-x^-,\tau) = 0. \tag{7.22}$$

The American call problem formulated in this way is almost identical to the American put problem in the previous section. We simply quote its linear complementarity and variational inequality formulations.

The linear complementarity formulation of the problem is

$$\begin{gathered}\left(\frac{\partial u}{\partial \tau}-\frac{\partial^2 u}{\partial x^2}\right)(u(x,\tau)-g(x,\tau))=0,\\ \left(\frac{\partial u}{\partial \tau}-\frac{\partial^2 u}{\partial x^2}\right)\geq 0, \qquad (u(x,\tau)-g(x,\tau))\geq 0,\end{gathered} \tag{7.23}$$

with the initial and boundary conditions (7.19) and (7.22)

$$u(x,0)=g(x,0),$$

$$u(-x^-,\tau)=g(-x^-,\tau), \quad u(x^+,\tau)=g(x^+,\tau)$$

and the conditions that

$$u(x,\tau) \text{ and } \frac{\partial u}{\partial x}(x,\tau) \text{ are continuous.} \tag{7.24}$$

To formulate the problem as a variational inequality we introduce the space of test functions $\mathcal{K}$ consisting of functions $\phi(x,\tau)$ that satisfy

- $\phi(x,\tau)$ and $\partial\phi/\partial\tau$ are both continuous and $\partial\phi/\partial x$ is piecewise continuous;
- $\phi(x,\tau)\geq g(x,\tau)$ for all x and τ;
- $\phi(x^+,\tau)=g(x^+,\tau)$ and $\phi(-x^-,\tau)=g(-x^-,\tau)=0$;
- $\phi(x,0)=g(x,0)$.

We then go through an almost identical series of steps to those given in the previous section, for the American put. We find that we can state the problem for an American call on an asset paying a continuous dividend as a variational inequality in two ways:

- Find $u(x,t) \in \mathcal{K}$ such that, for all $\phi(x,t) \in \mathcal{K}$, and for all $0 \leq t \leq \frac{1}{2}\sigma^2 T$,

$$\int_{-x^-}^{x^+} \frac{\partial u}{\partial \tau}(\phi - u) + \frac{\partial u}{\partial x}\left(\frac{\partial \phi}{\partial x} - \frac{\partial u}{\partial x}\right) dx \geq 0. \qquad (7.25)$$

Alternatively, the global formulation is

- Find $u(x,t) \in \mathcal{K}$ such that, for all $\phi \in \mathcal{K}$,

$$\int_0^{\frac{1}{2}\sigma^2 T} \int_{-x^-}^{x^+} \frac{\partial u}{\partial \tau}(\phi - u) + \frac{\partial u}{\partial x}\left(\frac{\partial \phi}{\partial x} - \frac{\partial u}{\partial x}\right) dx\, d\tau \geq 0. \quad (7.26)$$

Further reading

- For more on the theory of variational inequalities see Elliott & Ockendon (1982).
- Approximate solutions for American options have been found by Roll (1977), Whaley (1981), Barone-Adesi & Whaley (1987) and Johnson (1983).

Exercise

1. Set up the American call and put problems as variational inequalities using the original (S,t) variables. (This is not necessarily a good formulation as far as numerical solution is concerned.)

Chapter 8

Dividends and Time-dependent Parameters

8.1 Introduction

We begin this chapter with a further discussion of dividend structure and its effect on the random walk of the asset price and the price of an option. We discuss in some detail the effects of discrete dividend payments and the consequent jumps in the asset price. Then, by allowing the interest rate, the volatility and the dividend yield all to be known functions of time, we find explicit solutions for European vanilla options with some of our earlier restrictive assumptions dropped.

8.2 Dividends in the Black–Scholes framework

We mentioned in Chapter 3 that we only consider deterministic dividend payments in this book. However, even with this limitation there is a wide variety of structures possible for this payment, characterised by the dependence on S and t. Sometimes these payments are continuous in time and sometimes they are made at discrete times. The former is associated with indices, such as *FT-SE*, in which the large number of shares making up the index yield a fairly steady stream of dividend income. The latter is associated with single equities. We examine both of these cases in this chapter.

We first set out a framework for incorporating arbitrary known dividends into the models for assets and option prices. Let us suppose that in a time dt the underlying asset pays out a dividend $D(S,t)\,dt$. (The dependence on S allows us to consider as simple cases the fixed dividend payment (D independent of S) and the fixed dividend yield (D proportional to S). The dependence on time allows us to consider continuous and discrete payments. In Chapter 3 we discussed only the case $D = D_0S$, with D_0 constant.)

We follow the same modelling approach as in Chapter 3. Unless the asset price falls by the same amount as the dividend payment, there will be the possibility of arbitrage. If the asset price falls by more (less) than the dividend, an arbitrager could make a profit by selling (buying) the asset before the dividend is paid and buying (selling) it immediately after. The owners of the asset experience no net change in their overall wealth as a result of the dividend payment: the decrease in the value of their asset is precisely compensated for by the cash payment associated with the dividend.

With this modification, the random walk (2.1) for the asset price becomes

$$dS = \sigma S\,dX + (\mu S - D(S,t))\,dt. \tag{8.1}$$

Now we come to the option valuation problem. We have allowed for the effect of the dividend payment on the asset price but not its effect on the value of our hedged portfolio. Since we receive $D(S,t)\,dt$ for every asset held and since we hold $-\Delta$ of the underlying, our hedged portfolio changes by an amount

$$-\,D(S,t)\Delta\,dt, \tag{8.2}$$

which is the amount that the asset component of the portfolio receives. Thus, we must add (8.2) to our earlier $d\Pi$ to arrive at

$$d\Pi = dV - \Delta\,dS - D(S,t)\Delta\,dt.$$

The analysis proceeds exactly as before but with the addition of the new term $-D(S,t)\Delta\,dt$. For a European option, we find that

$$\frac{\partial V}{\partial t} + \tfrac{1}{2}\sigma^2 S^2\frac{\partial^2 V}{\partial S^2} + (rS - D(S,t))\frac{\partial V}{\partial S} - rV = 0. \tag{8.3}$$

When the option is American the equality in (8.3) becomes an inequality, as we saw in Chapter 3.

Returning to the effect that dividends have on the asset price, there are two simple and important examples we consider in more detail.

Let us restrict our attention, for the moment, to the case of proportional dividends, that is $D(S,t) = \bar{D}(t)S$. If we write

$$\hat{S} = Se^{\int^t \bar{D}(t')dt'} \tag{8.4}$$

then from Itô's lemma we have

$$d\hat{S} = \sigma\hat{S}\,dX + \mu\hat{S}\,dt.$$

Since this is just (2.1) for $\hat{S}$ instead of S, it shows the discounting effect of dividends on the asset price: the asset price is discounted by $e^{\int^t \bar{D}(t')dt'}$. Two choices for the function $\bar{D}(t)$ are particularly important: $\bar{D}(t) = D_0$ and $\bar{D}(t) = D_\delta^y\delta(t - t_d)$, where D_0 and D_δ^y are both constants[1]. The former is a continuous and constant dividend yield and the latter is a discrete and constant dividend yield. When the continuous dividend payment takes the form D_0S we can use (8.4) to find that the asset price is discounted by

$$e^{\int^t D_0\,dt'} = e^{D_0t}.$$

When the payment is discrete and of the form $D_\delta^y\delta(t - t_d)S$ we find that the asset is discounted by

$$e^{D_\delta^y\mathcal{H}(t-t_d)}. \tag{8.5}$$

(Thus if a company pays out half of the asset price at time t_d, this discretely paid constant dividend yield gives $e^{-D_\delta^y} = \frac{1}{2}$, $D_\delta^y = \log 2$.) At the moment that the dividend is paid out the asset price drops: there is a 'jump' in the asset price. Using t_d^- to denote *just before* the dividend payment and t_d^+ to denote *just after*, we can see from

[1]The superscript y here indicates a dividend yield ($D(S,t)$ proportional to S), while the subscript δ corresponds to a discrete dividend.

(8.5) that when $D(S,t) = D_\delta^y \delta(t - t_d)S$, the asset jumps from $S(t_d^-)$ before the dividend payment to

$$S(t_d^+) = S(t_d^-)e^{-D_\delta^y} \tag{8.6}$$

immediately after. We examine the consequences of this sudden jump in the next section.

8.3 Jump conditions for discrete dividends

We have just seen how a discrete dividend payment inevitably results in a jump in the value of the underlying asset across the dividend date. If the asset jumps discontinuously, then it is natural to ask what effect does this have on the option price? This brings us to the subject of **jump conditions**.

Jump conditions arise when there is a discontinuous change in one of the independent variables affecting the value of a derivative security. One cause of a jump is the discontinuous change in asset price due to the discrete payment of a dividend. The jump condition relates the values of the option across the jump; in this case it relates the values of the option before and after the dividend date. Jump conditions also arise in connection with many exotic options, as we see in later chapters.

Jump conditions may be derived in two equivalent ways. One method is via financial arguments, and is based on arbitrage considerations. The other way is a purely mathematical method, based on the manipulation of delta functions and first order hyperbolic partial differential equations. We consider the mathematical approach in Technical Point 2 at the end of this section, and here present the financial argument.

To be definite, we consider the effect of a discrete dividend yield, independent of S, paid on the asset underlying an option: $D(S,t) = D_\delta^y \delta(t - t_d)S$. Away from the dividend date the value of the option varies due to the random movement of the asset price; this variation is gradual in time since the movement of the asset price is continuous in time (albeit random). Across the dividend date, however, the value of the asset changes discontinuously. This change in asset price is given by (8.6).

Now consider the effect of this discontinuous change in the value of the asset on an option contingent on that asset. Let us write

$V(S,t)$ for the value of this option. To eliminate the same sort of arbitrage possibilities as those considered above, *the value of the option must be continuous as a function of time across the dividend date,* i.e. the value of the option is the same immediately before the dividend date as it is immediately after. Thus we arrive at the jump condition

$$V(S(t_d^-),t_d^-) = V(S(t_d^+),t_d^+). \tag{8.7}$$

This jump condition arises from eliminating arbitrage possibilities *for any given realisation of the asset and option values.* That is, the option value must be continuous in time for any realisation of the asset's random walk. We have just made the statement that the option price is continuous in time yet have called this a jump condition which implies discontinuity. How can we reconcile these two statements?

In this book, we analyse option models using partial differential equations with S and t as independent variables. We do this instead of thinking of S as a function of t as is implicit in (8.7) because we need to be able to consider all possible realisations of the asset's random walk. Bearing this in mind, let us now consider what happens to to the option value across a dividend date in a Black–Scholes model. Since we regard S and t as independent variables in such a formulation, this question can be phrased as

- How does V change across a dividend date for S fixed?

In fact, in any realisation, S would not be fixed across a dividend date. The question we have just posed is not quite appropriate to the problem, and it is better to ask

- How does V change as a function of S across a dividend date?

The answer is that V changes discontinuously according to (8.7) with $S(t_d^+)$ and $S(t_d^-)$ related by (8.6). That is we have

$$V(S,t_d^-) = V(Se^{-D_y^y},t_d^+). \tag{8.8}$$

This says that the value of the option at asset value S immediately before the dividend payment is the same as the value of the option immediately after the dividend payment, but at asset value $Se^{-D_y^y}$.

Thus, for fixed S the value of the option changes discontinuously across a dividend date. Notice, however, that (8.8) is equivalent to insisting that the option value is continuous in time for any realisation of the asset's random walk.

It is certainly true that the holder of the option does not receive any benefit from the dividend payment, and so the option price must reflect this forgone benefit. The fact that the option price is continuous for each realisation of the asset's random walk, even though the asset value is not, does not mean that the option value is unaffected by dividend payments. The effect of the jump condition (8.7) is felt throughout the life of the option, propagated by the partial differential equation that governs its value.

Finally in this section, we consider the jump condition when the discrete dividend payment is a more general known function of the asset price, $D_\delta(S)$. As above, the value of the asset must fall across the dividend date. The stochastic differential equation (8.1) describing the random walk followed by the asset must be modified accordingly. This is easily done by including a delta function term of the form $D_\delta(S)\delta(t-t_d)$, i.e.

$$dS = \sigma S\,dX + (\mu S - D_\delta(S)\delta(t-t_d))\,dt \tag{8.9}$$

to account for the discrete dividend payment and its affect on the asset value. Integrating across the dividend date, we find that

$$\int_{S(t_d^-)}^{S(t_d^+)} \frac{dS}{D_\delta(S)} = \int_{t_d^-}^{t_d^+} \frac{\sigma S}{D_\delta(S)}\,dX + \int_{t_d^-}^{t_d^+} \frac{\mu S}{D_\delta(S)}\,dt - \int_{t_d^-}^{t_d^+} \delta(t-t_d)\,dt.$$

Since t_d^- and t_d^+ differ only infinitesimally, the only nonzero term on the right-hand side is the one containing the delta function, and hence we obtain

$$\int_{S(t_d^+)}^{S(t_d^-)} \frac{dS}{D_\delta(S)} = -\int_{t_d^-}^{t_d^+} \delta(t-t_d)\,dt.$$

Interchanging the limits of integration gives the equation

$$\int_{S(t_d^-)}^{S(t_d^+)} \frac{dS}{D_\delta(S)} = 1 \tag{8.10}$$

relating the value of an asset before and after the dividend date for a general dividend payment $D_\delta(S)$.

For any given realisation the value of the option is continuous, and hence the appropriate jump condition is

$$V(S(t_d^+), t_d^+) = V(S(t_d^-), t_d^-)$$

with $S(t_d^+)$ and $S(t_d^-)$ related by (8.10).

Technical Point 1: avoiding negative asset prices.
A dividend payment taking the form of a known amount, independent of S, *on a known date, can be represented by*

$$D(S,t) = D_\delta^p \delta(t - t_d);$$

an amount D_δ^p is paid out at time t_d. Since D_δ^p is paid out we expect the asset price to drop by the same amount across $t = t_d$. Therefore

$$S(t_d^+) = S(t_d^-) - D_\delta^p. \tag{8.11}$$

But what happens if $S(t_d^-) < D_\delta^p$? In this case the asset price after the dividend payment is negative. This situation amounts to a company, whose share price is \$1, say, announcing a dividend payment of ten cents in two weeks' time while subsequently the asset price plummets to only five cents. Although the probability of this happening may be small it is still nonzero. The result is negative asset prices if (8.1) is valid.

Clearly, negative asset prices are financially unrealistic and the modelling of dividend payments must take this into account. Thus we should never choose a $D(S,t)$ that results in negative asset prices. Generally, if D takes the form

$$D(S,t) = D_\delta(S)\delta(t - t_d)$$

then the jump in the asset price is given by

$$\int_{S(t_d^-)}^{S(t_d^+)} \frac{dS}{D_\delta(S)} = 1.$$

We can guarantee that $S(t_d^+)$ is not negative by choosing $D_\delta(S)$ so that

$$\int_0^{S(t_d^-)} \frac{dS}{D_\delta(S)}$$

is infinite for any positive value of $S(t_d^-)$. We are certainly safe if, for example, $D(S,t) = O(S)$ as $S \to 0$. Although it is very simple, the model $D_0(S,t) = D_\delta^p \delta(t - t_d)$ is not always realistic.

Technical Point 2: alternative derivation of the jump condition.

We can arrive at the same result by considering the Black–Scholes equation directly. The modified Black–Scholes equation allowing for discrete dividends is

$$\frac{\partial V}{\partial t} + \tfrac{1}{2}\sigma^2 S^2 \frac{\partial^2 V}{\partial S^2} + (rS - D)\frac{\partial V}{\partial S} - rV = 0, \tag{8.12}$$

where

$$D = D_\delta(S)\delta(t - t_d).$$

This corresponds to an S-dependent dividend paid at $t = t_d$. Away from the time t_d (8.12) is insensitive to the presence of dividends; that is, the equation is simply the Black–Scholes equation without dividends, (3.9). This is not true at time $t = t_d$. Formally, we see that the term

$$-D\frac{\partial V}{\partial S} = -D_\delta(S)\delta(t - t_d)\frac{\partial V}{\partial S}$$

becomes large at this time (recall that the delta function is infinite here). This large term must be balanced by another large term in equation (8.12). It can only be balanced by the time derivative. Thus (8.12) contains two unbounded terms at $t = t_d$: the term proportional to the delta function and the time derivative of V. Near t_d these dominant terms are approximated by the equation

$$\frac{\partial V}{\partial t} - D_\delta(S)\delta(t - t_d)\frac{\partial V}{\partial S} = 0.$$

This first order partial differential equation has characteristics in the (S,t)-plane given by the solution of the ordinary differential equation

$$\frac{dS}{dt} = -D_\delta(S)\delta(t - t_d),$$

that is,

$$\int_{S(t)}^{S(t_d)} \frac{dS'}{D_\delta(S')} = \mathcal{H}(t - t_d). \tag{8.13}$$

Along these curves $V(S,t)$ is constant. But (8.13) is also the equation (8.10) which defines the jump in the asset price. Thus, since V is continuous along characteristics, the realised path of V is also continuous.

8.4 A generalisation with explicit formulæ

In this section we show how to derive explicit formulæ for options with time varying interest rate, volatility and dividend yield. First, we set the scene by describing the effect that a nonzero dividend yield has on the two boundary conditions.

The simplest generalisation of the European option problem is to incorporate a continuous and constant dividend yield as mentioned above; in this case $D(S,t) = D_0 S$ and is, for the moment, not a function of time. We have seen how the Black–Scholes equation is modified to (3.21) and it can easily be seen that for a call option the final condition is still (3.10), and that the boundary condition at $S = 0$ remains as (3.11). The only change to the boundary conditions is that

$$V(S,t) \sim S e^{-D_0(T-t)} \quad \text{as} \quad S \to \infty.$$

We now temporarily introduce a new variable in order to simplify this equation. With $\bar{S} = S e^{-D_0(T-t)}$, the Black–Scholes equation with dividends $D = D_0 S$ becomes

$$\frac{\partial V}{\partial t} + \tfrac{1}{2}\sigma^2 \bar{S}^2 \frac{\partial^2 V}{\partial \bar{S}^2} + (r - D_0)\bar{S}\frac{\partial V}{\partial \bar{S}} - rV + D_0 \bar{S}\frac{\partial V}{\partial \bar{S}} = 0,$$

i.e.

$$\frac{\partial V}{\partial t} + \tfrac{1}{2}\sigma^2 \bar{S}^2 \frac{\partial^2 V}{\partial \bar{S}^2} + r\bar{S}\frac{\partial V}{\partial \bar{S}} - rV = 0.$$

This is, of course, simply the Black–Scholes equation *without dividends.* Thus the formulæ for European calls and puts can be derived from the zero-dividend case by replacing S by $S e^{-D_0(T-t)}$. This discounting simply reflects the fact that the holder of the asset receives the dividend income, whereas the holder of an option does not.

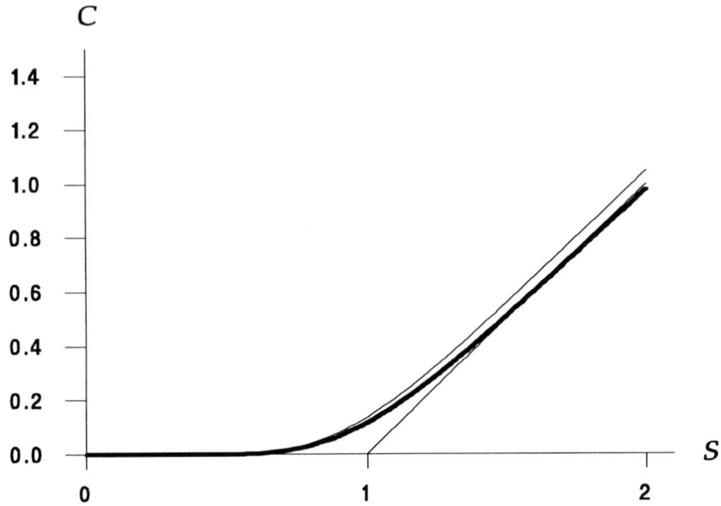

Figure 8.1: A comparison of European call option values with (lower curve) and without dividends (upper curve). There are six months to expiry, $E = 1$, $\sigma = 0.4$ and $r = 0.1$. The bold curve has $D_0 = 0.07$.

When D_0 is a function of time, $\bar{D}(t)$, the boundary condition at infinity for a call becomes

$$V(S,t) \sim Se^{-\int_t^T \bar{D}(\tau)\,d\tau} \quad \text{as} \quad S \to \infty,$$

and we simply replace S by

$$Se^{-\int_t^T \bar{D}(\tau)\,d\tau}$$

in all explicit formulæ.

In Figure 8.1 we see the European call option values as functions of S with six months to expiry, $\sigma = 0.4$ and $r = 0.1$; the top curve is the value of the option in the absence of dividends and the lower bold curve has a constant and continuous dividend yield $D_0 = 0.07$.

Now let us see what happens if we allow the interest rate r and the volatility σ to be known functions of time. This may be a suitable model for an investor with a strong view of the market or of an individual asset. The Black–Scholes equation (3.9) remains valid even if we replace r and σ by $r(t)$ and $\sigma(t)$. Furthermore, we can still solve this equation in this far more general situation.

The boundary and final conditions for the call and put remain exactly as before with one exception. Since r appears explicitly in (3.14), the boundary condition at $S=0$ for the put, we must be more careful in deriving this condition. When r is a function of time the correct condition is

$$P(0,t) = Ee^{-\int_t^T r(\tau)d\tau}.$$

Since the payoff at expiry is certainly E if S is zero, the value of the put option on $S=0$ the present value of the payoff under non-constant interest rates.

We can now demonstrate how to derive explicit formulæ when *all* of σ, r and $\bar{D}$ are functions of time[2]. The equation to be solved is

$$\frac{\partial V}{\partial t} + \tfrac{1}{2}\sigma^2(t)S^2\frac{\partial^2 V}{\partial S^2} + (r(t) - \bar{D}(t))S\frac{\partial V}{\partial S} - r(t)V = 0, \qquad (8.14)$$

where we have shown the dependence on t explicitly. Let us make the following substitutions:

$$\bar{S} = Se^{\alpha(t)},$$
$$\bar{V} = Ve^{\beta(t)},$$
$$\bar{t} = \gamma(t),$$

where α, β and γ are to be chosen carefully so as to eliminate all time-dependent coefficients from (8.14). In these new variables (8.14) becomes

$$\dot{\gamma}(t)\frac{\partial \bar{V}}{\partial \bar{t}} + \tfrac{1}{2}\sigma(t)^2\bar{S}^2\frac{\partial^2 \bar{V}}{\partial \bar{S}^2} + (r(t) - \bar{D}(t) + \dot{\alpha}(t))\bar{S}\frac{\partial \bar{V}}{\partial \bar{S}} - (r(t) + \dot{\beta}(t))\bar{V} = 0, \qquad (8.15)$$

where $\dot{} = d/dt$. Now eliminate the coefficients of $\bar{V}$ and $\partial\bar{V}/\partial\bar{S}$ by choosing

$$\alpha(t) = -\int_t^T (\bar{D}(\tau) - r(\tau))\,d\tau,$$

[2]Some readers may have already derived these formulæ by a different procedure, in the exercises at the end of Chapter 5.

$$\beta(t) = \int_t^T r(\tau)\,d\tau,$$

and remove the remaining time dependence by setting

$$\gamma(t) = \int_t^T \sigma^2(\tau)\,d\tau.$$

With these choices (8.15) becomes

$$\frac{\partial \bar{V}}{\partial \bar{t}} = \tfrac{1}{2}\bar{S}^2 \frac{\partial^2 \bar{V}}{\partial \bar{S}^2} \tag{8.16}$$

and has coefficients which are *independent of time.* This equation contains no reference to σ, r or D_0. If $\bar{V}(\bar{S}, \bar{t})$ is any solution of (8.16), then the corresponding solution of (8.15), in original variables, is

$$V = e^{-\beta(t)}\bar{V}\left(Se^{\alpha(t)}, \gamma(t)\right). \tag{8.17}$$

Let us now denote by V_{BS} any solution of the Black–Scholes equation for constant r, σ and zero dividends. In view of the above, this solution can be written in the form

$$V_{BS} = e^{-r(T-t)}\bar{V}_{BS}\left(Se^{-r(T-t)}, \sigma^2(T-t)\right) \tag{8.18}$$

for some function $\bar{V}_{BS}$. By comparing (8.17) and (8.18) we see that to go from an explicit solution of the Black–Scholes equation with constant r and σ and zero dividends we simply perform the following substitutions:

- wherever we see r in the explicit formula replace it by

$$\frac{1}{T-t}\int_t^T r(\tau)\,d\tau;$$

- wherever we see σ^2 in the explicit formula replace it by

$$\frac{1}{T-t}\int_t^T \sigma^2(\tau)\,d\tau;$$

- wherever we see S in the explicit formula replace it by

$$Se^{-\int_t^T \bar{D}(\tau)d\tau}.$$

Technical Point: trading volatility.
In practice volatility is not constant, nor is it predictable for timescales of more than a few months. This, of course, limits the validity of any model that assumes the contrary. This problem may be reduced by pricing options using implied volatility as described at the end of Chapter 3. Thus one trading strategy is to calculate implied volatilities from prices of all options on the same underlying and the same expiry date and then to buy the one with the lowest volatility and sell the one with the highest. The hope is then that the prices move so that implied volatilities become more or less comparable and the portfolio makes a profit.

More sophisticated modelling involves describing volatility itself as a random variable satisfying some stochastic differential equation. This results in a **two-factor model**. *If the volatility is random then it is no longer possible to construct the perfect hedge in which a portfolio grows by a deterministic amount. This is because there is no volatility instrument with which to hedge the randomness due to changes in volatility*[3].

Further reading

- For the original derivation of the Black–Scholes formulæ with time-dependent parameters see Merton (1973).
- In this book we have assumed that dividends are known. For a model with *stochastic* dividends see Geske (1978).
- Gemmill (1992) discusses the practical implications of discrete dividend payments.

[3]The CBOE has been developing a volatility index which measures the implied volatility from eight S&P 100 index options and then calculates a weighted volatility index. Thus it is hoped that in the future it will be possible to go some way towards hedging risk from both asset *and* volatility changes.

Chapter 9

Exotic Options

9.1 Exotic and path-dependent options

In this chapter we describe some of the more common exotic and path-dependent options. In subsequent chapters we consider partial differential equation models for their valuation. With this goal in mind, it is useful here to consider a classification of the varieties of exotic and path-dependent options.

A **path-dependent option** is an option whose payoff at exercise or expiry depends, in some non-trivial way, on the past history of the underlying asset price as well as its price at exercise or expiry.

We have already considered one type of path-dependent option in detail: the American option. This is clearly path-dependent since there is a finite probability of the option being exercised before expiry and thus ceasing to exist. This occurs if the asset price ever enters the range where it is optimal to exercise. In general, any option contract can specify either European or American exercise rights, and in this sense we can think of American early exercise rights as a feature of an option. An American early exercise feature turns any option into a potentially path-dependent option.

Broadly speaking, an **exotic option** is an option that is not a vanilla put or call. Conceptually, the simplest exotic options are the **binary** or **digital** options. These are options that have payoffs that are more general than and different from from those of vanilla options. They may have either European or American style exercise features. Originally the term binary described an option that was, effectively, a straight bet on whether the underlying asset value would be above (a binary call) or below (a binary put) the exercise price; the payoff was independent of how far above or below the exercise price the asset value was at the time of exercise. Now, however, the term is used to describe any option with a payoff more general than the payoff for a put or a call.

Another relatively simple class of exotic options consists of **barrier options**. These are options where either the right to exercise is forfeited if the underlying asset value crosses a certain value (an **out barrier**), or the option only comes into existence if the asset value crosses a certain value (an **in barrier**). An example is a **down-and-out option**, where the right to exercise is lost if the asset price ever falls to or below some given down-and-out barrier. The option cannot be exercised thereafter and is worthless.

A barrier feature makes an option path-dependent. If the asset price ever crosses an out barrier, the option becomes worthless and effectively ceases to exist. In the case of an in barrier, the option is worthless unless the asset price crosses the in barrier and effectively the option does not exist until the in barrier is crossed.

It is useful to think of barriers, whether in or out, simply as features of the option contract. In principle, a barrier can be applied to any option, whether a vanilla option, a binary or one of the class of path-dependent exotic options that we shall shortly describe.

An option with an American early exercise feature is path-dependent but not necessarily exotic. Similarly there are exotic options, such as binaries, that are exotic but not path-dependent. As suggested above, the term exotic is loosely used to denote something out of the ordinary and usually not (currently) quoted on an exchange. Such options are usually traded over-the-counter, meaning that option brokers bring together both sides of a contract and construct a product which does not exist as an exchange-traded option. For example, while a vanilla American call is path-dependent, it is not considered exotic since it is exchange traded, whereas a European binary option is not path-dependent but it is considered exotic. There are, of course, exotic options which are also path-dependent.

The following is a list of some common exotic or path-dependent options which can all be put into the same framework and valued quite easily (albeit numerically, if necessary):

- binaries (exotic);
- compounds (exotic);
- choosers (exotic);
- barriers (exotic, path-dependent);
- Asians (exotic, path-dependent);
- lookbacks (exotic, path-dependent).

The first three of these are all only trivially path-dependent and we describe only the methodology behind their valuation. Barrier options, however, are discussed in detail in Chapter 10. The last two, Asians and lookbacks, are both path-dependent and exotic (and from a mathematical point of view, particularly interesting); they each have a chapter to themselves, Chapters 11 and 12 respectively.

This is by no means an exhaustive list of exotic options. The number of options is continuing to grow rapidly and now includes range forwards, ladders, exchange, two-colour rainbow and cliquet, among others. Some of these (for example, the rainbow and exchange) depend on the values of many underlying assets, rather than a single underlying asset (see Barrett, Moore & Wilmott 1992). In this and the following three chapters we aim to address questions that are of fundamental importance in the modelling and analysis of exotic options rather than to catalogue solutions for the more esoteric options. Any such catalogue would in any case quickly become out of date.

We now consider in some greater detail the options listed above.

9.1.1 Binary options

Binary or **digital** options are the simplest type of exotic options and are not path-dependent unless they have an early exercise feature or a barrier feature. A binary option differs from a vanilla option in that the payoff at expiry (or at exercise if the option is American) can be an arbitrary non-negative function of asset price, S. If the payoff at time T is given by $\Lambda(S)$ then the method of Chapter 5 yields the explicit formula

$$\frac{e^{-r(T-t)}}{\sigma\sqrt{2\pi(T-t)}}\int_0^\infty \Lambda(S')e^{-\left(\log(S'/S)-(r-\frac{1}{2}\sigma^2)(T-t)\right)^2/2\sigma^2(T-t)}\frac{dS'}{S'} \qquad (9.1)$$

for the value of a European binary option. This formula obviously includes vanilla calls and puts as particular cases. The delta is given by the derivative of (9.1) with respect to S. In deriving (9.1), we have assumed that σ and r are constant and that the underlying pays no dividends. The inclusion of a dividend term is not difficult, and if σ or r are known functions of t then the methods described in Chapter 8 may be applied to obtain exact formulæ.

We mention two specific examples of particularly popular binary options, those with payoffs

$$B\mathcal{H}(S-E) \quad \text{and} \quad \frac{1}{d}\left(\mathcal{H}(S-E)-\mathcal{H}(S-E-d)\right).$$

The former, already mentioned above, can be interpreted as a simple bet on the asset price; if $S > E$ at expiry the payoff is B and otherwise it is zero. It is called a **cash-or-nothing call**. The latter, sometimes known as a **supershare**, has payoff $1/d$ if $E < S < E+d$ at expiry and zero otherwise[1]. Although these options are easy to value using (9.1) they can present problems in hedging near the time of expiry, caused by the discontinuities in the payoff function (these discontinuities also present problems for American versions of the options). Let us consider the difficulties associated with hedging an option having payoff $B\mathcal{H}(S-E)$.

By differentiating $\mathcal{H}(S-E)$ with respect to S we see that as $t \to T$ the delta of the option tends to the function $B\delta(S-E)$. Away from $S = E$ this function is zero, and therefore close to expiry we expect that we should not to have to hedge this portfolio. However, if S is close to E near expiry there is a high probability that the asset price will cross the value E, perhaps many times, before expiry. Each time this value is crossed the delta goes from nearly zero to very large and back to nearly zero. The Black–Scholes model assumes that the portfolio is continuously hedged with a number of assets equal to

[1] In the limit $d \to 0$ the payoff becomes a delta function.

the delta; this is clearly impractical if, at one moment, the portfolio contains no assets, then is rehedged to contain a large number of the assets only for that position to be liquidated shortly afterwards. Yet, if this rehedging is not done, the payoff at expiry is either zero or one and cannot be known for certain[2]. It is therefore open to question whether options with discontinuous payoffs can be valued according to the simple Black–Scholes formula (9.1).

In some cases American binary options are simple to value; they also provide an exception to the smoothness condition at the free boundary. Suppose as above that the binary has payoff B if $S > E$ and 0 otherwise. Suppose also that the payoff for early exercise is the same as the payoff at expiry. With the early exercise feature one would exercise as soon as S exceeded E; there is a clear disadvantage in not exercising the option since firstly the asset price might fall back below E, and secondly there is the loss of potential interest on the payoff that is not compensated for by the prospect of a larger payoff. Thus the free boundary is always at $S = E$. The problem for $S > E$ is trivial; the value of the option is always B. The problem for $S < E$ is just Black–Scholes with $V = B$ at $S = E$, $V = 0$ at $S = 0$ and $V = 0$ at expiry. This is now a fixed boundary value problem and is easy to solve explicitly. The delta for such an option is certainly not continuous. Of course, as explained in the Technical Point at the end of Section 3.8, we do not really have an exception to the smoothness condition; the obstacle itself has a discontinuity and so our earlier no-arbitrage analysis is not valid.

More generally, binary options include options whose payoffs simulate the payoffs for various combinations, spreads, straddles and straps. More complicated payoffs can also be considered; the only place in which the effect of a more general payoff is seen is the function $\Lambda(S)$.

9.1.2 Compound options

A **compound option** may be described simply as an option on an option. We consider only the case where the underlying option is a vanilla put or call and the compound option can be described as

---

[2]There is a similar but less important effect close to expiry for vanilla options if the asset price is close to the exercise price.

a vanilla put or call on the underlying option. The extension to more complicated path-dependent or exotic features for a compound option written on exotic or path-dependent underlying options is relatively straightforward.

Since there are two types of vanilla options—calls and puts—we can construct four different classes of basic compound option: calls on calls, calls on puts and so forth. We now consider a particular case. Let T_1 be the time at which we can, if we wish, exercise the compound option to purchase the underlying vanilla option for an amount E_1. This underlying option may be exercised at time T_2 for an amount E_2 in return for an asset with price S. This call on a call option is very simple to value within the Black–Scholes framework.

The time interval which we need to consider in order to value the compound option is divided into two parts. Working back from expiry at $t = T_2$, we first find the value of the vanilla call option that we receive if we do in fact exercise the compound option at time $t = T_1$. This underlying call option has exercise price E_2 and expiry date T_2. There is an explicit formula for its value; even if there were not, we could find the solution by numerical means (so we could consider an American underlying option, for example). Thus, at time T_1, we can calculate the value of the underlying call option; let us call this $C(S, T_1)$. If, at time T_1, the asset price is such that $C(S, T_1) > E_1$ then we would clearly exercise our compound option and obtain the underlying call. If, however, at time T_1 the asset price is such that $C(S, T_1) < E_1$ then we would not exercise the compound option. Thus the payoff for the compound option at time T_1 is

$$\max(C(S, T_1) - E_1, 0). \tag{9.2}$$

Because the compound option's value is governed *only* by the random walk of the underlying asset price S, it too must satisfy the Black–Scholes equation. The only difference from a vanilla option is in the final condition: we use (9.2) as the final data in solving for the compound option for $t < T_1$.

The method of solution is similar for calls on puts, puts on calls and puts on puts and, in principle, exotics on exotics. American features do not change this solution strategy in any way other than in introducing a constraint.

9.1.3 Chooser options

Chooser options or **as-you-like-it options** are only slightly more complicated than compound options. Although they are, strictly speaking, path-dependent they can still be valued by solving the Black–Scholes equation.

A chooser option gives its owner the right to purchase, for an amount E_1 at time T_1 *either* a call *or* a put with exercise price E_2 at time T_2. A more general structure can readily be imagined, and presents no serious difficulties.

These options are valued in a similar manner to compound options. First we solve the underlying option problems; there are now two of these, one for the underlying call and one for the underlying put. We denote these solutions by $C(S,t)$ and $P(S,t)$ respectively, and use them as the final data for the first option problem. Clearly, one will exercise the chooser option if either $C(S,t) > E_1$ or $P(S,t) > E_1$, and one will elect to purchase the more valuable of the two. The chooser option again satisfies the Black–Scholes equation with final data at time T_1 given by

$$\max(C(S,T_1) - E_1, P(S,T_1) - E_1, 0).$$

9.1.4 Barrier options

We devote the whole of Chapter 10 to **barrier options** and so we only describe them in outline here. These options are only weakly path-dependent and satisfy the Black–Scholes equation[3]. Barrier options differ from vanilla options in that part of the option contract is triggered if the asset price hits some barrier, $S = X$, say, at any time prior to expiry. As well as being either calls or puts barrier options are categorised as follows:

- **up-and-in**: the option expires worthless *unless* the barrier $S = X$ is reached from *below* before expiry;
- **down-and-in**: the option expires worthless *unless* the barrier $S = X$ is reached from *above* before expiry;

[3]We are only considering vanilla options with barrier features here. There is no reason why a barrier feature cannot be applied to any option, whether vanilla or exotic. The underlying principles are exactly the same since the barrier features affect only the boundary conditions in a partial differential equation formulation.

- **up-and-out**: the option expires worthless *if* the barrier $S = X$ is reached from *below* before expiry;
- **down-and-out**: the option expires worthless *if* the barrier $S = X$ is reached from *above* before expiry.

Some barrier options specify a **rebate**, usually a fixed amount paid to the holder if the barrier is reached.

9.1.5 Asian options

Asian options are the first fully path-dependent exotic options that we consider. They have payoffs which depend on the history of the random walk of the asset price via some sort of average. One such option is the **average strike call**, whose payoff is the difference between the asset price at expiry and its average over some period prior to expiry if this difference is positive, and zero otherwise.

Several factors affect the definition of average; among these are:

- The period of averaging. Over what time range before expiry is the average taken?
- Arithmetic or geometric averaging. The average can be defined as the mean of the asset price (the arithmetic average) or the exponential of the mean of the logarithm of the asset price (the geometric average).
- Weighted or unweighted averaging. Is the average simply the mean of asset prices over the averaging period or are some prices given a greater weighting in the average? We might for example choose to give a greater weighting to recent prices.
- Discrete or continuous sampling of the asset price. It is easier to take the mean of a small number of asset prices rather than the average over all realised asset prices. The average might, for example, be the mean of the closing asset prices at the end of every week before expiry instead of the average of the asset price measured every tick.

Different choices lead to different values for options. This list covers most of those used in practice.

We devote the whole of Chapter 11 to the analysis and valuation of Asian options.

9.1.6 Lookback options

A **lookback option** has a payoff which depends not only on the asset price at expiry but also on the maximum or the minimum of the asset price over some time prior to expiry. Usually the payoffs are structurally very similar to those of vanilla options. For example, a put option may have payoff

$$\max(J - S, 0)$$

where J is a suitably defined maximum. As with Asian options we can distinguish between discrete and continuous sampling of the asset price to obtain the maximum.

Lookback options are discussed fully in Chapter 12.

9.2 A unifying framework

Now we introduce the framework in which all of the path-dependent options mentioned above can be valued. These ideas are put into practice in Chapters 11 (Asian options) and 12 (lookbacks).

Let us first consider a fairly general class of European options with payoff depending on S and on

$$\int_0^T f(S(\tau), \tau)\, d\tau, \tag{9.3}$$

where f is a given function of the variables S and t. The integration in (9.3) is taken over the path of S from the initiation of averaging at $t = 0$ to expiry at $t = T$. An example is an average strike call option, where the payoff at expiry is

$$\max\left(S - \frac{1}{T}\int_0^T S(\tau)\, d\tau, 0\right).$$

We introduce the new variable

$$I = \int_0^t f(S(\tau), \tau)\, d\tau. \tag{9.4}$$

Since the history of the asset price is independent of the current price, we may treat I, S and t as independent variables; different realisations of the random walk lead to different values of I. Observe that this definition (9.4) is simply (9.3) with the expiry date T replaced by t.

We anticipate that the value of an exotic path-dependent option can be written as $V(S, I, t)$. That is, the option value is a function of *three* independent variables: time t, the current asset price S and the history of the asset price I. We intend applying Itô's lemma to V and to do this we need to know the stochastic differential equation for I. This is found quite easily by considering the change in I as t and S change by small amounts. Clearly,

$$I(t + dt) = I + dI = \int_0^{t+dt} f(S(\tau), \tau)\, d\tau.$$

To $O(dt)$ this can be written as

$$I + dI = \int_0^t f(S(\tau), \tau) d\tau + f(S(t), t)\, dt,$$

so that

$$dI = f(S, t)\, dt. \tag{9.5}$$

This is the stochastic differential equation for I; it so happens that there is no random component. We are now in a position to value any option that depends on I.

First we apply Itô's lemma to the function $V(S, I, t)$ to show that

$$dV = \sigma S \frac{\partial V}{\partial S} dX + \left(\tfrac{1}{2}\sigma^2 S^2 \frac{\partial^2 V}{\partial S^2} + \mu S \frac{\partial V}{\partial S} + \frac{\partial V}{\partial t} + f(S, t) \frac{\partial V}{\partial I} \right) dt. \tag{9.6}$$

This is derived in exactly the same way as equation (3.3). Note that the new term, which is proportional to the rate of change of V with respect to I, does not introduce any new *stochastic* terms into the random walk followed by V.

Recalling that the option is European, we now set up a risk-free portfolio, consisting of one option and a short position with a number Δ of the underlying. The delta is still equal to $\partial V/\partial S$, and we find that arbitrage considerations lead to

$$\frac{\partial V}{\partial t} + f(S, t) \frac{\partial V}{\partial I} + \tfrac{1}{2}\sigma^2 S^2 \frac{\partial^2 V}{\partial S^2} + (rS - D(S, I, t)) \frac{\partial V}{\partial S} - rV = 0. \tag{9.7}$$

We have allowed for an arbitrary dividend structure: D can now also be a function of the path-dependent variable, I.

To pose the problem fully for our class of path-dependent options we must specify suitable and sufficient boundary and final conditions. The boundary conditions depend on the particular choice of option and so we delay detailed consideration until we encounter specific examples.

We can, however, give the general final condition. At expiry we know the exact form of the payoff and hence the option value as a function of S and I. We have

$$V(S,I,T) = \Lambda(S,I,T)$$

where the function Λ is the known payoff function. In the case of the average strike call we would take $I = \int_0^T S(\tau)\,d\tau$ and then

$$\Lambda(S,I,T) = \max(S - I/T, 0).$$

We now extend the analysis to American options. Suppose that we wish to value an American version of the average strike option. In any such contract the payoff on early exercise is specified in advance. Let us suppose that the early exercise payoff for this average strike call is

$$\max(S - I/t, 0).$$

This is a natural choice for this particular option since it depends on the asset price average to date, the running average. For some options, especially those depending on discretely measured path-dependent quantities, the payoff is not so obvious. Nevertheless, let us suppose that in our general framework the payoff takes the form

$$\Lambda(S,I,t),$$

where Λ is a function known in advance and specified in the option contract.

As in Chapter 3 for American vanilla options, the American path-dependent option valuation problem is a simple modification of the European case. To this end, we introduce the partial differential operator

$$\mathcal{L}_{EX} = \frac{\partial}{\partial t} + f(S,t)\frac{\partial}{\partial I} + \tfrac{1}{2}\sigma^2 S^2 \frac{\partial^2}{\partial S^2} + (rS - D(S,I,t))\frac{\partial}{\partial S} - r.$$

This operator is a generalisation of the Black–Scholes operator. It measures the difference between the rates of return on a risk-free Δ-hedged portfolio and a bank deposit of equivalent value. As for the vanilla option case, the rate of return from a Δ-hedged portfolio cannot exceed the rate of return from a bank deposit, but it need not equal it. Thus

$$\mathcal{L}_{EX}(V) \leq 0.$$

Arbitrage considerations show that we must always have

$$V(S, I, t) \geq \Lambda(S, I, t).$$

If the rate of return from the portfolio equals the rate of return from a bank deposit, $\mathcal{L}_{EX}(V) = 0$, then it is not optimal to exercise the option. This can only be the case if it is more valuable held than exercised, $V > \Lambda$. If the rate of return from the portfolio is less than the return from a bank deposit, $\mathcal{L}_{EX}(V) < 0$, then it is optimal to exercise the option. This can only be the case if $V = \Lambda$ (if $V > \Lambda$ then it would be more profitable to sell the option, and we can never have $V < \Lambda$). Thus either $\mathcal{L}_{EX}(V) = 0$ and $V - \Lambda > 0$ or $\mathcal{L}_{EX}(V) < 0$ and $V - \Lambda = 0$. Either way, we always have

$$\mathcal{L}_{EX}(V) \cdot (V - \Lambda) = 0.$$

Thus the problem for the American version of our class of path-dependent exotic options can be written in linear complementarity form as

$$\mathcal{L}_{EX}(V) \cdot (V - \Lambda) = 0, \quad \mathcal{L}_{EX}(V) \leq 0, \quad (V - \Lambda) \geq 0, \tag{9.8}$$

with V and $\partial V/\partial S$ continuous (assuming Λ is continuous) and with final condition

$$V(S, I, T) = \Lambda(S, I, T).$$

The condition that the delta, i.e. the derivative of V with respect to S, must always be continuous follows from the same arbitrage argument as earlier: changes in V due to movements in S are $O(\sqrt{dt})$; this is much greater than changes due to both t and I, and so the S

derivative must be continuous. This assumes, as stated above, that the payoff function $\Lambda(S, I, t)$ is continuous.

Technical point: changing the averaging period.
In the discussion above, we assume that the life of the option coincides with the averaging period: the option comes into being at $t = 0$, *the lower limit of the integral in the definition of* I, *and expires at the upper limit* $t = T$. *This is an unnecessary restriction, though, and we can easily incorporate a more general relationship between the two time periods into the framework just described.*

Suppose that the option depends on the average

$$\int_{T_1}^{T_2} f(S(\tau), \tau)\, d\tau.$$

This definition is similar to (9.3), except that f *need only be defined for* $T_1 \le t \le T_2$, *where we assume that* $0 \le T_1 \le T_2 \le T$. *It might, for example arise from an option whose payoff depends on an average of the asset price over a specified period such as the middle third of its life or a particular calendar month. By extending the definition of* f *so that it vanishes for values of* t *outside the specified range, we automatically put this option into the framework discussed above. We must still solve*

$$\frac{\partial V}{\partial t} + f(S, t)\frac{\partial V}{\partial I} + \tfrac{1}{2}\sigma^2 S^2 \frac{\partial^2 V}{\partial S^2} + (rS - D)\frac{\partial V}{\partial S} - rV = 0, \qquad (9.9)$$

where, as before,

$$I = \int_0^T f(S(\tau), \tau)\, d\tau,$$

but with the extended definition of f *in both equations. (The modification for American options is similar.)*

Let us see how this works in more detail. Suppose that $0 < T_1 < T_2 < T$, *so that the averaging period is wholly contained in the lifetime of the option. We work backwards from expiry. Firstly, for* $T_2 < t < T$ *we have* $f = 0$, *and so we solve the basic Black–Scholes equation with* I *as a parameter, and with the final data* $\Lambda(S, I, T)$. *Then we use the option values at* $t = T_2$ *as final data for equation*

(9.9), which we solve for $T_1 < t < T_2$. Finally, the solution just calculated serves as final data for the basic Black–Scholes equation for $0 < t < T_1$, again treating I as a parameter. Although, in principle, we need to find the solution for all positive values of I in all three time periods, in practice I is often taken to be zero before sampling has started. Thus, when we solve for $0 < t < T_1$, we can discard all the values for which $I > 0$, and in the last step we only need to solve a two-dimensional problem.

9.3 Discrete sampling

The effect of discrete payments of dividends is considered in Section 8.7 and shown to imply jump conditions. In Chapters 11 and 12 on Asian and lookback options respectively we see the importance of discrete versus continuous sampling of the path-dependent quantity. As with discrete dividends, discrete sampling leads to jump conditions as shown in Chapters 11 and 12.

We now introduce a useful way of representing discretely measured quantities within the framework developed above. Let t_i, $i = 1, \ldots, N$, denote N discrete sampling dates. The value of a path-dependent exotic option will now depend on the discrete sum

$$I = \sum_{i=1}^{N} \hat{f}_i(S(t_i)),$$

for some function $\hat{f}$, rather than on the continuous integral

$$I = \int_0^T f(S(\tau), \tau)\, d\tau.$$

For example, consider an Asian option with a payoff that depends on a discretely measured arithmetic average of the realised asset prices, i.e. on

$$\frac{1}{N} \sum_{i=1}^{N} S(t_i).$$

It would then be sensible to assume that the value of the option depends on I where

$$I = \sum_{i=1}^{j(t)} S(t_i),$$

and where $j(t)$ is the largest integer such that $t_{j(t)} \leq t$.

Within our framework it is a very simple matter to allow for discretely measured path-dependent quantities. In Chapter 8 we demonstrated how to allow for discretely-paid dividends in the continuum models. The analysis of that chapter showed how two independent arguments, one financial and one mathematical, led to jump conditions at the dividend date. The same analysis is possible when path-dependent quantities are sampled discretely and again results in a jump condition.

For example, consider the discretely sampled average strike option, which is covered in depth in Chapter 11. With the definition

$$I = \sum_{i=1}^{j(t)} S(t_i), \tag{9.10}$$

for the running sum we find that, across a sampling date t_i, the option value must satisfy the jump condition

$$V(S, I, t_i^-) = V(S, I + S, t_i^+)$$

where we have used the notation t_i^- and t_i^+ to denote just before and just after the sampling date. Again this follows from an arbitrage argument or a mathematical argument. The former states that the realised path of the option price cannot be discontinuous. The latter follows from the equivalent definition of I as

$$\int_0^t S(\tau) \sum_{i=1}^{N} \delta(\tau - t_i)\, d\tau.$$

This puts discrete sampling into our general framework with

$$f(S, t) = S \sum_{i=1}^{N} \delta(t - t_i).$$

We may consider more complicated discretely sampled functions of price history by writing

$$\sum_{i=1}^{j(t)} f_i(S(t_i)) = \int_0^t f(S(\tau), \tau) \sum_{i=1}^{N} \delta(\tau - t_i)\, d\tau.$$

for some suitable function $f(S, t)$.

Further reading

- Ingersoll (1987) discusses the partial differential equation approach to valuing some exotic options.

- For a treatment of compound options see Geske (1979). For options contingent on *two* assets see Stulz (1982).

- The general framework for path-dependent options is discussed in Dewynne & Wilmott (1993 a).

- Information about practical issues, such as hedging of exotics, is given in the compilation of articles published by *Risk* magazine (1993).

Exercises

1. Find explicit solutions for American binaries with payoffs

   (a) $\mathcal{H}(S - E)$;
   (b) $\mathcal{H}(E - S)$.

2. What happens to a compound option if $T_1 = T_2$?

3. What is the put-call parity result for compound options?

4. The European **asset-or-nothing** call pays S if $S > E$ at expiry, and nothing if $S \leq E$. What is its value?

Chapter 10

Barrier Options

10.1 The different types of barrier option

For our first in-depth discussion of a path-dependent option we consider a simple barrier option. We have mentioned in the previous chapter that the basic forms of these options are 'down-and-out', 'down-and-in', 'up-and-out' and 'up-and-in'. These options have the property that the right to exercise either appears ('in') or disappears ('out') on some boundary in (S, t) space, above ('up') or below ('down') the current asset price. An example is a European option whose value becomes zero if the asset price ever goes as low as $S = X$. If the payoff is otherwise the same as that for a call option then we call this product a European 'down-and-out' call. An 'up-and-out' has similar characteristics except that it becomes worthless if the asset price ever exceeds a prescribed amount. These options can be further complicated by making the knockout boundary a function of time and by having a rebate if the barrier is activated. In the latter case the holder of the option receives a specified amount Z if the barrier is reached.

We only discuss European options in any detail and we find a number of explicit formulæ for the values of various barrier options. The problem can be readily generalised to incorporate early exercise, although we must then find solutions numerically. In principle, barrier features may be applied to any options.

10.2 An out barrier

We first consider the case of a European style down-and-out call option with payoff at expiry of $\max(S-E,0)$, provided that S never falls below X during the life of the option. If S ever reaches X then the option becomes worthless. We consider only the case where $E > X$. This option has an explicit formula for its fair value.

For as long as S is greater than X, the value of the option $V(S,t)$ satisfies the Black–Scholes equation (3.9). As before, the final condition for this equation is

$$V(S,T) = \max(S-E,0).$$

As S becomes large the likelihood of the barrier being activated becomes negligible and so

$$V(S,t) \sim S \quad \text{as} \quad S \to \infty.$$

So far, the problem is identical to that for a vanilla call. However, the valuation problem differs in that the second boundary condition is applied at $S = X$ rather than at $S = 0$. If S ever reaches X then the option is worthless; thus on this line the value of the option is zero,

$$V(X,t) = 0.$$

This completes the formulation of the problem; we now find the explicit solution.

We use the change of variables first introduced in Section 5.3. That is, we let

$$S = Ee^{x}, \quad t = T - \tau/\tfrac{1}{2}\sigma^2, \quad V = Ee^{\alpha x+\beta\tau}u(x,\tau)$$

with $\alpha = -\frac{1}{2}(k_1-1)$, $\beta = -\frac{1}{4}(k_1+1)^2$ and $k_1 = r/\frac{1}{2}\sigma^2$. In these new variables the barrier option problem becomes

$$\frac{\partial u}{\partial \tau} = \frac{\partial^2 u}{\partial x^2} \tag{10.1}$$

with

$$u(x,0) = \max\left(e^{\frac{1}{2}(k_1+1)x} - e^{\frac{1}{2}(k_1-1)x}, 0\right) = u_0(x), \quad x \geq \log(X/E), \tag{10.2}$$

$$u(x,t) \sim e^{(1-\alpha)x-\beta\tau} \quad \text{as} \quad x \to \infty, \tag{10.3}$$

and

$$u(\log(X/E),t) = 0. \tag{10.4}$$

The last boundary condition is new and we deal with it by the **method of images**.

We have several times related the problem of valuing simple call and put options to the flow of heat in an infinite bar. Boundary condition (10.4) is, however, imposed at a finite value of x and the analogy is now with heat flow in a *semi*-infinite bar held at zero temperature at $x = \log(X/E)$.

The flow of heat in a bar is unaffected by the coordinate system used, so equation (10.4) is invariant under translation, from x to $x + x_0$, or reflection, from x to $-x$. Thus, if $u(x,\tau)$ is a solution of (10.1), so are $u(x + x_0, \tau)$ and $u(-x + x_0, \tau)$ for any constant x_0. In the method of images we solve a semi-infinite problem by first solving an infinite problem made up of *two* semi-infinite problems with equal and opposite initial temperature distributions: one half is hot, the other cold. The net effect is cancellation at the join: the temperature there is guaranteed to be zero.

We can apply this method to the barrier option problem. We reflect the initial data about the point $x_0 = \log(X/E)$ (the 'join' of the two bars), at the same time changing its sign, thereby automatically satisfying (10.4). Thus, instead of solving (10.1)–(10.4) on the interval $\log(X/E) < x < \infty$, we solve (10.1) subject to

$$u(x,0) = u_0(x) - u_0(2\log(X/E) - x),$$

that is,

$$u(x,0) = \begin{cases} \max\left(e^{\frac{1}{2}(k_1+1)x} - e^{\frac{1}{2}(k_1-1)x}, 0\right) & \text{for } x > \log(X/E) \\ -\max\Big(e^{(k_1+1)(\log(X/E)-\frac{1}{2}x)} \\ \qquad -e^{(k_1-1)(\log(X/E)-\frac{1}{2}x)}, 0\Big) & \text{for } x < \log(X/E) \end{cases} \tag{10.5}$$

for all x. In this way we guarantee that $u(\log(X/E), 0) = 0$.

We now write the solution of the European call problem (with no barriers) as

$$C(S,t) = Ee^{\alpha x + \beta\tau}u_1(x,\tau),$$

where $u_1(x,\tau)$ is the appropriate solution of the heat equation. Thus, we have

$$u_1(x,\tau) = e^{-\alpha x-\beta\tau}C(S,t)/E$$

where $C(S,t)$ is given by the Black–Scholes formula (see Section 3.7.2). Next we can write the solution to the barrier option value as

$$V(S,t) = Ee^{\alpha x+\beta\tau}\left(u_1(x,\tau)+u_2(x,\tau)\right)$$

where $u_2(x,\tau)$ is the solution of the problem with antisymmetric initial data. The solution of this problem can be found in terms of u_1 by using the invariance of the equation (10.1) under translation and changes of sign. We must have

$$\begin{aligned} u_2(x,\tau) &= -u_1(2\log(X/E)-x,\tau) \\ &= -e^{-\alpha(2\log(X/E)-\log(S/E))-\beta\tau}C(X^2/S,t)/E, \end{aligned}$$

since replacing x by $2\log(X/E)-x$ is equivalent to replacing S by X^2/S. Finally, bringing all these together and writing the solution purely in terms of S and t, we have

$$V(S,t) = C(S,t) - \left(\frac{S}{X}\right)^{-(k_1-1)} C(X^2/S,t).$$

It is trivial to see that $V(X,t)=0$; it can also be verified that the equation and final condition are also satisfied. (The final condition is only satisfied for $S>X$, of course.)

This demonstrates the use of the method of images to find an explicit formula for a down-and-out call option. Other 'out' options can be valued similarly. However, 'in' options must be treated slightly differently.

10.3 An in barrier

An 'in' option expires worthless *unless* the asset price reaches the barrier before expiry. If the asset value crosses the line $S=X$ at some time prior to expiry then the option becomes a vanilla option with the appropriate payoff.

Let us now consider a down-and-in European call option. The option value $V(S,t)$ still satisfies the basic Black–Scholes equation (3.9) and all we have to do to pose the problem fully is to determine the correct final and boundary conditions. We use the notation $C(S,t)$ to denote a European vanilla call with the same expiry date and exercise price as the barrier call.

The option is worthless as $S \to \infty$. This is because the larger that S is, the less likely it is to fall through the barrier before expiry and activate the option. Thus one boundary condition is

$$V(S,t) \to 0 \quad \text{as} \quad S \to \infty.$$

If S has been greater than X right up to expiry then the option expires worthless. The final condition, for $S > X$, is therefore

$$V(S,T) = 0.$$

Finally, should the asset price reach $S = X$ at some time before expiry the option immediately turns into a vanilla call and must thus have the same value as this call. The second boundary condition is therefore

$$V(X,t) = C(X,t).$$

If $S < X$ at any point then the barrier has been crossed, the option is activated and the value of the option is exactly the same as a vanilla call. Thus, we have only to solve for the value in $S > X$. This completes the formulation of the European down-and-in barrier call.

In order to solve the down-and-in explicitly we first write

$$V(S,t) = C(S,t) - \bar{V}(S,t).$$

Since the Black–Scholes equation and boundary conditions are linear we know that $\bar{V}$ must satisfy the Black–Scholes equation with final condition

$$\bar{V}(S,T) = C(S,T) - V(S,T) = C(S,T) = \max(S - E, 0);$$

and boundary conditions

$$\begin{aligned} \bar{V}(S,t) &= C(S,t) - V(S,t) \sim S - 0 = S, \quad \text{as } S \to \infty \\ \bar{V}(X,t) &= C(X,t) - V(X,t) = C(X,t) - C(X,t) = 0. \end{aligned}$$

This is the problem for the down-and-*out* barrier option. In other words, in this case, a European 'in' plus a European 'out' equals a vanilla. This is obvious from a financial point of view as the value of a portfolio consisting of one in-option and one out-option (with the same barrier, exercise price and expiry dates) is obviously equal to the value of a vanilla call (with the same exercise price and expiry dates). This is because only one of the two barrier options can have be active at expiry and whichever it is, its value is the value of a vanilla call.

More explicit formulæ can be found in Rubinstein (1992). The American versions of these options exist but do not have explicit formulæ. Nevertheless, their numerical solution is no harder than for vanilla options.

Further reading

- Rubinstein (1992) contains a catalogue and explicit formulæ for a large number of barrier options.

Exercises

1. How is a boundary condition changed if the option pays a rebate of Z if the barrier is triggered?

2. Find explicit formulæ for all varieties of European barrier options (in/out, up/down, call/put) including a rebate, dividends and time-varying interest rate and volatility.

3. By seeking solutions of the Black–Scholes equation which are independent of time, show that there are 'perpetual' barrier options, i.e. ones whose values are independent of t. These options have no expiry date ($T = \infty$). Find their explicit formulæ and include a continuously paid constant dividend yield on the underlying.

Chapter 11

Asian Options

11.1 Options depending on averages

A typical example of an Asian option is a contract giving the holder the right to buy an asset for its average price over some prescribed period. Such a product is of obvious appeal to a company which must buy a commodity at a fixed time each year, yet has to sell it regularly throughout the year. In this case the underlying asset is the commodity. The same type of option is also used in foreign exchange markets by companies which have continuous sales in one currency but must purchase raw materials in a different currency and at a fixed date. Here, the underlying is the exchange rate. These options allow investors to eliminate losses (and, of course, at the same time, profits) from movements in an underlying asset without the need for continuous rehedging.

In this chapter we derive differential equations for the value of many Asian options. The common feature is that the exercise price is always some form of average of the price of the underlying over some period prior to exercise. The exercise price may depend on geometric or arithmetic averages, which may be measured either continuously or discretely. As well as deriving the equations we also examine several problems in more detail, in particular the continuously sampled arithmetic average strike option with either European and American exercise features, and the European geometric average strike with either continuous or discrete sampling. In general Asian options depend on three independent variables (see Chapter 9), but we find that these particular options permit similarity reductions where the value of the option is in each reduced to a function of *two* variables. This enables us to derive explicit solutions for options depending on geometric averages. (These are not the only similarity solutions derivable for Asian options. Many other types of Asian option can be simplified and solved in this way and these are left as exercises for the reader.) We conclude the chapter with an example of an average rate option, which does not admit a similarity reduction.

11.2 Continuously sampled averages

11.2.1 Arithmetic averaging

The basic model for valuing Asian options is discussed in Section 9.2, and the general form of the partial differential equation governing the option value is equation (9.7). In particular, for an option depending on the continuously sampled arithmetic average

$$\frac{1}{t}\int_0^t S(\tau)\,d\tau,$$

we introduce the variable

$$I = \int_0^t S(\tau)\,d\tau.$$

Following the analysis of Section 9.2, the partial differential equation for the value of such an option is

$$\frac{\partial V}{\partial t} + S\frac{\partial V}{\partial I} + \tfrac{1}{2}\sigma^2 S^2 \frac{\partial^2 V}{\partial S^2} + (rS - D(S,I,t))\frac{\partial V}{\partial S} - rV = 0. \quad (11.1)$$

Figure 11.1 shows a realisation of the random walk followed by an asset together with two versions of its running arithmetic average. One is the continuous arithmetic running average defined above, which is initiated at the start of the graph; the figure also shows the discrete version of this average, which is discussed in Section 11.3.2.

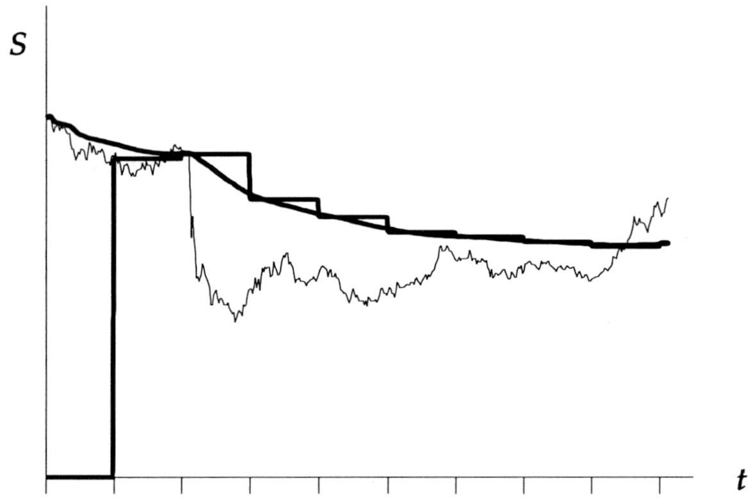

Figure 11.1: An asset price random walk, its continuously measured arithmetic running average and a discrete arithmetic running average.

11.2.2 Geometric averaging

The continuously sampled geometric average[1] is defined to be

$$\exp\left(\frac{1}{t}\int_0^t \log S(\tau)\,d\tau\right);$$

it is the limit as $n \to \infty$ of the usual discrete geometric average

$$\left(\prod_{i=1}^{n} S(t_i)\right)^{\frac{1}{n}}$$

(see Section 11.3.3). When this determines the payoff of the option, we define

$$I = \int_0^t \log S(\tau)\,d\tau$$

[1]Strictly speaking, we should make S dimensionless in this formula; however, the additive constant that arises from the units of S always cancels out. We can think of S as dimensionless in the units of currency under consideration.

and the partial differential equation for the value of the option is

$$\frac{\partial V}{\partial t}+\log S\frac{\partial V}{\partial I}+\tfrac{1}{2}\sigma^2S^2\frac{\partial^2 V}{\partial S^2}+(rS-D(S,I,t))\frac{\partial V}{\partial S}-rV=0. \quad (11.2)$$

Figure 11.2 shows a realisation of an asset price random walk with the continuous and discrete versions of its geometric running average.

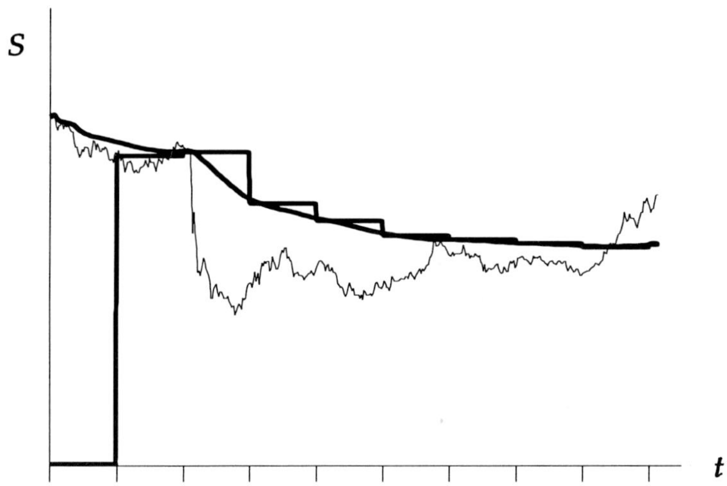

Figure 11.2: An asset price random walk, its continuous geometric running average and a discrete geometric running average.

11.3 Discretely sampled averages

In practice it can be difficult to calculate the average of an asset price from its complete time series: prices can change every 30 seconds or so, with the occasional misquotation of prices. Thus, it is more common in an option contract to determine the average from a small subset of the complete time series for the asset price, for example the average over the daily or weekly closing prices.

We have already modelled the continuous average as an integral, consistently with the assumption that asset and option values are time-continuous quantities. By a discrete average we mean the sum, rather than the integral, of a finite number of values of the asset during the life of the option. Such a definition of average is easily included within the framework of our model. The discrete sampling of averages bears close similarities with the discrete payment of dividends. In particular, both give rise to jump conditions across payment/sampling dates.

11.3.1 Jump conditions

In this section we demonstrate the financial argument leading to the jump condition for discretely sampled Asian options. First, however, let us briefly discuss the nature of the jump condition. We ask the question:

- Does the value of the option actually jump across the sampling date?

The answer to this question is, as for the case of discrete dividend payments, both yes and no, depending on the way the option value is viewed in relation to the underlying. It is certainly true that $V(S, I, t)$ need not be continuous *for fixed* S *and* I as t varies. In that sense there is indeed a jump in V, and the answer to the question is 'yes'. However, in the course of any realisation of the asset price in which all of S, I and t vary, the option price does *not* change discontinuously, and the answer is 'no'. This latter statement is a simple consequence of the absence of arbitrage opportunities; if the value of an option jumped discontinuously across a known sampling date it would present an obvious arbitrage opportunity.

These two, apparently contradictory, statements can be reconciled once it is recognised that across the sampling date the discretely sampled average changes discontinuously. The average changes discontinuously because I is measured discretely. The discontinuity of I and the continuity of $V(S(t), I(t), t)$ for any *realisation* of the random walk forces $V(S, I, t)$ (viewed as a function of t with S and I fixed) to change discontinuously across sampling dates.

We now determine the jump condition for an Asian option with discrete arithmetic averaging; this derivation is easily generalised to Asian options with more complicated discrete averaging, for example discrete geometric averaging, and even to lookbacks.

The discretely sampled arithmetic running sum may be defined as

$$I = \sum_{i=1}^{j(t)} S(t_i),$$

where t_i are the sampling dates and $j(t)$ is the largest integer such that $t_{j(t)} < t$. In terms of I and $j(t)$, the discretely sampled arithmetic average is $I/j(t)$.

We introduce the notation I_i to denote the value of the running sum I for $t_i < t < t_{i+1}$. Thus, I_i represents the (constant) value of I for the period immediately after a sample taken at t_i until the next sample is taken at t_{i+1}. We may write

$$I_i = I_{i-1} + S(t_i), \tag{11.3}$$

and so I is updated at time t_i by adding to it the value of S at that time. Since I_i is constant for the period t_i^+ (just after a sample is taken) to t_{i+1}^- (immediately before the next sample), it is effectively a parameter in the value of the option during this time, in the same way that the exercise price is a parameter in the value of a vanilla option. During this period, the only random variable that is changing is S and the option price must therefore satisfy the basic Black–Scholes equation during this time. From (11.3) it is clear that I is discontinuous at t_i as we noted above. However, since the *realised* option price is continuous across t_i we have

$$V(S(t_i^+), I_i, t_i^+) = V(S(t_i^-), I_{i-1}, t_i^-), \tag{11.4}$$

where $S(t_i^-)$ and I_{i-1} are the values of S and I immediately before sampling and $S(t_i^+)$ and I_i are the values immediately after sampling. Using (11.3) this can be written as

$$V(S, I_{i-1}, t_i^-) = V(S, I_{i-1} + S, t_i^+). \tag{11.5}$$

Since I_{i-1} does not change from t_{i-1}^+ to t_i^- we can drop its suffix $i-1$ in (11.5) with no possibility of confusion and arrive at the jump condition

$$V(S, I, t_i^-) = V(S, I + S, t_i^+). \tag{11.6}$$

This is the jump condition for the discretely sampled arithmetic Asian option. Notice that in (11.4) we think of S and I arising from a realisation of the random walk (so that they vary in time) and in (11.6) we think of them as fixed.

This derivation can be applied to any option which depends on a discretely updated parameter. For example, if the option depends on an I determined by a general equation of the form

$$I_i = w_i(S(t_i), I_{i-1}),$$

(where the functions w_i are known in advance) the jump condition is simply

$$V(S, I, t_i^-) = V(S, w_i(S, I), t_i^+).$$

In particular, for the discretely sampled geometric average where the running sum is

$$I = \sum_{i=1}^{j(t)} \log S(t_i)$$

we find that

$$V(S, I, t_i^-) = V(S, I + \log S, t_i^+).$$

We can see that, although the particular definition of the discrete average affects the details of the jump conditions across sampling dates, it does not affect the general procedure for solution. This is because the path-dependent quantity, I, is updated discretely and is therefore constant between sampling dates. The partial differential equation for the option value between sampling dates is just the basic Black–Scholes equation with I treated as a parameter. Thus the strategy for valuing any Asian option is as follows:

- Solve

$$\frac{\partial V}{\partial t} + \tfrac{1}{2}\sigma^2 S^2 \frac{\partial^2 V}{\partial S^2} + (rS - D(S, I, t))\frac{\partial V}{\partial S} - rV = 0$$

  between sampling dates, using the value of the option immediately before the next sampling date as final data. This gives the value of the option until immediately after the present sampling date.

- Then apply the appropriate jump condition across the current sampling date to deduce the option value immediately before the present sampling date.

- Repeat this process as necessary to arrive at the current value of the option.

11.3.2 Arithmetic averaging

As well as the continuously sampled arithmetic average, Figure 11.1 shows a discrete arithmetic running average defined by

$$\frac{1}{j(t)} \sum_{i=1}^{j(t)} S(t_i),$$

which can also be written as

$$\frac{1}{\int_0^t \sum_{i=1}^N \delta(\tau - t_i)\, d\tau} \int_0^t \sum_{i=1}^N S(\tau)\delta(t - t_i)\, d\tau.$$

In the figure the sampling dates t_i are evenly spaced at 50-day intervals. With this choice of the running average the average is only updated at each t_i.

When the average is only updated at discrete times option prices must satisfy jump conditions across the sampling dates. We have found the jump condition from financial arguments above. Here we briefly show how the jump condition may be derived from purely mathematical arguments.

Define

$$I = \int_0^t \sum_{i=1}^N \delta(\tau - t_i) S(\tau)\, d\tau.$$

With this definition, the value of I at $t = T$ is simply the sum of the values of S at the N dates t_i. Thus, I is given by

$$I = \sum_{i=1}^{j(t)} S(t_i).$$

This is, of course, the definition of the running sum that we have used earlier. The rest of the analysis is similar to the earlier discussion of the simple option with discrete dividends.

From Chapter 9 we see that the option value satisfies the equation

$$\frac{\partial V}{\partial t} + \sum_{i=1}^N \delta(t - t_i) S \frac{\partial V}{\partial I} + \tfrac{1}{2}\sigma^2 S^2 \frac{\partial^2 V}{\partial S^2} + (rS - D(S, I, t)) \frac{\partial V}{\partial S} - rV = 0. \tag{11.7}$$

Away from the sampling dates, t_i, the option differential equation is simply the Black–Scholes equation, and so I appears only as a parameter. However, across a sampling date t_i the equation can be approximated by

$$\frac{\partial V}{\partial t} + \delta(t - t_i) S \frac{\partial V}{\partial I} = 0.$$

The characteristics of this first order equation are given by

$$I - S\mathcal{H}(t - t_i) = \text{ constant.} \tag{11.8}$$

This is equivalent to (11.3): I is increased by S at time t_i. Since V is constant along these characteristics we have

$$V(S, I, t_i^-) = V(S, I + S, t_i^+)$$

as before.

11.3.3 Geometric averaging

Figure 11.2 also shows a discrete geometric running average defined by

$$\exp\left(\frac{\sum_{i=1}^{j(t)} \log S(t_i)}{j(t)}\right).$$

Another way of writing this is

$$\exp\left(\int_0^t \sum_{i=1}^N \delta(\tau - t_i) \log S(\tau)\, d\tau \Big/ \int_0^t \sum_{i=1}^N \delta(\tau - t_i)\, d\tau\right).$$

With this choice of the running average, the average is only updated at each t_i. In the example of Figure 11.2, the time between sampling of the average is 50 days.

Again, we briefly demonstrate the mathematical argument leading to the jump condition across a sampling date. Define the running variable I by

$$I = \int_0^t \sum_{i=1}^N \delta(\tau - t_i) \log S(\tau)\, d\tau.$$

Across a sampling date, t_i, the partial differential equation for the option value is approximated by the first order hyperbolic equation

$$\frac{\partial V}{\partial t} + \delta(t - t_i) \log S \frac{\partial V}{\partial I} = 0.$$

(Away from a sampling date it is simply the usual Black–Scholes equation.) Using the method of characteristics, the general solution of this first order equation is easily found to imply the jump condition

$$V(S, I, t_i^-) = V(S, I + \log S, t_i^+).$$

This is, or course, the same condition we derived above by financial reasoning.

11.4 Similarity reductions for arithmetic Asian options

The value of an Asian option depends on three variables S, I and t. This is true whether the quantity I is measured arithmetically or geometrically, continuously or discretely. Typically the value of these options must be calculated numerically, and this is the subject of Chapter 22. In cases where the option valuation problem is genuinely in three dimensions any computer program will be much slower than that for a vanilla option, due to the extra dimension. This cannot be avoided. However, some options have a particular mathematical structure that permits a reduction in the dimensionality of the problem by use of a similarity variable; we discuss two such options in detail in the following three sections. We saw in Chapter 5 how a problem in two dimensions could be reduced to a problem in only one dimension because of the structure of the differential equation and its boundary and initial conditions. In the case of the arithmetically sampled Asian option we can reduce the problem from three to two dimensions when both of the following conditions hold:

- the payoff has the form $I^\alpha F(S/I, t)$ for some constant α and some function F;
- the dividend has the form $D = S\hat{D}(S/I, t)$.

Here, as always in the case of arithmetically averaged Asian options,

$$I = \int_0^t S(\tau)\, d\tau.$$

If these two conditions hold we only need to find solutions of a two-dimensional problem. In fact, for continuous averaging, we find that

$V = I^{\alpha}W(\xi, t)$, where $\xi = S/I$, and

$$\frac{\partial W}{\partial t} + \tfrac{1}{2}\sigma^2\xi^2\frac{\partial^2 W}{\partial \xi^2} + \left((r - \hat{D} + \alpha)\xi - \xi^2\right)\frac{\partial W}{\partial \xi} + rW = 0.$$

For discrete averaging $V = I^{\alpha}W(\xi, t)$, where again $\xi = S/I$, and

$$\frac{\partial W}{\partial t} + \tfrac{1}{2}\sigma^2\xi^2\frac{\partial^2 W}{\partial \xi^2} + (r - \hat{D})\xi\frac{\partial W}{\partial \xi} + rW = 0,$$

with jump condition

$$W(\xi, t_i^-) = (1 + \xi)^{\alpha}W((1 + \xi)^{-1}, t_i^+).$$

Since these problems are only two-dimensional they are much quicker to solve numerically than the original three-dimensional ones; in practice they may be evaluated as rapidly as vanilla options.

11.5 The continuously sampled average strike option

For our main example of an Asian option we examine in depth the average strike option, where the payoff depends on the arithmetic average of an asset price. The option is named as it is because the payoff at expiry for the European version is the same as that for a simple option, but with the constant exercise price E replaced by

$$\frac{1}{T}\int_0^T S(\tau)\,d\tau.$$

That is, the payoff at expiry is

$$\max\left(S - \frac{1}{T}\int_0^T S(\tau)\,d\tau,\ 0\right)$$

for a call, and

$$\max\left(\frac{1}{T}\int_0^T S(\tau)\,d\tau - S,\ 0\right)$$

for a put. We give details only for the call.

The option value superficially depends on the three variables S, I and t, where I is the running sum

$$I = \int_0^t S(\tau)\,d\tau.$$

As mentioned above, this option value actually only depends on the two variables, S/I and t. This is because the average strike option admits a similarity reduction; if there are no dividends it satisfies both criteria in the last section. This gives it a particular elegance and enables us to take the analysis quite a long way. (At the end of this chapter we discuss the average rate option where the option value is genuinely a function of three variables.)

In this section we set up models for the European and American versions of the option. In order to value the American version we must first decide on the payoff for early exercise; the average up to expiry is not known before expiry. The natural choice for the call is

$$\max\left(S - \frac{1}{t}\int_0^t S(\tau)\,d\tau,\, 0\right); \tag{11.9}$$

this is the running average from time 0 to t. This also gives the correct payoff at expiry.

We can write the payoff for the call option as

$$S \max\left(1 - \frac{1}{St}\int_0^t S(\tau)\,d\tau,\, 0\right).$$

With this in mind we make the change of variables

$$R = \frac{1}{S}\int_0^t S(\tau)\,d\tau, \tag{11.10}$$

so that the payoff for early exercise and at expiry may be written respectively as

$$S \max\left(1 - \frac{R}{t}, 0\right), \quad S \max\left(1 - \frac{R}{T}, 0\right).$$

(Note that, written in terms of R, the payoff for the call option looks more like that of a *put*.) We now find the stochastic differential equation satisfied by R. As t increases to $t + dt$, R changes to

$$R + dR = \frac{1}{S + dS}\int_0^{t+dt} S(\tau)\,d\tau.$$

Using (2.1) this may be expanded to $O(dt)$, to give

$$dR = -\sigma R\,dX + \left(1 + R(\sigma^2 - \mu)\right)dt. \tag{11.11}$$

This is the random walk followed by R and it does not depend on S explicitly. In view of the forms of the payoff functions above, we are led to postulate that the option value takes the form

$$V(S,R,t) = SH(R,t).$$

We can find the partial differential equation for $H(R,t)$ in one of two equivalent ways. One is to set up a portfolio with one average strike option and a number of the underlying and derive the equation from first principles. A second, quicker derivation is simply to substitute $V = SH$ into (11.1) and seek a solution H that is independent of S. Either way we find that

$$\Delta = H - R\partial H/\partial R$$

and

$$\frac{\partial H}{\partial t} + \tfrac{1}{2}\sigma^2 R^2 \frac{\partial^2 H}{\partial R^2} + (1 - rR)\frac{\partial H}{\partial R} \leq 0. \tag{11.12}$$

(Recall that we have assumed that the underlying pays no dividend.) If the option is European we have strict equality in (11.12). If it is American we may have inequality in (11.12) but the constraint

$$H(R,t) \geq \max\left(1 - \frac{R}{t}, 0\right) = \Lambda(R,t) \tag{11.13}$$

must be satisfied. Moreover, if the option price ever meets the early exercise payoff it must do so smoothly. That is, the function $H(R,t)$ and its first R-derivative must be continuous everywhere.

11.5.1 Boundary conditions for the European option

For the European option we must impose boundary conditions at both $R = 0$ and as $R \to \infty$. The boundary condition as $R \to \infty$ is simple. Since S is bounded for finite t, the only way that R can tend to infinity is for S to tend to zero. In this case the option will not be exercised, and so

$$H(\infty, t) = 0.$$

To determine the boundary condition at $R = 0$ we need to take a close look at equation (11.12) as $R \to 0$. Recall the discussion of the boundary condition at $S = 0$ for the vanilla option. This followed since if ever S is zero then it remains zero for all time; the payoff is known with certainty. This, however, is not the case for the random walk in R. Put $R = 0$ in (11.11) and we find that $dR = dt > 0$, so the variable R immediately moves away from $R = 0$ into $R > 0$. Thus, even if $R = 0$ now, there is no reason why it should remain zero until expiry. Therefore we no longer know the value of the option when $R = 0$ with certainty. All we know is that the value of the option must be finite.

We can use the condition that the option value is finite at $R = 0$ to deduce a boundary condition there from the differential equation. First, note that for R small the term $R\partial H/\partial R$ is negligible compared with $\partial H/\partial R$. We can thus ignore this term (in fact, this is independent of whether H is finite or not). We may also ignore the $R^2\partial^2 H/\partial R^2$ term as $R \to 0$ for the following reason. Suppose that $R^2\partial^2 H/\partial R^2$ tends to a nonzero limit as $R \to 0$; we can assume without loss of generality that

$$\lim_{R\to 0} R^2 \frac{\partial^2 H}{\partial R^2} = O(1).$$

For small R we would then have

$$\frac{\partial^2 H}{\partial R^2} = O(\frac{1}{R^2})$$

which may be easily integrated to show that $H = O(\log R)$ as $R \to 0$. This is, of course, inconsistent with H being finite. Thus we conclude that only the terms $\partial H/\partial t$ and $\partial H/\partial R$ can contribute near $R = 0$. In other words

$$\frac{\partial H}{\partial t} + \frac{\partial H}{\partial R} = 0 \quad \text{on} \quad R = 0. \qquad (11.14)$$

This is the second boundary condition[2].

The equation (11.12), final and boundary conditions at $R = 0$ and $R = \infty$ are sufficient to determine the value H of a European

[2]Other balances are possible near $R = 0$, for example

$$\frac{\partial H}{\partial R} + \tfrac{1}{2}\sigma^2 R^2 \frac{\partial^2 H}{\partial R^2} \sim 0.$$

This, and other balances, are either inconsistent with the equation (i.e. ignored terms are, in fact, not small), or lead to exponentially large option prices. The latter are financially unrealistic.

option uniquely. It is possible to write down an exact analytic expression for the problem as an infinite sum of confluent hypergeometric functions. We do not give this exact solution because the confluent hypergeometric function is not a widely known function, the solution is represented in terms of an infinite sum and because, from a practical point of view, it is quicker to obtain values by applying numerical methods directly to the partial differential equation. In Figure 11.3 we see H against R at three months before expiry and with three months' averaging completed; $\sigma = 0.4$ and $r = 0.1$. This curve was computed numerically by the methods described in Chapter 22.

In the case of an American option, we have to solve the partial differential inequality (11.12) subject to the constraint (11.13), the final condition and the condition that $H \to 0$ as $R \to \infty$. We cannot do this analytically and we must find the solution numerically.

In the next sections we examine the behaviour of European and American average strike options in more detail.

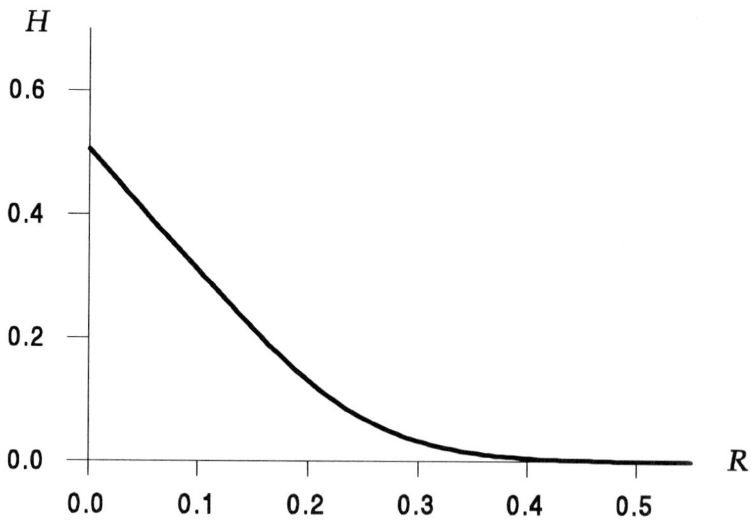

Figure 11.3: The European average strike call option; H versus R with $\sigma = 0.4$ and $r = 0.1$ at three months before expiry; there has already been three months' averaging.

11.5.2 Put-call parity for the European average strike

The payoff at expiry for a portfolio of one European average strike call held long and one put held short is

$$S\max(1 - R/T, 0) - S\max(R/T - 1, 0).$$

Whether R is greater or less than T at expiry, this payoff is simply

$$S - \frac{RS}{T}.$$

The value of this portfolio is identical to one consisting of one asset and a financial product whose payoff is

$$-\frac{RS}{T}.$$

In order to value this product we seek a solution of the average strike equation of the form

$$H = a(t) + b(t)R \tag{11.15}$$

and with $a(T) = 0$ and $b(T) = -1/T$; such a solution would have the required payoff of $-RS/T$. Substituting (11.15) into (11.12) and satisfying the boundary conditions, we find that

$$a(t) = -\frac{1}{rT}\left(1 - e^{-r(T-t)}\right), \quad b(t) = -\frac{1}{T}e^{-r(T-t)}.$$

We conclude that

$$C - P = S - \frac{S}{rT}\left(1 - e^{-r(T-t)}\right) - \frac{1}{T}e^{-r(T-t)}\int_0^t S(\tau)d\tau,$$

where C and P are the values of the European arithmetic average strike call and put. This is put-call parity for the European average strike option.

11.6 Analysis of the American average strike option

The constraint in the case of the American average strike option, written in terms of the scaled asset price R, is

$$\Lambda(R,t) = \max\left(1 - \frac{R}{t}, 0\right). \tag{11.16}$$

By determining where and when the function $\Lambda(R,t)$ in (11.16) satisfies the inequality (11.12) we can make qualitative statements about the position of the free boundary. Substituting (11.16) into (11.12), we find that, for $R < t$,

$$\frac{\partial \Lambda}{\partial t} + \tfrac{1}{2}\sigma^2 R^2 \frac{\partial^2 \Lambda}{\partial R^2} + (1 - rR)\frac{\partial \Lambda}{\partial R} = \frac{R}{t^2} - \frac{1}{t} + \frac{rR}{t} = F(R,t),$$

say. In Figure 11.4 we show the regions in (R,t) space where $F(R,t)$ is positive and negative.

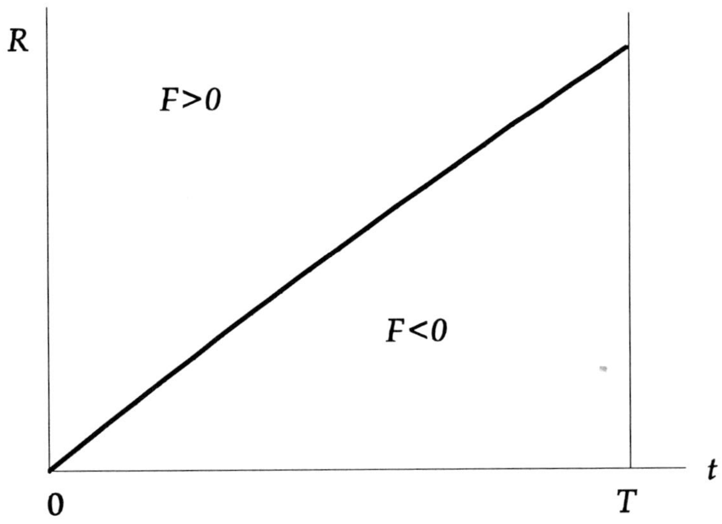

Figure 11.4: The regions where the obstacle $\Lambda(R,t)$ does and does not satisfy the inequality.

Since an American version of the option satisfies (11.12) with inequality, the free boundary $R = R_f(t)$ must be contained entirely within the region where $F(R,t) \leq 0$. Comparison with the analysis of Chapter 6 for the American vanilla option shows that, in particular, the free boundary emanates from the point $R = T/(1 + rT)$ at time $t = T$, since there $F = 0$. Thus $R_f(T) = T/(1 + rT)$. We anticipate that the problem for $H(R,t)$ is as shown schematically in Figure 11.5.

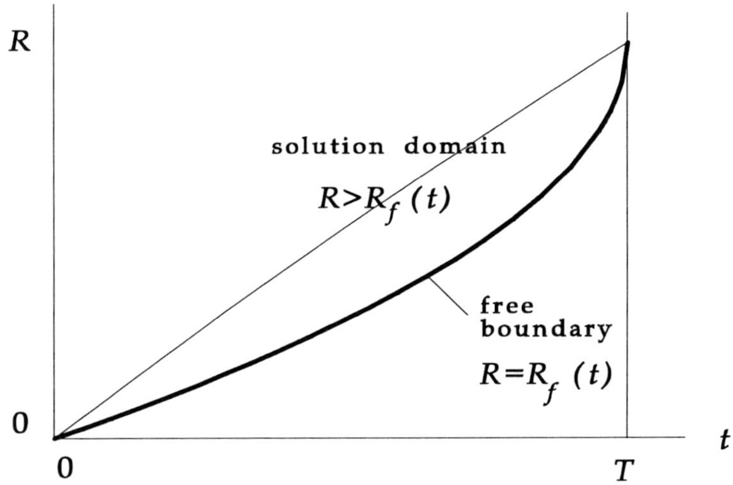

Figure 11.5: A schematic diagram for the problem for $H(R,t)$ showing the free boundary.

11.6.1 Local analysis of the free boundary near expiry

We can perform an analysis similar to that in Section 6.4 to determine the local behaviour of the free boundary at times close to expiry, i.e. near $t = T$ and $R = R_f(T)$.

It is convenient to change to a new dependent variable

$$\bar{H} = H - 1 + R/t.$$

For $(T-t)/T \ll 1$ and $|R - T/(1+rT)| \ll 1$, equation (11.12), which is valid above the free boundary as shown in Figure 11.5, can be approximated by

$$\tfrac{1}{2}\sigma^2 R_f(T)^2 \frac{\partial^2 \bar{H}}{\partial R^2} + \frac{\partial \bar{H}}{\partial t} = (R - R_f(T))\frac{1+rT}{T^2}.$$

Near expiry, other terms in (11.12) are smaller than those retained.

This local problem is almost identical to the local model for the American vanilla option of Section 6.4. There, the behaviour of the free boundary close to expiry is determined by the solution of

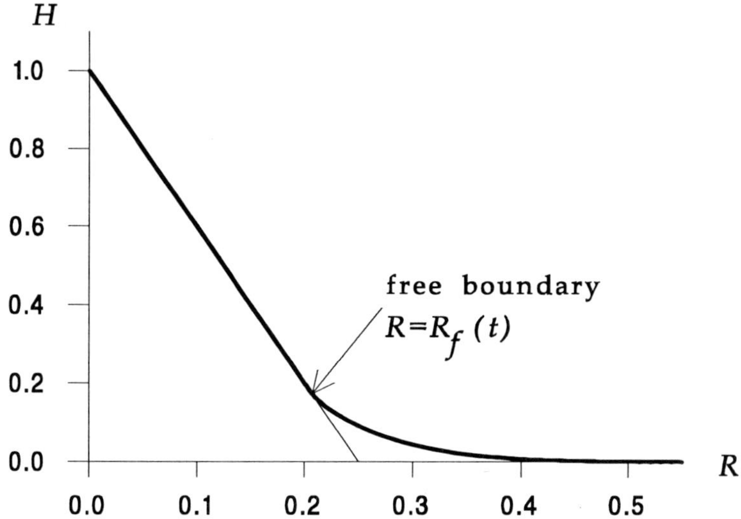

Figure 11.6: The scaled American arithmetic average strike call option value $H(R,t)$; $\sigma = 0.4$, $r = 0.1$. There are three months to expiry, and three months' averaging has already been carried out. The payoff is also shown; the graph of $H(R,t)$ meets it smoothly.

a diffusion equation with a source term. From that analysis we see that near expiry the free boundary is given by

$$R_f(t) = \frac{T}{1+rT} + \xi_0 \frac{\sigma T}{\sqrt{2}(1+rT)} \sqrt{(T-t)},$$

where $\xi_0 = 0.9034\ldots$. In Figure 11.6 we show the function H against R, computed by the methods described in Chapter 22. There are three months to expiry with three months' averaging already carried out; $\sigma = 0.4$ and $r = 0.1$.

Technical Point: local analysis near initiation of averaging.

At $t = 0$, *the function* $\max(1 - R/t, 0)$ *is discontinuous at* $R = 0$. *A numerical scheme may therefore encounter difficulties as* $t \to 0$. *We may, however, predict the effects of this singularity by a careful* *analysis of the problem in the limit $t \to 0$.*

In order to make the constraint time-independent, and for this Technical Point only, *we change to a new coordinate ξ defined by*

$$R = t\xi.$$

The constraint function becomes

$$\Lambda = \max(1 - \xi, 0),$$

and when $H > \Lambda$, H satisfies the partial differential equation

$$\frac{\partial H}{\partial t} + \tfrac{1}{2}\sigma^2\xi^2\frac{\partial^2 H}{\partial \xi^2} + \left(-\frac{\xi}{t} + \frac{1}{t} - r\xi\right)\frac{\partial H}{\partial \xi} = 0. \qquad (11.17)$$

As $t \to 0^+$, we approximate (11.17) by its dominant part, giving

$$\frac{\partial H}{\partial t} + \left(-\frac{\xi}{t} + \frac{1}{t}\right)\frac{\partial H}{\partial \xi} = 0; \qquad (11.18)$$

the other terms are negligible. The solution of (11.18) has the form

$$H = F(t(\xi - 1))$$

for some function F. This represents convection to the right for $\xi > 1$ and to the left for $\xi < 1$. Thus for small t the value of H at $\xi = 1$, i.e. at $R = t$, does not change.

In the absence of a constraint H tends to the constant $\alpha = F(0)$ as $t \to 0^+$, for $\xi = O(1)$. Therefore, we anticipate that the large curvature that is needed to satisfy the constraint is confined to a small region around the point where $H = \alpha$ meets the constraint function Λ. This point is $\xi = 1 - \alpha$; see Figure 11.7.

To analyse the behaviour of H near this point we again change coordinates, this time choosing

$$\xi = 1 - \alpha + t\eta.$$

The dominant terms in (11.17) for small t give the approximation

$$\tfrac{1}{2}\sigma^2(1-\alpha)^2\frac{\partial^2 H}{\partial \eta^2} + \alpha\frac{\partial H}{\partial \eta} = 0.$$

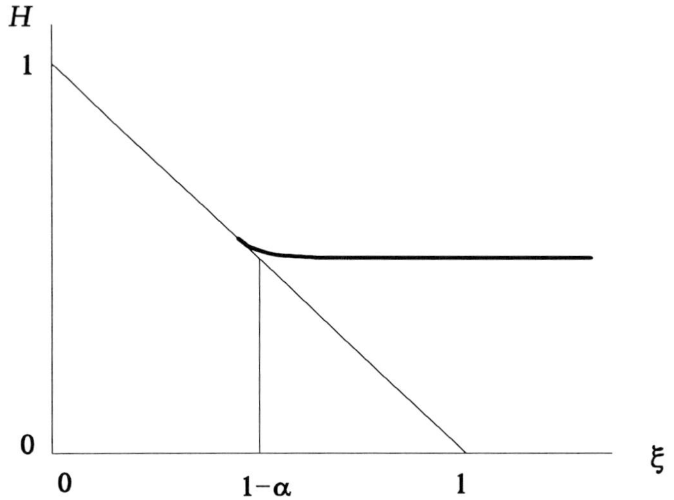

Figure 11.7: Local behaviour of H near initiation of averaging.

This can be integrated explicitly to yield

$$H \sim A + B \exp\left(\frac{-2\alpha\eta}{\sigma^2(1-\alpha)^2}\right),$$

where the constants A and B are found by joining this solution smoothly to the function Λ. In the new coordinates,

$$\Lambda = \max(\alpha - t\eta, 0).$$

We find that

$$A = \alpha, \quad B = \frac{\sigma^2(1-\alpha)^2}{e\alpha}t,$$

and the free boundary is at $\eta = \eta^*$, where

$$\eta^* = -\frac{\sigma^2(1-\alpha)^2}{2\alpha}.$$

Thus

$$H \sim \alpha + \frac{t\sigma^2(1-\alpha)^2}{2\alpha} \exp\left(-\frac{2\alpha(R/t-\alpha)}{\sigma^2(1-\alpha)^2 t} - 1\right),$$

for

$$R > (1-\alpha)t - \frac{\sigma^2(1-\alpha)^2 t^2}{2\alpha}.$$

Unfortunately, the value of α cannot be determined by a local analysis. Although our analysis gives the local structure qualitatively, the parameter α depends on the final data, which cannot be included in our local analysis about $t = 0$. Nevertheless, an analysis such as this is of use when it comes to checking numerical schemes. The intricacy of the mathematics suggests that any numerical scheme for valuing average strike options must take special care at the initiation of the averaging.

11.7 Average strike foreign exchange options

As our second example we briefly consider average strike foreign exchange options, both European and American. The specific option we consider is one that gives the right to buy one unit of a foreign currency for the average domestic price over some period. In this context S denotes the exchange rate and the payoff is

$$\max\left(1 - \frac{1}{ST}\int_0^T S(\tau)\,d\tau, 0\right), \tag{11.19}$$

measured in the foreign currency.

This problem, like the previous one, can be written in terms of the two variables R and t where

$$R = \frac{1}{S(t)}\int_0^t S(\tau)\,d\tau.$$

The payoff at expiry can be written as

$$\max(1 - R/T, 0)$$

and we take the early exercise payoff to be

$$\max(1 - R/t, 0).$$

As before, we look for an option value $V(R,t)$ in which S does not occur explicitly. Assuming this form for the solution and substituting into (11.1) we find that

$$\frac{\partial V}{\partial t} + \tfrac{1}{2}\sigma^2 R^2 \frac{\partial^2 V}{\partial R^2} + \frac{\partial V}{\partial R} - rV + (\sigma^2 - r + r_f) R \frac{\partial V}{\partial R} \le 0, \qquad (11.20)$$

with strict equality for a European option. The delta is given by

$$\Delta = -\frac{R}{S}\frac{\partial V}{\partial R}.$$

We have assumed that foreign currency receives interest continuously at the constant rate r_f, i.e. we have taken $D(S, I, t) = r_f$.

Now we must determine the correct final and boundary conditions. The easiest to decide is the final condition

$$V(R, T) = \max\left(1 - \frac{R}{T}, 0\right),$$

which is the payoff function. The first boundary condition is also obvious; as $R \to \infty$ the option will not be exercised and so

$$V(R, t) \to 0 \quad \text{as} \quad R \to \infty.$$

As with the previous example of the average strike option, the local behaviour of the option price at $R = 0$ determines the correct boundary condition there. For the option price to remain finite we need

$$\frac{\partial V}{\partial t} + \frac{\partial V}{\partial R} - rV = 0$$

on $R = 0$.

If the option is American then we do not require strict equality in (11.20), but we do require the constraint

$$V(R, t) \ge \max\left(1 - \frac{R}{t}, 0\right).$$

The American average strike FX-option leads to a free boundary problem and there is a free boundary $R = R_f(t)$ on which V and $\partial V / \partial R$ must be continuous.

11.8 Average rate options

The typical average rate option is very similar to the average strike option in that the payoff depends on a suitably defined average of the asset price. The difference is in the structural form of the payoff. Whereas the average strike is the same as a vanilla option except with the exercise price replaced by the average, the average rate has the same payoff as the vanilla but with the asset price replaced by the average. That is, an arithmetic average rate call option has payoff given by

$$\max(I/T - E, 0)$$

at expiry. Such options are usually more difficult to value than average strike options because, in general, they do not admit similarity reductions: typically, it is not possible to reduce the number of independent variables from three to two. This is certainly the case when the average is measured arithmetically. Generally, therefore, such problems must be solved numerically as described in Chapter 22. However, when the average is measured geometrically, it is possible to reduce the problem to one in two variables and we now show how to find explicit formulæ.

11.8.1 Geometric averaging and discrete sampling

It is known that there are explicit solutions for the value of average rate options when the average is measured geometrically (see Rubinstein 1992). This is because the logarithm of the asset price follows a random walk with variance which is independent of the asset price. There is also an intimate link between sums of logarithms and the geometric average. In this and the next section we demonstrate how to find these exact solutions from the partial differential equation formulation of the problem.

The explicit formulæ only exist for European options. Let us therefore consider a European average rate option with payoff at expiry given by

$$V(S, I, T) = \Lambda(I).$$

Observe that the payoff is here only a function of I and not of S; this makes an explicit solution possible.

The governing equation is

$$\frac{\partial V}{\partial t}+\sum_{i=1}^{N}\delta(t-t_i)\log S\frac{\partial V}{\partial I}+\tfrac{1}{2}\sigma^2S^2\frac{\partial^2 V}{\partial S^2}+rS\frac{\partial V}{\partial S}-rV=0, \quad (11.21)$$

that is, equation (9.7) with

$$f(S,t)=\sum_{i=1}^{N}\delta(t-t_i)\log S.$$

As usual, t_i denote the times at which the discrete samples are taken for the average and N denotes the total number of samples taken.

We seek a solution of (11.21) of the form

$$V(S,I,t)=F(y,t),$$

where

$$y=\frac{I+l(t)\log S}{N},$$

and where $l(t)$ is to be determined. With y and t as the independent variables, we can write (11.21) as

$$\begin{aligned}\frac{\partial F}{\partial t}+\frac{dl/dt\ \log S}{N}\frac{\partial F}{\partial y}+\frac{1}{N}\sum_i\delta(t-t_i)\log S\frac{\partial F}{\partial y}\\ +\frac{\sigma^2l^2(t)}{2N^2}\frac{\partial^2F}{\partial y^2}+\frac{l(t)}{N}\left(r-\tfrac{1}{2}\sigma^2\right)\frac{\partial F}{\partial y}-rF=0.\end{aligned} \quad (11.22)$$

The choice

$$l(t)=\int_t^T\sum_i\delta(\tau-t_i)d\tau$$

eliminates $\log S$ from the equation. Since the times t_i are known, this function is known. It is a step function which increases in value by one at each sampling date. The upper limit in this integral has been taken as T, so that at expiry $l=0$, $y=I$ and the payoff is a function of y only.

When the log terms have been eliminated, what remains is a modified diffusion equation with coefficients that are independent of the variable y. These coefficients are, however, functions of time, t. Therefore, what remains after the log terms are removed from

(11.22) is simply the Black–Scholes equation, under a logarithmic transformation with time-dependent volatility and interest rate and with a nonzero, time-dependent dividend yield. In particular, the effective volatility is given by

$$\frac{\sigma l(t)}{N}.$$

In Chapter 8 we saw that the Black–Scholes formulæ need only very simple modifications to yield explicit formulæ for time varying volatility, interest rate and dividend yield. For options with more complicated payoffs than calls or puts it is still possible to solve the constant coefficient partial differential equation by taking advantage of the general solution of the Black–Scholes equation with arbitrary final condition as given in Chapter 10.

The following rules show exactly how to modify simple Black–Scholes formulæ to value a similar geometric average rate option:

- Take the Black–Scholes formula for a vanilla option having the same payoff as the Asian but, of course, in terms of $e^{I/N}$ instead of S; for example,

  $$\max(e^{I/N} - E, 0) \quad \text{instead of} \quad \max(S - E, 0).$$

  Call this formula $V_{BS}(S, t; r, \sigma)$. (In the example described above, $V_{BS}(S, t; r, \sigma)$ is the formula for an option with payoff $\max(S - E, 0)$, i.e. a European call.)

- Wherever σ^2 appears in the formula for V_{BS}, replace it by

  $$\frac{1}{N^2(T-t)} \int_t^T \sigma^2 l^2(\tau)\, d\tau.$$

- Wherever r appears in the formula, replace it by

  $$\frac{1}{T-t} \int_t^T \left(r - \tfrac{1}{2}\sigma^2\right) \frac{l(\tau)}{N} + \frac{\sigma^2}{2N^2} l^2(\tau)\, d\tau.$$

- Multiply the resulting formula by

  $$\exp\left(- \int_t^T r - \frac{l(\tau)}{N} \left(r - \tfrac{1}{2}\sigma^2\right) - \frac{\sigma^2}{2N^2} l^2(\tau)\, d\tau \right).$$

- Replace S by $e^{I/N} S^{l(t)/N}$.

11.8.2 Geometric averaging and continuous sampling

When the geometric average is sampled continuously, I is given by

$$I = \int_0^t \log S(\tau)\, d\tau$$

and for a European option we must solve

$$\frac{\partial V}{\partial t} + \log S \frac{\partial V}{\partial I} + \tfrac{1}{2}\sigma^2 S^2 \frac{\partial^2 V}{\partial S^2} + rS\frac{\partial V}{\partial S} - rV = 0.$$

Again, if the payoff is a function of I only, we can seek a solution of the form $F(y,t)$, where now

$$y = \frac{I + (T-t)\log S}{T}.$$

With this independent variable the differential equation becomes a parabolic partial differential equation with coefficients that are independent of y.

Again explicit formulæ may be found, and the following rules show how to convert an explicit formula for a vanilla option into an explicit formula for a geometric average rate option:

- Take the Black–Scholes formula for a vanilla option having the same payoff as the Asian, but in terms of $e^{I/T}$ instead of S; for example

  $$\max(e^{I/T} - E, 0) \quad \text{instead of} \quad \max(S - E, 0).$$

  Call this $V_{BS}(S,t;r,\sigma)$. (In the example above, $V_{BS}(S,t;r,\sigma)$ is the formula for an option with payoff $\max(S-E,0)$, i.e. a European call.)

- Wherever σ^2 appears in the formula for V_{BS}, replace it by

  $$\frac{1}{T-t}\int_t^T \sigma^2 \frac{(T-\tau)^2}{T^2}\, d\tau.$$

  Thus, if σ is constant, the effective volatility is $\sigma^2(T-t)^2/3T^2$.

- Wherever r appears in the formula, replace it by

$$\frac{1}{T-t}\int_t^T \left(r-\tfrac{1}{2}\sigma^2\right)\frac{(T-\tau)}{T}\,d\tau.$$

  When r and σ are constant, the effective interest rate is thus $(\frac{1}{2}\sigma^2 - r)(T-t)/2T$.

- Multiply the resulting formula by

$$\exp\left(-\int_t^T \left(r-\frac{(T-\tau)}{T}\left(r-\tfrac{1}{2}\sigma^2\right)\right)d\tau\right).$$

  When r and σ are constant this factor is

$$\exp\Big(-(\sigma^2+(r-\tfrac{1}{2}\sigma^2)(T+t))(T-t)/2\Big).$$

- Replace S by $e^{I/T}S^{(T-t)/T}$.

11.8.3 The arithmetic average

The arithmetically averaged average rate option is harder to value than its geometrically averaged equivalent. It is not generally possible to eliminate one of the independent variables and the problem must always be solved in three dimensions. However, the arithmetic average rate problem is very easy to solve numerically once it has been posed in partial differential equation form. In this final section of this chapter we present some results for the value of a European arithmetic average rate put with discrete sampling. Details of the numerical method are in Chapter 22.

Such an option has a payoff of the form

$$V(S,I,T)=\max(E-I/N,0),$$

where, in this example,

$$I=\sum_{i=1}^{N} S(t_i).$$

This option value genuinely depends on all three independent variables S, I and t. In this example we neglect any dividends. We must solve the basic Black–Scholes equation with I as a parameter, together with the boundary conditions

$$V(0, I, t) = e^{-r(T-t)} \max(E - I/N, 0),$$

$$V(S, I, t) \to 0 \quad \text{as} \quad S \to \infty.$$

The jump conditions to be applied across the sampling dates are

$$V(S, I, t_i^-) = V(S, I + S, t_i^+).$$

In Figure 11.8 we show the value of the European arithmetic average rate put with $r = 0.1$, $\sigma = 0.2$ and $E = 1$ with one year before expiry. The average is defined as the arithmetic mean of the asset prices at 3.5, 7.5 and 11.5 months before expiry. With I as the running sum of the asset prices at the sampling dates, the payoff is given by

$$\max(1 - I/3, 0). \tag{11.23}$$

(In this case the number of sampling dates is 3.) In Figure 11.9 we show the corresponding delta, $\partial V/\partial S$.

At one year to expiry there have been no samples taken and so $I = 0$. Thus the value of the option as a function of S is the cross-section through Figure 11.8 along $I = 0$. Why then have we plotted a three-dimensional graph? The answer is that in solving the present problem we have also solved other average rate put option valuation problems in which the sampling started before one year to expiry. We can see this as follows. Consider an average rate put option with $N > 3$ samples, the last three of which occur at 3.5, 7.5 and 11.5 months before expiry with all the other samples being taken more than one year before expiry. Suppose that this option has exercise price E'. Thus the payoff is

$$\max(E' - I/N, 0).$$

This can be written as

$$\frac{3}{N} \max\left(\frac{NE'}{3} - \frac{I}{3}, 0\right).$$

This payoff is the same as (11.23) with $E = E'N/3$ and with a scaling factor $3/N$. Of course, in this example at one year to expiry

I is nonzero; there have been $N-3$ samples taken. Thus Figure 11.8 also gives the value an average rate put (after the scaling factor has been removed) with exercise price $E' = 3E/N$. We must show the full three-dimensional plot to convey the structure of this option. Note that it does not matter when the previous $N-3$ samples were taken, only the running sum to date.

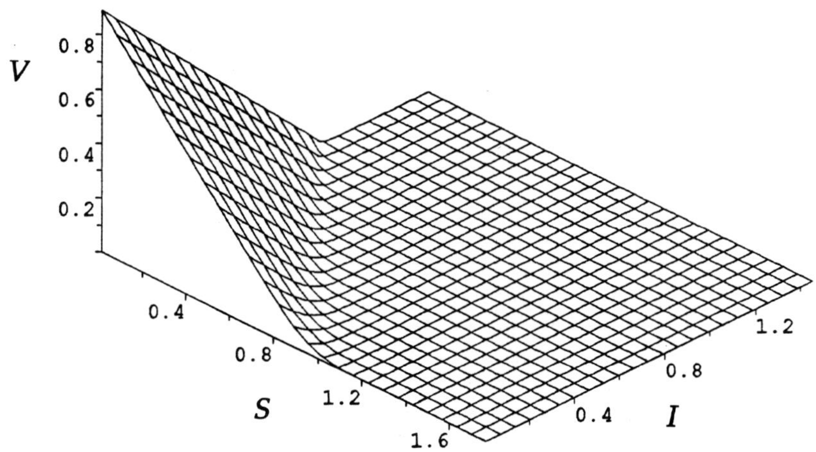

Figure 11.8: The value of a European average rate put as a function of both S and I; see the text for details of the contract.

Further reading

- Some exact solutions can be found in Boyle (1991).
- Ingersoll (1987) presents the partial differential equation formulation of some average strike options and demonstrates the similarity reduction.
- For other methods of evaluating Asian options see Geman & Yor (1992).
- The application of the numerical Monte Carlo method is described by Kemna & Vorst (1990).

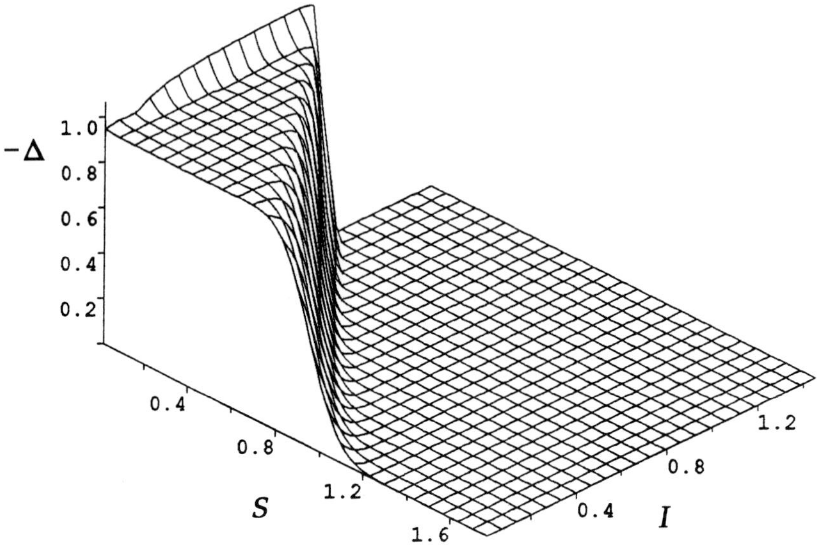

Figure 11.9: Minus the delta of a European average rate put as a function of both S and I; see the text for details of the contract.

- More examples of the methods described here can be found in Dewynne & Wilmott (1993 c, d).
- For an approximate valuation of arithmetic Asian options see Levy (1990) who replaces the density function for the distribution of the average by a lognormal function.

Exercises

1. Recall the jump conditions for the discretely sampled arithmetic average strike option. In this case the option price has a similarity reduction of the form $V(S, I, t) = SH(S/I, t)$. Write the jump conditions in terms of $H(\xi, t)$, where $\xi = S/I$.

2. Find similarity variables for the discretely and continuously sampled *geometric* Asian options. What form must the payoff function take?

3. Repeat the local analyses for the American foreign exchange continuously sampled average strike call and put options.

Chapter 12

Lookback Options

12.1 The lookback put

A lookback option is a derivative product whose payoff depends on the maximum or minimum realised asset price over the life of the option. For example, a **lookback put** has a payoff at expiry that is the difference of the maximum realised price and the price at expiry; this may be written as

$$\max(J - S, 0)$$

where J is the maximum realised price of the asset:

$$J = \max_{0 \le \tau \le t} S(\tau).$$

As for the Asian options considered in the previous chapter, the maximum or minimum realised asset price may be measured continuously or, more commonly, discretely.

Such options give the holder an extremely advantageous payoff. Using lookback options, one can construct a product enabling the investor to buy at the low and sell at the high. They are therefore relatively expensive. They were first described in the academic literature by Goldman, Sosin & Gatto (1979), who presented an explicit formula for a European option where the maximum is measured continuously throughout the life of the option.

We continue in the spirit of the analysis in Chapters 9 and 11. The general framework established in those chapters is sufficiently robust to include both European and American exercise features and continuous and discrete sampling; we now apply this framework to lookback options. As in the previous chapter we find that European lookbacks lead to partial differential equations with final and boundary conditions, whereas for American lookbacks we obtain a partial differential inequality subject to a constraint and, consequently, a linear complementarity problem. With discrete sampling we find that, as before, jump conditions apply across sampling dates. In general the option value is a function of the three variables S, J and t, but we find that if the payoff and dividend payments have the correct form then the problem admits a similarity reduction to two independent variables. When a similarity reduction can be found the option value may, in some cases, be determined explicitly. Even if it cannot be found explicitly, the similarity reduction allows more efficient numerical solution.

As in the examples in Chapter 11 on Asian options we consider, amongst others, the lookback *strike* and the lookback *rate*, in both call and put varieties. If J is the sampled maximum, the **lookback strike** put option has a payoff similar to a vanilla put but with J replacing the exercise price E, i.e. the payoff is

$$V(S, J, T) = \max(J - S, 0).$$

(This option admits a similarity reduction in the variables S/J and t.) Similarly, the **lookback rate** put has payoff similar to the vanilla put but with J replacing S, i.e.

$$V(S, J, T) = \max(E - J, 0),$$

where E is prescribed. (This option does not admit a similarity reduction and must be solved in three dimensions.)

We continue to work in the general framework introduced in Chapter 9 and then consider some special cases. At the end of the chapter we consider two perpetual options which depend on the maximum realised asset price, the 'Russian' and the 'stop-loss'. Both of these have simple exact solutions.

We concentrate on valuing a put option. The equivalent call option depends on the realised minimum of the asset price

$$J = \min_{0 \le \tau \le t} S(\tau)$$

but is otherwise so similar to the put option that we leave its valuation as an exercise.

12.2 Continuous sampling of the maximum

In this section we consider a put option that depends on the maximum value of the asset where the maximum is measured continuously. This measurement is shown schematically in Figure 12.1. Observe that the asset price is necessarily less than the maximum when the maximum is updated continuously:

$$0 \leq S \leq J.$$

This section also serves as an introduction to the case where the maximum is sampled at discrete times.

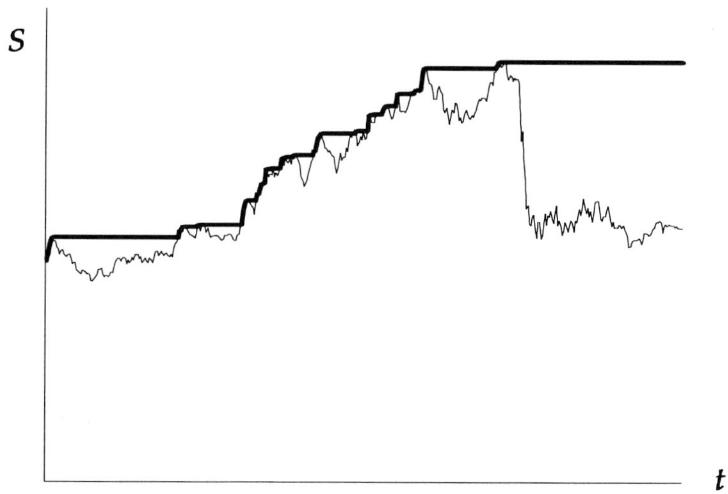

Figure 12.1: An example of continuous measurement of the maximum.

Since the lookback put is a path-dependent option, its value P is not simply a function of S and t, as is the case for a simple option. If the independent variable J is the maximum realised asset value over the life of the option, P also depends on J since it depends on

J at expiry. Thus

$$P = P(S, J, t).$$

It may not be immediately obvious how our general exotic option framework, for which the path-dependent quantity has been defined as an integral, can accommodate the lookback case. This is not as difficult as might be supposed. Let us define

$$J_n = \left(\int_0^t S(\tau)^n d\tau \right)^{1/n}. \tag{12.1}$$

This places the lookback option in our general setting if, using the notation of Chapter 9, we take

$$I = (J_n)^n$$

with $f(S,t) = S^n$. The strategy is to consider an option whose value depends on J_n and then take the limit as $n \to \infty$. In this limit we obtain a model for the lookback option. This is because in the limit as n tends to infinity we have[1]

$$J = \lim_{n \to \infty} J_n = \max_{0 \le \tau \le t} S(\tau).$$

We now derive the partial differential equation satisfied by an option whose value $P(S, J_n, t)$ depends on S, J_n and t. By letting n tend to infinity in this equation, we find the value of the lookback put, $P(S, J, t)$. Since we consider both European and American options, we present the valuation problem in a linear complementarity framework.

First we derive the stochastic differential equation satisfied by J_n. In the time t to $t + dt$, J_n changes by an amount dJ_n given by

$$J_n + dJ_n = \left(\int_0^{t+dt} S(\tau)^n d\tau \right)^{1/n}.$$

[1]At this point it is important to note that $S(\tau)$ is a *continuous* realisation of the random walk (2.1). If $S(\tau)$ in this integral is not continuous the result need not follow. We have not previously had cause to discuss the continuity of realisations of (2.1), and it is not obvious that we can make the assumption that $S(\tau)$ is continuous. A full discussion of the matter of continuous realisations is outside the scope of this text, and we refer the reader to Øksendal (1992). The basic result is that we can assume the continuity without loss of generality.

From this and (2.1) we see that

$$dJ_n = \frac{1}{n} \frac{S^n}{(J_n)^{n-1}} \, dt. \tag{12.2}$$

Thus J_n is a deterministic variable as there are no random terms in (12.2). We need (12.2) to apply Itô's lemma to P.

As we have done many times before we construct a hedged portfolio consisting of one option and a number $-\Delta$ of the underlying asset:

$$\Pi = P - \Delta S.$$

In the time from t to $t + dt$ the value of this portfolio changes by an amount $d\Pi$ given by

$$d\Pi = dP - \Delta \, dS - \Delta D(S, J_n, t) \, dt.$$

(We have again included a dividend of $D(S, J_n, t)$ on the underlying asset.) Choosing

$$\Delta = \frac{\partial P}{\partial S}$$

and using Itô's lemma to expand dP, remembering that P depends on the three variables S, J_n and t, we find that

$$d\Pi = \frac{\partial P}{\partial t} dt + \frac{1}{n} \frac{S^n}{(J_n)^{n-1}} \frac{\partial P}{\partial J_n} dt + \tfrac{1}{2}\sigma^2 S^2 \frac{\partial^2 P}{\partial S^2} dt - D(S, J_n, t) \frac{\partial P}{\partial S} dt. \tag{12.3}$$

When the option is American there may be times when it is optimal to exercise the option before expiry. We can only insist that the return is at most that to be received from a risk-free account, thus

$$d\Pi \leq r\Pi \, dt = r \left(P - S \frac{\partial P}{\partial S} \right) dt. \tag{12.4}$$

In the case of a European option we have equality in (12.4). Bringing together (12.3) and (12.4) we arrive at

$$\frac{\partial P}{\partial t} + \frac{1}{n} \frac{S^n}{(J_n)^{n-1}} \frac{\partial P}{\partial J_n} + \tfrac{1}{2}\sigma^2 S^2 \frac{\partial^2 P}{\partial S^2} + (rS - D(S, J_n, t)) \frac{\partial P}{\partial S} - rP \leq 0. \tag{12.5}$$

We now take the limit $n \to \infty$. Since $S \leq \max S = J$, in this limit the coefficient of $\partial V/\partial J_n$ tends to zero. Thus in this limit the partial differential inequality becomes

$$\frac{\partial P}{\partial t} + \tfrac{1}{2}\sigma^2 S^2 \frac{\partial^2 P}{\partial S^2} + (rS - D(S,J,t))\frac{\partial P}{\partial S} - rP \leq 0. \qquad (12.6)$$

This is simply the usual Black–Scholes inequality; for a European option it is the Black–Scholes equation. The independent variable J only appears as a parameter in this equation, but it also features in the boundary and final conditions.

The final condition for the equation is simply the payoff at expiry. The lookback put has

$$P(S,J,T) = \max(J - S, 0). \qquad (12.7)$$

This is the final condition regardless of whether the option is European or American or whether the sampling is continuous or discrete.

When the maximum is sampled continuously it is impossible for the asset price ever to exceed the sampled maximum; thus $S \leq J$. Therefore the problem is only posed on the region $0 \leq S \leq J$.

It is interesting to note that because $S \leq J$, the lookback put with a continuously sampled maximum is, in a sense, not an option: with probability one, it will be exercised. (The only case where it may not be exercised is in the unlikely event that the maximum realised asset value occurs at expiry.) A similar remark applies to the lookback strike call option.

12.2.1 The European case

When the option is European, arbitragers can hold both sides of the portfolio and so the inequality in (12.6) becomes equality. We have a final condition from (12.7), and boundary conditions are to applied at $S = 0$ and $S = J$.

If S is zero then it can never become greater than zero. The payoff at time T is known with certainty to be J. Hence the interest-rate discounted present value of the option is

$$P(0,J,t) = Je^{-r(T-t)}. \qquad (12.8)$$

The remaining boundary condition comes from considering the behaviour of the random walk close to the boundary $S = J$. Suppose that, at some time prior to expiry, S is close to its maximum realised so far, i.e. S is close to J. It can be shown that the probability that the current value of the maximum is still the maximum at expiry is zero. Since the present value of the maximum is not the final maximum, the value of the option must be insensitive to small changes in J. The remaining boundary condition is therefore

$$\frac{\partial P}{\partial J} = 0 \quad \text{on} \quad S = J. \tag{12.9}$$

These final and boundary conditions give a unique value for the option.

The explicit solution was found by Goldman, Sosin & Gatto (1979) when $D = 0$ and by Garman (1993) when $D = D_0 S$ with D_0 constant. When $D = 0$ the solution for the lookback put is

$$S\left(-1 + N(d_3)(1 + k_1^{-1})\right) + Je^{-r(T-t)}\left(N(d_1) - k_1^{-1}\left(\frac{S}{J}\right)^{1-k_1} N(d_2)\right),$$

where

$$d_1 = \frac{\log(J/S) - (r - \frac{1}{2}\sigma^2)t}{\sigma\sqrt{T-t}},$$

$$d_2 = \frac{\log(S/J) - (r - \frac{1}{2}\sigma^2)t}{\sigma\sqrt{T-t}},$$

$$d_3 = \frac{\log(J/S) + (r + \frac{1}{2}\sigma^2)t}{\sigma\sqrt{T-t}}$$

and

$$k_1 = r/\tfrac{1}{2}\sigma^2.$$

This formula can be derived by an extension of the method of images.

12.2.2 The American case

When early exercise is a possibility, the exercise price of the option must be specified for times prior to expiry. The natural specification for a lookback put is

$$\Lambda(S, J, t) = \max(J - S, 0).$$

When the option is American the possibility of early exercise means that we have inequality in (12.6). There may be times at which it is optimal to exercise the option as well as times when it should be held. For the lookback put we see that if S is less than some critical value $S_f(J,t)$ then it is, in fact, optimal to exercise.

Arbitrage considerations show that the value of the option must satisfy the constraint

$$P(S,J,t) \geq \Lambda(S,J,t) \tag{12.10}$$

since this is the payoff for early exercise. Further, all of P, $\partial P/\partial S$ and $\partial P/\partial J$ must be continuous.

The final condition (12.7) is satisfied at $t = T$ and, should the boundaries at $S = 0$ and/or $S = J$ ever lie in the hold region, the boundary conditions at $S = 0$, (12.8), and/or at $S = J$, (12.9), must also be satisfied. This completes the formulation of the American option problem.

For times before expiry $t < T$, $S = 0$ cannot lie in the hold region. This follows from (12.8) and (12.10); if $S = 0$ does lie in the hold region then

$$P(0,J,t) = Je^{-r(T-t)} < \Lambda(0,J,t) = J,$$

contrary to (12.10). Thus there must be an optimal exercise boundary $S_f(J,t)$ separating an early exercise region where $S < S_f(J,t)$ from a hold region where $S > S_f(J,t)$.

We can write this problem in linear complementarity form (and thereby eliminate explicit reference to $S_f(J,t)$) as follows. Define the linear operator $\mathcal{L}$ by

$$\mathcal{L}(P) = \frac{\partial P}{\partial t} + \tfrac{1}{2}\sigma^2 S^2 \frac{\partial^2 P}{\partial S^2} + (rS - D(S,J,t))\frac{\partial P}{\partial S} - rP;$$

this is, of course, the basic Black–Scholes operator. The American lookback put problem can be written as

$$\mathcal{L}(P) \leq 0 \quad \text{and} \quad (P - \Lambda(S,J,t)) \geq 0, \tag{12.11}$$

together with

$$\mathcal{L}(P) \cdot (P - \Lambda) = 0, \tag{12.12}$$

and the final condition

$$P(S, J, T) = \Lambda(S, J, T), \tag{12.13}$$

with the boundary condition

$$\frac{\partial P}{\partial J}(J, J) = 0. \tag{12.14}$$

The problem is only valid for $0 \le S \le J$; all of P, $\partial P/\partial S$ and $\partial P/\partial J$ must be continuous.

12.3 Discrete sampling of the maximum

Having set up the models for continuous sampling we now modify them to allow for discrete measurement of the maximum. This is a more practical model and corresponds to most lookback option contracts. Figure 12.2 shows an example of discrete measurement of the maximum. The ticks on the horizontal time axis represent the times at which the maximum is sampled. As we can see, the asset price can now exceed the sampled maximum if it does so between sampling dates. With J still denoting the maximum, albeit sampled discretely, it is no longer true that S must always be less than J. This is a very important difference between the continuously and discretely sampled cases: the domain on which the problem is posed is quite different. The payoff for the lookback put is still $\max(J - S, 0)$ but there now arises the possibility that the option will not be exercised; it will not be exercised at expiry if $S > J$.

When the maximum is sampled discretely we still obtain the Black–Scholes equation or inequality in S and t, with J entering only as a parameter. Across the sampling dates there is a jump condition. The financial argument for the jump condition is similar to that used in Chapter 8 for discrete dividends and Chapter 11 for Asian options. Arbitrage considerations show that the realised value of the option cannot be discontinuous. Thus $P(S, J, t)$ must be continuous as S, J and t vary. Across a sampling date the discretely sampled maximum is updated according to the rule

$$J(t_i) = \max(J(t_{i-1}), S),$$

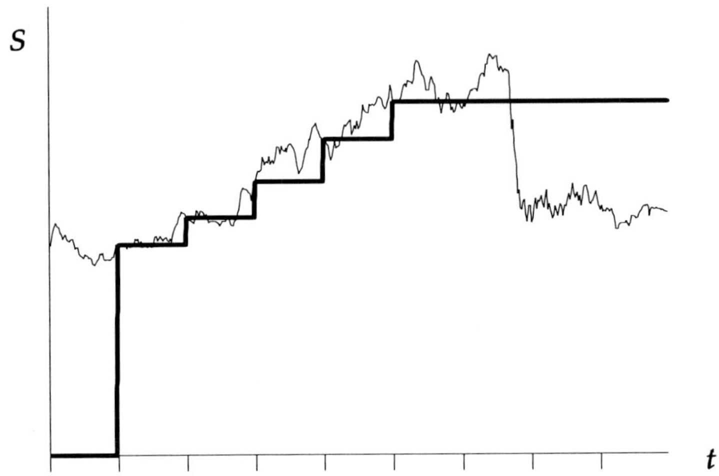

Figure 12.2: A schematic diagram of the discretely measured maximum. The ticks on the time axis are the sampling dates; J does not change between these dates.

where $J(t_i)$ is the value of J just after sampling at time t_i. Note that J then remains constant until immediately after t_{i+1}. Continuity of the realised put option price may be stated as

$$P(S(t_i^-), J(t_{i-1}), t_i^-) = P(S(t_i^+), J(t_i^+), t_i^+).$$

Writing J for $J(t_{i-1})$, this is equivalent to the jump condition

$$P(S, J, t_i^-) = P(S, \max(J, S), t_i^+)$$

in a Black–Scholes framework where S and J are considered independent variables.

We can also derive this jump condition from a mathematical argument. In order to parallel the analysis of the above section in the case of discrete sampling we define a new variable that measures the maximum value of the underlying asset at *discrete* times. Suppose that the maximum of the asset price is taken at times

$0 < t_1, \ldots, t_N < T$. Define

$$J_n = \left(\sum_{i=1}^{j(t)} S(t_i)^n \right)^{1/n}$$

where as in Chapter 11 $j(t)$ denotes the largest value of i such that $t_i < t$. In the limit as $n \to \infty$ we find that[2]

$$J = \lim_{n\to\infty} J_n = \max\left(S(t_1), S(t_2), \ldots, S(t_{j(t)})\right).$$

We may place this in the partial differential equation framework of Chapter 9 by observing that an equivalent definition of J_n is

$$J_n = \left(\int_0^t f(\tau) S(\tau)^n d\tau \right)^{1/n}, \qquad (12.15)$$

with

$$f(t) = \sum_{i=1}^{N} \delta(t - t_i).$$

In the limit as $n \to \infty$ we have

$$J = \lim_{n\to\infty} J_n = \max_{1 \le i \le j(t)} S(t_i).$$

With these definitions and using the analysis of Chapter 9, the inequality satisfied by $P(S, J_n, t)$ becomes

$$\frac{\partial P}{\partial t} + \frac{1}{n} \sum_{i=1}^{N} \delta(t - t_i) \frac{S^n}{(J_n)^{n-1}} \frac{\partial P}{\partial J_n}$$

$$+ \tfrac{1}{2}\sigma^2 S^2 \frac{\partial^2 P}{\partial S^2} + (rS - D(S, J_n, t)) S \frac{\partial P}{\partial S} - rP \le 0. \qquad (12.16)$$

We now consider the effect of discrete sampling while n is finite. As with discrete dividends and discrete sampling of other path-dependent quantities, we arrive at a jump condition across the sampling date. We need only consider the case where it is optimal to hold the option prior to a given sampling date t_i (otherwise, the option

[2] Since the sum here is discrete and finite, the continuity of S as a function of t is not an issue.

will not exist.) It may be the case that it becomes optimal to exercise immediately after the sampling date; this depends on whether the jump condition pushes the option value below its intrinsic value or not.

Across a sampling date t_i we find that (12.3) is approximately the first order hyperbolic equation

$$\frac{\partial P}{\partial t} + \frac{1}{n}\delta(t - t_i)\frac{S^n}{(J_n)^{n-1}}\frac{\partial P}{\partial J_n} = 0. \tag{12.17}$$

The characteristics are given by

$$\left(\frac{J_n}{S}\right)^n = \mathcal{H}(t - t_i) + \text{ constant},$$

and along these characteristics P is constant. From this follows the jump condition

$$P(S, J_n, t_i^-) = P(S, S(1 + (J_n/S)^n)^{1/n}, t_i^+). \tag{12.18}$$

In taking the limit $n \to \infty$ we must distinguish between the two cases $S > J_n$ and $S \leq J_n$. When $S \leq J_n$, which is always the case for continuous sampling, the second argument on the right-hand side of (12.18) simply tends to J. When $S > J_n$, however, this argument tends to S. We can conclude that the jump condition across the sampling dates t_i is

$$P(S, J, t_i^-) = P(S, \max(S, J), t_i^+). \tag{12.19}$$

12.3.1 The European case

The governing equation is simply the Black–Scholes equation, with J occurring only as a parameter. The final condition remains (12.7) but is now applied for all values of S and not just $S \leq J$. The boundary condition at $S = 0$ is again (12.8). There is no longer a boundary condition at $S = J$, since S is no longer constrained to be less than J; instead we must consider the behaviour of the option value as $S \to \infty$.

In the time between the last sampling and expiry, the value of the option decreases monotonically to zero with increasing S; no new maximum can be sampled, and the payoff is zero if $S \geq J$ at expiry.

This is not true at any other time. Indeed, it is possible for the delta of a lookback put option to be positive, unlike the delta for the simple vanilla put option. This is because, from the holder's point of view, the best thing that can happen is for the asset to register a new maximum at a sampling date and then drop significantly. The value of the option may therefore have a global minimum at a finite value of S. As far as the boundary condition is concerned all we can, and need, say is that the value of the option can grow at most linearly with S as $S \to \infty$. This is a sufficient boundary condition and, indeed, we cannot say *a priori* what the constant of proportionality is.

Another way to look at this is to consider what happens near the final sampling date. Between the final sampling and expiry the option value satisfies the Black–Scholes equation with a known exercise price $E = J$. Thus the solution to the problem during this time is simply the Black–Scholes European vanilla put value, for which there is an analytic expression. Call the solution, for the time between the final sampling and expiry, $P_{BS}(S, J, t)$. Now consider the jump condition (12.19) across the last sampling date. We have

$$P(S, J, t_N^-) = P_{BS}(S, \max(S, J), t_N^+),$$

where t_N is the final sampling date. We can use this to calculate $P_{BS}(S, \max(S, J), t_N^+)$ exactly, and this jump condition enables us to solve for the option value between the final and penultimate sampling dates. That is, using $P_{BS}(S, \max(S, J), t_N^+)$ we may calculate $P(S, J, t_N^-)$ from the jump condition. We then use this as final data, and solve the Black–Scholes equation back to the next sampling date t_{N-1}^+ (see Chapter 8 where a similar procedure was applied to discrete dividend payments).

Now consider the value of the option in the period between the final and penultimate sampling dates. Since J in P_{BS} is the final realised maximum it is certainly known and finite. Thus as $S \to \infty$ we have

$$P(S, J, t_i^-) = P_{BS}(S, S, t_i^+).$$

The right-hand side of this expression becomes unbounded, being proportional to S, as $S \to \infty$; it represents the value of a put with an arbitrarily large exercise price which is at the money with a finite time left to expiry. This illustrates the limiting behaviour of P for large S; it is linear in S. When we come to solve the problem numerically we may use either the boundary condition

$$\frac{S}{P}\frac{\partial P}{\partial S} \sim 1 \quad \text{as} \quad S \to \infty \tag{12.20}$$

or the condition that

$$\frac{\partial^2 P}{\partial S^2} \to 0 \quad \text{as} \quad S \to \infty. \tag{12.21}$$

12.3.2 The American case

This case can again be formulated as a linear complementarity problem. It is essentially the same as (12.11), (12.12) and (12.13) but with some exceptions. We must further impose the jump condition (12.19) and the boundary conditions (12.8) and (12.20) should $S = 0$ and/or $S = \infty$ lie in the hold region. Since the boundary condition (12.8) violates the constraint $P \geq \Lambda$, there is always an optimal exercise boundary; for small S it is always optimal to exercise early. For sufficiently large S it is never optimal to exercise early.

12.4 Transformation to a single state variable

The formulation of the problem has so far used the 'primitive variables' S, J, t. In this section we show how to recast some lookback problems in terms of only two variables; we thus seek similarity reductions and solutions.

The lookback option model presented so far is very general in that it permits the following:

- an arbitrary dividend structure $D(S, J, t)$;
- an arbitrary payoff (at expiry or earlier) $\Lambda(S, J, t)$;

these are simple modifications to the discussion presented above.

If we make some restrictions on the class of dividend and payoff structures that are admissible, we may take the analysis further and find classes of lookbacks that depend on only time and a single state variable. The restrictions that we make are

- a dividend yield of the form $D(S, J, t) = S\hat{D}(S/J, t)$;
- a payoff of the form $\Lambda(S, J, t) = J\bar{\Lambda}(S/J, t)$.

Note that the lookback put has payoff

$$J \max(1 - S/J, 0)$$

and therefore satisfies the second requirement.

With these restrictions we may find a solution of the form

$$P(S, J, t) = JW(\xi, t), \tag{12.22}$$

where

$$\xi = S/J. \tag{12.23}$$

In the following we only describe the European option; the modification for an American option is simple and left as an exercise. To keep the analysis as uncluttered as possible, we examine the zero-dividend case; again the inclusion of nonzero dividends with the structure given above is simple and is left as an exercise.

With these definitions for W and ξ we find that the partial differential equation for $W(\xi, t)$ is

$$\frac{\partial W}{\partial t} + \tfrac{1}{2}\sigma^2\xi^2\frac{\partial^2 W}{\partial \xi^2} + r\xi\frac{\partial W}{\partial \xi} - rW = 0 \tag{12.24}$$

and the boundary condition at $S = 0$ becomes

$$W(0, t) = e^{-r(T-t)}. \tag{12.25}$$

The final condition for a lookback put becomes

$$W(\xi, T) = \max(1 - \xi, 0). \tag{12.26}$$

When the maximum is measured continuously, the boundary condition at $S = J$ becomes a boundary condition at $\xi = 1$ and is

$$\frac{\partial W}{\partial \xi} = W \quad \text{on} \quad \xi = 1. \tag{12.27}$$

If the maximum is measured discretely, the boundary condition as $S \to \infty$ becomes a boundary condition as $\xi \to \infty$, and is

$$\frac{\xi}{W}\frac{\partial W}{\partial \xi} \sim 1 \quad \text{as} \quad \xi \to \infty. \tag{12.28}$$

The jump condition across sampling dates becomes

$$W(\xi, t_i^-) = \max(\xi, 1)\, W(\min(\xi, 1), t_i^+). \tag{12.29}$$

12.5 Some examples

In this section we give some results for simple lookback puts. The numerical analysis is to be found in Chapters 18-21 for lookbacks which admit similarity reductions, and in Chapter 22 for more general lookback options which depend on three independent variables S, J and t.

In Figures 12.3 and 12.4 we see comparisons between American and European option prices using different sets of sampling times. In each case the values shown are at one year before expiry with zero dividend yield, $r = 0.1$ and $\sigma = 0.2$. Figure 12.3 shows option values for the American option and Figure 12.4 for the equivalent European option.

ξ	A	B	C	O
0.9	0.125	0.120	0.114	0.104
1.0	0.105	0.095	0.081	0.048
1.1	0.111	0.098	0.082	0.021

Figure 12.3: American lookback put values for $r = 0.1$, $\sigma = 0.2$, $T = 1.0$. Cases A, B and C correspond to sampling at different times (see text for details). Case O corresponds to no sampling; this is the simple put with exercise price 1.0.

There are three examples of the sampling of the maximum and one simple vanilla put problem for comparison. The latter is Case O; this is exactly equivalent to a vanilla put option with unit exercise

ξ	A	B	C	O
0.9	0.101	0.094	0.087	0.074
1.0	0.089	0.079	0.067	0.038
1.1	0.095	0.083	0.068	0.017

Figure 12.4: European lookback put values for $r = 0.1$, $\sigma = 0.2$, $T = 1.0$. Cases A, B and C correspond to sampling at different times (see text for details). Case O corresponds to no sampling; this is the simple put with exercise price 1.0.

price. Otherwise we have

Case A: sampling at times 0.5, 1.5, 2.5, ... 10.5, 11.5 months;

Case B: sampling at times 1.5, 3.5, 5.5, 7.5, 9.5, 11.5 months;

Case C: sampling at times 3.5, 7.5, 11.5 months.

The tables should be read as follows. Suppose the value of an American lookback put option with discrete sampling under sampling strategy B is required. Recall that the value of the option is given by

$$P = JW(S/J, t).$$

If we want the value of the option at one year to expiry when the asset price is 180 and the current maximum is 200 then we must look along the row $\xi = S/J = 180/200 = 0.9$. The value of the option is then $200 \times 0.120 = 24$.

Observe that the option price decreases as the number of samples decreases (from A to C). This is financially obvious, since the fewer samples the lower the final payoff is likely to be. Decreasing the frequency of measurement of the maximum decreases their cost. This may be important since one of the commercial criticisms of lookback options is that they are too expensive. Also note that the option price reaches a minimum close to $\xi = 1$. The option delta can become positive since it is beneficial for the holder of the option if the asset price rises just before a sampling date and then falls. As expected, American prices are everywhere greater than European.

12.6 Two 'perpetual options'

We have seen one explicit formula for a simple lookback put and in the exercise at the end of this chapter we make suggestions for finding more. In this section we find two more explicit formulæ, for a 'Russian' option and a 'stop-loss' option. Both of these lookback options share the property that they are perpetual options, i.e. they do not have an expiry date but rather an infinite time horizon. (Another perpetual option was the perpetual barrier option, an exercise in Chapter 10.)

12.6.1 Russian options

A **Russian option** (see Duffie & Harrison 1992) is a perpetual American option which, at any time chosen by the owner, pays out the maximum realised asset price up to that date. We only consider the continuously sampled maximum case as it is unlikely that an explicit solution exists if the sampling is discrete. The explicit solution also requires that the dividend is independent of time, hence we only consider a constant dividend yield $D(S, J, t) = D_0 S$. This is easiest case for which an explicit solution may be found. As the time horizon the solution is infinite we may take the option value to be *independent of time:* $V = V(S, J)$. (With discrete sampling at periodic intervals the solution would also be periodic.)

As before, let J be the maximum realised value of the asset price. When it is optimal to hold and the option exists, we solve the time-independent Black–Scholes equation

$$\tfrac{1}{2}\sigma^2 S^2 \frac{\partial^2 V}{\partial S^2} + (r - D_0) S \frac{\partial V}{\partial S} - rV = 0$$

with the boundary condition

$$\frac{\partial V}{\partial J} = 0 \quad \text{on} \quad J = S.$$

The solution must also satisfy

$$V \geq J$$

since the option is American and the right-hand side of this inequality is the early exercise payoff. Thus, if there is a free boundary (and as we show, there is), both V and $\partial V / \partial S$ must be continuous there.

Let us seek a solution in the form

$$V = JW(\xi)$$

where $\xi = S/J$. Then we have

$$\tfrac{1}{2}\sigma^2\xi^2 W'' + (r - D_0)\xi W' - rW = 0, \qquad (12.30)$$

where $'$ denotes $d/d\xi$. Suppose that the free boundary is at $\xi = \xi_0$. The boundary conditions become

$$W - W' = 0 \quad \text{at} \quad \xi = 1$$

and

$$W = 1 \quad \text{and} \quad W' = 0 \quad \text{at} \quad \xi = \xi_0.$$

The general solution of (12.30) is found by trying $W = \text{const.}\xi^\alpha$ for constant α. This yields a quadratic equation for α, whose roots are

$$\alpha_\pm = \frac{1}{\sigma^2}\left(-r + D_0 + \tfrac{1}{2}\sigma^2 \pm \sqrt{(r - D_0 - \tfrac{1}{2}\sigma^2)^2 + \tfrac{1}{2}\sigma^2 r}\right). \qquad (12.31)$$

The solution to the boundary value problem is then easily found to be

$$W = \frac{1}{\alpha_+ - \alpha_-}\left(\alpha_+\left(\frac{\xi}{\xi_0}\right)^{\alpha_-} - \alpha_-\left(\frac{\xi}{\xi_0}\right)^{\alpha_+}\right),$$

where the free boundary conditions give

$$\xi_0 = \left(\frac{\alpha_+(1-\alpha_-)}{\alpha_-(1-\alpha_+)}\right)^{1/(\alpha_- - \alpha_+)}.$$

When the dividend yield is zero, i.e. $D_0 = 0$, the problem does not have a solution. It is, clearly, never optimal to hold such an option when the underlying does not pay dividends.

12.6.2 The stop-loss option

A **stop-loss option** may be thought of as a perpetual barrier lookback with a rebate that is a fixed proportion of the maximum realised value of the asset price. Thus, if S reaches a maximum value J and then falls back to λJ, where $\lambda < 1$, the option pays the owner S (which at that time is equal to λJ). It has an obvious use to lock in a good proportion of a profit while relieving the owner of the uncertainty of guessing when the maximum is reached. Note that the option is not triggered until this fall occurs.

Since the option pays the owner the amount S when S reaches λJ we have

$$V(\lambda J, J) = \lambda J. \tag{12.32}$$

We again write $V = JW(\xi)$ where, as before, $\xi = S/J$. The differential equation is again (12.30), (12.32) becomes

$$W(\lambda) = \lambda,$$

and the remaining boundary condition is

$$W - W' = 0 \quad \text{at} \quad \xi = 1.$$

The solution is

$$W = \lambda \frac{\xi^{\alpha_+}(1-\alpha_-) - \xi^{\alpha_-}(1-\alpha_+)}{\lambda^{\alpha_+}(1-\alpha_-) - \lambda^{\alpha_-}(1-\alpha_+)},$$

where $\alpha_\pm$ are given by (12.31). When $D_0 = 0$ the solution is

$$W = \xi$$

irrespective of λ, i.e. $V = S$: the option is equivalent to the underlying.

Further reading

- Some more explicit solutions are given by Conze & Viswanathan (1991).

- More numerical results can be found in Dewynne & Wilmott (1993 b).

- The stop-loss option when the maximum is measured discretely is covered in Fitt, Wilmott & Dewynne (1993).

Exercises

1. Derive the explicit formula for the value of a European lookback put.

2. Find explicit formulæ in the following cases, all with continuous sampling of the maximum or minimum:
   (a) lookback call, with payoff $\max(S - J, 0)$, where J is the asset price minimum;
   (b) lookback calls and puts with constant dividend yield;
   (c) lookback calls and puts with time varying volatility, interest rate and dividend yield.

Chapter 13

Options with Transaction Costs

13.1 Discrete hedging

We have derived the Black–Scholes partial differential equation for simple option prices, we have discussed the general theory behind the diffusion equation and, in the last few chapters, we have generalised the Black–Scholes model to exotic options. We continue this generalisation with a model which incorporates the effects of **transaction costs** on a hedged portfolio. We only describe the model for vanilla options but it can easily be modified for exotic options.

One of the key assumptions of the Black–Scholes analysis is that the portfolio is rehedged continuously: we take the limit $dt \to 0$. If the costs associated with rehedging (e.g. bid-offer spread on the underlying) are independent of the timescale of rehedging then the infinite number of transactions needed to maintain a hedged position until expiry leads to infinite total transaction costs. Since the Black–Scholes analysis is based on a hedged portfolio, the consequences of significant costs associated with rehedging are important. Different people have different levels of transaction costs; as a general rule there are economies of scale, so that the larger the trader's book, the less significant are her costs. Thus, contrary to the basic Black–Scholes model, we may expect that there is no unique option value. Instead, the value of the option depends on the investor.

Leland (1985) has proposed a very simple modification to the

Black–Scholes model for vanilla calls and puts (extended to portfolios of options by Hoggard, Whalley & Wilmott (1993)) which introduces discrete revision of the portfolio and transaction costs. In the main his assumptions are those mentioned in Chapter 3 for the Black–Scholes model with the following exceptions:

- The portfolio is revised every δt where now δt is a finite fixed time-step; note that we do not take $\delta t \to 0$. For example, the portfolio may be rehedged every day at 9:00 a.m.

- The random walk is given in discrete time by

$$\delta S = \sigma S \phi \sqrt{\delta t} + \mu S \, \delta t$$

  where ϕ is drawn from a standardised normal distribution.

- Transaction costs in buying or selling the asset are proportional to the monetary value of the transaction. Thus if ν shares are bought ($\nu > 0$) or sold ($\nu < 0$) at a price S, then the transaction costs are $k|\nu|S$, where k is a constant depending on the individual investor. A more complex cost structure can be incorporated into the model with only a small amount of effort (see the exercise at the end of this chapter).

- The hedged portfolio has an *expected* return equal to that from a bank deposit.

We now derive a model for portfolios of European options incorporating transaction costs. We can follow the Black–Scholes analysis up to equation (3.6) but in equation (3.7) we must allow for the cost of the transaction. If Π denotes the value of the hedged portfolio and $\delta\Pi$ the change in the portfolio over the timestep δt, then we must subtract the cost of any transaction from the right-hand side of the equation for $\delta\Pi$.

After a time-step the change in the value of the hedged portfolio is then

$$\delta\Pi = \sigma S \left(\frac{\partial V}{\partial S} - \Delta \right) \phi \sqrt{\delta t} + \left(\tfrac{1}{2}\sigma^2 S^2 \frac{\partial^2 V}{\partial S^2} \phi^2 + \mu S \frac{\partial V}{\partial S} + \frac{\partial V}{\partial t} - \mu \Delta S \right) \delta t - kS \mid \nu \mid . \tag{13.1}$$

Here we have subtracted off the transaction costs (which are always positive, hence the modulus sign $|\ \ |$ above). Since we have not gone to the limit $\delta t = 0$ we cannot replace the square of the random variable ϕ by its expected value, 1. The remainder of the above equation is the same as in Chapter 3.

Let us follow the same hedging strategy as before and choose $\Delta = \partial V/\partial S$. The number of assets held is therefore

$$\Delta = \frac{\partial V}{\partial S}(S,t)$$

where this has been evaluated at time t and asset value S. After a timestep δt and rehedging, the number of assets we hold becomes

$$\frac{\partial V}{\partial S}(S+\delta S, t+\delta t).$$

This has been evaluated at the new time and asset price. On subtracting one from the other we find the number of assets we have bought or sold. This is

$$\nu = \frac{\partial V}{\partial S}(S+\delta S, t+\delta t) - \frac{\partial V}{\partial S}(S,t).$$

We can apply Taylor's theorem to expand the first term for small δS and δt. Since $\delta S = \sigma S \phi \sqrt{\delta t} + O(\delta t)$, the dominant term is that which is proportional to δS; this term is $O(\sqrt{\delta t})$ whereas the other terms are $O(\delta t)$. We find that to leading order the number of assets bought (sold) is

$$\nu \approx \frac{\partial^2 V}{\partial S^2}(S,t)\,\delta S \approx \frac{\partial^2 V}{\partial S^2}\sigma S \phi \sqrt{\delta t}.$$

Thus the expected transaction cost in a time-step, $\mathcal{E}[kS|\nu|]$, is

$$\sqrt{\frac{2}{\pi}}k\sigma S^2 \left|\frac{\partial^2 V}{\partial S^2}\right| \sqrt{\delta t}. \qquad (13.2)$$

(The factor $\sqrt{2/\pi}$ comes from calculating the expected value of $|\phi|$ using (2.2).) With our choice of Δ and (13.2) as the expected transaction cost, we can calculate the expected change in the value of our portfolio from (13.1):

$$\mathcal{E}[\delta\Pi] = \left(\frac{\partial V}{\partial t} + \tfrac{1}{2}\sigma^2 S^2 \frac{\partial^2 V}{\partial S^2} - \sqrt{\frac{2}{\pi}}\frac{k\sigma S^2}{\sqrt{\delta t}}\left|\frac{\partial^2 V}{\partial S^2}\right|\right)\delta t. \qquad (13.3)$$

Observe that except for the modulus sign, the new term above, which is proportional to the transaction costs, is of the same form as the second S derivative that has appeared before.

If we assume that the holder of the option *expects* to make as much from his portfolio as if he had put the money in the bank, then we can replace the $\mathcal{E}[\delta\Pi]$ in (13.3) with $r(V - S\partial V/\partial S)\,\delta t$ as before to yield an equation for the value of the option:

$$\frac{\partial V}{\partial t} + \tfrac{1}{2}\sigma^2 S^2 \frac{\partial^2 V}{\partial S^2} - \sqrt{\frac{2}{\pi}}\frac{k\sigma S^2}{\sqrt{\delta t}}\left|\frac{\partial^2 V}{\partial S^2}\right| + rS\frac{\partial V}{\partial S} - rV = 0. \qquad (13.4)$$

The financial interpretation of the additional term not appearing in the Black–Scholes equation is clear if we recall the comments in the section on hedging. The second derivative of the option price with respect to the asset price is the gamma, $\Gamma = \partial^2 V/\partial S^2$. This is a measure of the degree of mishedging of the hedged portfolio. The leading order component of randomness has been eliminated—this is delta-hedging—leaving behind a small component proportional to the gamma. Thus the gamma is related to the amount of rehedging that takes place in the next time interval and hence to the costs expected.

The equation—which is a *nonlinear* parabolic partial differential equation, one of the few such in finance—is also valid for a portfolio of derivative products. This is the only time in this book that we notice any difference between single options and a portfolio of options. The reason for this is simply that, since (13.4) is nonlinear, the value of a portfolio which is the sum of individual options is not the same as sum of the values of the individual components. We can best see this by taking a very extreme case.

Suppose we have a position in two call options with the same exercise price and the same expiry date and on the same underlying asset. However, one of these is held long and the other short. Our net position is therefore zero. Our book of options is so large that we do not notice the cancellation effect of the two opposite positions and so decide to hedge each of them separately. Because of transaction costs we lose money at each rehedge on both options. At expiry we have a negative net balance, since the two payoffs cancel out but the costs remain. This contrasts greatly with our net balance at expiry if we realise that our positions are opposite. In the latter case we never rehedge, which leaves us with no transaction costs and a net balance of zero at expiry.

We give numerical results for a portfolio of options below. First, however, we consider the effect of costs on a single option held long. We know that

$$\frac{\partial^2 V}{\partial S^2} > 0$$

for a single call or put held long in the absence of transaction costs, as can be shown by differentiating (3.16) and (3.17). Let us postulate that this is true for a single call or put when transaction costs are present. We thus drop the modulus sign from (13.4) for the moment. With the notation

$$\breve{\sigma}^2 = \sigma^2 - 2\sqrt{\frac{2}{\pi}}\frac{k\sigma}{\sqrt{\delta t}}. \tag{13.5}$$

the equation for the value of the option is identical to the Black–Scholes value with the exception that the actual variance σ^2 is replaced by the modified variance $\breve{\sigma}^2$. Thus our assumption that $\partial^2 V/\partial S^2 > 0$ even in the presence of transaction costs is true for a single vanilla option. This is one way of valuing a long position on an option with transaction costs.

For a short option position we change all the signs in the above analysis with the exception of the transaction cost term, which must always be a drain on the portfolio. We then find that the option is valued using the new variance

$$\hat{\sigma}^2 = \sigma^2 + 2\sqrt{\frac{2}{\pi}}\frac{k\sigma}{\sqrt{\delta t}}. \tag{13.6}$$

The results (13.5) and (13.6) show that a long position in a single call or put has an apparent volatility that is less than the actual volatility. This is because when the asset price rises the owner of the option must sell some of the asset to remain delta hedged; however, the effect of the bid-offer spread on the underlying is to reduce the price at which the asset is sold and so the effective increase in the asset price is less than the actual increase. The converse is true for a short option position.

Staying with a single call or put, we can get some idea of the total transaction costs associated with the above strategy by examining the difference between the value of an option with the modified variance and that with the usual variance; that is, the difference between the value of the option taking into account the costs and the Black–Scholes value. Thus consider

$$V(S,t) - \hat{V}(S,t)$$

with the obvious notation. Expanding this expression for small k we find that it becomes

$$\frac{\partial V}{\partial \sigma}(\sigma - \hat{\sigma}) + \cdots.$$

Since we know the formula for a European call option we find the expected spread to be

$$\frac{2kSN(d_1)\sqrt{(T-t)}}{\sqrt{2\pi\delta t}},$$

where

$$N(x) = \frac{1}{\sqrt{2\pi}}\int_{-\infty}^{x} e^{-\frac{1}{2}y^2}\,dy$$

and

$$d_1 = \frac{\log(S/E) + (r + \frac{1}{2}\sigma^2)(T-t)}{\sigma\sqrt{T-t}}.$$

Perhaps the most important quantity which appears in this model is

$$K = \frac{k}{\sigma\sqrt{\delta t}}. \tag{13.7}$$

If $K \gg 1$ then the transaction costs term swamps the basic variance. This implies that costs are too high and that the chosen δt is too small. The portfolio is being rehedged too often[1].

If $K \ll 1$ then the costs term only affects the basic variance marginally. This implies very low transaction costs. Hence δt is too large, and it should be decreased to minimise risk. The portfolio is being rehedged too seldom.

[1]If the transaction costs are very large or the portfolio is rehedged very often then it is possible to have $k > 2\sigma\sqrt{2\delta t/\pi}$. If this is the case then the diffusion equation has a negative coefficient for a long option position and is thus ill-posed. This is because, although the asset price may have risen, its effective value due to the addition of the costs will have actually dropped.

13.2 Portfolios of options

We now consider the valuation of portfolios of options. For a general portfolio of options, the curvature of V with respect to S is not of one sign. In this case we cannot drop the modulus sign. Since the problem is nonlinear we must in general solve equation (13.4) numerically, except in some very special cases such as the single option mentioned above. Numerical techniques are the subject of later chapters of this book and for the moment we simply present some results.

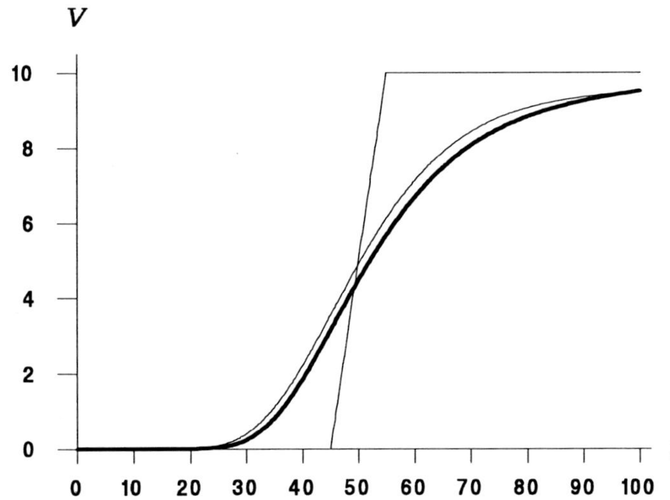

Figure 13.1: The value of a bullish vertical spread with (bold) and without transaction costs. The payoff is also shown.

In Figures 13.1 and 13.2 we show the value of a long bullish vertical spread (one long call with $E = 45$ and one short call with $E = 55$) and the delta at six months before expiry for the two cases, with and without transaction costs. The volatility is 0.4 and the interest rate 0.1. The bold curve shows the values in the presence of transaction costs and the other curve in the absence of transaction costs. In this example $K = 0.25$. The latter is simply the Black–Scholes value for the combination of the two options. The bold line approaches the other line as the transaction costs decrease.

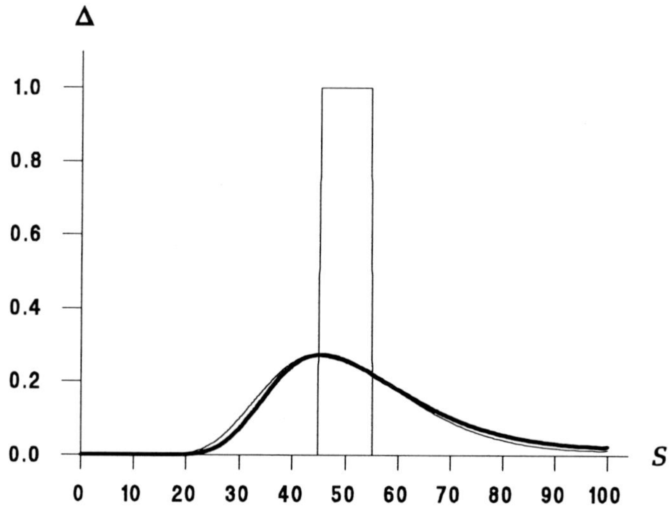

Figure 13.2: The delta for a bullish vertical spread prior to and at expiry with (bold) and without transaction costs.

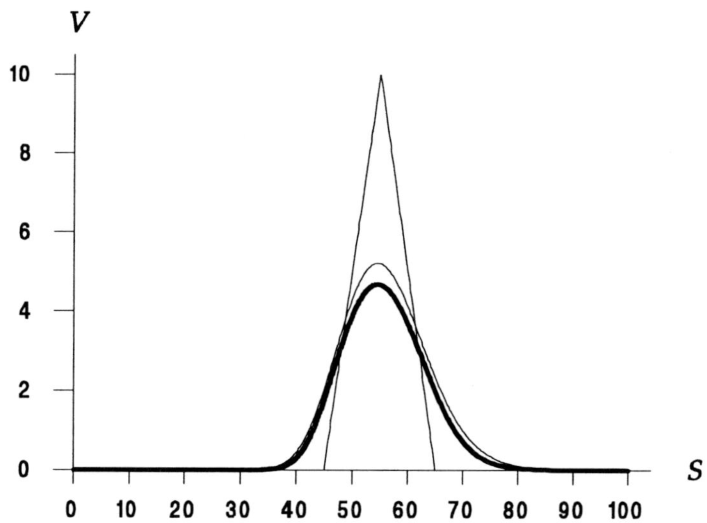

Figure 13.3: The value of a butterfly spread with (bold) and without transaction costs.

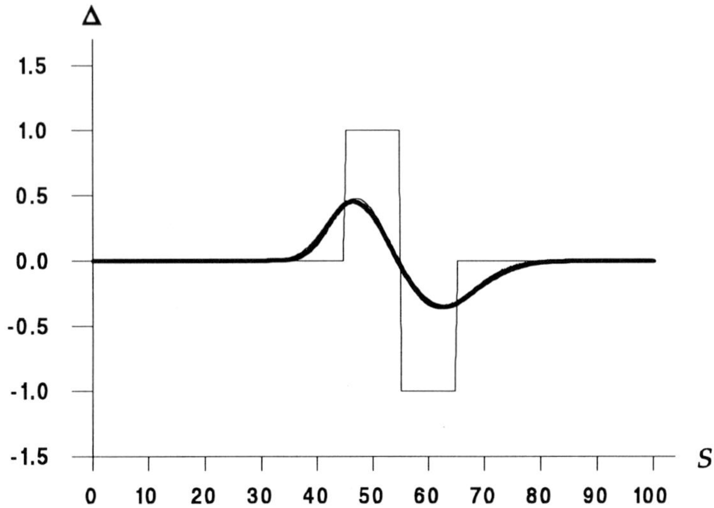

Figure 13.4: The delta for a butterfly spread with (bold) and without transaction costs.

In Figures 13.3 and 13.4 we show the value of a long butterfly spread and its delta, before and at expiry. A butterfly spread is made up of three types of options with three different exercise prices. In this example the portfolio contains one long call with $E = 45$, two short calls with $E = 55$ and another long call with $E = 65$. The results are with one month until expiry for the two cases, with and without transaction costs. The volatility, the interest rate and K are as in the previous example. Other examples may be found in Hoggard, Whalley and Wilmott (1993).

Further reading

- All the material of this chapter is based on the model of Leland (1985).
- Boyle & Emanuel (1980) explain some of the problems associated with the *discrete* rehedging of an option portfolio.
- Gemmill (1992) gives an example taken from practice of the effect of transaction costs on a hedged portfolio.

- Whalley & Wilmott (1993) discuss various hedging strategies and derive more nonlinear equations using ideas similar to those in this chapter.
- For alternative approaches involving 'optimal strategies' see Hodges & Neuberger (1989) and Davis & Norman (1990).

Exercise

1. Generalise the analysis of this chapter to include transaction costs which have three components: a fixed cost at each transaction, a cost proportional to the number of assets traded and a cost proportional to the value of the assets traded (only the last is included in our analysis here). Show that under this general cost structure option prices can become negative. Is this financially reasonable? In the light of this, can the model be improved? (See Whalley & Wilmott (1993) for a discussion of this subject.)

Chapter 14

Interest Rate Derivative Products

14.1 Introduction

In this chapter we introduce the subject of bond pricing. We do this first under the assumption of constant interest rate. This simplification allows us to discuss the effect of coupons on the prices of bonds and the appearance of the yield curve, which we define shortly. Later in the chapter we relax the assumption of constant interest rates and present a model which allows the short term interest rate, the spot rate, to follow a random walk. This leads to a parabolic partial differential equation for the prices of bonds and to models for bond options and many other interest rate derivative products.

14.2 Basics of bond pricing

A **bond** is a contract, paid for up front, which yields a known amount on a known date in the future, the **maturity date**[1], $t = T$. The bond may also pay a known cash dividend (the **coupon**) at fixed times during the life of the contract. If there is no dividend payment the bond is known as a **zero-coupon bond**. Bonds may be issued by both governments or companies. The main purpose of a bond issue is the raising of capital, and the up-front premium can be thought of as a loan to the government or the company.

[1]Convention has it that bonds 'mature' while options 'expire'.

The problem of valuing a bond can be illustrated by the question

- How much should one pay now to get a guaranteed \$1 in 10 years' time?

As with option models we aim to find the fair value of the contract. In this example the life-span of the bond is 10 years, in contrast to a typical equity option's life-span of nine months or less. For this reason the modelling of any time-dependent process must be more accurate when pricing bonds. It is not true, for instance, that interest rates remain constant for 10-year periods. However, we begin this chapter with the simplest model for a bond using the assumption that r is a known function of time. Having established a theoretical framework, we then introduce a model for stochastic interest rate movements.

14.2.1 Bond pricing with known interest rates

We continue to use the notation V to represent the price of the contract, in this case a bond. If the interest rate $r(t)$ and coupon payment $K(t)$ are known functions of time, the bond price is also a function of time only: $V = V(t)$. (The bond price is, of course, also a function of maturity date T, but we suppress that dependence except when it is important.) If this bond pays the owner $\$Z$ at time $t = T$ then we know that $V(T) = Z$. We now derive an equation for the value of the bond at a time before maturity, $t < T$.

Suppose we hold one bond. The change in the value of that bond in a time-step dt (from t to $t + dt$) is

$$\frac{dV}{dt}\,dt.$$

If during this period we have received a coupon payment of $K(t)\,dt$, which can include both continuous and discrete payments, our holdings including cash change by an amount

$$\left(\frac{dV}{dt} + K(t)\right) dt.$$

Arbitrage considerations again lead us to equate this with the return from a bank deposit receiving interest at a rate $r(t)$. Thus we conclude that

$$\frac{dV}{dt} + K(t) = r(t)V;$$

the right-hand side is the return we would have received had we converted our bond into cash at time t. The solution of this ordinary differential equation is easily found with the help of the integrating factor $e^{-\int^t r(\tau)d\tau}$ to be

$$V(t) = e^{-\int_t^T r(\tau)d\tau}\left(Z + \int_t^T K(t')e^{\int_{t'}^T r(\tau)d\tau}dt'\right); \tag{14.1}$$

the arbitrary constant of integration has been chosen to ensure that $V(T) = Z$. Note that a positive coupon payment increases the value of the bond at time t.

Now suppose that there exist zero-coupon bonds with all possible maturity dates. Still supposing that the interest rate is deterministic, we have

$$V(t,T) = Ze^{-\int_t^T r(\tau)d\tau}, \tag{14.2}$$

from (14.1) with $K = 0$ (we have now made the dependence on T explicit). If the bond prices are quoted today, at time t, for all values of the maturity date T then we know the left-hand side of (14.2) for all values of T. Thus

$$-\int_t^T r(\tau)\,d\tau = \log(V(t,T)/Z). \tag{14.3}$$

If $V(t,T)$ is differentiable with respect to T, then differentiating (14.3) we have

$$r(T) = \frac{-1}{V(t,T)}\frac{\partial V}{\partial T}. \tag{14.4}$$

If the market prices of the zero-coupon bonds genuinely reflect a known, deterministic interest rate then that interest rate at future dates is given from the bond prices by (14.4). Since the interest rate r is positive we must have

$$\frac{\partial V}{\partial T} < 0.$$

Thus the longer a bond has to live, the less it is now worth; this result is financially clear.

14.3 The yield curve

Despite all our assumptions to the contrary, interest rates are not deterministic. For short-dated derivative products such as options the errors associated with assuming a deterministic, or even constant, rate are small, typically 2%. In dealing with products with a longer lifespan we must address the problem of random interest rates. The first step is to decide on a suitable measure for future values of interest rates, one that enables traders to communicate effectively about the same quantity. In the previous section we have seen a definition, (14.4), which gives an interest rate from bond price data but this relies on bond prices being differentiable with respect to the maturity date.

The **yield curve** is another measure of future values of interest rates. With the value of zero-coupon bonds $V(t,T)$ taken from real data, define

$$Y(t,T) = -\frac{\log(V(t,T)/V(T,T))}{T-t}, \tag{14.5}$$

where t is the current time. The yield curve is the plot of Y against maturity date T. The dependence of the yield curve on the time to maturity, $T-t$, is called the **term structure of interest rates**. This definition for Y has advantages over the measure (14.4) since

- bond prices, $V(t,T)$, do not have to be differentiable;
- a continuous distribution of bonds with all maturities is not required.

Y has the same dimensions as interest rates, i.e. inverse time. The two measures of future interest rates, (14.4) and (14.5), are the same when interest rates are constant.

It is common experience from market data that yield curves typically come in three distinct shapes, each associated with different economic conditions:

- increasing—this is the most common form for the yield curve. Future interest rates are higher than the short term rate since it should be more rewarding to tie money up for a long time than for a short time;

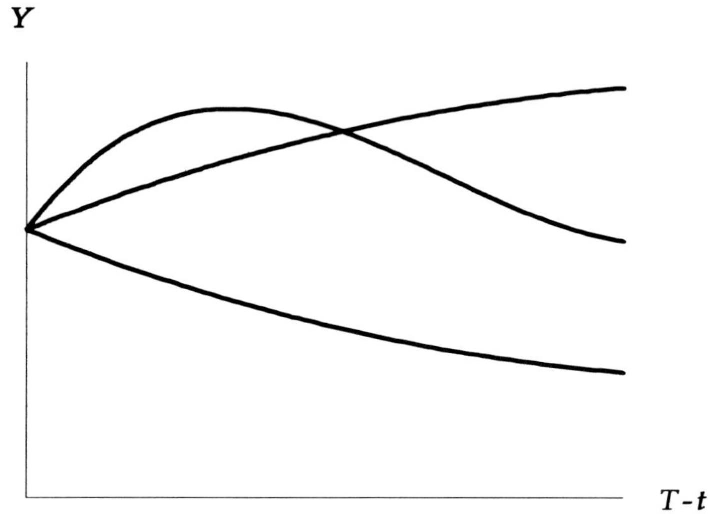

Figure 14.1: Typical yield curves: increasing, decreasing and humped.

- decreasing—this is typical of periods when the short rate is high but expected to fall;
- humped—again the short rate is expected to fall.

These are all illustrated in Figure 14.1.

14.4 Stochastic interest rates

In view of our uncertainty about the future course of the interest rate, it is natural to model it as a random variable. For the rest of this chapter we assume that this is the case. To be technically correct we should specify that r is the interest rate received by the shortest possible deposit. If one is willing to tie money up for a long period of time then usually one gets a higher overall rate to offset the risk that the short rate will rise rapidly. (This would give an upward sloping yield curve.) The interest rate for the shortest possible deposit is commonly called the **spot rate**.

The subject of modelling interest rates is still in its infancy and we do not have the space here to discuss it in any depth. For these reasons we simply quote a fairly general interest rate model which, for reasons we mention below, has become popular.

In the same way that we proposed a model for the asset price as a lognormal random walk let us suppose that the interest rate r is governed by a stochastic differential equation of the form

$$dr = w(r,t)\,dX + u(r,t)\,dt. \tag{14.6}$$

The functional forms of $w(r,t)$ and $u(r,t)$ determine the behaviour of the spot rate r. We use this random walk to derive a partial differential equation for the price of a bond in a similar way to our derivation of the Black–Scholes equation. Later we choose functional forms for u and w that give a reasonable model for the spot rate.

14.5 The bond pricing equation

When interest rates follow the stochastic differential equation (14.6). a bond has a price of the form $V(r,t)$; the dependence on T will only be made explicit when necessary.

Pricing a bond is technically harder than pricing an option since *there is no underlying asset with which to hedge.* In this situation the only alternative is to hedge with bonds of different maturity dates. For this reason we must set up a portfolio containing *two* bonds with different maturities T_1 and T_2. The bond with maturity T_1 has price V_1 and the bond with maturity T_2 has price V_2. We hold one of the former and a number $-\Delta$ of the latter. Thus

$$\Pi = V_1 - \Delta V_2. \tag{14.7}$$

The change in this portfolio in a time dt is

$$\begin{aligned} d\Pi = {} & \frac{\partial V_1}{\partial t}dt + \frac{\partial V_1}{\partial r}dr + \tfrac{1}{2}w^2\frac{\partial^2 V_1}{\partial r^2}dt \\ & - \Delta\left(\frac{\partial V_2}{\partial t}dt + \frac{\partial V_2}{\partial r}dr + \tfrac{1}{2}w^2\frac{\partial^2 V_2}{\partial r^2}dt\right), \end{aligned} \tag{14.8}$$

where we have applied Itô's lemma to functions of r and t.

From (14.8) we see that the choice

$$\Delta = \frac{\partial V_1/\partial r}{\partial V_2/\partial r}$$

eliminates the random component in $d\Pi$. We then have

$$\begin{aligned} d\Pi &= \left(\frac{\partial V_1}{\partial t} + \tfrac{1}{2}w^2 \frac{\partial^2 V_1}{\partial r^2} - \frac{\partial V_1/\partial r}{\partial V_2/\partial r} \left(\frac{\partial V_2}{\partial t} + \tfrac{1}{2}w^2 \frac{\partial^2 V_2}{\partial r^2} \right) \right) dt \\ &= r \left(V_1 - \frac{\partial V_1/\partial r}{\partial V_2/\partial r} V_2 \right) dt, \\ &= r\Pi \, dt \end{aligned}$$

where we have used arbitrage arguments to set the return on the portfolio equal to the risk-free rate, the spot rate.

Gathering together all V_1 terms on the left-hand side and all V_2 terms on the right-hand side we find that

$$\left(\frac{\partial V_1}{\partial t} + \tfrac{1}{2}w^2 \frac{\partial^2 V_1}{\partial r^2} - rV_1 \right) \Big/ \frac{\partial V_1}{\partial r} = \left(\frac{\partial V_2}{\partial t} + \tfrac{1}{2}w^2 \frac{\partial^2 V_2}{\partial r^2} - rV_2 \right) \Big/ \frac{\partial V_2}{\partial r}$$

This is one equation in two unknowns. However, the left-hand side is a function of T_1 and the right-hand side is a function of T_2. The only way for this to be possible is for both sides to be independent of the maturity date. Thus, dropping the subscript from V,

$$\left(\frac{\partial V}{\partial t} + \tfrac{1}{2}w^2 \frac{\partial^2 V}{\partial r^2} - rV \right) \Big/ \frac{\partial V}{\partial r} = a(r,t)$$

for some function $a(r,t)$. In view of later developments it is convenient to write

$$a(r,t) = w(r,t)\lambda(r,t) - u(r,t);$$

for given $w(r,t)$ (nonzero) and $u(r,t)$ this is always possible. The function $\lambda(r,t)$ is as yet unspecified.

The zero-coupon bond pricing equation is therefore

$$\frac{\partial V}{\partial t} + \tfrac{1}{2}w^2 \frac{\partial^2 V}{\partial r^2} + (u - \lambda w)\frac{\partial V}{\partial r} - rV = 0. \qquad (14.9)$$

In order to solve (14.9) uniquely we must pose one final and two boundary conditions. The final condition corresponds to the payoff on maturity and so

$$V(r,T) = Z.$$

Boundary conditions depend on the form of $u(r,t)$ and $w(r,t)$ and are discussed later for a special model.

It is a simple matter to incorporate coupon payments into the model. The result is

$$\frac{\partial V}{\partial t} + \tfrac{1}{2}w^2\frac{\partial^2 V}{\partial r^2} + (u - \lambda w)\frac{\partial V}{\partial r} - rV + K = 0,$$

where K is the coupon payment and may be a function of r and t. We leave the demonstration of this as an exercise for the reader.

14.5.1 The market price of risk

We can now give an elegant interpretation of the hitherto mysterious function $\lambda(r,t)$. Instead of holding the hedged portfolio that we constructed above, suppose that we hold just one bond with maturity date T. In a time-step dt this bond changes in value by

$$dV = w\frac{\partial V}{\partial r}dX + \left(\frac{\partial V}{\partial t} + \tfrac{1}{2}w^2\frac{\partial^2 V}{\partial r^2} + u\frac{\partial V}{\partial r}\right)dt.$$

From (14.9) this may be written as

$$dV = w\frac{\partial V}{\partial r}dX + \left(w\lambda\frac{\partial V}{\partial r} + rV\right)dt,$$

or

$$dV - rV\,dt = w\frac{\partial V}{\partial r}(dX + \lambda\,dt). \tag{14.10}$$

The appearance of dX in (14.10) shows that this is not a riskless portfolio. The right-hand side may be interpreted as the excess return above the risk-free rate for accepting a certain level of risk. In return for taking the extra risk the portfolio profits by an extra $\lambda\,dt$ per unit of extra risk, dX. For this reason the function λ is often called the **market price of risk**.

Technical Point: the market price of risk for assets.
In Chapter 3 we derived the Black–Scholes equation by constructing a portfolio with one option and a number $-\Delta$ of the underlying asset. Suppose that instead we were to follow the analysis above with a portfolio of two options with different maturity dates (or different exercise prices, for that matter), so that

$$\Pi = V_1 - \Delta V_2.$$

As above, we find that

$$\frac{\partial V}{\partial t} + \tfrac{1}{2}\sigma^2 S^2 \frac{\partial^2 V}{\partial S^2} + (\mu - \lambda_S \sigma) S \frac{\partial V}{\partial S} - rV = 0; \tag{14.11}$$

this is simply (14.9) with S instead of r, μS instead of u, λ_S instead of λ and σS instead of w. Now recall that hedging options is easier than hedging bonds because of the existence of an underlying asset. In other words, $V = S$ must itself be a solution of (14.11). Substituting $V = S$ into (14.11) we find that

$$(\mu - \lambda_S \sigma) S - rS = 0,$$

i.e.

$$\lambda_S = \frac{\mu - r}{\sigma};$$

this is the market price of risk for assets. Now putting $\lambda_S = (\mu - r)/\sigma$ into (14.11) we arrive at

$$\frac{\partial V}{\partial t} + \tfrac{1}{2}\sigma^2 S^2 \frac{\partial^2 V}{\partial S^2} + rS \frac{\partial V}{\partial S} - rV = 0;$$

this is the Black–Scholes equation, which contains no reference to μ or λ_S.

14.6 Solutions of the bond pricing equation

Experience shows that the coefficients in (14.6) must have a more complicated form than the rather simple coefficients in the basic random walk for asset prices that we have used so far. Compensating for this is the fact that in the yield curve we have some detailed information about the behaviour of r, and it is important to be able to use this data effectively. The solution of the 'inverse problem', namely to derive the random walk from the yield curve, is much easier if we have explicit formulæ that relate bond prices to interest rates. Thus, we only consider certain special functional forms for w and u, which can be shown to be the most general such forms compatible with a particularly tractable class of solutions of the bond pricing equation. We assume that w and u have the form

$$w(r,t) = \sqrt{\alpha(t) r - \beta(t)}, \tag{14.12}$$

$$u(r,t) = \left(-\gamma(t)r + \delta(t) + \lambda(r,t)\sqrt{\alpha(t)r - \beta(t)}\right). \qquad (14.13)$$

The functionsα, β, γ, δ and λ that appear in (14.12) and (14.13) are functions of time[2]. They are at our disposal to fit the data as well as possible. By suitably restricting these time-dependent functions, we can ensure that the random walk (14.6) for r has the following economically plausible properties:

- We can avoid negative interest rates: the spot rate can be bounded below by a positive number if we insist that $\alpha(t) > 0$ and $\beta \geq 0$. The lower bound is then β/α. (In the special case $\alpha(t) = 0$ we must take $\beta(t) \leq 0$.) Note that r can still go to infinity, albeit with probability zero.

- We can make the spot rate **mean reverting**. For large (small) r the interest rate will tend to decrease (increase) towards the mean, which may be a function of time.

In addition, we require that if r reaches its lower bound β/α, it thereafter increases. This requirement can be shown to force

- $\delta(t) \geq \beta(t)\gamma(t)/\alpha(t) + \alpha(t)/2$,

and it is discussed further below.

The stochastic differential equation (14.6) has been considered by Pearson & Sun (1989), Duffie (1992), Klugman (1992) and Klugman & Wilmott (1993). It incorporates the models of

- Vasicek (1977) ($\alpha = 0$, no time dependence in the parameters);

- Cox, Ingersoll & Ross (1985) ($\beta = 0$, no time dependence in the parameters);

- Hull & White (1990) (either $\alpha = 0$ or $\beta = 0$ but all parameters time-dependent);

[2]The function δ is *not* the delta function: this should not cause confusion as the latter is not needed in this chapter.

With the model (14.12) and (14.13) we can state that the boundary conditions for (14.9) are, first, that

$$V(r,t) \to 0 \quad \text{as} \quad r \to \infty,$$

and, second, that on $r = \beta/\alpha$ V remains finite[3].

All of the models mentioned above take special functional forms for the coefficients of dt and dX in the stochastic differential equation for r, so that the solution of (14.9) is of the simple form[4]

$$V(r,t) = ZA(t,T)e^{-rB(t,T)}. \tag{14.14}$$

(We have explicitly shown the dependence of A and B on T.) Indeed the model with all of α, β, γ and δ non-zero is the most general stochastic differential equation for r which leads to a solution of (14.9) of the form (14.14). (We do not prove this; the proof is simple and is left as an exercise at the end of this chapter.)

We omit the details, but the substitution of (14.12), (14.13) and (14.14) into (14.9) and equating powers of r yields the following equations for A and B:

$$\frac{1}{A}\frac{\partial A}{\partial t} = \delta(t)B + \tfrac{1}{2}\beta(t)B^2 \tag{14.15}$$

and

$$\frac{\partial B}{\partial t} = \tfrac{1}{2}\alpha(t)B^2 + \gamma(t)B - 1. \tag{14.16}$$

In order to satisfy the final data that $V(r,T) = Z$ we must have

$$A(T,T) = 1 \quad \text{and} \quad B(T,T) = 0.$$

---

[3]When r is bounded below by β/α, a local analysis of the partial differential equation can be carried out near $r = \beta/\alpha$ (see the exercises at the end of this chapter). Briefly, balancing the terms $\frac{1}{2}(\alpha r - \beta)\partial^2 V/\partial r^2$ and $(\delta - \gamma r)\partial V/\partial r$ shows that finiteness of V at $r = \beta/\alpha$ is a sufficient boundary condition only if $\delta \geq \beta\gamma/\alpha - \alpha/2$. The calculation is similar to the local analysis of the arithmetic average strike option near $R = 0$.

[4]The existence of a simple explicit solution, while being an obvious advantage in a model, is not usually a good reason for accepting a model as representative of the real world. However, the *inverse* nature of fitting yield curves makes these models useful.

14.6.1 Analysis for constant parameters

The solution for arbitrary α, β, γ and δ is found by integrating the two ordinary differential equations (14.15) and (14.16). Generally this cannot be done explicitly but a simple case is when α, β, γ and δ are all constant. In this case it is found that

$$\frac{2}{\alpha}\log A = a\psi_2 \log(a-B) + (\psi_2 - \tfrac{1}{2}\beta)b\log((B+b)/b) + \tfrac{1}{2}B\beta - a\psi_2 \log a, \tag{14.17}$$

and

$$B(t,T) = \frac{2(e^{\psi_1(T-t)} - 1)}{(\gamma + \psi_1)(e^{\psi_1(T-t)} - 1) + 2\psi_1}, \tag{14.18}$$

where

$$b, a = \frac{\pm\gamma + \sqrt{\gamma^2 + 2\alpha}}{\alpha},$$

and

$$\psi_1 = \sqrt{\gamma^2 + 2\alpha} \quad \text{and} \quad \psi_2 = \frac{\delta + a\beta/2}{a+b}$$

(since B is independent of β it is identical to the expression found by Cox, Ingersoll & Ross (1985)).

When all four of the parameters are constant it is obvious that both A and B are functions of only the one variable $\tau = T - t$; this would not necessarily be the case if any of the parameters were time-dependent.

A wide variety of yield curves can be predicted by the model, including increasing, decreasing and humped. As $\tau \to \infty$,

$$B \to \frac{2}{\gamma + \psi_1}$$

and the yield curve Y has long term behaviour given by

$$Y \to \frac{2}{(\gamma + \psi_1)^2}\left(\delta(\gamma + \psi_1) + \beta\right).$$

Thus for constant and fixed parameters the model leads to a fixed long term interest rate, independent of the spot rate.

14.6.2 Fitting the parameters

The general stochastic process developed in this chapter involves four time-dependent parameters, α, β, γ and δ. If these parameters are assumed to be constant then explicit forms for A, B and hence bond prices are easily obtained.

However, it is reasonable to conjecture that the market's expectations about future interest rates are time-varying. This time dependence may, for example, arise from the cyclical nature of the economy. We now give an overview of a possible approach to incorporating one time-dependent parameter in the general model while the other three parameters are kept constant. When introducing time-dependent parameters, careful consideration must be given to what information is available from and relevant to the market.

The methodology of this section is as follows. We insist that α, β and γ are constant and allow δ to be a function of time. We see that this gives sufficient freedom to fit the market yield curve exactly.

The first step is to determine α and β. There is sufficient information in historic data to find these if we know the lower bound for interest rates and the volatility of the spot rate. Having determined α and β we then go on to find γ. This is found by considering the correlation between the spot rate and the slope of the yield curve. Finally, the function $\delta(t)$ is chosen to fit the full yield curve exactly. This involves the solution of an integral equation.

Bounding r below

Suppose that we are interested in valuing a 10 year bond. Over the next 10 years it is possible that an investor has a view about the likely lower bound for interest rates. Alternatively, it may be reasonable to postulate that a lower bound for interest rates over this period is similar to the smallest value achieved in the past 10 years. This is analogous to using the historic volatility over a period comparable to the life of the option as a volatility measure in option pricing. In any event, let us suppose that a lower bound has been decided on. In this case the quantity

$$\beta/\alpha$$

is 'known'.

The spot rate volatility
The spot rate volatility is simply

$$\sqrt{\alpha r - \beta}.$$

Again, this is easy to estimate, if it is assumed not to be time-dependent. Thus from the historic lower bound and the current volatility we have sufficient information to estimate both α and β.

The volatility of the yield curve slope
It is easy to solve (14.15) and (14.16) by Taylor series for values of t close to T. Such an analysis shows that the yield curve Y, which is now given by

$$Y = \frac{-\log A + rB}{T - t},$$

can be approximated for times close to maturity by

$$Y \sim r - \tfrac{1}{2}(T - t)\left(\gamma r - \delta(0)\right) + \cdots.$$

We can see from this that the slope of the yield curve at the short end (i.e. at $T = t$) is given by

$$s = \tfrac{1}{2}(\delta(0) - \gamma r). \tag{14.19}$$

Note that this model predicts that this slope depends on the spot rate itself.

If the spot rate is indeed mean-reverting, which is the case if $\gamma(t)$ is positive, an increase in the spot rate r leads to a decrease in the slope (14.19): if the spot rate increases, the yield curve flattens. Moreover, as the spot rate follows a random walk, so does the slope of the short rate. Since the two are linked by the deterministic equation (14.19), these changes are perfectly correlated:

$$ds = -\tfrac{1}{2}\gamma\, dr.$$

An examination of the data for r and s gives γ as minus twice the covariance of ds and dr divided by the variance of dr. It may happen that the data give a negative value for γ, so that the spot rate random walk and the local yield curve slope random walk are positively correlated: if the spot rate drops then the yield curve steepens. This is suggestive of a spot rate which is not mean-reverting.

The whole yield curve

So far we have fitted the constant parameters α, β and γ in a simple and practical manner. We now come to choose $\delta(t)$ so as to fit the term structure in the market exactly. We see that this leads to an integral equation for $\delta(t)$ which must be solved numerically except in simple cases.

We can integrate (14.15) explicitly to find that

$$\log A = -\tfrac{1}{2}\beta \int_t^T B^2(T-s)\,ds - \int_t^T \delta(s)B(T-s)\,ds \qquad (14.20)$$

where $B(T-t)$ is given by (14.18) with the obvious notation; it is only a function of $T-t$. This expression is known exactly except for the final integral term involving $\delta(t)$.

Suppose that we wish to fit the yield curve once only, at time t^*. At this time the spot rate is r^*, the known yield curve is $Y^*(T)$ and the four parameters in the model are denoted by α^*, β^*, γ^* and $\delta^*(t)$. If we now substitute the known yield curve into (14.20) we find that $\delta^*(t)$ satisfies the integral equation

$$\int_{t^*}^T \delta^*(s)B(T-s)\,ds = (Br^* - Y^*)(T-t^*) - \tfrac{1}{2}\beta^* \int_{t^*}^T B^2(T-s)\,ds. \qquad (14.21)$$

This must be solved for $t^* \leq T < \infty$. Once the solution of this equation has been found we know all of α, β, γ and $\delta(t)$. Substitution of these into (14.18) gives the expression for B and then into (14.20) gives A. The price of any bond is then given by

$$ZA(t,T)e^{-rB(t,T)}.$$

It is possible to solve (14.21) exactly by taking Laplace transforms since the equation is of Volterra type with a convolution kernel (see Keener 1988). Unfortunately, B does not have a simple transform and thus this method is impractical. Fortunately, the integral equation is not difficult to solve numerically (see Baker 1977), but we do not discuss this any further here.

We have fitted the yield curve exactly at time t^*. In so doing we have found the three constant parameters α, β and γ and the time-dependent parameter δ. The model is only strictly valid if, when we come to refit these parameters at a later date, they remain the same. This is unlikely to be the case and is because the basic model (14.6) has been chosen for its analytic properties and not on the basis of any economic modelling. This is a weakness of many currently popular models.

14.7 The extended Vasicek model of Hull & White

In the Vasicek (1977) model as extended to include time-dependent parameters by Hull & White (1990), $\alpha(t) = 0$ and $\beta < 0$. Although Hull & White advocate a very sophisticated choice of $\beta(t)$, $\gamma(t)$ and $\delta(t)$ (all time-dependent) to fit spot rate volatility, yield curve volatility for all maturities etc., we only allow δ to be time-dependent as suggested above.

With $\alpha = 0$, $B(T-t)$ simplifies to

$$B(T-t) = \frac{1}{\gamma}\left(1 - e^{-\gamma(T-t)}\right)$$

and the integral equation for δ^* becomes

$$\int_{t^*}^{T} \delta^*(s)\left(1 - e^{-\gamma(T-s)}\right) ds = F^*(T). \tag{14.22}$$

Here F^* is a known function of T, given by the right-hand side of (14.21), which in particular depends on integrals of B and the yield curve. For this integral equation to have a solution we must have $F(0) = 0$. That this is indeed the case can be seen from the right-hand side of (14.21).

Although (14.22) may be solved by Laplace transform methods as suggested above, it is particularly easy to solve by differentiating the equation twice with respect to T to find that

$$\delta^*(T) = F^{*\prime\prime}(T) + \gamma F^{*\prime}(T),$$

where $'$ denotes d/dT.

14.8 Bond options

The theoretical model for the spot rate presented above allows us to value contingent claims such as bond options. A **bond option** is identical to an equity option except that the underlying asset is a bond. Both European and American versions exist.

As a simple example, we derive the differential equation satisfied by a call option, with exercise price E and expiry date T, on a zero coupon bond with maturity date $T_B \geq T$. Before finding the value of the option to buy a bond we must find the value of the bond itself.

Let us write $V_B(r, t, T_B)$ for the value of the bond. Thus, V_B satisfies

$$\frac{\partial V_B}{\partial t} + \tfrac{1}{2}w^2 \frac{\partial^2 V_B}{\partial r^2} + (u - \lambda w)\frac{\partial V_B}{\partial r} - rV_B = 0 \tag{14.23}$$

with

$$V_B(r, T_B, T_B) = Z$$

and suitable boundary conditions. Now write $C_B(r, t)$ for the value of the call option on this bond. Since C_B also depends on the random variable r, it too must satisfy equation (14.23). The only difference is that the final value for the option is

$$C_B(r, T) = \max(V_B(r, T, T_B) - E, 0).$$

This idea can readily be generalised, as we now see.

14.9 Other interest rate products

There is a large, and ever-growing, number of different interest rate derivative products. We do not have the space to include any but the most common. However, the following examples show the way in which many such products can be incorporated into the same partial differential equation framework.

14.9.1 Swaps

An interest rate **swap** is an agreement between two parties to exchange the interest rate payments on a certain amount, the principal, for a certain length of time. One party pays the other a fixed rate of interest in return for a variable interest rate payment. For example, A pays 9% of $1,000,000 p.a. to B and B pays r of the same amount to A. This agreement is to last for three years, say. We now value such swaps in general.

Suppose that A pays the interest on an amount Z to B at a fixed rate r^* and B pays interest to A at the floating rate r. These payments continue until time T. Let us denote the value of this swap to A by $ZV(r,t)$.

We can accommodate this product into our interest rate framework by observing that in a time-step dt A receives $Z(r-r^*)\,dt$. If we think of this payment as being similar to a coupon payment on a simple bond then we find that

$$\frac{\partial V}{\partial t}+\tfrac{1}{2}w^2\frac{\partial^2 V}{\partial r^2}+(u-\lambda w)\frac{\partial V}{\partial r}-rV+r-r^*=0,$$

with final data

$$V(r,T)=0.$$

Note that r can be greater or less than r^* and so $V(r,t)$ need not be positive. Indeed, a swap is not necessarily an asset but can be a liability depending on, for example, the current state of the yield curve.

14.9.2 Caps and floors

A **cap** is a loan at the floating interest rate but with the proviso that the interest rate charged is guaranteed not to exceed a specified value, the **cap**, which we denote by r^*. The loan of Z is to be paid back at time T. We readily find that the value of the capped loan, $ZV(r,t)$, satisfies

$$\frac{\partial V}{\partial t}+\tfrac{1}{2}w^2\frac{\partial^2 V}{\partial r^2}+(u-\lambda w)\frac{\partial V}{\partial r}-rV+\min(r,r^*)=0, \qquad (14.24)$$

with

$$V(r,T)=1.$$

A **floor** is similar to a cap except that the interest rate does not go *below* r^*. To value this contract simply replace min by max in (14.24).

14.9.3 Swaptions, captions and floortions

Having valued swaps, caps and floors it is easy to value options on these instruments: **swaptions**, **captions** and **floortions**. Suppose that our swap (cap or floor) which expires at time T_S has value $V_S(r,t)$ for $t \leq T_S$. An option to buy this swap (a call swaption) for an amount E at time $T < T_S$ has value $V(r,t)$ where

$$\frac{\partial V}{\partial t} + \tfrac{1}{2}w^2\frac{\partial^2 V}{\partial r^2} + (u - \lambda w)\frac{\partial V}{\partial r} - rV = 0,$$

with

$$V(r,T) = \max(V_S(r,T) - E, 0).$$

Thus we solve for the value of the swap itself first, and then use this value as the final data for the value of the swaption. Captions and floortions are treated similarly.

Further reading

We have given only a brief account of the rapidly-developing subject of interest rate modelling. The interested reader will find many more details in the original papers listed below.

- See the original papers by Dothan (1978), Vasicek (1977), Cox, Ingersoll & Ross (1985), Ho & Lee (1986) and Black, Derman & Toy (1990).
- A more sophisticated choice of time-dependent parameters is described by Hull & White (1990).
- Klugman & Wilmott (1993) solve the integral equation asymptotically for small α.
- See Hull (1993) for details of other interest rate products and their uses in practice.

Exercises

1. Derive the most general functional forms for $u(r,t)$ and $w(r,t)$ that lead to a solution of (14.9) in the form

$$ZA(t,T)e^{-rB(t,T)}.$$

[Hint: Substitute this form into the bond pricing equation with arbitrary u and w and equate functions of T and r separately.]

2. Verify the local analysis of the bond pricing equation near $r = \beta/\alpha$.

3. Suppose that a bond pays a coupon $K(r,t)$. Show that the bond pricing equation is modified to

$$\frac{\partial V}{\partial t} + \tfrac{1}{2}w^2\frac{\partial^2 V}{\partial r^2} + (u - \lambda w)\frac{\partial V}{\partial r} - rV + K = 0.$$

Chapter 15

Convertible Bonds

15.1 The convertible bond

In this chapter we discuss the valuation of convertible bonds. With the assumption of known interest rates, these bonds are very similar to American vanilla options. We illustrate the ideas with constant interest rates and, at the end of the chapter, we briefly bring together convertible bonds and stochastic interest rates in a two-factor model.

A **convertible bond** has many of the same characteristics as an ordinary bond but with the additional feature that the bond may, at any time of the owner's choosing, be exchanged for a specified asset. This exchange is called **conversion**. The convertible bond on an underlying asset (with price S) returns Z, say, at time T *unless* at some previous time the owner has converted the bond into n of the underlying asset[1]. The bond may also pay a coupon to the holder.

Since the bond price depends on the value of that asset we have

$$V = V(S,t);$$

the contract value now depends on an asset price. It also depends on the time to maturity, but we usually suppress this dependence. Repeating the Black–Scholes analysis, with a portfolio consisting of

[1]We have implicitly assumed that the number of assets controlled by all the existing convertible bonds is small and that conversion does not affect the value of the issuing company. For further details see Cox & Rubinstein (1985), Gemmill (1992), the Technical Point below and the discussion of dilution in the section on warrants in Chapter 3.

one convertible bond and $-\Delta$ assets, we find that the change in the value of the portfolio is

$$d\Pi = \frac{\partial V}{\partial t}dt + \frac{\partial V}{\partial S}dS + \tfrac{1}{2}\sigma^2 S^2 \frac{\partial^2 V}{\partial S^2}dt - \Delta\, dS + (K(S,t) - D(S,t)\Delta)\, dt$$

where we have included a coupon payment of $K(S,t)\,dt$ on the bond and a dividend payment of $D(S,t)\,dt$ on the asset. As before, we choose

$$\Delta = \frac{\partial V}{\partial S}$$

to eliminate risk from this portfolio.

The return on this risk-free portfolio is at most that from a bank deposit and so

$$\frac{\partial V}{\partial t} + \tfrac{1}{2}\sigma^2 S^2 \frac{\partial^2 V}{\partial S^2} + (rS - D(S,t))\frac{\partial V}{\partial S} - rV + K(S,t) \le 0$$

for the bond price. This inequality is recognised as the basic Black–Scholes inequality but with the addition of the coupon payment term. The final condition is

$$V(S,T) = Z.$$

Recalling that the bond may be converted into n assets we have the constraint

$$V \ge nS.$$

In addition to this constraint, we require the continuity of V and $\partial V/\partial S$.

Thus the convertible bond is similar to an American option problem. It is interesting to note that the final data itself does not satisfy the pricing constraint. Thus, although the value *at* maturity may be Z the value *just before* is

$$\max(nS, Z).$$

Boundary conditions are

$$V(S,t) \sim nS \quad \text{as} \quad S \to \infty$$

and

$$V(0,t) = Ze^{-r(T-t)};$$

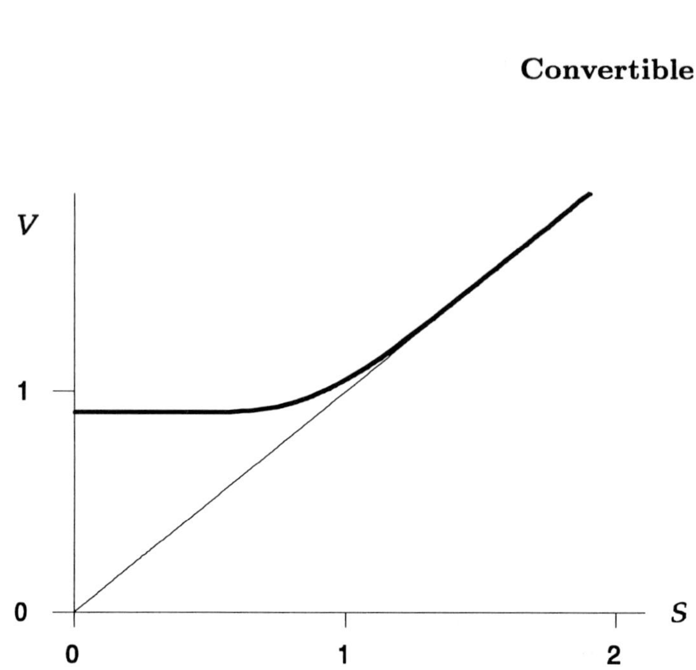

Figure 15.1: The value of a convertible bond with constant interest rate. See text for details.

this last condition assumes (as can be verified *a posteriori*) that it is not optimal to exercise when $S = 0$.

This problem is as easy to solve numerically as an American option problem (see Chapters 20 and 21). It can be shown that an increase in D (respectively K) makes early exercise more (less) likely. When $K = D = 0$ the constraint only comes into play at expiry and the convertible bond can be valued explicitly as a combination of cash and a European call option. In Figures 15.1 and 15.2 are shown the values of a convertible bonds with $Z = 1$, $n = 1$, $r = 0.1$, $\sigma = 0.25$ and with one year before maturity. In both cases there are no coupon payments. In Figure 15.1 there is no dividend paid on the underlying but in Figure 15.2 we have $D_0 = 0.05$. Thus in the latter case there is a free boundary: for sufficiently large S the bond should be converted.

Sometimes the bond may only be converted during specified periods This is called **intermittent conversion**. If this is the case then the constraint only needs to be satisfied during these times; at other times the contract is European.

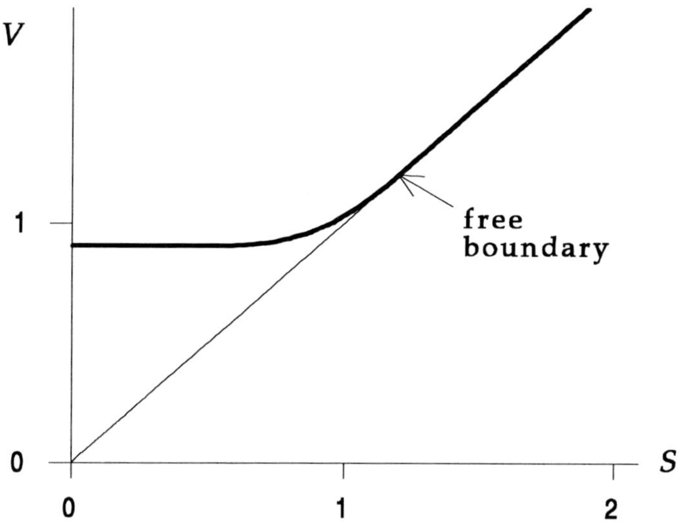

Figure 15.2: The value of a convertible bond with constant interest rate and a dividend paid on the underlying. See text for details.

15.1.1 Call and put features

The convertible bond permits the holder to swap the bond for a certain number of the underlying asset at any time of *his or her* choosing. Some bonds also have a **call feature** which gives the company the right to purchase back the bond at any time (or during specified periods) for a fixed sum. Thus the bond with a call feature is worth less than the bond without since it cedes a right to the company. Such a call feature is easily modelled.

Suppose that the bond can be repurchased by the company for an amount M_1. The elimination of arbitrage opportunities leads to

$$V(S,t) \le M_1.$$

Thus we must solve an obstacle problem in which our bond price is bounded below by nS and above by M_1. Again, V and $\partial V/\partial S$ must be continuous. As with the intermittent conversion feature it is also simple to incorporate the intermittent call feature, according to which the company can only repurchase the bond during certain time periods.

Some convertible bonds incorporate a **put feature**. This is a further right belonging to the owner of the bond. It allows the holder to return the bond to the issuing company for an amount M_2, say. Now we must impose the constraint

$$V(S,t) \geq M_2.$$

This feature increases the value of the bond.

15.2 Convertible bonds with random interest rate

When interest rates are stochastic, a convertible bond has a value of the form

$$V = V(S,r,t),$$

with the dependence on T suppressed. The value of the convertible bond is now a function of both S and r as independent variables (previously, r was just a parameter).

We assume that the asset price is governed by the standard model

$$dS = \sigma S\,dX_1 + \mu S\,dt, \tag{15.1}$$

and the interest rate by

$$dr = w(r,t)\,dX_2 + u(r,t)\,dt. \tag{15.2}$$

Since we are only modelling the bond, and do not intend finding explicit solutions, we allow u and w to be any functions of r and t. Observe that in (15.1) and (15.2) the Wiener processes have been given subscripts. This is because we are allowing S and r to be governed by two different random variables; this is a **two-factor model**. Thus, although dX_1 and dX_2 are both drawn from normal distributions with zero mean and variance dt, they are not necessarily the same random variable. They are, however, correlated by

$$\mathcal{E}[dX_1\,dX_2] = \rho\,dt,$$

with $-1 \leq \rho(r,S,t) \leq 1$. We can still think of (15.1) and (15.2) as recipes for generating random walks for S and r, but now at each time-step we must draw two random numbers.

In order to manipulate $V(S,r,t)$ we need to know how Itô's lemma applies to functions of two random variables. As might be expected, the usual Taylor series expansion together with a few rules of thumb results in the correct expression for the small change in any function of both S and r. These rules of thumb are

- $dX_1^2 = dt$;
- $dX_2^2 = dt$;
- $dX_1\,dX_2 = \rho\,dt$.

Applying Taylor's theorem to $V(S + dS, r + dr, t + dt)$ we find that

$$\begin{aligned} dV = & \frac{\partial V}{\partial t}dt + \frac{\partial V}{\partial S}dS + \frac{\partial V}{\partial r}dr \\ & + \tfrac{1}{2}\frac{\partial^2 V}{\partial S^2}dS^2 + \frac{\partial^2 V}{\partial S \partial r}dS\,dr + \tfrac{1}{2}\frac{\partial^2 V}{\partial r^2}dr^2 + \cdots. \end{aligned}$$

To leading order,

$$\begin{aligned} dS^2 &= \sigma^2 S^2 dX_1^2 = \sigma^2 S^2 dt, \\ dr^2 &= w^2 dX_2^2 = w^2 dt \end{aligned}$$

and

$$dS\,dr = \sigma S w\,dX_1\,dX_2 = \rho\sigma S w\,dt.$$

Thus Itô's lemma for the two random variables governed by (15.1) and (15.2) becomes

$$\begin{aligned} dV = & \frac{\partial V}{\partial t}dt + \frac{\partial V}{\partial S}dS + \frac{\partial V}{\partial r}dr \\ & + \tfrac{1}{2}\sigma^2 S^2 \frac{\partial^2 V}{\partial S^2}dt + \rho\sigma S w \frac{\partial^2 V}{\partial S \partial r}dt + \tfrac{1}{2}w^2 \frac{\partial^2 V}{\partial r^2}dt. \end{aligned}$$

Now we come to the pricing of the convertible bond. Let us construct a portfolio consisting of one bond with maturity T_1, $-\Delta_2$ bonds with maturity date T_2 and $-\Delta$ of the underlying asset. Thus

$$\Pi = V_1 - \Delta_2 V_2 - \Delta S.$$

The analysis is much as before; the choice

$$\Delta_2 = \frac{\partial V_1/\partial r}{\partial V_2/\partial r}$$

and

$$\Delta = \frac{\partial V_1}{\partial S} - \frac{\partial V_1/\partial r}{\partial V_2/\partial r}\frac{\partial V_2}{\partial S}$$

eliminates risk from the portfolio. Terms involving T_1 and T_2 may be grouped together separately to find that, dropping the subscripts,

$$\frac{\partial V}{\partial t} + \tfrac{1}{2}\sigma^2 S^2 \frac{\partial^2 V}{\partial S^2} + \rho\sigma S w \frac{\partial^2 V}{\partial S \partial r} + \tfrac{1}{2}w^2 \frac{\partial^2 V}{\partial r^2} + rS\frac{\partial V}{\partial S} + (u - w\lambda)\frac{\partial V}{\partial r} - rV = 0.$$

Again, $\lambda(r, S, t)$ is the market price of risk.

This is the bond pricing equation. Note that it contains the known interest rate problem ($u = 0 = w$, i.e. Black–Scholes) and the simple bond problem ($\partial/\partial S = 0$) as special cases. More generally, when the underlying asset pays dividends and the bond pays a coupon we have

$$\frac{\partial V}{\partial t} + \tfrac{1}{2}\sigma^2 S^2 \frac{\partial^2 V}{\partial S^2} + \rho\sigma S w \frac{\partial^2 V}{\partial S \partial r} + \tfrac{1}{2}w^2 \frac{\partial^2 V}{\partial r^2} + (rS - D)\frac{\partial V}{\partial S} + (u - w\lambda)\frac{\partial V}{\partial r} - rV + K = 0.$$

The final condition and American constraints are exactly as before; there is one constraint for each of the convertibility feature and the call feature. Since this is a diffusion equation with two 'space-like' state variables S and r—that is, there are double derivatives of V with respect to each of S and r, as well as a cross-term—we need to impose boundary conditions on the edge of the (S, r) space. In other words, we must prescribe $V(0, r, t)$ and $V(\infty, r, t)$ for all t, $V(S, \infty, t)$ for all S and t and a second boundary condition on a fixed r boundary, again for all S and t. Some of these boundary conditions are very obvious and others are a result of insisting that V remain finite. For example, for a convertible bond with no call feature we have

$$V(S, r, t) \sim nS \quad \text{as} \quad S \to \infty;$$

$V(0, r, t)$ is given by the solution of the simple bond problem (no convertibility and stochastic interest rates);

$$V(S, r, t) \to 0 \quad \text{as} \quad r \to \infty;$$

and the last boundary condition, to be applied on the lower r boundary, is equivalent to finiteness of V.

Technical Point: the issue of new shares.
We have assumed in this chapter that the existence of convertible bonds does not affect the market worth of the company. In reality, the conversion of the bond into n shares requires the company to issue n new shares. This contrasts with options for which the exercise leaves the number of shares unchanged. We do not include any of the details here; however, if we let S be the worth of the company's assets, without the bond obligation and N be the number of shares before conversion, we arrive at the following problem.

The convertible bond pricing equation (with known or stochastic interest rate) is to be solved with

$$V \geq \frac{nS}{n+N}, \tag{15.3}$$

$$V \leq S \tag{15.4}$$

and

$$V(S,T) = Z.$$

Constraint (15.3) bounds the bond price below by its value on conversion and constraint (15.4) allows the company to declare bankruptcy if the bond becomes too valuable. The factor $N/(n+N)$ is known as the dilution. A typical convertible bond value is shown in Figure 15.3. In this example we have $Z = 1$, $r = 0.1$, $\sigma = 0.25$, $D_0 = 0.05$, there is one year to maturity and the dilution factor is 0.5. *In the limit $n/N \rightarrow 0$ this model is identical to the one considered above.*

Note that the total worth of the company is $S - V$ and the share price is thus $(S - V)/N$ and not *S.*

Further reading

- For details of the effect of the issue of new shares on the value of convertible bonds see Brennan & Schwartz (1977) and Gemmill (1992).

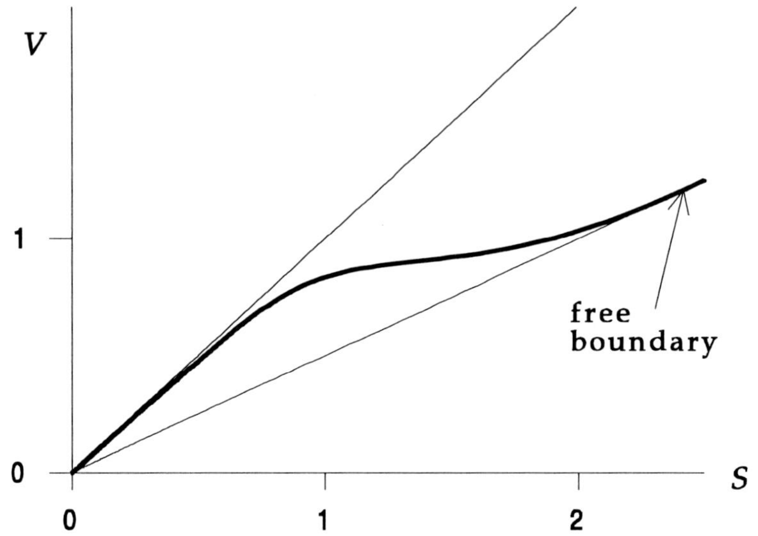

Figure 15.3: The value of a convertible bond versus company's assets, allowing for dilution on issue of new shares.

Exercises

1. Assuming that interest rates are constant, find an explicit formula for the value of a convertible bond with zero coupon and zero dividend on the underlying and generalise this result to include a coupon payment.

   [Hint: Assume that the bond is a European option with payoff $\max(nS, Z)$. Write this in terms of cash plus a vanilla call option and show that the constraint $V \geq nS$ is always satisfied.]

2. Perform a local analysis of the same kind as those in Chapter 6 to find the position of the free boundary close to maturity. Allow for both a dividend payment on the underlying and a coupon payment on the bond.

Chapter 16

Numerical Methods

16.1 Introduction

In the following seven chapters we consider various techniques for the numerical solution of mathematical models of derivative securities. Most of the models presented in this book do not admit simple closed form solutions and for such models numerical solution is the only means of obtaining quantitative results[1].

We discuss various numerical techniques for solving partial differential equation models and construct algorithms to solve these models. We start by considering the numerical solution of simple European puts and calls. This may seem rather restrictive, but it has the advantage of illustrating quite general techniques in a familiar setting.

It is important to be aware that not all numerical methods perform well on all problems. A poor numerical method will usually give an answer, but it may not be the correct answer. The danger is that it may not be obvious that the answer is incorrect. An example arises in Section 18.7, where a naive direct discretisation of the Black–Scholes equation predicts negative option prices. These negative option values are incorrect. What is less obvious is that the positive option values adjacent to the negative ones are also incor-

[1] Some models admit exact solutions only in terms of infinite series of relatively obscure special functions; in general it is more efficient to solve these numerically from a partial differential equation formulation rather than to approximate the infinite series.

rect. Less obvious still is the fact that, even if the calculated option values are all positive, they may still be incorrect. We spend some time discussing the question of the appropriateness of a particular method for a particular problem.

We consider only finite differences in the following chapters; we describe finite-element methods in Appendix D. There are, of course, other methods for the numerical solution of option pricing problems. Among these are the **Monte Carlo methods**; these involve generating large numbers of numerically simulated realisations of the random walk followed by the underlying asset. They have the disadvantage that early exercise features are difficult or impossible to implement.

The convergence of Monte Carlo methods is well understood and, from the numerical analyst's point of view, the main consideration for Monte Carlo simulations is the implementation of a non-biased random number generator (see Hammersley & Handscomb 1992). We do not discuss them further in this book as they are relatively slow and inflexible compared to the methods we do discuss. For a discussion of Monte Carlo methods applied to option pricing, see Boyle (1977).

Another popular class of methods are the various **lattice methods** which include the binomial and trinomial methods. These models assume that the underlying stochastic process is discrete. In these cases, the models can be written down directly as discrete sets of difference equations, and these can then be implemented directly on a computer.

Although the lattice methods are highly efficient methods for valuing simple calls and puts, they are somewhat less efficient when valuing more complicated options. All commonly used lattice methods are special cases of explicit finite-difference schemes. For these reasons lattice methods are discussed separately in Appendix C.

16.2 General considerations for numerical solution

The models that we consider solving in the following chapters assume that the underlying stochastic processes are continuous and these models lead to partial differential equations These are all, essentially, extensions of the basic Black–Scholes models. The numerical considerations for this type of model are:

- To construct a finite approximation to the partial differential equation that can be implemented as an algorithm on a computer. This is the **discretisation** or approximation problem.
- To consider whether or not the discretised model is sensitive to small errors that arise because of the finite precision of computer arithmetic. If the discretised equations are sensitive to small errors, then the discretisation is useless. This is the **stability** problem.
- To consider the degree to which the solutions of the discretised equations approximate the solutions of the partial differential equation. In particular, to consider whether as we refine the discretisation, the solutions of the discretised equations tend to the solutions of the partial differential equation. This is the **convergence** problem.

By **discretisation** we mean any method of reducing a continuous partial differential equation to a discrete set of difference equations that can be solved on a computer. We only consider two types of discretisations, namely **finite differences** and **finite elements**. Finite elements are discussed in detail in Appendix D and only finite differences are discussed in the main text. The reason for this is that both methods lead to identical numerical schemes in the context of the problems that we are considering.

16.3 Efficiency

Another important consideration is the efficiency of the solution technique. We can, to some extent, measure this by two indicators:

- The amount of computer memory required by the solution algorithm;
- The number of arithmetical calculations performed by the solution algorithm. This determines the execution speed of the algorithm.

Typically, in the course of solving an option valuation problem, we divide the remaining life of the option into M discrete time intervals. As we let $M \to \infty$ we expect to obtain the exact solution, assuming that the algorithm we are using is convergent. The efficiency of the algorithm may be measured by expressing the amount of computer memory and number of arithmetical operations required as a function of M. If these quantities vary linearly with M, we say that they are $O(M)$, whereas if one varies quadratically and one exponentially with M we express this by saying the former is $O(M^2)$ and the latter is exponential in M.

Exponential increase in the memory or time required is a very bad thing—taking an extra time-step typically means doubling the amount of memory and/or the time taken to find the answer. Any algorithm that has exponential dependence (in memory or time) on the number of time-steps is not a practical solution method at all.

One may question the point of regarding what is, after all, a discrete stochastic process (asset values are discrete quantities, and there is a lower bound on transaction times) as a continuous process at all if it leads to a problem that has to be re-discretised in order to be solved. This is a matter of scales. If the discrete transaction time and price quanta are small compared to the overall time and price scales then an accurate binomial or trinomial model is easy to write down but it will be so huge that it will be unrealistic to solve it. In these circumstances the continuum approximation gives an accurate approximation to the (huge) discrete problem. (It is also the case that lattice methods for valuing path-dependent options are hugely inefficient except in a few special cases; their execution times increase exponentially with the number of time-steps.)

Most continuum models are more easily analysed than discrete models; it is easy to discretise a partial differential equation so that the errors induced can be estimated (the convergence problem). The continuous models lead to smaller discrete models, and there is a well-understood theory of convergence and error analysis for discretisations of continuous partial differential equations. Nevertheless, it is interesting that the discretised versions of the continuous models (assuming a sensible approach to the discretisation) can themselves be interpreted as discrete probabilistic models.

16.4 Outline

In the following three chapters we consider finite-difference methods for European options The method is discussed in general in Chapter 17. There are two distinct classes of finite-difference methods, **explicit finite-difference** methods and **implicit finite-difference** methods. We discuss both of these, the former in Chapter 18 and the latter Chapter 19.

In Chapter 20 we consider numerical methods for free boundary problems (specifically, for the obstacle problem). We introduce the Projected SOR algorithm for solving linear complementarity problems and variational inequalities, and show how to solve the obstacle problem numerically.

In Chapter 21 we then move onto the real issue in question, the numerical valuation of American options. We apply the methods developed for the simple obstacle problem to American options. When reformulated as linear complementarity problems or as variational inequalities, American option problems may be solved by exactly the same methods developed to solve obstacle problems. We give both finite-difference and finite-element algorithms for solving, respectively, the linear complementarity and variational inequality formulations.

The finite-element method emerges naturally from the variational formulation of the American option problem, so we only consider it in the context of the valuation of American options. Since, however, the algorithm for valuing American options that arises from the finite-element method is identical to the algorithm arising from finite-difference methods, we discuss the finite-element method separately in Appendix D. Finally we consider some more complicated issues which may arise in the numerical valuation of exotic options; we consider the numerical valuation of an average strike option as an example.

Further reading

- For a very good discussion of the Monte Carlo method see Hammersley & Handscomb (1992). Also see Boyle (1977) for an introduction to the method as applied to option pricing.
- See the book by Smith (1985) for more about the numerical so-

lution of partial differential equations of elliptic and hyperbolic type as well as parabolic.

- The books by Johnson & Riess (1982) and Stoer & Bulirsch (1993) give excellent background material on some of the basic considerations of numerical analysis: accuracy of computer arithmetic, convergence and efficiency of algorithms and stability of numerical methods.

Chapter 17

Finite-difference Approximations

17.1 Introduction

Although it is only slightly more difficult to solve the Black–Scholes equation numerically than to solve the diffusion equation numerically, the analyses of the numerical schemes for the diffusion equation are considerably simpler than the corresponding analyses for the Black–Scholes equation. Also, there is a sense in which the 'obvious' way to solve the diffusion equation numerically is 'correct' and the 'obvious' way to solve the Black–Scholes equation is not 'correct'. This statement is quantified in due course.

Recall from Sections 5.4 and 6.3 that, by using the change of variables

$$\begin{gathered} S = Ee^x, \qquad t = T - \tau/\tfrac{1}{2}\sigma^2, \\ V(S,t) = Ee^{-\frac{1}{2}(k_2-1)x-(\frac{1}{4}(k_2-1)^2+k_1)\tau}u(x,\tau) \end{gathered} \tag{17.1}$$

where

$$k_1 = r/\tfrac{1}{2}\sigma^2 \quad \text{and} \quad k_2 = (r - D_0)/\tfrac{1}{2}\sigma^2, \tag{17.2}$$

the Black–Scholes equation

$$\frac{\partial V}{\partial t} + \tfrac{1}{2}\sigma^2 S^2 \frac{\partial^2 V}{\partial S^2} + (r - D_0)S\frac{\partial V}{\partial S} - rV = 0$$

for any European option paying a constant dividend yield can be transformed into the diffusion equation

$$\frac{\partial u}{\partial \tau} = \frac{\partial^2 u}{\partial x^2}.$$

The payoff function for the option determines the initial[1] conditions for $u(x,\tau)$, and the boundary conditions for the option determine the conditions at infinity for $u(x,\tau)$ (that is, as $x \to \pm\infty$). For a put the initial and boundary conditions are

$$\begin{aligned} u(x,0) &= \max\left(e^{\frac{1}{2}(k_2-1)x} - e^{\frac{1}{2}(k_2+1)x}, 0\right), \\ \lim_{x\to\infty} u(x,\tau) &= 0, \qquad \lim_{x\to-\infty} u(x,\tau) \sim e^{\frac{1}{2}(k_2-1)x+\frac{1}{4}(k_2-1)^2\tau}. \end{aligned} \tag{17.3}$$

For a call the initial and boundary conditions are

$$\begin{aligned} u(x,0) &= \max\left(e^{\frac{1}{2}(k_2+1)x} - e^{\frac{1}{2}(k_2-1)x}, 0\right), \\ \lim_{x\to\infty} u(x,\tau) &\sim e^{\frac{1}{2}(k_2+1)x+\frac{1}{4}(k_2+1)^2\tau}, \qquad \lim_{x\to-\infty} u(x,\tau) = 0. \end{aligned} \tag{17.4}$$

We also consider a particular binary option, a cash or nothing call, with a payoff of B for $S > E$ and zero otherwise. Writing $b = B/E$, we have

$$\begin{aligned} u(x,0) &= \begin{cases} 0 & x < 0 \\ be^{\frac{1}{2}(k_2-1)x} & x \geq 0, \end{cases} \\ \lim_{x\to\infty} u(x,\tau) &\sim be^{\frac{1}{2}(k_2-1)x+\frac{1}{4}(k_2-1)^2\tau}, \qquad \lim_{x\to-\infty} u(x,\tau) = 0. \end{aligned} \tag{17.5}$$

The values of the option $V(S,t)$, in financial variables, may be recovered from the non-dimensional $u(x,\tau)$ using

$$\begin{aligned} V = {} & E^{\frac{1}{2}(1+k_2)} S^{\frac{1}{2}(1-k_2)} e^{\frac{1}{8}((k_2-1)^2+4k_1)\sigma^2(T-t)} \\ & \times u\left(\log\left(\frac{S}{E}\right), \tfrac{1}{2}\sigma^2(T-t)\right). \end{aligned}$$

[1]Recall that we have turned the Black–Scholes equation, which is backward parabolic, into a forward parabolic equation, so final conditions become initial conditions.

17.2 Simple finite differences

The idea underlying finite-difference methods is to replace the partial derivatives occurring in partial differential equations by finite-difference approximations. For example, the partial derivative $\partial u/\partial\tau$ may be defined to be the limiting difference

$$\frac{\partial u}{\partial \tau}(x,\tau) = \lim_{\delta\tau\to 0} \frac{u(x,\tau+\delta\tau) - u(x,\tau)}{\delta\tau}.$$

If, instead of regarding $\delta\tau$ as tending to zero, we regard it as nonzero but small (in a sense yet to be determined), we obtain the approximation

$$\frac{\partial u}{\partial \tau}(x,\tau) \approx \frac{u(x,\tau+\delta\tau) - u(x,\tau)}{\delta\tau}, \qquad \delta\tau \text{ small.} \tag{17.6}$$

This is called a **finite-difference approximation** or a **finite difference** of $\partial u/\partial\tau$ because it involves small, but not infinitesimal, differences of the dependent variable u. This particular finite-difference approximation is called a **forward difference**, since the differencing is in the forward τ direction: the values of u at τ and $\tau + \delta\tau$ only are used.

We also have

$$\frac{\partial u}{\partial \tau}(x,\tau) = \lim_{\delta\tau\to 0} \frac{u(x,\tau) - u(x,\tau-\delta\tau)}{\delta\tau}$$

so that the approximation

$$\frac{\partial u}{\partial \tau}(x,\tau) \approx \frac{u(x,\tau) - u(x,\tau-\delta\tau)}{\delta\tau}, \qquad \delta\tau \text{ small,} \tag{17.7}$$

is also a valid finite-difference approximation for the first τ partial derivative of u. We call this finite-difference approximation a **backward difference**. See Figure 17.1 for a geometric interpretation of differences.

We can similarly define **central differences**. We do this by observing that yet another definition of $\partial u/\partial\tau$ is

$$\frac{\partial u}{\partial \tau}(x,\tau) = \lim_{\delta\tau\to 0} \frac{u(x,\tau+\delta\tau) - u(x,\tau-\delta\tau)}{2\delta\tau}$$

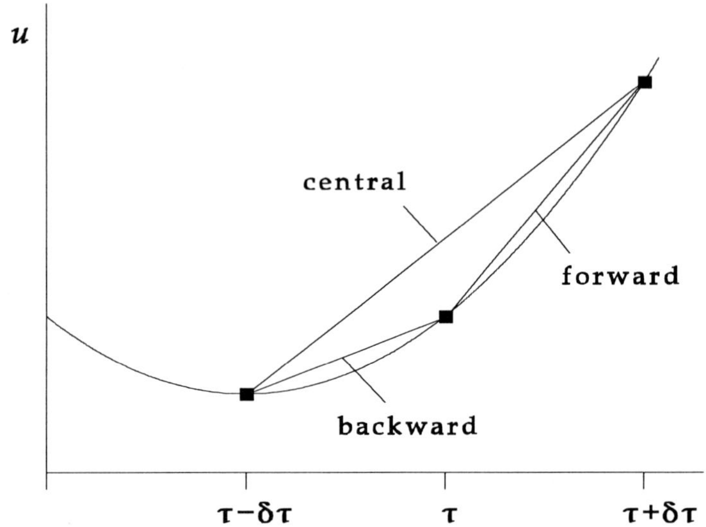

Figure 17.1: Forward, backward and central difference approximations.

and it gives rise to the central finite-difference approximation

$$\frac{\partial u}{\partial \tau}(x,\tau) \approx \frac{u(x,\tau+\delta\tau) - u(x,\tau-\delta\tau)}{2\delta\tau}, \quad \delta\tau \text{ small}, \tag{17.8}$$

also illustrated in Figure 17.1. Other types of finite-difference approximations for first partial derivatives exist, but we do not have cause to use them in this chapter.

When applied to the the diffusion equation forward and backward difference approximations for $\partial u/\partial\tau$ lead to **explicit** and **fully implicit** finite-difference schemes, respectively.

Central differences of the form (17.8) lead to schemes for the diffusion equation that are never used in practice because they always lead to bad numerical schemes (specifically, schemes that are inherently unstable). Central differences of the form

$$\frac{\partial u}{\partial \tau} \approx \frac{u(x,\tau+\delta\tau/2) - u(x,\tau-\delta\tau/2)}{\delta\tau} \tag{17.9}$$

arise in the **Crank–Nicolson** finite-difference scheme.

We can define finite-difference approximations for the x partial derivative of u in exactly the same way. The forward, backward and central finite-difference approximations are easily seen to be:

Forward difference:

$$\frac{\partial u}{\partial x}(x,\tau) \approx \frac{u(x+\delta x,\tau) - u(x,\tau)}{\delta x}; \tag{17.10}$$

Backward difference:

$$\frac{\partial u}{\partial x}(x,\tau) \approx \frac{u(x,\tau) - u(x-\delta x,\tau)}{\delta x}; \tag{17.11}$$

Central difference:

$$\frac{\partial u}{\partial x}(x,\tau) \approx \frac{u(x+\delta x,\tau) - u(x-\delta x,\tau)}{2\delta x}. \tag{17.12}$$

In each of these we assume that δx is in some sense small.

17.3 Finite differences for second derivatives

For second partial derivatives, such as $\partial^2 u/\partial x^2$, we can define finite-difference approximations by any of the following rules:

Forward difference:

$$\frac{\partial^2 u}{\partial x^2}(x,\tau) = \lim_{\delta x\to 0}\frac{1}{\delta x}\left(\frac{\partial u}{\partial x}(x+\delta x,\tau) - \frac{\partial u}{\partial x}(x,\tau)\right);$$

Backward difference:

$$\frac{\partial^2 u}{\partial x^2}(x,\tau) = \lim_{\delta x\to 0}\frac{1}{\delta x}\left(\frac{\partial u}{\partial x}(x,\tau) - \frac{\partial u}{\partial x}(x-\delta x,\tau)\right);$$

Central difference:

$$\frac{\partial^2 u}{\partial x^2}(x,\tau) = \lim_{\delta x\to 0}\frac{1}{\delta x}\left(\frac{\partial u}{\partial x}(x+\delta x/2,\tau) - \frac{\partial u}{\partial x}(x-\delta x/2,\tau)\right).$$

This gives us three ways of approximating the second partial derivative $\partial^2 u/\partial x^2$ in terms of the first partial derivatives $\partial u/\partial x$. We can approximate the first partial derivative $\partial u/\partial x$ in three different ways in terms of finite differences of u. This shows there are 27 possible ways of approximating $\partial^2 u/\partial x^2$ in terms of finite differences of u. Not all of these 27 ways are distinct.

Of all of these possibilities, the preferred ones are those that give rise to the symmetric central difference

$$\frac{\partial^2 u}{\partial x^2}(x,\tau) \approx \frac{u(x+\delta x,\tau) - 2u(x,\tau) + u(x-\delta x,\tau)}{(\delta x)^2}. \tag{17.13}$$

This approximation to $\partial^2 u/\partial x^2$ is preferred as its symmetry preserves the reflectional symmetry of the second partial derivative; it is left invariant by reflections of the form $x \to -x$.

17.4 Accuracy of finite-difference approximations

We have proposed making approximations of the form

$$\frac{\partial u}{\partial \tau}(x,\tau) \approx \frac{u(x,\tau+\delta\tau) - u(x,\tau)}{\delta\tau}.$$

where we assume that $\delta\tau$ is small. It is important to ask the question:

- How accurate are these approximations?

This determines how small $\delta\tau$ must in fact be. We can answer this question by considering Taylor's theorem. If we assume that $u(x,\tau)$ is sufficiently differentiable (and it can be shown that for $\tau > 0$ any solution of $\partial u/\partial\tau = \partial^2 u/\partial x^2$ with analytic spatial boundary conditions is infinitely differentiable), then Taylor's theorem asserts that

$$u(x,\tau+\delta\tau) = u(x,\tau) + \frac{\partial u}{\partial \tau}(x,\tau)\,\delta\tau + R_2\frac{(\delta\tau)^2}{2!}, \tag{17.14}$$

where the remainder term R_2 satisfies the inequality

$$|R_2| \le \max_{\tau\le\zeta\le\tau+\delta\tau}\left|\frac{\partial^2 u}{\partial \tau^2}(x,\zeta)\right|.$$

Assuming that $\partial^2 u/\partial\tau^2$ is continuous implies that R_2 is finite, and hence after some simple manipulations we find that

$$\frac{\partial u}{\partial \tau}(x,\tau) = \frac{u(x,\tau+\delta\tau) - u(x,\tau)}{\delta\tau} + \tfrac{1}{2}R_2\,\delta\tau. \tag{17.15}$$

We can do likewise for the backward difference (simply replace $\delta\tau$ by $-\delta\tau$ above), and we find that both forward and backward differences give approximations to $\partial u/\partial\tau$ where the error goes to zero like $R_2\,\delta\tau$ as $\delta\tau$ goes to zero. We write this as

$$\begin{aligned}\frac{\partial u}{\partial\tau}(x,\tau) &= \frac{u(x,\tau+\delta\tau)-u(x,\tau)}{\delta\tau}+O(\delta\tau),\\ \frac{\partial u}{\partial\tau}(x,\tau) &= \frac{u(x,\tau)-u(x,\tau-\delta\tau)}{\delta\tau}+O(\delta\tau).\end{aligned} \tag{17.16}$$

We can interpret the condition '$\delta\tau$ is small' to mean that terms of $O(\delta\tau)$ are negligible.

Similarly, backward and forward difference approximations to $\partial u/\partial x$ are accurate to $O(\delta x)$, by which we mean that the error in these finite-difference approximations goes to zero linearly with δx.

By considering the Taylor expansions

$$u(x+\delta x,\tau)=u(x,\tau)+\frac{\partial u}{\partial x}(x,\tau)\,\delta x+\frac{\partial^2 u}{\partial x^2}(x,\tau)\frac{(\delta x)^2}{2!}+R_3\frac{(\delta x)^3}{3!},$$

where $|R_3|$ is bounded by the maximum value of $|\partial^3 u/\partial x^3|$, and

$$\begin{aligned}u(x+\delta x,\tau)=u(x,\tau)&+\frac{\partial u}{\partial x}(x,\tau)\delta x+\frac{\partial^2 u}{\partial x^2}(x,\tau)\frac{(\delta x)^2}{2!}\\ &+\frac{\partial^3 u}{\partial x^3}(x,\tau)\frac{(\delta x)^3}{3!}+R_4\frac{(\delta x)^4}{4!},\end{aligned}$$

where $|R_4|$ is bounded by the maximum value of $|\partial^4 u/\partial x^4|$, we can show that the central difference approximations (17.12) and (17.13) are accurate to $O((\delta x)^2)$. That is

$$\begin{aligned}\frac{\partial u}{\partial x}(x,\tau) &= \frac{u(x+\delta x,\tau)-u(x-\delta x,\tau)}{2\delta x}+O((\delta x)^2),\\ \frac{\partial^2 u}{\partial x^2}(x,\tau) &= \frac{u(x+\delta x,\tau)-2u(x,\tau)+u(x-\delta x,\tau)}{(\delta x)^2}+O((\delta x)^2).\end{aligned} \tag{17.17}$$

Note that these central difference approximations exhibit quadratic convergence (the error goes to zero like $(\delta x)^2$ as δx goes to zero), whereas the forward and backward approximations (17.16) exhibit linear convergence. These expressions give rise to the possibility of rigorous error bounds for numerical solutions.

17.5 The finite-difference mesh

To continue with the finite-difference approximation to the diffusion equation we divide the x-axis into equally-spaced **nodes** a distance δx apart, and the τ-axis into equally spaced nodes a distance $\delta\tau$ apart. This divides the (x,τ) plane up into a mesh, where the **mesh points** have the form $(n\,\delta x, m\,\delta\tau)$; see Figure 17.2. We then concern ourselves only with the values of $u(x,\tau)$ at mesh points $(n\,\delta x, m\,\delta\tau)$. We write

$$u_n^m = u(n\,\delta x, m\,\delta\tau). \tag{17.18}$$

It is important to realise that this means we think of u_n^m as the value of the *exact* solution of the partial differential equation at the mesh point $(n\,\delta x, m\,\delta\tau)$. Thus, if at time-step $m\,\delta\tau$ the function $u(x, m\,\delta\tau)$ is as shown in Figure 17.3, then u_n^m takes on the discrete set of values also shown in Figure 17.3. We use finite differences to obtain a discrete set of equations which *approximate* the partial differential equation, but this gives us an only approximate system. Even if we solve this approximate system exactly, it does not give us the exact values of the u_n^m except, we hope, in the limit as $\delta\tau$ and δx tend to zero.

The finite-difference method does not actually rely on taking constant space steps δx, nor does it rely on taking constant time steps $\delta\tau$. This does, however, simplify matters. Moreover, as the finite-difference equations turn out to have a natural interpretation in terms of a random walk, the constant space step arises naturally if we are considering a process that arises from a normally distributed random walk. This is one reason for *not* using a direct discretisation of the untransformed Black–Scholes model—the underlying random walk there is lognormally distributed, so the natural step-size is not δS constant, but $\delta(\log S)$ constant.

Further reading

- Richtmyer & Morton (1967) and Smith (1985) are both very readable books on the subject of finite-difference methods.

- Brennan & Schwartz (1978) were the first to describe the application of finite difference methods to option pricing.

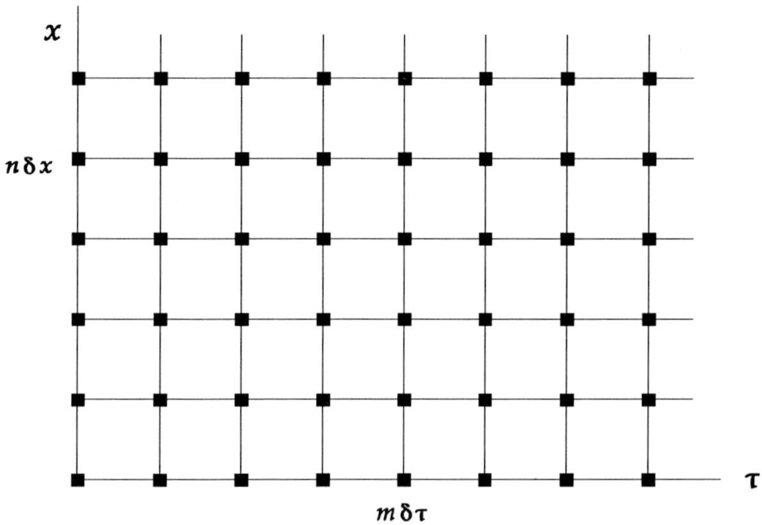

Figure 17.2: The mesh for a finite-difference approximation.

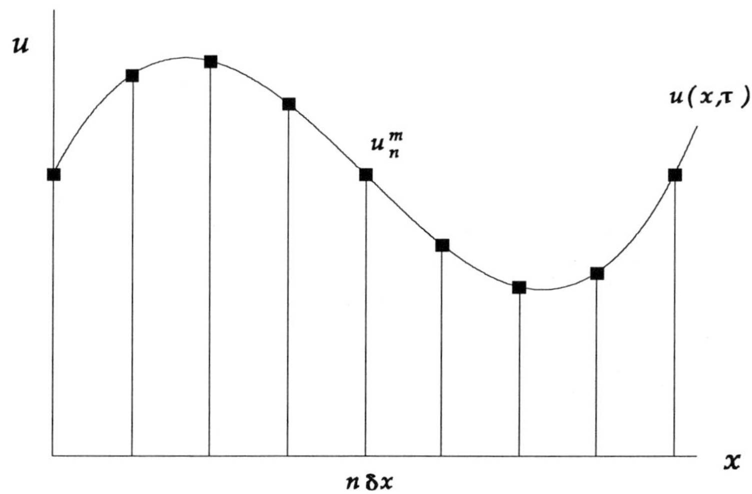

Figure 17.3: The finite-difference approximation at a fixed time-step.

- Geske & Shastri (1985) give a comparison of the efficiency of various finite-difference methods for option pricing.

Exercise

1. By considering the Taylor series expansions

$$
\begin{aligned}
u(x+\delta x,\tau) &= u(x,\tau)+\frac{\partial u}{\partial x}\delta x+\frac{\partial^2 u}{\partial x^2}\frac{(\delta x)^2}{2}+O((\delta x)^3),\\
u(x+2\delta x,\tau) &= u(x,\tau)+2\frac{\partial u}{\partial x}\delta x+2\frac{\partial^2 u}{\partial x^2}(\delta x)^2+O((\delta x)^3),
\end{aligned}
$$

in which the derivatives are evaluated at (x,τ), show that the approximation

$$
\frac{\partial u}{\partial x}(x,\tau)=\frac{-3u_n^m+4u_{n+1}^m-u_{n+2}^m}{2\,\delta x}
$$

is accurate to $O((\delta x)^2)$.

Chapter 18

The Explicit Finite-difference Method

18.1 The explicit finite-difference equations

Consider the general form of the transformed Black–Scholes model for the value of a European option,

$$\frac{\partial u}{\partial \tau} = \frac{\partial^2 u}{\partial x^2}, \tag{18.1}$$

with boundary and initial condition

$$\begin{gathered}\lim_{x \to -\infty} u(x,\tau) = f(x,\tau), \quad \lim_{x \to \infty} u(x,\tau) = g(x,\tau), \\ u(x,0) = u_0(x).\end{gathered} \tag{18.2}$$

We use the notation $f(x,\tau)$, $g(x,\tau)$ and $u_0(x)$ to emphasise that the following does not in anyway depend on the particular functions we are using. The precise forms for f, g and u_0 for puts, calls and a binary cash or nothing call are given in (17.3), (17.4) and (17.5) respectively.

Using a forward difference for $\partial u/\partial \tau$, equation (17.6), and a symmetric central difference for $\partial^2 u/\partial x^2$, equation (17.13), we find that the diffusion equation (18.1) becomes

$$\begin{aligned}&\frac{u(x,\tau+\delta\tau) - u(x,\tau)}{\delta\tau} + O(\delta\tau) \\ &\quad = \frac{u(x+\delta x,\tau) - 2u(x,\tau) + u(x-\delta x,\tau)}{(\delta x)^2} + O((\delta x)^2).\end{aligned}$$

Restricting our attention to the values of $u(x,\tau)$ on the regular mesh, with $u_n^m = u(n\,\delta x, m\,\delta\tau)$, this becomes

$$\frac{u_n^{m+1}-u_n^m}{\delta\tau}+O(\delta\tau)=\frac{u_{n+1}^m-2u_n^m+u_{n-1}^m}{(\delta x)^2}+O((\delta x)^2).$$

Ignoring terms of $O(\delta\tau)$ and $O((\delta x)^2)$, we can approximate this by

$$v_n^{m+1}=v_n^m+\alpha\left(v_{n+1}^m+v_{n-1}^m-2v_n^m\right), \tag{18.3}$$

where

$$\alpha=\frac{\delta\tau}{(\delta x)^2}. \tag{18.4}$$

We use v_n^m to emphasise that the solution of (18.3) is only an approximate solution of the differential equation, not the exact solution, since we have derived (18.3) by neglecting terms of $O(\delta\tau)$ and $O((\delta x)^2)$. That is, v_n^m is the solution of (18.3), whereas $u_n^m = u(n\,\delta x, m\,\delta\tau)$. This allows us to consider the **convergence** question:

- Does $v_n^m \to u_n^m$ as $\delta\tau \to 0$ and $\delta x \to 0$?

If, at time-step m, we know v_n^m for all values of n we can explicitly calculate v_n^{m+1}. This is why this method is called explicit. Note that v_n^{m+1} depends only on v_{n+1}^m, v_n^m and v_{n-1}^m. These relationships are illustrated in Figure 18.1, which also suggests that (18.3) may be considered as a random walk on a regular lattice.

If we choose a constant x-spacing δx, we cannot solve the problem for all $-\infty < x < \infty$ without taking an infinite number of x-steps. We get around this problem by taking a finite, but suitably large (to be made precise shortly), number of x-steps. We restrict our attention to the interval

$$-N^-\delta x \le x \le N^+\delta x$$

where $N^-\delta x$ and $N^+\delta x$ are large, and replace the boundary conditions in (18.2) by the approximate conditions

$$v_{-N^-}^m = f(-N^-\delta x, m\,\delta\tau), \quad v_{N^+}^m = g(N^+\delta x, m\,\delta\tau), \tag{18.5}$$

and the initial condition in (18.2) by the discretised initial conditions

$$v_n^0 = u_0(n\,\delta x), \quad -N^- \le n \le N^+. \tag{18.6}$$

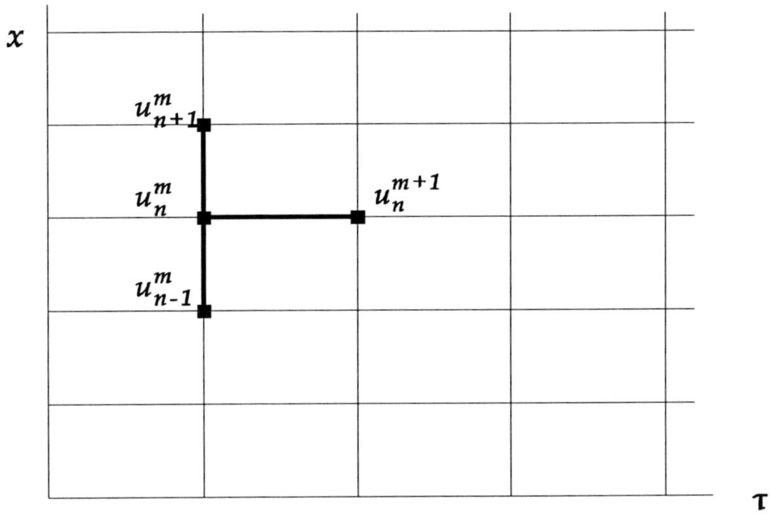

Figure 18.1: Explicit finite-difference discretisation.

18.2 Approximating an infinite mesh

One reason that we can approximate an infinite interval by a finite number of x-mesh points is that, from inspection of (18.3) and Figure 18.1, we can see that any errors in v^m_{N+} can influence only the values of v^i_j where $i + j \geq m + N^+$. This means that the errors introduced by approximating the infinite mesh by a finite one are confined to the regions illustrated in Figure 18.2.[1] Observe that, since we are only interested in options that have finite non-dimensional exercise times, we only have to solve (18.3) for $0 \leq m \leq M$ where the expiry time T determines M by

$$M\,\delta\tau = \tfrac{1}{2}\sigma^2 T.$$

We know the asymptotic form of $u(x, \tau)$ for large positive and negative x, so we do not have to calculate this. By making N^- and N^+ large enough we can always ensure that the error introduced by truncation of the infinite mesh is confined to triangles at each end of the mesh where the numerical solution is not required.

[1]Inspection of this figure should also show, in principle, why binomial and trinomial methods are simply special cases of the explicit finite-difference method.

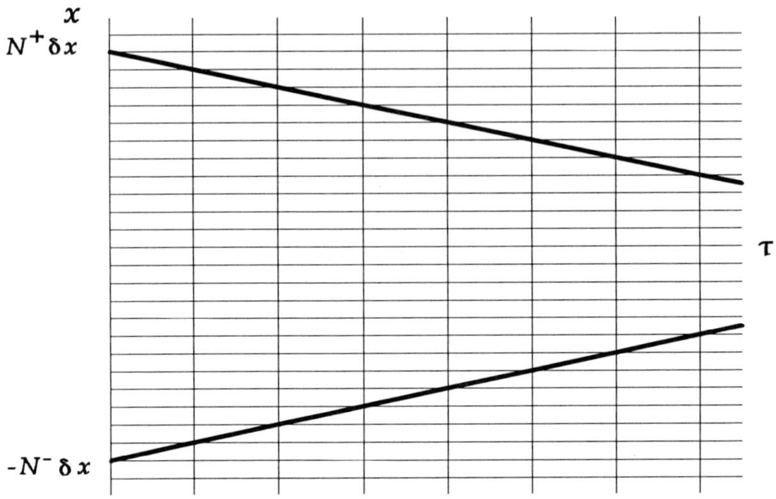

Figure 18.2: Region of boundary condition error dependence.

18.3 The explicit finite-difference algorithm

To obtain the finite-difference approximation for the option price, we divide the non-dimensional time to expiry of the option, $\frac{1}{2}\sigma^2 T$, into M equal time-steps so that

$$\delta\tau = \tfrac{1}{2}\sigma^2 T/M$$

and solve (18.3), subject to (18.5) and (18.6). This means we solve

$$v_n^{m+1} = v_n^m + \alpha(v_{n+1}^m - 2v_n^m + v_{n-1}^m), \quad -N^- < n < N^+, \quad 0 < m \le M.$$

We use the initial condition to find

$$v_n^0 = u_0(n\,\delta x), \; -N^- \le n \le N^+$$

and use these values to start the iterative procedure. We also have the boundary conditions

$$v_{-N^-}^m = f(-N^-\delta x, m\,\delta\tau), \; 0 < m \le M,$$
$$v_{N^+}^m = g(N^+\delta x, m\,\delta\tau), \; 0 < m \le M,$$

so that we do not have to solve for $v^m_{-N^-}$ or $v^m_{N^+}$; they are determined from the boundary conditions.

The algorithm is as follows:

1. Starting with the initial values of v^0_n, we apply (18.3) to solve for v^1_n for $-N^- < n < N^+$. We use the boundary conditions to determine $v^1_{N^-}$ and $v^1_{N^+}$. This completely determines v^1_n for $-N^- \leq n \leq N^+$.

2. Repeat the process to find v^2_n, and so on, until we have found v^M_n. Since the equations determining v^{m+1}_n in terms of the v^m_n's are explicit, this process can be easily coded for a computer to solve; a pseudo-code is given in Figure 18.3.

In Figure 18.4 we compare explicit finite-difference solutions for a European put with the exact Black–Scholes formula. This option has six months to expiry and an exercise price $E = 10$, the annual volatility is $\sigma = 0.2$ and risk-free annual interest rate $r = 0.05$. In each calculation the x-mesh spacing is first fixed and the time-step is determined from the quantity α, defined by (18.4). We have deliberately chosen to regard α and $\delta\tau$ as variable (rather than the more obvious choice of δx and $\delta\tau$) to illustrate an extremely important point. Notice that with $\alpha = 0.25$ and $\alpha = 0.5$ there is good agreement between computed and exact solutions. When $\alpha = 0.52$, the computed solution is nonsensical. This illustrates the **stability** problem.

18.4 The stability problem

The stability problem arises because we are using finite precision computer arithmetic to solve the difference equation (18.3). This introduces rounding errors into the *numerical* solution of (18.3). The system (18.3) is said to be **stable** if these rounding errors are not magnified at each iteration. If the rounding errors do grow in magnitude at each iteration of the solution procedure, then (18.3) is said to be **unstable**.

The important result is that the system (18.3) is

- stable if $0 < \alpha \leq \frac{1}{2}$ (**stability condition**),
- unstable if $\alpha > \frac{1}{2}$ (**instability condition**).

```
explicit_fd( values, dx, dt, M )
{
  alpha = dt/(dx*dx);

  /* set up initial values of array */

  for( i = -Nminus; i <= Nplus; ++i )
     oldv[i] = pay_off( i*dx );

  /* solve diffusion equation */

  for( time = 1; time <= M; ++time ) {

     newv[-Nminus] = f(-Nminus*dx,time*dt);
     newv[ Nplus ] = g( Nplus*dx, time*dt);

     for(i=-Nminus+1; i<Nplus; ++i)
        newv[i] = oldv[i] + alpha*
                  (oldv[i-1]-2*oldv[i]+oldv[i+1]);
     for(i=-Nminus; i <= Nplus; ++i)
        oldv[i] = newv[i];
  }
  /* and return values */

  for(i=-Nminus; i <= Nplus; ++i)
    values[i] = oldv[i];

}
```

Figure 18.3: Pseudo-code for explicit finite-difference solution for a European option.

S	$\alpha = 0.25$	$\alpha = 0.50$	$\alpha = 0.52$	exact
0.00	9.7531	9.7531	9.7531	9.7531
2.00	7.7531	7.7531	7.7531	7.7531
4.00	5.7531	5.7531	5.7531	5.7531
6.00	3.7532	3.7532	2.9498	3.7532
7.00	2.7567	2.7567	−17.4192	2.7568
8.00	1.7986	1.7985	95.3210	1.7987
9.00	0.9879	0.9879	350.5603	0.9880
10.00	0.4418	0.4419	625.0347	0.4420
11.00	0.1605	0.1607	−457.3122	0.1606
12.00	0.0483	0.0483	−208.9135	0.0483
13.00	0.0124	0.0123	40.5813	0.0124
14.00	0.0028	0.0027	−15.2150	0.0028
15.00	0.0006	0.0005	−3.1582	0.0006
16.00	0.0001	0.0001	0.7365	0.0001

Figure 18.4: Comparison of exact Black–Scholes solution and explicit finite-difference solutions for a European put with $E = 10$, $r = 0.05$, $\sigma = 0.20$ and with six months to expiry. Note the effect of taking $\alpha > \frac{1}{2}$.

The system (18.3) is also unstable if we choose $\alpha < 0$, but in this case we have a finite-difference approximation for a backward diffusion equation, which is itself an unstable equation.

Notice that this puts severe constraints on the size of time-steps. For stability we must have

$$0 < \frac{\delta\tau}{(\delta x)^2} \leq \tfrac{1}{2}.$$

This means that if we start with a stable solution on a mesh and double the number of x-mesh points, we must quarter the size of the time-step. Each iteration then takes twice as long (twice as many x-mesh spacings) and there are four times as many time-steps. Thus, doubling the number of x-mesh points means that finding the solution takes eight times as long. If we increase the number of x-points by a factor of K, then the number of calculations performed increases by a factor of K^3.

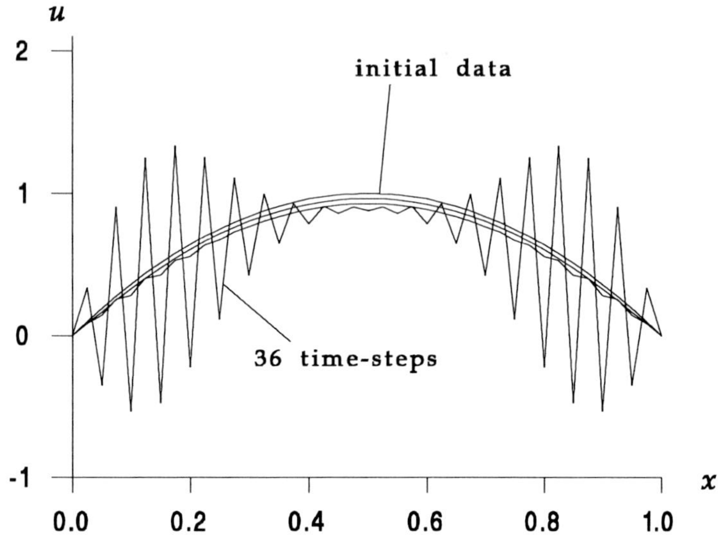

Figure 18.5: Growth of instabilities for explicit finite-difference method, applied to the diffusion equation with parabolic initial data and fixed boundary values. The value of α is 0.6.

When a numerical solution of the diffusion equation is unstable, it is entirely obvious that it is. Instability is characterised by exponentially growing oscillation as illustrated in Figure 18.5, in which $\alpha = 0.6$. This is important, because it turns out that the stability and convergence problems for the explicit finite-difference method for the diffusion equation are equivalent; the explicit finite-difference solution converges if and only if it is stable. Thus the fact that instability is obvious is useful; it is easy to see that a solution is unstable and hence deduce that it is not converging to the solution of the partial differential equation.

18.5 The stability of explicit finite differences

One way of understanding the stability problem, and of seeing why the onset of instability occurs as α exceeds $\frac{1}{2}$ is as follows. Suppose that we can find the exact solution of (18.3), using infinite precision arithmetic say. Let v_n^m be an exact solution. We then simulate the effect of **rounding errors** by introducing a small error into the initial data

$$\hat{v}_n^0 = v_n^0 + E_n^0,$$

where E_n^0 represents the small initial error, and write

$$\hat{v}_n^m = v_n^m + E_n^m$$

so that E_n^m represents the error at time-step m. If we assume that v_n^m and $\hat{v}_n^m$ are both exact solutions of (18.3), then we find that the error $E_n^m = \hat{v}^m - v_n^m$ also satisfies (18.3). Suppose that we try an error of the form[2]

$$E_n^m = \epsilon\lambda^m \sin n\omega,$$

so that $E_n^0 = \epsilon \sin n\omega$ is a small harmonic perturbation to the initial data[3]. We then find that

$$\lambda^{m+1} \sin n\omega = \lambda^m \sin n\omega + \alpha\lambda^m(\sin(n+1)\omega - 2\sin n\omega + \sin(n-1)\omega),$$

and rearranging gives

$$\lambda = 1 + \alpha\left(\frac{\sin(n+1)\omega - 2\sin n\omega + \sin(n-1)\omega}{\sin n\omega}\right).$$

Recalling that $\sin(A+B)+\sin(A-B) = 2\sin A\cos B$, we can rewrite this as

$$\lambda = 1 + 2\alpha(\cos\omega - 1) = 1 - 4\alpha\sin^2 \tfrac{1}{2}\omega.$$

If, on the one hand, $0 \le \alpha \le \frac{1}{2}$, then we always have $-1 \le \lambda \le 1$, no matter what frequency ω we choose. Thus, whatever ω is, we see that the error does not grow as m increases since

$$E_n^m = \epsilon\lambda^m \sin n\omega, \quad |\lambda| \le 1.$$

Indeed, we see that small initial errors decay. This has the important consequence that small errors in the initial (and boundary) data, however they are caused, will die out.

If we choose $\alpha > \frac{1}{2}$, on the other hand, we see that for certain choices of ω, $\lambda < -1$. For such an error we see that

$$|E_n^m| = |\epsilon\lambda^m \sin n\omega| \to \infty$$

[2]In this expression λ^m denotes λ raised to the power m.

[3]This is perfectly general since an arbitrary initial error can be written as a sum of such harmonic perturbations using Fourier analysis.

as m increases, since $|\lambda| > 1$. That is, if $\alpha > \frac{1}{2}$ then errors grow without bound. This is instability.

We also see that we can have $|\lambda| > 1$ if $\alpha < 0$, so $\alpha < 0$ is also unstable; this is equivalent, of course, to attempting to solve the *backward* diffusion equation.

18.6 Convergence of the explicit method

It is an important result that, provided we ensure that we let $\delta\tau$ and δx tend to zero in such a way that the ratio $\alpha = \delta\tau/(\delta x)^2$ remains between 0 and $\frac{1}{2}$, we can *prove* that the finite-difference approximation converges to the actual solution. It is also worth noting that if we do not keep the ratio α less than or equal to $\frac{1}{2}$ as we let δx and $\delta\tau$ tend to zero, the solution of the finite-difference equations (18.3) *does not* tend to solution of the partial differential equations. (That is, as noted above, the finite-difference approximation converges if and only if it is stable.) In a sense this latter point is irrelevant, since the exact solution of (18.3) is unstable for $\alpha > \frac{1}{2}$ (and also for $\alpha < 0$) so we would never be able to calculate it.

An important consequence of this **convergence** result is that we can make the discretisation errors, between the finite-difference scheme and the exact solution, as small as we want to make it by taking small enough time-steps (that is, by making $\delta\tau$ small enough), provided that we meet the condition

$$0 < \frac{\delta\tau}{(\delta x)^2} \leq \tfrac{1}{2}.$$

In reality, the finite precision arithmetic inherent in any computer implies that if we take $\delta\tau$ too small, then the rounding errors become the dominant error, so this theoretical result has its practical limitations. Against this is the fact that no-one would, in practice, take a value of $\delta\tau$ so small that rounding errors became more important than discretisation errors for the very simple reason that the number of time iterations necessary to solve a sensible problem would then be of the order of 10^8 or so.

To demonstrate that the explicit finite-difference scheme outlined above does indeed converge to the solution of partial differential equation we consider the difference between the exact solution $u(x,\tau)$

and the finite-difference approximation. To this end, we consider the **discretisation error**

$$D_n^m = u_n^m - v_n^m.$$

(Recall that v_n^m is the solution of the explicit finite-difference equations (18.3) and $u_n^m = u(n\,\delta x, m\,\delta\tau)$ is the value of the solution of the partial differential equation at the mesh points.)

Using the fact that the exact solution satisfies the partial differential equation, and the estimates given in (17.14), (17.15), (17.16) and (17.17), we find that

$$D_n^{m+1} = (1-2\alpha)D_n^m + \alpha(D_{n+1}^m + D_{n-1}^m) + \delta\tau\left(R_2\frac{\delta\tau}{2} + R_4\frac{(\delta x)^2}{12}\right).$$

Putting $\hat{R}_2 = |R_2/2|$ and $\hat{R}_4 = |R_4/12|$, this yields

$$\left|D_n^{m+1}\right| \le |(1-2\alpha)D_n^m| + \left|\alpha D_{n+1}^m\right| + \left|\alpha D_{n-1}^m\right| + \delta\tau\left(\hat{R}_2\delta\tau + \hat{R}_4(\delta x)^2\right).$$

Now if we let $\hat{D}_m$ be the largest error in absolute value at time-step m, and $\hat{D}_{m+1}$ be the largest error in absolute value at time-step $m+1$,

$$\hat{D}^m = \max_n\left|D_n^m\right|, \quad \hat{D}^{m+1} = \max_n\left|D_n^{m+1}\right|,$$

and so forth, we get

$$\hat{D}^{m+1} \le (|1-2\alpha| + 2|\alpha|)\hat{D}^m + \delta\tau\left(\hat{R}_2\delta\tau + \hat{R}_4(\delta x)^2\right).$$

Provided that $0 \le \alpha \le \frac{1}{2}$ we have

$$|1-2\alpha| + 2|\alpha| = 1$$

(and note that this is *not* true if $\alpha < 0$ or $\alpha > \frac{1}{2}$), and hence

$$\hat{D}^{m+1} \le \hat{D}^m + \delta\tau\left(\hat{R}_2\delta\tau + \hat{R}_4(\delta x)^2\right).$$

By induction it follows that

$$\hat{D}^{m+1} \le \hat{D}^0 + (m+1)\delta\tau\left(\hat{R}_2\delta\tau + \hat{R}_4(\delta x)^2\right),$$

so that if we assume zero error at time-step $m = 0$, which we can do since $v_n^0 = u_n^0$ from the initial condition, we see that

$$\hat{D}^{m+1} \leq (m+1)\delta\tau \left(\hat{R}_2 \delta\tau + \hat{R}_4 (\delta x)^2 \right) \to 0 \text{ as } \delta\tau \to 0.$$

This proves that the maximum error between u_n^m and v_n^m tends to zero as $\delta\tau \to 0$, provided $0 \leq \alpha \leq \frac{1}{2}$. Thus, the explicit finite-difference method converges to the solution of the partial differential equation as $\delta\tau \to 0$ with $(\delta x)^2 = \alpha\,\delta\tau$. Note that it is not the $(m+1)\,|\delta\tau|$ term that gives the convergence, since as $\delta\tau \to 0$, $m \to \infty$ in order that $(m+1)\delta\tau$ remains constant. It is the second term that gives convergence.

A simple modification to this argument shows that if $\alpha \geq \frac{1}{2}$ then the error actually grows without bound as we let $\delta\tau \to 0$ and m increase.

In practice we find that, assuming $0 < \alpha \leq \frac{1}{2}$, the above estimate for the growth of the maximum error is absurdly high. Generally speaking, the maximum error tends to zero, rather than increasing with the number of time-steps. This is, in part, illustrated by the exponential damping of errors mentioned above.

18.7 Probabilistic interpretation of explicit finite differences

The explicit difference scheme (18.3) has a natural interpretation as a discrete random walk. Imagine a random walk taking place on the (x, τ) mesh with equally spaced x-nodes, a distance δx apart, and equally spaced τ-nodes, a distance $\delta\tau$ apart, as in Figure 17.2. If we interpret v_n^m as the probability that a marker is at mesh position $(n\,\delta x, m\,\delta\tau)$ at time $m\,\delta\tau$, then writing (18.3) as

$$v_n^{m+1} = \alpha v_{n-1}^m + (1-2\alpha) v_n^m + \alpha v_{n+1}^m,$$

we see that (18.3) describes a random walk in which the marker can move to the right or the left with probability α or stay put with probability $(1-2\alpha)$. In particular, the critical value $\alpha = \frac{1}{2}$ (which marks the boundary between stability and instability) corresponds to a binomial walk, where the marker cannot stay put. Instability corresponds to $\alpha > \frac{1}{2}$ or $\alpha < 0$; in both cases this means a negative probability. The random walk gives rise to a normal distribution as $\delta\tau \to 0$ and in view of $\alpha = \delta\tau/(\delta x)^2$, the size natural x step size is order $\sqrt{\delta\tau}$. Thus, the finite-difference scheme accurately reflects the underlying assumptions about the stochastic variable $x = \log(S/E)$. In this sense the binomial and trinomial models are simply explicit finite-difference methods (consider the logarithm of the binomial and trinomial asset prices—these form a regularly spaced mesh).

It is possible to use finite-difference methods on the Black–Scholes equation directly. That is, using a *backward* difference approximation for time (because the Black–Scholes equation is *backward* parabolic) and central difference approximation for asset price S, the equation

$$\frac{\partial V}{\partial t} + \tfrac{1}{2}\sigma^2 S^2 \frac{\partial^2 V}{\partial S^2} + rS\frac{\partial V}{\partial S} - rV = 0$$

can be approximated by the explicit scheme

$$V_n^m = a_{n-1} V_{n-1}^{m+1} + b_n V_n^{m+1} + c_{n+1} V_{n+1}^{m+1}$$

where

$$\begin{aligned} a_{n-1} &= \tfrac{1}{2}\delta t\left(\sigma^2 n^2 - r\right) \\ b_n &= 1 - \delta t\left(\sigma^2 n^2 + r\right) \\ c_{n+1} &= \tfrac{1}{2}\delta t\left(\sigma^2 n^2 + r\right). \end{aligned}$$

Bearing in mind that we are solving for m decreasing and that we use the payoff function to determine V_n^M, there are two serious problems with such a discretisation. Firstly, it does not reflect the nature of the underlying random walk. The variable S is lognormally distributed and so the natural mesh does not have equally spaced S-jumps; rather it has equally spaced jumps in $\log S$.

Secondly, this equation is undesirable from the point of view of stability and convergence. The balance that decides stability is the balance between $\partial V/\partial t$ and $\frac{1}{2}\sigma^2 S^2 \partial^2 V/\partial S^2$. In order to obtain a stable solution we need

$$0 \le \delta t \le \frac{1}{\sigma^2 (N^+)^2}$$

(see the exercises at the end of the chapter). The maximum stable time step now depends only on the number of S-steps, but not the

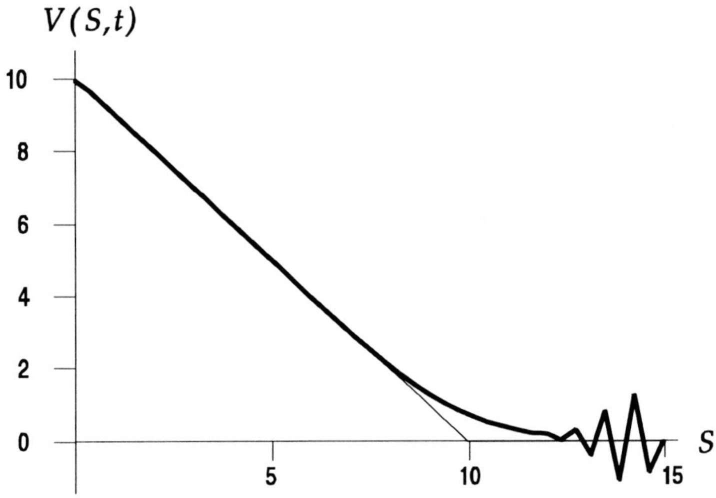

Figure 18.6: Instability problem for direct discretisation of Black–Scholes.

size of the S-step. Since the convergence of the method clearly does depend on the size of the S-step, the convergence and stability criteria are distinct. This is undesirable in that non-convergent schemes could still be stable.

Moreover, it is not obvious whether the scheme is stable. Indeed, the scheme can be stable for small S and unstable for large S. The instabilities in this system tend to be concentrated near the right-hand end of the mesh where n is large. Consider, for example, taking

$$\delta t = \frac{1}{\sigma^2 (N^+ - 3)^2}.$$

Then the system would be stable except at the nodes $n = N^+ - 2$, $n = N^+ - 1$ and $n = N^+$. A common manifestation of this problem is that negative option values are predicted for large values of S. This rather perverse behaviour cannot happen with the regular discretisation of the transformed equation where either the system is stable at every mesh point or it is unstable at every mesh point. The problem is illustrated in Figure 18.6, which shows a numerical solution of an

American put problem with $\sigma = 0.9$, $r = 0.1$, $E = 10$ and one year to expiry. With $\alpha = 0.9$ and 40 S-steps, the solution became unstable after 36 time-steps at S-step 33 ($S = 12.375$).

Technical Point: interpolation.

One apparent advantage of direct discretisation of the Black–Scholes equation is that the consequent numerical method returns values of the option at equally spaced values of the underlying. This is in contrast to the procedure we advocate above, namely transforming to the diffusion equation and solving on an equally spaced grid, because the values of the option are returned at geometrically spaced underlying values. The alert reader will have noticed that the put values in figure 18.4 *are listed at (more or less) equally spaced intervals in S and will, possibly, have thought this a little odd.*

In order to produce values of the put at equally spaced values of S we used **interpolation**. *Having solved the diffusion equation for u on an equally spaced x-grid, we find the value of the option for any value of S as follows. We first find the value of x corresponding to the S we require: $x = \log(S/E)$. This, we assume, lies between two grid points, say $x_{i-1} < x < x_i$. Then we approximate the value of u at x by assuming that u varies linearly from u_{i-1}^m to u_i^m as x varies from x_{i-1} to x_i. Thus we obtain the approximation*

$$u(x, m\,\delta\tau) \approx u_{i-1} + \left(\frac{u_i - u_{i-1}}{x_i - x_{i-1}}\right)(x - x_{i-1}).$$

Having found the value of u at x, it is then a simple matter to transform back into financial variables and obtain the value of V at the given S.

There are considerably more sophisticated methods of interpolation than the simple linear scheme we have proposed here, such as cubic splines and Lagrange interpolation. Linear interpolation is, however, accurate to the same order as our numerical scheme, i.e. $O((\delta x)^2)$, and as such suffices for our purposes. For further discussion and application of interpolation, see Section 22.3.

Further reading

- See Johnson & Riess (1982) and Smith (1985) for more discussion of the explicit finite-difference method.
- See Hill & Dewynne (1991) for further discussion of the relation between random walks, the diffusion equation and finite-difference methods.

Exercises

1. Write a computer program to value a European call using explicit finite differences.

2. Show that on a grid with K x-mesh points, it requires K multiplications (which are much slower operations than addition and subtraction on a computer) per time-step to solve (18.3).

3. Consider using the symmetric central-difference approximations
$$\frac{\partial u}{\partial \tau}(n\,\delta x, m\,\delta\tau) \sim \frac{u_n^{m+1} - u_n^{m-1}}{2\,\delta\tau} + O((\delta\tau)^2)$$
$$\frac{\partial^2 u}{\partial x^2}(n\,\delta x, m\,\delta\tau) \sim \frac{u_{n+1}^m - 2u_n^m + u_{n-1}^m}{(\delta x)^2} + O((\delta x)^2)$$
to solve the diffusion equation. Show that the resulting system of difference equations is
$$v_n^{m+1} = v_n^{m-1} + 2\alpha\left(v_{n+1}^m - 2v_n^m + v_{n-1}^m\right),$$
where, as usual, $\alpha = \delta\tau/(\delta x)^2$. Assuming an error of the form $E_n^m = \lambda^m \sin n\omega$, show that λ satisfies a quadratic equation. Deduce that if $\alpha \neq 0$, one of its roots has $|\lambda| > 1$ so that the scheme is always unstable.

4. Find an explicit finite-difference approximation for the equation
$$\frac{\partial V}{\partial t} + \tfrac{1}{2}\sigma^2 S^2 \frac{\partial^2 V}{\partial S^2} = 0$$
on the interval $0 < S < S_{max}$ divided into N equal steps of size $\delta S = S_{max}/N$. Deduce that the scheme is stable for *all* points on the mesh if and only if
$$0 < \delta t < 1/\sigma^2 N^2.$$

Chapter 19

Implicit Finite-difference Methods

19.1 The purpose of implicit methods

Implicit finite-difference methods are used to overcome the stability and convergence limitations imposed by the restriction

$$0 < \alpha = \frac{\delta\tau}{(\delta x)^2} \leq \tfrac{1}{2},$$

which applies to the explicit finite-difference method. Implicit finite-difference methods allow us to use a large number of x-mesh points without having to take ridiculously small time-steps. We discuss the fully implicit finite-difference method, the Crank–Nicolson finite-difference method and the implicit finite-difference θ-method which unifies the previous two.

Unlike the explicit method, implicit methods require the solution of *systems* of equations. We discuss the highly efficient numerical method of LU decompositions for solving the systems of equations that arise from implicit finite-difference schemes. The consequence is that, although an implicit finite-difference scheme is slightly more difficult to implement on a computer, it is almost as efficient as the explicit method in terms of arithmetical operations per time-step[1].

[1]In their most efficient forms explicit and implicit methods require $O(N)$ arithmetical operations per time-step, where N is the number of x-grid points.

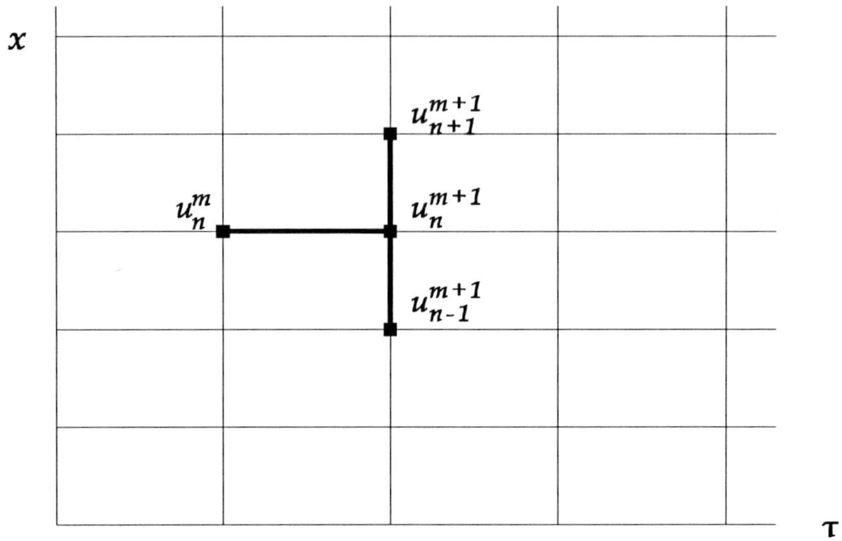

Figure 19.1: Implicit finite-difference discretisation.

Since fewer time-steps need to be taken, implicit finite-difference methods are usually more efficient than explicit methods.

19.2 The fully implicit method

The fully implicit finite-difference scheme, which is usually known as the **implicit finite-difference** method, uses the backward difference approximation (17.7) for the $\partial u/\partial\tau$ term and the symmetric central difference approximation (17.13) for the $\partial^2 u/\partial x^2$ term. This leads to the equation

$$\frac{u_n^m - u_n^{m-1}}{\delta\tau} + O(\delta\tau) = \frac{u_{n+1}^m - 2u_n^m + u_{n-1}^m}{(\delta x)^2} + O((\delta x)^2),$$

where we are using the same notation as in the previous chapter. We approximate this equation by the difference system

$$\frac{v_n^m - v_n^{m-1}}{\delta\tau} = \frac{v_{n+1}^m - 2v_n^m + v_{n-1}^m}{(\delta x)^2}.$$

After rearrangement, we obtain the implicit finite-difference equations in the form

$$v_n^m - \alpha(v_{n-1}^m - 2v_n^m + v_{n+1}^m) = v_n^{m-1}. \tag{19.1}$$

As before, the space-step and the time-step are related through the parameter

$$\alpha = \frac{\delta\tau}{(\delta x)^2}$$

and v_n^m is our numerical approximation to the exact value u_n^m. Now v_n^m, v_{n-1}^m and v_{n+1}^m all depend on v_n^{m-1} in an *implicit* manner: the new values cannot immediately be separated out and solved for explicitly in terms of the old values. The scheme is illustrated in Figure 19.1.

Let us consider the European option problems discussed in the previous chapter. We assume that we can truncate the infinite mesh at $x = -N^-\delta x$ and $x = N^+\delta x$, and take N^- and N^+ sufficiently large so that no significant errors are introduced[2]. As before we find the v_n^0 from the initial data,

$$v_n^0 = u_0(n\,\delta x), \quad -N^- \le n \le N^+,$$

and the $v_{-N^-}^m$ and $v_{N^+}^m$ from the boundary conditions

$$\begin{aligned} v_{-N^-}^m &= f(-N^-\delta x, m\,\delta\tau), \\ v_{N^+}^m &= g(N^+\delta x, m\,\delta\tau). \end{aligned}$$

The problem is then to find the v_n^m for $m \ge 1$ and $-N^- < n < N^+$

[2]Note, however, that the simple argument used in the previous section no longer works in this case. An error in, say, $v_{N^+}^0$ is propagated to every v_n^1. We argue this time that the boundary values for large x and large negative x will be very close to the boundary values at infinity, so that the errors we are introducing are small. This can be made more precise and rigorous using, for example, the fundamental solution of the diffusion equation. Intuitively it follows from the stability proof; the small errors introduced by truncation are damped exponentially at each time-step.

from (19.1). We can write it as the linear system

$$\begin{pmatrix} 1+2\alpha & -\alpha & 0 & \cdots & 0 \\ -\alpha & 1+2\alpha & -\alpha & & 0 \\ 0 & -\alpha & \ddots & \ddots & \\ \vdots & & \ddots & \ddots & -\alpha \\ 0 & 0 & & -\alpha & 1+2\alpha \end{pmatrix} \begin{pmatrix} v^m_{N^+-1} \\ \vdots \\ v^m_0 \\ \vdots \\ v^m_{-N^-+1} \end{pmatrix}$$

$$= \begin{pmatrix} v^{m-1}_{N^+-1} \\ \vdots \\ v^{m-1}_0 \\ \vdots \\ v^{m-1}_{-N^-+1} \end{pmatrix} + \alpha \begin{pmatrix} v^m_{N^+} \\ 0 \\ \vdots \\ 0 \\ v^m_{-N^-} \end{pmatrix}. \tag{19.2}$$

The vector on the extreme right-hand side of this equation arises from the end equations, for example

$$(1+2\alpha)v^m_{N^+-1} - \alpha v^m_{N^+-2} = v^{m-1}_{N^+-1} + \alpha v^m_{N^+},$$

and the fact that the boundary conditions determine both $v^m_{N^+}$ and $v^m_{-N^-}$. We can write (19.2) in the somewhat more compact form

$$\mathbf{M}\boldsymbol{v}^m = \boldsymbol{v}^{m-1} + \boldsymbol{b}^m \tag{19.3}$$

where $\boldsymbol{v}^m$ and $\boldsymbol{b}^m$ denote the $(N^+ + N^- - 2)$-dimensional vectors

$$\boldsymbol{v}^m = (v^m_{N^+-1}, \ldots, v^m_{-N^-+1}), \quad \boldsymbol{b}^m = \alpha(v^m_{N^+}, 0, 0, \ldots, 0, v^m_{-N^-}),$$

and $\mathbf{M}$ is the $(N^+ + N^- - 2)$-square symmetric matrix given in (19.2).

19.2.1 The invertibility of M

In order to solve for $\boldsymbol{v}^m$ in terms of $\boldsymbol{v}^{m-1}$ and $\boldsymbol{b}^m$, it is important that it be possible to invert the matrix $\mathbf{M}$. If $\mathbf{M}$ is not invertible, then (19.2) and (19.3) do not have a solution in general, and if they do have a solution it will not be unique. In practice we *do not solve* (19.3) *by inverting the matrix* $\mathbf{M}$, but it is important to know that we can, in principle, do the inversion.

A square matrix $\mathbf{A}$ whose elements are A_{ij} is called **strictly diagonally dominant** if

$$|A_{ii}| > \sum_{j=1, j\neq i}^{n} |A_{ij}| .$$

This means that the diagonal element in each row is greater in absolute value than the sum of the absolute values of the non-diagonal elements in the row. It is well known that a strictly diagonally dominant matrix is necessarily invertible (see for example Johnson & Riess 1982).

The diagonal elements of $\mathbf{M}$ are all $1 + 2\alpha$, whereas the non-diagonal elements are all either 0 or $-\alpha$. The matrix $\mathbf{M}$ is diagonally dominant for any $\alpha > 0$, since, obviously,

$$|1 + 2\alpha| > 2\,|\alpha| , \qquad \text{if } \alpha > 0.$$

Thus the matrix $\mathbf{M}$ in (19.3) is invertible.

Since $\mathbf{M}$ can be shown to be invertible we have, in principle,

$$\boldsymbol{v}^m = \mathbf{M}^{-1}(\boldsymbol{v}^{m-1} + \boldsymbol{b}^m), \tag{19.4}$$

where $\mathbf{M}^{-1}$ is such that $\mathbf{M}^{-1}\mathbf{M} = \mathbf{I}$. Thus we can find $\boldsymbol{v}^m$ given $\boldsymbol{v}^{m-1}$ and boundary conditions. Since the initial condition determines $\boldsymbol{v}^0$, we can find each $\boldsymbol{v}^m$ inductively.

19.2.2 Practical considerations

In practice there are far more efficient solution techniques than matrix inversion. The matrix $\mathbf{M}$ has the property that it is **tridiagonal**: that is, only the diagonal elements and the super- and sub-diagonal elements are non-zero. This has a number of important consequences.

Firstly, this means that we do not have to store all the zeros, just the non-zero elements. The inverse, $\mathbf{M}^{-1}$, of $\mathbf{M}$ is not tridiagonal and requires a great deal more storage. (Specifically, if $\mathbf{M}$ is an $N \times N$ tridiagonal matrix, it takes only $3N - 2$ memory words to store the diagonal, sub-diagonal and super-diagonal elements, whereas it takes N^2 memory words to store $\mathbf{M}^{-1}$. If $N = 1000$ this is the difference between 2998×8 bytes (approximately 24 kilobytes) and $1,000,000 \times 8$ bytes, or approximately 8 megabytes.)

Secondly, the tridiagonal structure of $\mathbf{M}$ means that there is a highly efficient algorithm called **LU decomposition** for solving (19.3) in $O(N)$ arithmetic operations per solution (specifically, about $4N$ operations). Leaving aside the problem of finding $\mathbf{M}^{-1}$ (which requires $O(N^3)$ operations), it requires $O(N^2)$ arithmetic operations to multiply a vector by a matrix as we would have to do in (19.4).

19.2.3 A general LU solver

A quite general method of solving a (non-singular) matrix equation of the form

$$\begin{pmatrix} a_{11} & a_{12} & \cdots & a_{1n} \\ a_{21} & a_{22} & \cdots & a_{2n} \\ \vdots & \vdots & & \vdots \\ a_{n1} & a_{n2} & \cdots & a_{nn} \end{pmatrix} \begin{pmatrix} x_1 \\ x_2 \\ \vdots \\ x_n \end{pmatrix} = \begin{pmatrix} q_1 \\ q_2 \\ \vdots \\ q_n \end{pmatrix}$$

arises from the observation that it is easy to solve matrix equations of the two forms

$$\begin{pmatrix} u_{11} & u_{12} & \cdots & u_{1n} \\ 0 & u_{22} & \cdots & u_{2n} \\ \vdots & & \ddots & \vdots \\ 0 & 0 & & u_{nn} \end{pmatrix} \begin{pmatrix} y_1 \\ y_2 \\ \vdots \\ y_n \end{pmatrix} = \begin{pmatrix} q_1 \\ q_2 \\ \vdots \\ q_n \end{pmatrix}$$

and

$$\begin{pmatrix} \ell_{11} & 0 & \cdots & 0 \\ \ell_{21} & \ell_{22} & & \vdots \\ \vdots & \vdots & \ddots & 0 \\ \ell_{n1} & \ell_{n2} & \cdots & \ell_{nn} \end{pmatrix} \begin{pmatrix} x_1 \\ x_2 \\ \vdots \\ x_n \end{pmatrix} = \begin{pmatrix} y_1 \\ y_2 \\ \vdots \\ y_n \end{pmatrix}.$$

Assuming that none of the diagonal terms u_{ii} and ℓ_{ii} are zero, then in the former case we start with the last equation and observe that at each step we can solve for the unknown y_i in terms of previously calculated y_j's. That is,

$$u_{nn}y_n = q_n$$

which gives

$$y_n = q_n/u_{nn}$$

and then from

$$u_{n-1\,n-1}y_{n-1} + u_{n-1\,n}y_n = q_{n-1}$$

we see, using the above expression for y_n, that

$$y_{n-1} = \frac{q_{n-1} - u_{n-1\,n}y_n}{u_{n-1\,n-1}} = \frac{q_{n-1} - u_{n-1\,n}q_n/u_{nn}}{u_{n-1\,n-1}}$$

and so on. This is called **backward substitution**. In the latter case we start with the first equation and observe that at each step we can solve for the unknown x_i in terms of already determined x_j's. That is,

$$\begin{aligned} \ell_{11}x_1 &= y_1 & \Rightarrow \quad x_1 &= y_1/\ell_{11} \\ \ell_{21}x_1 + \ell_{22}x_2 &= y_2 & \Rightarrow \quad x_2 &= (y_2 - \ell_{21}x_1)/\ell_{22} \\ & & &= (y_2 - \ell_{21}y_1/\ell_{11})/\ell_{22} \end{aligned}$$

and so on. This is called **forward substitution**

The idea for solving the original matrix equation is to find a decomposition of the original matrix in the form

$$\begin{pmatrix} a_{11} & a_{12} & \cdots & a_{1n} \\ a_{21} & a_{22} & \cdots & a_{2n} \\ \vdots & & \ddots & \vdots \\ a_{n1} & a_{n2} & \cdots & a_{nn} \end{pmatrix}$$

$$= \begin{pmatrix} 1 & 0 & \cdots & 0 \\ \ell_{21} & 1 & & 0 \\ \vdots & & \ddots & \vdots \\ \ell_{n1} & \ell_{n2} & \cdots & 1 \end{pmatrix} \begin{pmatrix} u_{11} & u_{12} & \cdots & u_{1n} \\ 0 & u_{22} & \cdots & u_{2n} \\ \vdots & & \ddots & \vdots \\ 0 & 0 & & u_{nn} \end{pmatrix}.$$

This is called an LU decomposition because we decompose the matrix into a lower triangular matrix multiplied by an upper triangular matrix. (Incidentally, the choice of diagonal elements $\ell_{ii} = 1$ makes the decomposition unique.) By multiplying out the matrices on the right-hand side we get equations for the u_{ij} and ℓ_{ij} that can easily be solved (under most circumstances, and certainly in the cases that we are interested in) in terms of a_{ij}.

Once this decomposition has been found, as it always can for strictly diagonally dominant matrices, we can write the matrix $\mathbf{A}$ as

$$\mathbf{A} = \mathbf{LU}$$

where $\mathbf{L}$ is a lower triangular matrix (with 1's on the diagonal) and $\mathbf{U}$ is upper triangular. The original system then has the form

$$\mathbf{A}\boldsymbol{x} = \mathbf{L}\mathbf{U}\boldsymbol{x} = \boldsymbol{q}.$$

Recall that we can solve the equation

$$\mathbf{L}\boldsymbol{y} = \boldsymbol{q}$$

using forward substitution. So we write

$$\mathbf{U}\boldsymbol{x} = \boldsymbol{y},$$

which we can solve using backward substitution, and this reduces the original problem to two much simpler problems

$$\mathbf{L}\boldsymbol{y} = \boldsymbol{q}, \quad \mathbf{U}\boldsymbol{x} = \boldsymbol{y}.$$

We then solve the former by forward substitution to find $\boldsymbol{y}$, and then the latter by backward substitution to find $\boldsymbol{x}$ from $\boldsymbol{y}$.

19.2.4 An LU solver for tridiagonal systems

While LU decomposition works for quite general matrices, it gives a particularly powerful and efficient means of solving *tridiagonal* systems. This is because we can find the decomposition $\mathbf{A} = \mathbf{LU}$ explicitly if $\mathbf{A}$ is tridiagonal, eliminating the need to calculate the decomposition numerically. We find that if we write a (non-singular) tridiagonal matrix in the LU form

$$\begin{pmatrix} a_1 & c_1 & 0 & \cdots & 0 \\ b_1 & a_2 & c_2 & & \vdots \\ 0 & b_2 & \ddots & \ddots & 0 \\ \vdots & & \ddots & \ddots & c_{n-1} \\ 0 & \cdots & 0 & b_{n-1} & a_n \end{pmatrix}$$

$$= \begin{pmatrix} 1 & 0 & 0 & \cdots & 0 \\ \ell_1 & 1 & 0 & & \vdots \\ 0 & \ell_2 & \ddots & \ddots & 0 \\ \vdots & & \ddots & \ddots & 0 \\ 0 & \cdots & 0 & \ell_{n-1} & 1 \end{pmatrix} \begin{pmatrix} u_1 & z_1 & 0 & \cdots & 0 \\ 0 & u_2 & z_2 & & \vdots \\ 0 & 0 & \ddots & \ddots & 0 \\ \vdots & & \ddots & u_{n-1} & z_{n-1} \\ 0 & \cdots & 0 & 0 & u_n \end{pmatrix}$$

then the u_i's z_i's and ℓ_i's are given by

$$u_1 = a_1, \quad u_i = a_i - \frac{c_{i-1}b_{i-1}}{u_{i-1}}, \quad 2 \leq i \leq n,$$

$$z_i = c_i, \quad \ell_i = b_i/u_i, \quad 1 \leq i \leq n-1.$$

The solution procedure is first to calculate the u_i's, then to form the intermediate quantities y_i from the forward substitution

$$y_1 = q_1, \quad y_i = q_i - \frac{b_{i-1}y_{i-1}}{u_{i-1}}, \quad 2 \leq i \leq n,$$

and then to find the solution using backward substitution by

$$x_n = y_n/u_n, \quad x_i = (y_i - c_i x_{i+1})/u_i.$$

This means that to solve a general tridiagonal matrix equation we need only store the nonzero diagonal, sub-diagonal and super-diagonal elements, and that we only have to calculate the quantities u_i and y_i explicitly in order to find the solution quantities x_i.

In our particular case we can make the algorithm even more effective by noting that we only have to form the u_i's once. In Figure 19.2 we give a pseudo-code for the LU decomposition and solution algorithm: the function `lu_find_u` need only be called once since the array `u` need only be found once. The function `lu_solve` may then be called as often as needed to solve the tridiagonal system $\mathbf{A}\boldsymbol{x} = \boldsymbol{q}$.

19.2.5 The implicit finite-difference algorithm

The solution scheme is thus to solve (19.2) for each time-step using the LU solver routine described in the previous section. This allows us to time-step through and calculate the current value of the option. The algorithm is illustrated in Figure 19.3.

In Figure 19.4 we compare implicit finite-difference solutions for a European put with a three month expiry time, exercise price $E = 10$, volatility $\sigma = 0.4$ and risk-free interest rate $r = 0.1$ with the exact Black–Scholes formula. As with the explicit method, the x-mesh spacing is first fixed and the time-step subsequently determined from α. We have chosen, as before, to regard α and $\delta\tau$ as variable to highlight an important point about stability. Whether $\alpha = 0.5$, $\alpha = 1.0$ or $\alpha = 5.0$, the computed solution agrees quite well with the exact solution. This illustrates the fact that the implicit scheme is stable where the explicit scheme is unstable (that is, for $\alpha > \frac{1}{2}$).

```
lu_find_u( a, b, c, u, N)
{
  /* set up the array u[]
     --- only have to do this once! */

    u[0] = a[0];

    for( i=1; i<n; ++i ) {
        u[i] = a[i] - b[i-1]*c[i-1]/u[i-1];
        if (u[i] == 0) return(ERROR);
    }

    return(NO_ERROR);
}


lu_solver(a,b,c,u,x,q,N)
{
  y[0] = q[0];

  for( i=1; i<n; i++ )
    y[i] = q[i]-b[i-1]*y[i-1]/u[i-1];

  x[n-1] = y[n-1]/u[n-1];

  for( i=n-2; i >=0; i-- )
    x[i] = (y[i]-c[i]*x[i+1])/u[i];

}
```

Figure 19.2: Pseudo-code for LU tridiagonal solver.

```
implicit_fd( values, dx, dt, M )
{
    alpha = dt/(dx*dx);

    for( i = -Nminus; i <= Nplus; ++i ) {
      /* initial value */
      values[i]=pay_off(i*dx);
      /* set up arrays for tridiagonal matrix */
      a[i] = 1+2*alpha;
      b[i] = c[i] = -alpha;
    }

    /* find u[] */
    lu_find_u( a, b, c, u, Nplus+Nminus-2);

    for( time = 1; t <= M; ++time ) {

      for( i = -Nminus+1; i < Nplus; ++i )
          q[i]=values[i];

      values[-Nminus] = f(-Nminus*dx,time*dt);
      values[ Nplus ] = g( Nplus*dx, time*dt);
      q[-Nminus+1] += a*values[-Nminus];
      q[ Nplus-1 ] += a*values[ Nplus ];

      /* solve */
      lu_solver(a, b, c, u, values, q, Nplus+Nminus-2);

    }
}
```

Figure 19.3: Pseudo-code for an implicit solver.

S	$\alpha = 0.50$	$\alpha = 1.00$	$\alpha = 5.00$	exact
0.00	9.7531	9.7531	9.7531	9.7531
2.00	7.7531	7.7531	7.7531	7.7531
4.00	5.7531	5.7531	5.7530	5.7531
6.00	3.7569	3.7570	3.7573	3.7569
8.00	1.9025	1.9025	1.9030	1.9024
10.00	0.6690	0.6689	0.6675	0.6694
12.00	0.1674	0.1674	0.1670	0.1675
14.00	0.0327	0.0328	0.0332	0.0326
16.00	0.0054	0.0055	0.0058	0.0054

Figure 19.4: Comparison of exact Black–Scholes and fully implicit finite-difference solutions for a European put with $E = 10$, $r = 0.1$, $\sigma = 0.4$ and three months to expiry. Even with $\alpha = 5.0$ the results are accurate to 2 decimal places.

19.2.6 Stability of the implicit scheme

We can show that the implicit finite-difference method is stable for any $\alpha > 0$. The basic arguments are simple variations on the arguments given in the previous section. The consequence is that we can solve the Black–Scholes equation transformed into the diffusion equation with larger time-steps using an implicit algorithm than we can using an explicit algorithm. This leads to more efficient numerical solutions.

To consider the stability of the implicit finite-difference method we again consider small harmonic perturbations to the exact solution of the difference equations (19.1) of the implicit scheme. If we write the equation (19.1) for the v_n^m's in the form

$$(1 + 2\alpha)v_n^m - \alpha v_{n-1}^m - \alpha v_{n+1}^m = v_n^{m-1}$$

and consider the effect of a small perturbation $\epsilon\lambda^m \sin n\omega$, then we find that

$$(1+2\alpha)\lambda^m \sin n\omega - \alpha\lambda^m \sin(n-1)\omega - \alpha\lambda^m \sin(n+1)\omega = \lambda^{m-1} \sin n\omega,$$

which gives

$$\lambda\left(1 + \alpha\left(2 - \frac{\sin(n-1)\omega + \sin(n+1)\omega}{\sin n\omega}\right)\right) = 1.$$

This can easily be rearranged to show that

$$\lambda = \left(1 + 4\alpha \sin^2 \tfrac{1}{2}\omega\right)^{-1},$$

so that $|\lambda| < 1$ for all frequencies of disturbance if $\alpha > 0$. This implies that all disturbances must die out, since $\lambda^m \to 0$ as m increases. (If $\alpha < 0$ then $|\lambda| > 1$, and the procedure is unstable. This is to be expected, however, since we are then attempting to solve a backward diffusion equation.) This argument is valid regardless of the source of the errors. In particular, it also applies to the small errors consequent on the truncation of the grid.

19.2.7 Convergence of the implicit scheme

The convergence of the implicit finite-difference approximation to the solution of the partial differential equation can be proved. Again, like the explicit finite-difference scheme, it is convergent if and only if it is stable. The argument is essentially the same as the argument for the convergence of the explicit solution. It is important to note, however, that since the maximum error varies like $\delta\tau$, we should expect that if we take $\delta\tau$ too large then the implicit finite-difference solution gives a poor approximation to the solution of the partial differential equation. We observe this in practice.

Again, the practical consequence of this convergence result is that we can make the error between the finite-difference implicit solution and the actual solution of the partial differential equation as small as we please, by taking small enough time-steps. There are practical limitations on this result due to finite precision arithmetic.

We define the discretisation error between the solution v_n^m of the implicit difference equations (19.1) and the values of the solution of the partial differential equation at the mesh points as before,

$$D_n^m = u_n^m - v_n^m.$$

Using the fact that the exact solution satisfies the partial differential equation, and the estimates given in (17.14), (17.15), (17.16) and (17.17), we find that

$$(1 + 2\alpha) D_n^m = D_n^{m-1} + \alpha(D_{n+1}^m + D_{n-1}^m) + \delta\tau\left(R_2\frac{\delta\tau}{2} + R_4\frac{(\delta x)^2}{12}\right).$$

Putting $\hat{R}_2 = |R_2/2|$ and $\hat{R}_4 = |R_4/12|$, this yields

$$|(1+2\alpha)D_n^m| \le \left|D_n^{m-1}\right| + \left|\alpha D_{n+1}^m\right| + \left|\alpha D_{n-1}^m\right| + \delta\tau\left(\hat{R}_2\delta\tau + \hat{R}_4(\delta x)^2\right).$$

Now if we let $\hat{D}^m$ be the largest error in absolute value at time step m, and assume only that $\alpha > 0$, we see that

$$(1+2\alpha)\hat{D}^m \le \hat{D}^{m-1} + 2\alpha\hat{D}^m + \delta\tau\left(\hat{R}_2\delta\tau + \hat{R}_4(\delta x)^2\right),$$

which clearly gives

$$\hat{D}^m \le \hat{D}^{m-1} + \delta\tau\left(\hat{R}_2\delta\tau + \hat{R}_4(\delta x)^2\right).$$

By induction it follows that if $\hat{D}^0 = 0$ then

$$\hat{D}^m \le m\,\delta\tau\left(\hat{R}_2\delta\tau + \hat{R}_4(\delta x)^2\right).$$

This proves that the maximum error between u_n^m and v_n^m tends to zero as $\delta\tau \to 0$, $\delta x \to 0$, assuming only that α remains finite.

19.3 The Crank–Nicolson method

The Crank–Nicolson finite-difference method is used to overcome the stability limitations imposed by the stability and convergence restrictions of the explicit finite-difference method, and to have $O((\delta\tau)^2)$ rates of convergence to the solution of the partial differential equation. (Recall that the rate of convergence of the implicit and explicit methods is $O(\delta\tau)$.)

The Crank–Nicolson implicit finite-difference scheme is essentially an average of the implicit and explicit methods. Specifically, if we use a forward difference approximation to the time partial derivative we obtain the explicit scheme

$$\frac{u_n^{m+1} - u_n^m}{\delta\tau} + O(\delta\tau) = \frac{u_{n+1}^m - 2u_n^m + u_{n-1}^m}{(\delta x)^2} + O((\delta x)^2),$$

and if we take a backward difference we obtain the implicit scheme

$$\frac{u_n^{m+1} - u_n^m}{\delta\tau} + O(\delta\tau) = \frac{u_{n+1}^{m+1} - 2u_n^{m+1} + u_{n-1}^{m+1}}{(\delta x)^2} + O((\delta x)^2).$$

The average of these two equations is

$$\frac{u_n^{m+1}-u_n^m}{\delta\tau}+O(\delta\tau)=$$
$$\left(\frac{u_{n+1}^m-2u_n^m+u_{n-1}^m}{2(\delta x)^2}+\frac{u_{n+1}^{m+1}-2u_n^{m+1}+u_{n-1}^{m+1}}{2(\delta x)^2}\right)+O((\delta x)^2). \tag{19.5}$$

This leads to the Crank–Nicolson method.

19.3.1 Accuracy of the Crank–Nicolson method

If, before proceeding, we think about the terms in (19.5) we can see that it is actually accurate to $O((\delta\tau)^2)$. The expression on the right-hand side of (19.5) is simply

$$\frac{1}{2}\left(\frac{\partial^2 u}{\partial x^2}(x,\tau+\delta\tau)+\frac{\partial^2 u}{\partial x^2}(x,\tau)\right).$$

If we now consider a forward and backward difference scheme of $\partial^2 u/\partial x^2$ about the point $(x,\tau+\delta\tau/2)$, using Taylor's theorem, we obtain

$$\frac{\partial^2 u}{\partial x^2}(x,\tau)=\frac{\partial^2 u}{\partial x^2}(x,\tau+\delta\tau/2)-\delta\tau\frac{\partial^3 u}{\partial x^2\partial\tau}(x,\tau+\delta\tau/2)+R_4(\delta\tau/2)^2$$

and

$$\frac{\partial^2 u}{\partial x^2}(x,\tau+\delta\tau)=\frac{\partial^2 u}{\partial x^2}(x,\tau+\delta\tau/2)+\delta\tau\frac{\partial^3 u}{\partial x^2\partial\tau}(x,\tau+\delta\tau/2)+S_4(\delta\tau/2)^2,$$

where R_4 and S_4 are error terms. Adding these equations shows that

$$\frac{\partial^2 u}{\partial x^2}(x,\tau+\delta\tau/2)=\frac{1}{2}\left(\frac{\partial^2 u}{\partial x^2}(x,\tau)+\frac{\partial^2 u}{\partial x^2}(x,\tau+\delta\tau)\right)+O((\delta\tau)^2).$$

We then note that

$$\frac{\partial u}{\partial\tau}(x,\tau+\delta\tau/2)=\frac{u(x,\tau+\delta\tau)-u(x,\tau)}{\delta\tau}+O((\delta\tau)^2)$$

(see, for example, equation (17.17)).

Thus if we interpret the finite-difference approximation (19.5) as being an approximation to

$$\frac{\partial u}{\partial\tau}(x,\tau+\delta\tau/2)=\frac{\partial^2 u}{\partial x^2}(x,\tau+\delta\tau/2),$$

we see that in fact

$$\frac{u_n^{m+1}-u_n^m}{\delta\tau}+O((\delta\tau)^2)=$$
$$\left(\frac{u_{n+1}^m-2u_n^m+u_{n-1}^m}{2(\delta x)^2}+\frac{u_{n+1}^{m+1}-2u_n^{m+1}+u_{n-1}^{m+1}}{2(\delta x)^2}\right)+O((\delta x)^2). \tag{19.6}$$

One reason for *not* regarding this as a 'true' central time difference is simply that we never solve for $u(x,\tau+\delta\tau/2)$; we only ever consider terms of the form $u(x,\tau\pm\delta\tau)$.

19.3.2 The Crank–Nicolson finite-difference equations

From either of (19.5) or (19.6) we see that the appropriate finite-difference scheme is

$$v_n^{m+1}-\tfrac{1}{2}\alpha(v_{n-1}^{m+1}-2v_n^{m+1}+v_{n+1}^{m+1})=v_n^m+\tfrac{1}{2}\alpha(v_{n-1}^m-2v_n^m+v_{n+1}^m) \tag{19.7}$$

where, as before, $\alpha=\delta\tau/(\delta x)^2$. Note that v_n^{m+1}, v_{n-1}^{m+1} and v_{n+1}^{m+1} are now determined implicitly in terms of all of v_n^m, v_{n+1}^m and v_{n-1}^m.

Solving this system of equations is, in principle, no different from solving the equations (19.1) for the implicit scheme. This is because everything on the right hand side of (19.7) can be evaluated explicitly if the v_n^m are known. The problem thus reduces to first calculating

$$Z_n^m=v_n^m+\tfrac{1}{2}\alpha(v_{n-1}^m-2v_n^m+v_{n+1}^m), \tag{19.8}$$

which is an explicit formula for Z_n^m, and then solving

$$v_n^{m+1}-\tfrac{1}{2}\alpha(v_{n-1}^{m+1}-2v_n^{m+1}+v_{n+1}^{m+1})=Z_n^m.$$

This second problem is essentially the same as solving (19.1).

Let us consider the same simple European option problems discussed in the previous sections. Again we assume that we can truncate the infinite mesh at $x=-N^-\delta x$ and $x=N^+\delta x$, and take N^- and N^+ sufficiently large so that no significant errors are introduced. As before we can calculate v_n^0 from the initial data by putting

$$v_n^0=u_0(n\,\delta x),\quad -N^-\le n\le N^+.$$

We know $v_{-N^-}^m$ and $v_{N^+}^m$ from the boundary conditions

$$v_{-N^-}^m=f(-N^-\delta x,m\,\delta\tau),\quad v_{N^+}^m=g(N^+\delta x,m\,\delta\tau).$$

We are then left with the problem of finding the v_n^m for $m \geq 1$ and $-N^- < n < N^+$ from (19.3). We can write the problem as a linear system

$$\mathbf{C}\boldsymbol{v}^{m+1} = \mathbf{D}\boldsymbol{v}^m + \boldsymbol{b}^m \tag{19.9}$$

where the matrices **C** and **D** are given by

$$\mathbf{C}= \begin{pmatrix} 1+\alpha & -\frac{1}{2}\alpha & 0 & \cdots & 0 \\ -\frac{1}{2}\alpha & 1+\alpha & -\frac{1}{2}\alpha & & \vdots \\ 0 & -\frac{1}{2}\alpha & \ddots & \ddots & 0 \\ \vdots & & \ddots & \ddots & -\frac{1}{2}\alpha \\ 0 & 0 & & -\frac{1}{2}\alpha & 1+\alpha \end{pmatrix},$$
$$\mathbf{D}= \begin{pmatrix} 1-\alpha & \frac{1}{2}\alpha & 0 & \cdots & 0 \\ \frac{1}{2}\alpha & 1-\alpha & \frac{1}{2}\alpha & & \vdots \\ 0 & \frac{1}{2}\alpha & 1-\alpha & \ddots & 0 \\ \vdots & 0 & \ddots & \ddots & \frac{1}{2}\alpha \\ 0 & 0 & & \frac{1}{2}\alpha & 1-\alpha \end{pmatrix} \tag{19.10}$$

and the vectors $\boldsymbol{v}^m$, $\boldsymbol{v}^{m+1}$ and $\boldsymbol{b}^m$ take the form

$$\boldsymbol{v}^{m+1} = \begin{pmatrix} v_{N^+-1}^{m+1} \\ \vdots \\ v_0^{m+1} \\ \vdots \\ v_{-N^-+1}^{m+1} \end{pmatrix}, \qquad \boldsymbol{v}^m = \begin{pmatrix} v_{N^+-1}^{m} \\ \vdots \\ v_0^{m} \\ \vdots \\ v_{-N^-+1}^{m} \end{pmatrix},$$

$$\boldsymbol{b}^m = \tfrac{1}{2}\alpha \begin{pmatrix} v_{N^+}^m + v_{N^+}^{m+1} \\ 0 \\ \vdots \\ 0 \\ v_{-N^-}^m + v_{-N^-}^{m+1} \end{pmatrix}. \tag{19.11}$$

The vector on the extreme right-hand side of equation (19.9), $\boldsymbol{b}^m$, arises from the boundary conditions applied at the ends, as in the implicit finite-difference method.

19.3.3 Practical considerations

Since $\mathbf{C}$ can be shown to be invertible (it is clearly diagonally dominant) we have, in principle,

$$\boldsymbol{v}^{m+1} = \mathbf{C}^{-1}(\mathbf{D}\boldsymbol{v}^m + \boldsymbol{b}^m), \tag{19.12}$$

so that we can find $\boldsymbol{v}^{m+1}$ given $\boldsymbol{v}^m$ and boundary conditions. Thus, since the initial condition determines $\boldsymbol{v}^0$, we can find each $\boldsymbol{v}^m$ inductively.

This is *not* what is done in practice. In practice, we first form the vector $\boldsymbol{Z}^m$ using

$$\boldsymbol{Z}^m = \mathbf{D}\boldsymbol{v}^m + \boldsymbol{b}^m.$$

Since we have simple explicit formulæ for $\boldsymbol{Z}^m$, we do not implement this as matrix multiplication but, rather, in a direct method implied by the formulæ of equation (19.8). Then we use an LU tridiagonal solver to solve the system

$$\mathbf{C}\boldsymbol{v}^{m+1} = \boldsymbol{Z}^m.$$

This allows us to time-step through the solution.

In Figure 19.6 we compare Crank–Nicolson finite-difference solutions for a European put with four months to expiry, exercise price 10, volatility $\sigma = 0.45$ and risk-free interest rate $r = 0.1$ with the exact Black–Scholes formula. Notice that with $\alpha = 0.50$, $\alpha = 1.0$ and even $\alpha = 10.0$, the computed solution agrees very well with the exact solution. This demonstrates the fact that the Crank–Nicolson scheme is stable where the explicit scheme is unstable (that is, for $\alpha > 0.5$). Moreover, its accuracy is greater than that of the fully implicit scheme.

We can show that the Crank–Nicolson scheme is both stable and convergent for all values of $\alpha > 0$. The proofs of stability and convergence are essentially the same as for the explicit method and the implicit method. For brevity, we only give the proof of stability.

It should be noted, however, that in theory the Crank–Nicolson scheme is convergent to the exact solution in the sense that the discretisation error $u_n^m - v_n^m$ is of order $(\delta\tau)^2$,

$$u_n^m - v_n^m = O((\delta\tau)^2) \quad \text{as} \quad \tau \to \infty.$$

This result explains the high degree of accuracy displayed in table 19.6

```
crank_fd( values, dx, dt, M )
{
    alpha = dt/(dx*dx);

    for( i = -Nminus; i <= Nplus; ++i ) {
      /* initial value */
      values[i]=pay_off(i*dx);
      /* set up arrays for tridiagonal matrix */
      a[i] = 1+alpha;
      b[i] = c[i] = -alpha/2;
    }

    /* find u[] */
    lu_find_u( a, b, c, u, Nplus+Nminus-2);

    for( time = 1; t <= M; ++time ) {

      for( i = -Nminus+1; i < Nplus; ++i )
          z[i]=(1-alpha)*values[i]+alpha*
               (values[i+1]+values[i-1])/2.0

      values[-Nminus] = f(-Nminus*dx,time*dt);
      values[ Nplus ] = g( Nplus*dx, time*dt);

      /*solve*/
      lu_solver(a, b, c, u, values, z, Nplus+Nminus-2);
    }

    /* values of option are returned in values[] */

}
```

Figure 19.5: Pseudo-code for a Crank–Nicolson solver.

S	$\alpha = 0.50$	$\alpha = 1.00$	$\alpha = 10.00$	exact
0.00	9.6722	9.6722	9.6722	9.6722
2.00	7.6721	7.6721	7.6721	7.6722
4.00	5.6722	5.6722	5.6723	5.6723
6.00	3.6976	3.6976	3.6975	3.6977
8.00	1.9804	1.9804	1.9804	1.9806
10.00	0.8605	0.8605	0.8566	0.8610
12.00	0.3174	0.3174	0.3174	0.3174
14.00	0.1047	0.1047	0.1046	0.1046
16.00	0.0322	0.0322	0.0321	0.0322

Figure 19.6: Comparison of exact Black–Scholes and Crank–Nicolson finite-difference solutions for a European put with $E = 10$, $r = 0.1$, $\sigma = 0.45$ and four months to expiry. Even with $\alpha = 10$, the numerical and exact results differ only marginally.

19.3.4 Stability of the Crank–Nicolson method

As before we consider the stability of the Crank–Nicolson scheme by examining the effect of small harmonic perturbations to the exact solution of the difference equations (19.7) for the Crank–Nicolson scheme.

If we write the equation (19.7) for the v_n^m's in the form

$$(1+\alpha)v_n^{m+1} - \tfrac{1}{2}\alpha(v_{n-1}^{m+1} + v_{n+1}^{m+1}) = (1-\alpha)v_n^m + \tfrac{1}{2}\alpha(v_{n-1}^m + v_{n+1}^m)$$

and consider the effect of a small perturbation $\epsilon\lambda^m \sin n\omega$ then, after some algebra, we find that

$$\lambda\,(1+\alpha-\alpha\cos\omega)\sin n\omega = (1-\alpha+\alpha\cos\omega)\sin n\omega.$$

Rearranging shows that

$$\lambda = \frac{1-2\alpha\sin^2\frac{1}{2}\omega}{1+2\alpha\sin^2\frac{1}{2}\omega}$$

so that $|\lambda| < 1$ for all frequencies of disturbance. This implies stability, since all disturbances decrease as m increases.

19.4 The θ-method

There is a generalisation of the Crank–Nicolson method, usually called the **θ-method.** It takes the form

$$v_n^{m+1} - \theta\alpha(v_{n-1}^{m+1} - 2v_n^{m+1} + v_{n+1}^{m+1}) = v_n^m + (1-\theta)\alpha(v_{n-1}^m - 2v_n^m + v_{n+1}^m)$$

where $0 \leq \theta \leq 1$. This can be thought of as a θ-weighted average of the explicit and fully implicit finite-difference methods. When $\theta = 0$, it gives the explicit method, when $\theta = \frac{1}{2}$ it gives Crank–Nicolson and when $\theta = 1$ it gives the implicit method. It can be shown that the θ-method is stable for all $\alpha > 0$ if $\frac{1}{2} \leq \theta \leq 1$. For $0 < \theta < \frac{1}{2}$ it is stable if

$$0 < \alpha \leq \frac{1}{2(1-2\theta)}, \qquad (0 < \theta < \tfrac{1}{2}).$$

The θ-method is convergent whenever it is stable. The proofs of these statements are simple adaptations of the proofs for the explicit, implicit and Crank–Nicolson cases. Implementing the θ-method is essentially the same as implementing the Crank–Nicolson method.

It is not particularly sensible to use the θ-method with values of $\theta < \frac{1}{2}$, since this involves all the extra complications of solving implicit sets of equations without any great improvement in stability over the explicit method. We use the θ-method in the following section for solving the American put problem, in order to avoid having to go through the explicit, fully-implicit and Crank–Nicolson methods individually.

Further reading

- As well as those books mentioned in previous chapters the reader should see Richtmyer & Morton (1967)

Exercises

1. Write a computer program to value a European call using the implicit and Crank–Nicolson algorithms.

2. Show that, using the LU solver described in Section 19.2.4, the implicit scheme requires $4N$ multiplications or divisions per time-step (where N is the number of x-mesh points). (Assume

that the quantities u_i do not have to be calculated each time-step.)

3. Show that, using the LU solver described in Section 19.2.4, the Crank–Nicolson scheme requires $5N$ multiplications or divisions per time-step .

4. Prove the convergence of the Crank–Nicolson scheme.

5. Show that the θ-method is stable for all $\alpha > 0$ if $\theta \geq \frac{1}{2}$, and that it is stable for $0 < \alpha < \frac{1}{2}(1 - \theta)$ if $0 < \theta < \frac{1}{2}$.

Chapter 20

Methods for Free Boundary Problems

20.1 Introduction

Using finite-difference methods for European options is relatively straightforward as there is no possibility of early exercise. As we have seen, the possibility of early exercise may lead to free boundaries. The chief problem with free boundaries, from the point of view of numerical analysis, is that we do not know where they are. This makes it difficult to impose the free boundary conditions, since we have to determine where to impose them as part of the solution procedure. (Recall that in Chapters 18–19 we simply imposed the boundary conditions at fixed grid points.)

There are two distinct strategies for the numerical solution of free boundary problems. One is to attempt to track the free boundary as part of the time-stepping process. In the context of valuation of American options this is not a particularly attractive method as the free boundary conditions are both implicit—that is, they do not give a direct expression for the free boundary or its time derivatives[1]. We simply note the existence of such methods here, and refer the reader to Crank (1984) for a discussion of various boundary tracking

[1]An example of a free boundary problem with an explicit free boundary condition is the Stefan problem, where the one of the free boundary conditions is an equation for the velocity of the free boundary; see for example Crank (1984) or Elliott & Ockendon (1982).

strategies for implicit free boundary problems; the 'oxygen consumption problem' is the canonical implicit free boundary problem and boundary tracking strategies for this problem are discussed at some length there.

The other strategy is to attempt to find a transformation that reduces the problem to a fixed boundary problem from which the free boundary can be inferred afterwards. There are many transformations that do this, but we consider only two particularly elegant methods involving the use of **linear complementarity problems** and **variational inequalities.** The full details for the method using variational inequalities, the **finite-element method**, can be found in Appendix D since, in practice, the two methods lead to identical numerical methods.

As in our treatment of the theory, our strategy is to introduce the methods with reference to the simplest free boundary problem, namely the obstacle problem, before applying the same ideas to more complicated, time-dependent, American option free boundary problems.

20.2 Finite-difference solution of the obstacle problem

Recall the obstacle problem, discussed in Chapters 3 and 7. With reference to Figure 20.1, we consider a string stretched over an obstacle. If $u(x)$ is the displacement of the string and $f(x)$ is the height of the obstacle, then as in Chapter 7, the problem may be written in the linear complementarity form

$$u''(u-f)=0, \quad -u''\geq 0, \quad (u-f)\geq 0, \tag{20.1}$$

subject to the conditions that

$$u(-1)=u(1)=0, \quad u, u' \text{ are continuous.} \tag{20.2}$$

By referring to Figure 20.1 we can also see the utility of methods that have no explicit dependence on the position of the free boundary. In this figure as it now stands there are four free boundaries, two on each of the obstacle's humps. Suppose that the left-hand end of the string, at $x=-1$, were raised slowly. It would not have to be moved far before the string would lift off the left-hand hump leaving only *two* free boundaries, on the right-hand hump. In a complicated

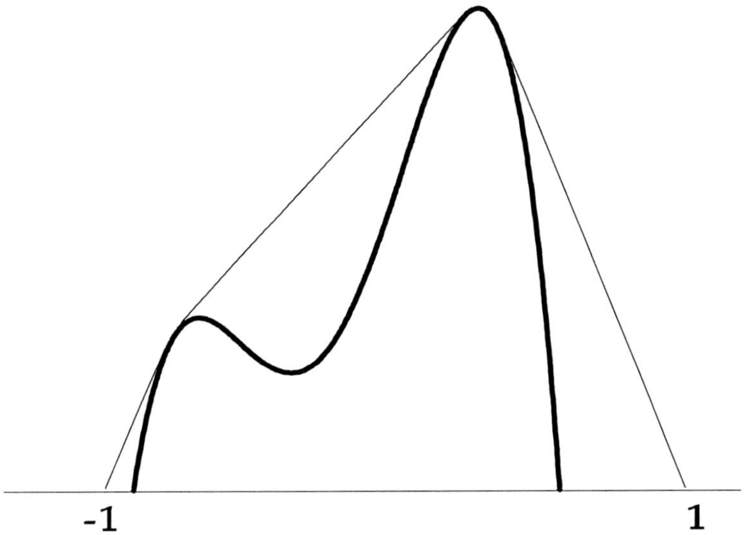

Figure 20.1: Example of an obstacle problem.

obstacle problem (or with a portfolio of American options) we may not know *a priori* how many free boundaries there are going to be. Some numerical methods require the number of free boundaries to be known. This is not the case with linear complementarity formulations and variational inequalities and this is one of the reasons we favour these methods.

We approximate the second derivative in the linear complementarity formulation (20.1), (20.2) by finite differences and thus obtain a finite-difference approximation to the problem. With symmetric central differences on a regular mesh,

$$-1 = -N\,\delta x < (-N+1)\,\delta x < \ldots < n\,\delta x < \ldots < N\,\delta x = 1,$$

we use the approximation

$$u'' = \frac{u_{n+1} - 2u_n + u_{n-1}}{(\delta x)^2} + O((\delta x)^2),$$

where $u_n = u(n\,\delta x)$ as in Figure 20.2. With the notation $f_n = f(n\,\delta x)$, and with v_n as the finite-difference approximation to u_n, we

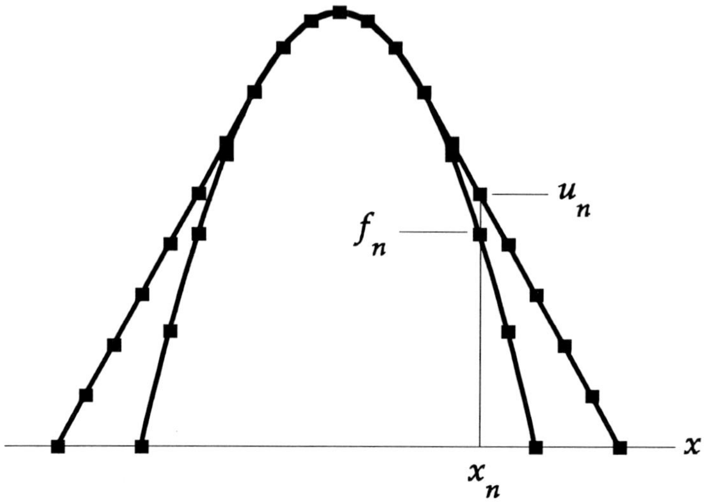

Figure 20.2: Finite-difference discretisation for the obstacle problem. For simplicity, this obstacle has only one hump.

obtain

$$-v_{n+1}+2v_n-v_{n-1} \geq 0, \quad v_n \geq f_n, \quad (v_n-f_n)(v_{n+1}-2v_n+v_{n-1}) = 0,$$

for $-N < n < N$, and

$$v_{-N} = v_N = 0.$$

This can be written in the matrix form

$$\mathbf{B}\boldsymbol{v} \geq \mathbf{0}, \quad \boldsymbol{v} \geq \boldsymbol{f}, \quad (\boldsymbol{v}-\boldsymbol{f})\cdot\mathbf{B}\boldsymbol{v} = 0, \tag{20.3}$$

where

$$\mathbf{B} = \begin{pmatrix} 2 & -1 & 0 & \cdots & 0 \\ -1 & 2 & -1 & & \vdots \\ 0 & -1 & 2 & \ddots & 0 \\ \vdots & & \ddots & \ddots & -1 \\ 0 & \cdots & 0 & -1 & 2 \end{pmatrix},$$

$$\boldsymbol{v} = \begin{pmatrix} v_{N-1} \\ \vdots \\ \vdots \\ \vdots \\ v_{-N+1} \end{pmatrix}, \quad \boldsymbol{f} = \begin{pmatrix} f_{N-1} \\ \vdots \\ \vdots \\ \vdots \\ f_{-N+1} \end{pmatrix}. \tag{20.4}$$

The notation $\boldsymbol{x} \geq \mathbf{0}$ means that every component of the vector $\boldsymbol{x}$ is non-negative ($x_i \geq 0$), and $\boldsymbol{v} \geq \boldsymbol{f}$ means each component of $\boldsymbol{v}$ is greater than or equal to the corresponding component of $\boldsymbol{f}$ (i.e. $v_i \geq f_i$).

In dealing with American options we encounter a very similar system. There is a quite general means of solving constrained linear problems such as (20.3), called **projected SOR**.

20.3 The projected SOR solution scheme

The acronym SOR stands for Successive Over Relaxation, and SOR is a method frequently used to solve certain classes of matrix equation (see Stoer & Bulirsch (1993) for example). The projected SOR algorithm is discussed in some detail in Elliott & Ockendon (1982) and Crank (1984).

Consider a quite general version of (20.3),

$$\mathbf{A}\boldsymbol{x} \geq \boldsymbol{b}, \quad \boldsymbol{x} \geq \boldsymbol{c}, \quad (\boldsymbol{x} - \boldsymbol{c}) \cdot (\mathbf{A}\boldsymbol{x} - \boldsymbol{b}) = 0.$$

Assuming only that the matrix $\mathbf{A}$ is invertible and that it is positive definite (i.e. $\boldsymbol{x} \cdot (\mathbf{A}\boldsymbol{x}) > 0$ for any $\boldsymbol{x} \neq \mathbf{0}$) it can be shown that there is one and only one solution vector $\boldsymbol{x}$ for this problem (see Elliott & Ockendon (1982) for a proof and references).

The algorithm for finding the solution is iterative. Start with an initial guess $\boldsymbol{x}^0 \geq \boldsymbol{c}$ (the algorithm may not converge if $\boldsymbol{x}^0 < \boldsymbol{c}$). During each iteration we form a new vector

$$\boldsymbol{x}^{k+1} = (x_1^{k+1}, x_2^{k+1}, \ldots, x_n^{k+1}),$$

from the current vector $\boldsymbol{x}^k$,

$$\boldsymbol{x}^k = (x_1^k, x_2^k, \ldots, x_n^k),$$

by the following two-step process. For each $i = 1, 2, \ldots, n$ we *sequentially* form the intermediate quantity y_i^{k+1}, given by

$$y_i^{k+1} = \frac{1}{A_{ii}}\left(b_i - \sum_{j=1}^{i-1} A_{ij}x_j^{k+1} - \sum_{j=i+1}^{n} A_{ij}x_j^k\right)$$

and then define the new x_i^{k+1} to be

$$x_i^{k+1} = \max\left(c_i, x_i^k + \omega(y_i^{k+1} - x_i^k)\right).$$

Note that it is important to perform these two steps in sequence; we need the new value of x_{i-1}^{k+1} in order to find x_i^{k+1}. The only difference between this method and the classical SOR method is the test to make sure that $x_i^{k+1} \geq c_i$. The constant ω is called a relaxation parameter, and provided that $\boldsymbol{x}^0 \geq \mathbf{c}$ and $0 < \omega < 2$, the method converges. (It can be shown that the convergence can be optimised by choosing a particular value of $\omega \in (1, 2)$ which depends on the matrix $\mathbf{A}$.)

At each iteration this defines a new vector $\boldsymbol{x}^{k+1} \geq \mathbf{c}$; as $k \to \infty$ $\boldsymbol{x}^k \to \boldsymbol{x}$, the solution of the problem. In practice, naturally enough, we do not iterate forever. We stop once we have satisfied a condition of the form

$$\left|\boldsymbol{x}^{k+1} - \boldsymbol{x}^k\right| < \epsilon$$

where $\epsilon > 0$ is some pre-chosen small tolerance. We then take $\boldsymbol{x}^{k+1}$ as the solution.

20.4 Projected SOR for the obstacle problem

The algorithm for solving the obstacle problem is a simple version of this general projected SOR algorithm. It relies on the fact that the only nonzero matrix elements B_{ij} are the diagonal elements, $B_{ii} = 2$, the super-diagonal elements, $B_{i\,i+1} = -1$, and the sub-diagonal elements $B_{i+1\,i} = -1$. Therefore, the projected SOR solution algorithm for (20.3) is as follows:

```
projected_sor( values, obstacle, N, omega, eps )
{
  do {
    error = 0.0;
    values[-N] = 0.0;
    values[ N] = 0.0;

    for( i = -N+1; i < N; ++i ) {
      y = (values[i-1]+values[i+1])/2.0;
      y = max( obstacle[i], values[i]
                 +omega*(y-values[i]) );
      error += (values[i]-y)*(values[i]-y);
      values[i]=y;
    }
  } while ( error > eps*eps );
}
```

Figure 20.3: Pseudo-code for projected SOR solution of the obstacle problem.

1. Start with an initial guess $\boldsymbol{v}^0 \geq \boldsymbol{f}$ and a relaxation parameter ω.

2. Given $\boldsymbol{v}^k = (v^k_{1-N}, \ldots, v^k_{N-1})$, put
$$y^{k+1}_{1-N} = v^k_{2-N}/2,$$
and let v^{k+1}_{1-N} be
$$v^{k+1}_{1-N} = \max\left(f_{1-N}, v^k_{1-N} + \omega(y^{k+1}_{1-N} - v^k_{1-N})\right).$$

3. Then, in sequence, form v^{k+1}_i for $2 - N \leq i \leq N - 2$ by first calculating
$$y^{k+1}_i = (v^{k+1}_{i-1} + v^k_{i+1})/2,$$
(note the use of v^{k+1}_{i-1} rather than v^k_{i-1}—as soon as we update part of the solution vector we use it) and then setting
$$v^{k+1}_i = \max\left(f_i, v^k_i + \omega(y^{k+1}_i - v^k_i)\right).$$

4. To find v_{N-1}^{k+1}, first find

$$y_{N-1}^{k+1} = v_{N-2}^{k+1}/2,$$

and then put

$$v_{N-1}^{k+1} = \max\left(f_{N-1}, v_{N-1}^{k} + \omega(y_{N-1}^{k+1} - v_{N-1}^{k})\right).$$

5. Test to see whether $\left|\boldsymbol{v}^{k+1} - \boldsymbol{v}^{k}\right|$ is small enough for convergence to be assumed, that is, check whether or not

$$\sum_{i=1-N}^{N-1} \left(v_i^{k+1} - v_i^{k}\right)^2 \leq \epsilon^2.$$

If the test fails, return to step 2, replacing $\boldsymbol{v}^k$ by $\boldsymbol{v}^{k+1}$. If the test succeeds, stop.

The algorithm is illustrated in the pseudo-code shown in Figure 20.3, and it was used to generate the solution for the obstacle of Figure 20.1.

Further reading

- For the theoretical and practical discussion (including the numerical analysis) of free boundary problems see Crank (1984), Elliott & Ockendon (1982) and Kinderlehrer & Stampacchia (1980).
- The Projected SOR algorithm was originally devised by Cryer (1971) in the context of quadratic optimisation.

Exercises

1. Write a computer program to solve the obstacle problem, for an arbitrary function $f(x)$, using the projected SOR algorithm.
2. Compare the numerical solution of the problem with the exact solution when $f(x) = \frac{1}{2} - x^2$ and $\frac{1}{2} - \sin^2(\pi x/2)$. (See the first exercise at the end of Chapter 6.)

Chapter 21

Methods for American Options

21.1 Introduction

We now focus on the real issue at hand, how to find the value of an American-style option. After the change of variables (17.1) and using the dimensionless parameters (17.2) the problems for American puts, calls and binaries (with constant dividend yield) are as follows.

For the put,

$$\begin{aligned} \frac{\partial u}{\partial \tau} &= \frac{\partial^2 u}{\partial x^2}, \\ u(x,0) &= \max\left(e^{\frac{1}{2}(k_2-1)x} - e^{\frac{1}{2}(k_2+1)x}, 0\right), \\ u(x,\tau) &\geq e^{\frac{1}{4}((k_2-1)^2+4k_1)\tau} \max\left(e^{\frac{1}{2}(k_2-1)x} - e^{\frac{1}{2}(k_2+1)x}, 0\right), \\ \lim_{x\to\infty} u(x,\tau) &= 0. \end{aligned} \tag{21.1}$$

For the call,

$$\begin{aligned} \frac{\partial u}{\partial \tau} &= \frac{\partial^2 u}{\partial x^2}, \\ u(x,0) &= \max\left(e^{\frac{1}{2}(k_2+1)x} - e^{\frac{1}{2}(k_2-1)x}, 0\right), \\ u(x,\tau) &\geq e^{\frac{1}{4}((k_2-1)^2+4k_1)\tau} \max\left(e^{\frac{1}{2}(k_2+1)x} - e^{\frac{1}{2}(k_2-1)x}, 0\right), \\ \lim_{x\to-\infty} u(x,\tau) &= 0. \end{aligned} \tag{21.2}$$

For the binary with payoff B for $S > E$ (the cash or nothing call),

$$\begin{gathered}\frac{\partial u}{\partial \tau} = \frac{\partial^2 u}{\partial x^2}, \\ u(x,0) = \begin{cases} 0 & x < 0 \\ b e^{\frac{1}{2}(k_2-1)x} & x \geq 0, \end{cases}\end{gathered} \tag{21.3}$$

$$u(x,\tau) \geq e^{\frac{1}{4}((k_2-1)^2+4k_1)\tau} u(x,0), \qquad \lim_{x\to-\infty} u(x,\tau) = 0, \tag{21.4}$$

where $b = B/E$ is the dimensionless binary payoff.

We can write all of these option valuation problems in the more compact linear complementarity form

$$\begin{gathered}\left(\frac{\partial u}{\partial \tau} - \frac{\partial^2 u}{\partial x^2}\right) \geq 0, \quad (u(x,\tau) - g(x,\tau)) \geq 0, \\ \left(\frac{\partial u}{\partial \tau} - \frac{\partial^2 u}{\partial x^2}\right)(u(\tau,x) - g(x,\tau)) = 0.\end{gathered} \tag{21.5}$$

Here the transformed payoff constraint function, $g(x,\tau)$, is given by

$$g(x,\tau) = e^{\frac{1}{4}((k_2-1)^2+4k_1)\tau} \max\left(e^{\frac{1}{2}(k_2-1)x} - e^{\frac{1}{2}(k_2+1)x}, 0\right)$$

for the put,

$$g(x,\tau) = e^{\frac{1}{4}((k_2-1)^2+4k_1)\tau} \max\left(e^{\frac{1}{2}(k_2+1)x} - e^{\frac{1}{2}(k_2-1)x}, 0\right)$$

for the call and

$$g(x,\tau) = e^{\frac{1}{4}((k_2-1)^2+4k_1)\tau} \begin{cases} 0 & x < 0 \\ b e^{\frac{1}{2}(k_2-1)x} & x \geq 0 \end{cases}$$

for the binary option. The initial, fixed and free boundary conditions become

$$\begin{gathered}u(x,0) = g(x,0), \\ u(x,\tau),\ \frac{\partial u}{\partial x}(x,\tau) \text{ are as continuous as } g(x,\tau),\ \frac{\partial g}{\partial x}(x,\tau), \\ \lim_{x\to\pm\infty} u(x,\tau) = \lim_{x\to\pm\infty} g(x,\tau).\end{gathered} \tag{21.6}$$

This framework extends in the obvious way to more general payoff functions.

The advantage of the the linear complementarity formulation (21.5) is that there is no explicit mention of the free boundary. If we can solve the linear complementarity problem then we find the free boundary, $X(\tau)$ by the condition that defines it, namely that

$$u(X(\tau),\tau) = g(X(\tau),\tau), \quad \text{but} \quad u(x,\tau) > g(x,\tau) \text{ for } x > X(\tau)$$

for the put, and

$$u(X(\tau),\tau) = g(X(\tau),\tau), \quad \text{but} \quad u(x,\tau) > g(x,\tau) \text{ for } x < X(\tau)$$

for the call and binary. The formulation remains valid if there are several free boundaries, or indeed if there are none at all.

21.2 Finite-difference formulation

In order to obtain a numerical method to solve the American put free boundary problem, we can, as before, adopt several different approaches. One simple way is to divide the (x,τ) plane into a regular finite mesh as usual, and take a finite-difference approximation of the linear complementarity equations (21.5). This is the only approach we use in this chapter.

We start by discretising the linear complementarity form of the problem, (21.5). Since most of this discretisation is a trivial extension of the finite-difference formulations given in the previous three chapters, we only give a short account of it here. We approximate terms of the form $\partial u/\partial\tau - \partial^2 u/\partial x^2$ by finite differences on a regular mesh with step sizes $\delta\tau$ and δx, and truncating so that x lies between $-x^-$ and x^+ where

$$-x^- = -N^-\delta x \le x = n\,\delta x \le N^+\delta x = x^+,$$

and N^- and N^+ are suitably large numbers.

In order to avoid going through the cases of explicit, implicit and Crank–Nicolson methods separately, we use the general finite-difference θ-approximations

$$\frac{\partial u}{\partial\tau} = \frac{u_n^{m+1} - u_n^m}{\delta\tau} + O(\delta\tau),$$

and

$$\frac{\partial^2 u}{\partial x^2} = \theta\left(\frac{u_{n+1}^{m+1} - 2u_n^{m+1} + u_{n-1}^{m+1}}{(\delta x)^2}\right) + (1-\theta)\left(\frac{u_{n+1}^{m} - 2u_n^{m} + u_{n-1}^{m}}{(\delta x)^2}\right) + O((\delta x)^2),$$

where $0 \le \theta \le 1$ and, as usual, $u_n^m = u(n\,\delta x, m\,\delta\tau)$. The cases $\theta = 0$, $\theta = \frac{1}{2}$ and $\theta = 1$ give, respectively, the explicit, the Crank–Nicolson and the implicit finite-difference approximations. We write

$$g_n^m = g(n\,\delta x, m\,\delta\tau) \tag{21.7}$$

for the discretised payoff function.

As in the previous chapters on finite-difference methods, we use the notation v_n^m to denote the solution of our finite-difference approximation to the exact solution u_n^m. The condition $u(x,\tau) \ge g(x,\tau)$ implies that

$$v_n^m \ge g_n^m \quad \text{for } m \ge 1, \tag{21.8}$$

and the boundary and initial conditions (21.6) imply that

$$v_{-N^-}^m = g_{-N^-}^m, \quad v_{N^+}^m = g_{N^+}^m, \quad v_n^0 = g_n^0. \tag{21.9}$$

We use finite differences to discretise the partial derivatives in problem (21.5). Using the finite-difference approximation

$$\frac{\partial u}{\partial\tau} - \frac{\partial^2 u}{\partial x^2} \approx \frac{v_n^{m+1} - v_n^m}{\delta\tau} - \theta\left(\frac{v_{n+1}^{m+1} - 2v_n^{m+1} + v_{n-1}^{m+1}}{(\delta x)^2}\right) - (1-\theta)\left(\frac{v_{n+1}^{m} - 2v_n^{m} + v_{n-1}^{m}}{(\delta x)^2}\right),$$

we see that the condition $\partial u/\partial\tau - \partial^2 u/\partial x^2 \ge 0$ is approximated by

$$v_n^{m+1} - \alpha\theta(v_{n+1}^{m+1} - 2v_n^{m+1} + v_{n-1}^{m+1}) \ge v_n^m - \alpha(1-\theta)(v_{n+1}^m - 2v_n^m + v_{n-1}^m).$$

As usual,

$$\alpha = \frac{\delta\tau}{(\delta x)^2}$$

and if $\theta < \frac{1}{2}$ then stability restrictions on the size of α apply (namely, $0 < \alpha < \frac{1}{2}(1-\theta)$). We define

$$b_n^m = v_n^m - \alpha(1-\theta)(v_{n+1}^m - 2v_n^m + v_{n-1}^m), \tag{21.10}$$

so that we have

$$v_n^{m+1} - \alpha\theta(v_{n+1}^{m+1} - 2v_n^{m+1} + v_{n-1}^{m+1}) \geq b_n^m. \tag{21.11}$$

Note that at time-step $(m+1)\delta\tau$ we can find b_n^m explicitly, since we know the values of v_n^m. The linear complementarity condition that

$$\left(\frac{\partial u}{\partial \tau} - \frac{\partial^2 u}{\partial x^2}\right)(u(x,\tau) - g(x,\tau)) = 0$$

is approximated by

$$\left(v_n^{m+1} - \alpha\theta(v_{n+1}^{m+1} - 2v_n^{m+1} + v_{n-1}^{m+1}) - b_n^m\right)\left(v_n^{m+1} - g_n^{m+1}\right) = 0. \tag{21.12}$$

21.3 Solution of the finite-difference problem

We can write the finite-difference approximation (21.8)–(21.12) as a constrained matrix problem, that is, in the same general form as the finite-difference approximation (20.3) for the obstacle problem. We can then solve this problem using the projected SOR method.

Let $\boldsymbol{v}^m$ denote the vector of approximate values at time-step $m\,\delta\tau$ and $\boldsymbol{g}^m$ the vector representing the constraint at this same time:

$$\boldsymbol{v}^m = \begin{pmatrix} v_{-N^-+1}^m \\ \vdots \\ v_{N^+-1}^m \end{pmatrix}, \quad \boldsymbol{g}^m = \begin{pmatrix} g_{-N^-+1}^m \\ \vdots \\ g_{N^+-1}^m \end{pmatrix}. \tag{21.13}$$

We do not include the terms $v_{-N^-}^m$ and $v_{N^+}^m$ since these are explicitly determined by the boundary conditions (21.9), $v_{-N^-}^m = g_{-N^-}^m$ and $v_{N^+}^m = g_{N^+}^m$. Let the vector $\boldsymbol{b}^m$ be given by

$$\boldsymbol{b}^m = \begin{pmatrix} b_{-N^-+1}^m \\ \vdots \\ b_{N^+-1}^m \end{pmatrix}, \tag{21.14}$$

where the quantities b_n^m are determined from (21.10). The b_n^ms may be written as

$$b_n^m = v_n^m + \alpha(1-\theta)(v_{n+1}^m - 2v_n^m + v_{n-1}^m) \quad \text{for} \quad -N^- + 2 < n \leq N^+ - 2, \tag{21.15}$$

and for the end conditions at $n = -N^- + 1$ and $n = N^+ - 1$, we have to include the effect of the boundary conditions at $n = -N^-$ and $n = N^+$. This means that $b^m_{-N^-+1}$ and $b^m_{N^+-1}$ differ from the general pattern by the inclusion of an extra term, and are given by

$$\begin{aligned} b^m_{-N^-+1} &= v^m_{-N^-+1} + \alpha(1-\theta)(g^m_{-N^-} - 2v^m_{-N^-+1} + v^m_{-N^-+2}) + \alpha\theta g^{m+1}_{-N^-}, \\ b^m_{N^+-1} &= v^m_{N^+-1} + \alpha(1-\theta)(g^m_{N^+} - 2v^m_{N^+-1} + v^m_{N^+-2}) + \alpha\theta g^{m+1}_{N^+}. \end{aligned} \tag{21.16}$$

If we introduce the $(N^- + N^+ - 2)$-square, tridiagonal, symmetric matrix

$$\mathbf{C} = \begin{pmatrix} 1+2\alpha\theta & -\alpha\theta & 0 & \cdots & 0 \\ -\alpha\theta & 1+2\alpha\theta & -\alpha\theta & & \vdots \\ 0 & -\alpha\theta & \ddots & \ddots & 0 \\ \vdots & & \ddots & 1+2\alpha\theta & -\alpha\theta \\ 0 & \cdots & 0 & -\alpha\theta & 1+2\alpha\theta \end{pmatrix}, \tag{21.17}$$

we can rewrite our discrete approximation (21.8)–(21.12) to the linear complementarity problem (21.5)–(21.6) in matrix form, as

$$\begin{gathered} \left(\mathbf{C}\boldsymbol{v}^{m+1} - \boldsymbol{b}^m\right) \geq \mathbf{0}, \quad \left(\boldsymbol{v}^{m+1} - \boldsymbol{g}^{m+1}\right) \geq \mathbf{0}, \\ \left(\boldsymbol{v}^{m+1} - \boldsymbol{g}^{m+1}\right) \cdot \left(\mathbf{C}\boldsymbol{v}^{m+1} - \boldsymbol{b}^m\right) = 0. \end{gathered} \tag{21.18}$$

As before, we take the expression $\boldsymbol{Z} \geq \mathbf{0}$, where $\boldsymbol{Z}$ is a vector, to mean that the vector has no negative components.

This is, of course, of exactly the same form as the discretisation of the linear complementarity version of the obstacle problem. We can solve it in exactly the same way, using projected SOR. The time stepping is implicit in the scheme: the vector $\boldsymbol{b}^m$ contains the information from the time-step $m\,\delta\tau$ that determines the value of $\boldsymbol{v}^{m+1}$ at time-step $(m+1)\delta\tau$.

At each time-step we can calculate $\boldsymbol{b}^m$ from already known values of $\boldsymbol{v}^m$. We can calculate $\boldsymbol{g}^m$ for any $m\,\delta\tau$, and thus to time-step the system we have only to be able solve the problem (21.18). This can be done using the projected SOR algorithm outlined in the previous chapter. To implement the projected SOR algorithm for problem (21.18) we have only to note that the nonzero elements of the (positive definite symmetric) matrix $\mathbf{C}$ are only the diagonal elements, $C_{ii} = 1 + 2\alpha\theta$, and the sub- and super-diagonal elements, $C_{i\,i\pm1} = -\alpha\theta$.

```
/* projected SOR algorithm for American options */

P_sor(v,b,g,N,alpha,theta,omega)
{
     a = alpha*theta;

     do {
         error = 0.0;
         v[-N] = g[-N];
         v[ N] = g[ N];

         for( i = -N+1; i < N; ++i ) {
             y = (b[i]+a*(v[i-1]+v[i+1])/(1+2*a);
             y = max( g[i], v[i]+omega*(y-v[i]) );
             error += (v[i]-y)*(v[i]-y);
             v[i]=y;
         }
     } while ( error > eps*eps );
}
```

Figure 21.1: Pseudo-code for projected SOR algorithm for an American option problem.

The algorithm for time-stepping from $\boldsymbol{v}^m$ to $\boldsymbol{v}^{m+1}$ is a simple modification to the projected SOR solution of the obstacle problem. Specifically,

1. Given $\boldsymbol{v}^m$, first form the vector $\boldsymbol{b}^m$ using formulæ (21.14), (21.15) and (21.16), and calculate the constraint vector $\boldsymbol{g}^{m+1}$ using (21.7) and (21.13).

2. Let $\boldsymbol{V}^j = (V^j_{-N^-+1}, \ldots, V^j_{N^+-1})$ denote our iterative vectors, so that we start with $\boldsymbol{V}^0$ and as we apply the projected SOR algorithm we generate $\boldsymbol{V}^{j+1}$ from $\boldsymbol{V}^j$. We know that $\boldsymbol{V}^j \to \boldsymbol{v}^{m+1}$ as $j \to \infty$. Start with $\boldsymbol{V}^0 = \max(\boldsymbol{v}^m, \boldsymbol{g}^{m+1})$. (Recall that it is important that $\boldsymbol{V}^0 \geq \boldsymbol{g}^{m+1}$—if not then the method may not converge.)

3. Form, in sequence, the quantities U_i^{j+1} by

$$U_i^{j+1} = \left(b_i^m + \alpha\theta V_{i-1}^{j+1} + \alpha\theta V_{i+1}^j\right)/(1 + 2\alpha\theta)$$

   (note, again, that we use V_{i-1}^{j+1} rather than V_{i-1}^j) and then find V_i^{j+1} from

$$V_i^{j+1} = \max\left(g_i^{m+1}, V_i^j + \omega(U_i^{j+1} - V_i^j)\right),$$

   where $1 < \omega < 2$ is a given relaxation parameter.

4. Test whether or not $\left|\boldsymbol{V}^{j+1} - \boldsymbol{V}^j\right|$ is smaller than a pre-chosen tolerance ϵ, that is, test whether

$$\sum_i \left(V_i^{j+1} - V_i^j\right)^2 \leq \epsilon^2.$$

   If it is, go on to step 5. If it is not, go back to step 3 and repeat the process with $\boldsymbol{V}^{j+1}$ instead of $\boldsymbol{V}^j$.

5. When the vectors $\boldsymbol{V}^j$ have converged to the required tolerance, put $\boldsymbol{v}^{k+1} = \boldsymbol{V}^{j+1}$.

6. Return to step 1 until the desired number of time-steps have been completed.

```
/* Value an American option */

American_option(theta, N, M, dt, dx, v)
{
    tau = 0.0; alpha = dt/(dx*dx);

    /* set up initial value */

    for(i = -N; i <= N; ++i ) {
        x[i] = i * dx;
        v[i] = payoff( x[i], tau );
    }

    /* time step */

    for(i = 1, tau=i*dt; i <= M; ++i ) {
        for( j=-N+1; j < N; ++j ) {
            g[j] = payoff(x[i],tau);
            b[j] = v[j] + alpha*(1-theta)*
                   (v[j+1]+v[j-1]-2*v[j]);
        }
        g[-N] = payoff(x[-N],tau);
        g[ N] = payoff(x[ N],tau);
        b[1-N] += alpha*theta*g[-N];
        b[N-1] += alpha*theta*g[ N];
        P_sor(v,b,g,N,alpha,theta,omega,eps);
    }
}
```

Figure 21.2: Pseudo-code for solution of an American option problem.

In Figure 21.2 we give a pseudo-code implementation of this algorithm.

Technical Point: SOR and European options.
The projected SOR method is a generalisation of the SOR or **Successive Over-Relaxation** *method. The two methods are identical except that the step*

$$V_i^{j+1} = \max\left(g_i^{m+1}, V_i^j + \omega(U_i^{j+1} - V_i^j)\right),$$

that occurs in the projected SOR algorithm, becomes

$$V_i^{j+1} = V_i^j + \omega(U_i^{j+1} - V_i^j),$$

in the SOR algorithm. The SOR algorithm solves the problem

$$\mathbf{C}\boldsymbol{v}^{m+1} = \boldsymbol{b}^m \qquad (21.19)$$

without *the constraint that $\boldsymbol{v}^{m+1} \geq \boldsymbol{g}^{m+1}$. Thus, we could value a European option using the SOR algorithm, since (21.19) is simply the finite-difference θ-method approximation to the diffusion equation. This approach is slightly less efficient than the LU algorithm advocated in the earlier chapters; typically an SOR solver for a European option is about twice as slow as an LU solver.*

One advantage of the SOR algorithm over the LU algorithm when valuing European options is that the computer code is identical to the code for an American version except for a single line. Indeed, using SOR or projected SOR, it is trivial to modify the code for a European or American option to value an option which may be exercised early, but only on predetermined dates. Such an option is referred to as a **Bermudan option**. *During a period where the option may be exercised early, the constraint that its value exceeds the payoff applies. This implies that we use projected SOR during such a period. When early exercise is forbidden, the payoff constraint does not apply, and we use ordinary SOR. The difference between the two algorithms amounts to taking a* max *in the projected SOR method and not taking a* max *in the SOR method. For completeness, in Figure* 21.4 *we give the SOR algorithm for a European option in*

```
/* SOR algorithm for European options */

SOR(v,b,g,N,alpha,theta,omega)
{
    a = alpha*theta;

    do {
        error = 0.0;
        v[-N] = g[-N];
        v[ N] = g[ N];

        for( i = -N+1; i < N; ++i ) {
            y = (b[i]+a*(v[i-1]+v[i+1])/(1+2*a);
            y = v[i]+omega*(y-v[i]);
            error += (v[i]-y)*(v[i]-y);
            v[i]=y;
        }
    } while ( error > eps*eps );
}
```

Figure 21.3: Pseudo-code for SOR algorithm for a European option problem.

Figure 21.3 *and a general projected SOR algorithm that allows the early exercise constraint to be turned either on or off at each time step. This latter code may be used to value Bermudan options.*

21.4 Numerical examples

In Figure 21.5 we give values for the American put with interest rate $r = 0.10$, volatility $\sigma = 0.5$ and exercise price $E = 10$. The calculation uses the Crank–Nicolson version of the method and α was taken to be 1.

In Figure 21.6 we show a numerically computed solution of an American call problem with $E = 10$, $r = 0.25$, $\sigma = 0.8$, $D_0 = 0.2$ and lifetime of one year, together with the corresponding European

```
/* generalised SOR algorithm for American,
   European and Bermudan options             */

G_sor(v,b,g,N,alpha,theta,omega,early_exercise)
{
     a = alpha*theta;

     do {
         error = 0.0;
         v[-N] = g[-N];
         v[ N] = g[ N];

         for( i = -N+1; i < N; ++i ) {
             y = (b[i]+a*(v[i-1]+v[i+1])/(1+2*a);
             if( early_exercise == TRUE)
                 y = max( g[i], v[i]+omega*(y-v[i]) );
             else
                 y = v[i]+omega*(y-v[i]);
             error += (v[i]-y)*(v[i]-y);
             v[i]=y;
         }
     } while ( error > eps*eps );
}
```

Figure 21.4: Pseudo-code for generalised SOR algorithm for American, European and Bermudan option problems.

Asset Price	Payoff Value	3 months		6 months	
		Amer.	Euro.	Amer.	Euro.
0.00	10.0000	10.0000	9.7531	10.0000	9.5123
2.00	8.0000	8.0000	7.7531	8.0000	7.5123
4.00	6.0000	6.0000	5.7531	6.0000	5.5128
6.00	4.0000	4.0000	3.7569	4.0000	3.5583
8.00	2.0000	2.0200	1.9024	2.0951	1.9181
10.00	0.0000	0.6913	0.6694	0.9211	0.8703
12.00	0.0000	0.1711	0.1675	0.3622	0.3477
14.00	0.0000	0.0332	0.0326	0.1320	0.1279
16.00	0.0000	0.0055	0.0054	0.0460	0.0448

Figure 21.5: Crank–Nicolson solution for an American put with $E = 10$, $r = 0.1$, $\sigma = 0.4$ and with expiry times of three and six months.

value. The smooth separation of the option value from the payoff function can be seen at the point S_f. (We determine the position of the free boundary *a posteriori* by finding the x-node $x_n = n\,\delta x$ at which $v_n^m > g_n^m$ but for which $v_{n-1}^m \leq g_{n-1}^m$. Further resolution is possible by assuming a linear formula for u_n^m and g_n^m. We can approximate the position of the free boundary by the intersection of the straight line segments joining g_{n-1}^m, g_n^m and v_{n-1}^m, v_n^m.)

21.5 Convergence of the method

A detailed analysis of the convergence of the finite-difference approximation to the linear complementarity form of the American option problem is somewhat beyond the aims of this book. A rigorous proof of the convergence involves the use of a good deal of abstract functional analysis and is most easily presented within the framework of the finite-element formulation of the variational inequality formulation of the problem. Since the numerical algorithms for solving the linear complementarity formulation by finite differences and for solving the variational inequality formulation by finite elements are identical (as proved in Appendix D), the convergence of the algorithm presented here can be established in this manner. Such a detailed analysis of the convergence may be found in Elliott & Ockendon (1982) or Crank (1984). Suffice it to say that, if the method

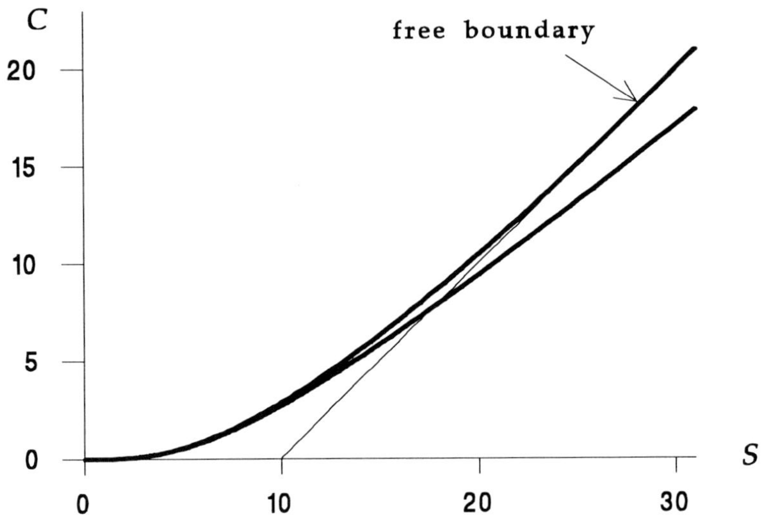

Figure 21.6: Numerically calculated solution of an American call problem with $E = 10$, $r = 0.25$, $D_0 = 0.2$, $\sigma = 0.8$ and expiry date of one year. The parameter values have been chosen to exaggerate the difference between the American option and its European counterpart (also shown).

is stable then it converges as $\delta\tau \to 0$, $\delta x \to 0$.

Further reading

- See Crank (1984) and Elliott & Ockendon (1982) for more general information about numerical solution of parabolic linear complementarity problems and free boundary problems.

Exercises

1. Write a computer program to value a call option that may be exercised early, but only during the second and fourth weeks of each month. Use the θ-method and modified projected SOR.

2. Determine, experimentally, the optimal value of the SOR parameter ω using the program developed in question 1.

Chapter 22

Methods for Exotic Options

22.1 Introduction

Many of the other partial differential equation models for derivative securities presented in this book may be solved numerically with minor modifications to the simple numerical schemes described in the previous chapters. Some, however, require more substantial modification.

In this chapter we briefly discuss some of the modifications necessary. They apply to models in higher dimensions, and incorporate jump conditions from discrete sampling (where the problem is the implementation of the jump condition) and the application of boundary conditions involving partial derivatives. All of these are minor variants on the theme outlined in the earlier chapters.

As an example where more substantial modification is necessary, we consider in detail the problem for average strikes. This problem cannot be reduced to the diffusion equation in any way that is easy or sensible. We therefore have to think about another method of discretising the problem. This is complicated by the nature of one of the boundary conditions, and careful attention has to be paid to the characteristics of the underlying partial differential equation in order to obtain a sensible discretisation. This example serves as a warning that not all partial differential equation models are easy to solve numerically.

22.2 Three-dimensional models

We begin by considering the model for a European lookback put option, although similar ideas apply to the American lookback option. (Indeed, the only difference is that we would use the projected SOR algorithm for the American option instead of the LU decomposition algorithm for the European option.)

Recall that lookback problems can sometimes be written in terms of a similarity variable S/J. When this is possible we need only solve the basic Black–Scholes partial differential equation by exactly those numerical methods we have so far discussed. In this case the numerical method will be as quick to run as any vanilla option. However, if the dividends or the payoff at expiry do not take certain simple forms we must necessarily solve a problem with *three* independent variables. In what follows we show how to solve such problems numerically. For comparison with the earlier discussion of Chapter 12 we describe the method as applied to the lookback put option.

The problem may be written as

$$\frac{\partial P}{\partial t} + \tfrac{1}{2}\sigma^2 S^2 \frac{\partial^2 P}{\partial S^2} + rS\frac{\partial P}{\partial S} - rP = 0$$

where $P = P(S, J, t)$ and

$$P(S, J, T) = \max(J - S, 0),$$

with

$$P(0, J, t) = Je^{-r(T-t)}, \qquad \frac{\partial P}{\partial J}(J, J, t) = 0.$$

Here the variable J (the maximum realised value of the underlying) only enters into the problem through the payoff condition and the boundary conditions. We may transform the Black–Scholes equation into the diffusion equation in the manner described in Section 5.4 and, also putting $J = Ee^y$, we obtain

$$\frac{\partial u}{\partial \tau} = \frac{\partial^2 u}{\partial x^2},$$

with initial condition

$$u(x, y, 0) = e^{\frac{1}{2}(k_1-1)x}\max(e^y - e^x, 0)$$

and boundary conditions

$$\lim_{x\to-\infty} u(x,y,\tau) = \lim_{x\to-\infty} e^{y+\frac{1}{2}(k_1-1)x+\frac{1}{4}(k_1-1)^2\tau},$$

$$\frac{\partial V}{\partial y}(y,y,\tau) = 0;$$

here $k_1 = r/\frac{1}{2}\sigma^2$. The problem is only defined for $x \le y$, since $S \le J$ by definition of J.

We can solve the diffusion equation in exactly the manner described in the previous chapters. Since, however, u depends on y as well as x and τ, we must allow for this. This means that we must work on a three-dimensional grid, that is in (x, y, τ)-space. As before, we take a finite τ-step, and finite x- and y-steps, and form a mesh whose points are $(i\,\delta x, j\,\delta y, m\,\delta\tau)$. Since the variable y occurs in the boundary and initial conditions, and in particular since the problem is only defined for $x \le y$, it is sensible to take $\delta x = \delta y$. We consider the values of u at the grid points $(i\,\delta x, j\,\delta y, m\,\delta\tau)$ and define

$$u_{i,j}^m = u(i\,\delta x, j\,\delta y, m\,\delta\tau).$$

In order to represent the values of u at time-step $m\,\delta\tau$ it is necessary to use a two-dimensional array, rather than a one-dimensional array; see Figure 22.1.

The solution method for the diffusion equation is essentially the same as in the previous chapters, but it is necessary to solve it for each value of y since u varies with y. Thus we can construct an explicit finite-difference approximation to the diffusion equation as

$$\frac{v_{i,j}^{m+1} - v_{i,j}^m}{\delta\tau} = \frac{v_{i+1,j}^m - 2v_{i,j}^m + v_{i-1,j}^m}{(\delta x)^2}.$$

The only difference between this and the previous chapters is that this finite difference equation must be solved for each distinct value of j. This means that the number of operation involved increases dramatically in comparison with a single-factor model. Similar comments apply to implicit and Crank–Nicolson finite-difference approximations. The idea is illustrated in the pseudo-code shown in Figure 22.2; notice that we use two two-dimensional arrays to contain the

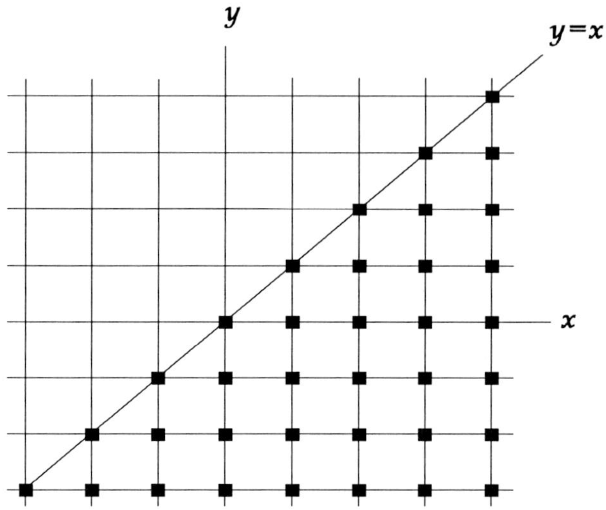

Figure 22.1: Finite-difference grid at fixed time for a European lookback.

old and new option values during each time-step and compare this with Figure 18.3.

We have so far avoided mention of the boundary condition at $x = y$, namely that $\partial u/\partial y = 0$. We can implement this relatively easily, using the approximation

$$\frac{\partial u}{\partial y} = \frac{u_{i,j}^m - u_{i,j-1}^m}{\delta y} + O(\delta y).$$

This gives us the finite difference approximation

$$\frac{v_{j,j}^m - v_{j,j-1}^m}{\delta y} = 0$$

or, equivalently,

$$v_{j,j}^m = v_{j,j-1}^m.$$

This is also illustrated in Figure 22.2.

```
lookback
{
  alpha = dt/(dx*dx);

  /* initialise arrays */

  for( j = -Nminus; j <= Nplus; ++j) {
      for( i = -Nminus; i <= j; ++i )
          oldv[i,j] = pay_off( i*dx, j*dx );

  /* solve diffusion equation */

  for( time = 1; time <= M; ++time ) {

    for( j=-Nminus; j <= Nplus; ++j ) {

      newv[-Nminus,j] = boundary_value(-Nminus*dx,j*dx);

      for(i=-Nminus+1; i<j; ++i)
        newv[i,j] = oldv[i,j] + alpha*(oldv[i-1,j]
                    +oldv[i+1,j]-2*oldv[i,j]);

      newv[j,j] = newv[j,j-1];

     for(i=-Nminus; i <= Nplus; ++i)
        oldv[i] = newv[i];

    }
  }
}
```

Figure 22.2: Pseudo-code for explicit finite-difference solution for a European lookback.

22.3 Jump conditions

Jump conditions arise in models that contain some form of discrete sampling, for example, discrete dividend payments or discrete sampling dates for exotics such as lookbacks or average strikes. A typical example is the jump condition arising from a discrete dividend yield,

$$V(S,t_d^-) = V(e^{-D_\delta^y}S, t_d^+)$$

where t_0 is the dividend date and D_δ^y the dividend yield. In the transformed variables of Section 5.4, this condition becomes

$$u(x,\tau_d^+) = e^{-\eta D_\delta^y}u(x - D_\delta^y, \tau_d^-),$$

where $\eta = \frac{1}{2}(1-k_1)$. In the former case we know $V(S,t)$ at a finite number of values of S at $t = t_d^+$, and we wish to find $V(S,t)$ at these values of S at $t = t_d^-$, in the latter case we know $u(x,\tau)$ at a finite number of values of x at τ_d^- and wish to find it τ_d^+. In either case, it is extremely unlikely that the value of $e^{-D_\delta^y}S$ or $x - D_\delta^y$ will correspond to one of the finite number of values of S or x for which the option value is known; see Figure 22.3. We must attempt to find an approximate value by interpolation.

Notice that the value of the option after the jump is always in terms of its value before the jump but for smaller values of S or x (assuming, of course, that the dividends are positive). Thus we can consider the problem as follows:

- Given the value of a function $f(x)$ at the points $x = i\,\delta x$, for $i = -N, \dots, N$, how can we approximate its value at $x = y$ where $y \neq x_i$?

The simplest answer, which is also accurate to the order that we require, is to use linear interpolation, which works as follows. First find x_i and x_{i+1} such that $x_i < y < x_{i+1}$. (If we are lucky enough to find an $x_i = y$ then no approximation is necessary; however, this is extremely unlikely to happen in practice.) Then assume that the point $(y, f(y))$ lies on the straight line segment between $(x_i, f(x_i))$ and $(x_{i+1}, f(x_{i+1}))$; see Figure 22.4. This implies that

$$\frac{f(y) - f(x_i)}{y - x_i} = \frac{f(x_{i+1}) - f(x_i)}{x_{i+1} - x_i}$$

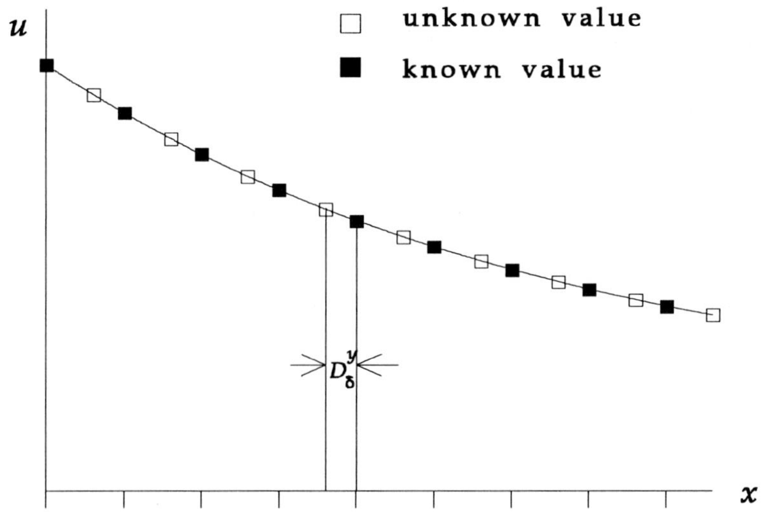

Figure 22.3: Jump condition across a sampling date on a finite difference grid.

and hence that

$$f(y) = f(x_i) + \left(\frac{f(x_{i+1}) - f(x_i)}{x_{i+1} - x_i}\right)(y - x_i).$$

In our finite-difference approximations we work to an accuracy of $O((\delta x)^2)$. We can show that linear interpolation is accurate to this order of approximation. From Taylor's theorem

$$f(x_{i+1}) = f(x_i) + (x_{i+1} - x_i)\frac{df}{dx}(x_i) + O((\delta x)^2)$$
$$f(y) = f(x_i) + (y - x_i)\frac{df}{dx}(x_i) + O((\delta x)^2)$$

where $\delta x = (x_{i+1} - x_i) > (y - x_i)$. We therefore find that

$$\frac{df}{dx}(x_i) = \frac{f(x_{i+1}) - f(x_i)}{x_{i+1} - x_i} + O(\delta x).$$

Thus we have

$$f(y) = f(x_i) + \left(\frac{f(x_{i+1}) - f(x_i)}{x_{i+1} - x_i}\right)(y - x_i) + O((\delta x)^2),$$

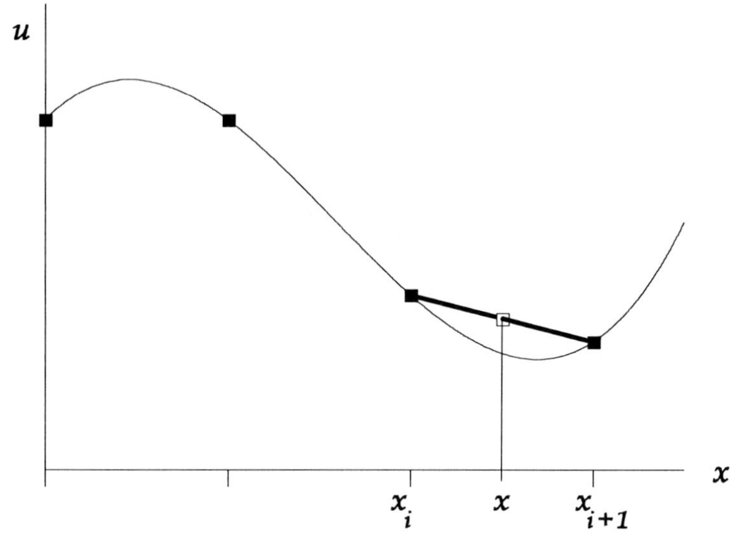

Figure 22.4: Linear interpolation between grid points.

since $O(\delta x)\,(y - x_i) = O((\delta x)^2)$. Linear interpolation is therefore consistent with the order of approximation used in the finite-difference solution method. Using higher order interpolation formulæ is not sensible, since this gives an order of accuracy that is not preserved by the underlying solution method for the diffusion equation.

22.4 Average strike options

As shown in Section 11.5 the problem for a European average strike call, with arithmetic averaging, may be reduced to the partial differential equation

$$\frac{\partial H}{\partial t} + \tfrac{1}{2}\sigma^2 R^2 \frac{\partial^2 H}{\partial R^2} + \frac{\partial H}{\partial R} - rR\frac{\partial H}{\partial R} = 0. \tag{22.1}$$

This is subject to the boundary conditions

$$\lim_{R\to 0} H(R,t) \text{ is finite}, \quad \lim_{R\to\infty} H(R,t) = 0, \tag{22.2}$$

and the final condition

$$H(R,T) = \max\left(1 - \frac{R}{T}, 0\right). \tag{22.3}$$

Similarly the problem for the American average strike, with the early exercise payoff

$$\max\left(S(t) - \frac{1}{t}\int_0^t S(\tau)\,d\tau, 0\right),$$

may be reduced to the following linear complementarity problem: with $\Lambda(R,t) = \max(1 - R/t, 0)$,

$$\begin{gathered}(\Lambda(R,t) - H(R,t)) \le 0, \\ \left(\frac{\partial H}{\partial t} + \tfrac{1}{2}\sigma^2 R^2 \frac{\partial^2 H}{\partial R^2} + \frac{\partial H}{\partial R} - rR\frac{\partial H}{\partial R}\right) \le 0, \\ (H - \Lambda)\left(\frac{\partial H}{\partial t} + \tfrac{1}{2}\sigma^2 R^2 \frac{\partial^2 H}{\partial R^2} + \frac{\partial H}{\partial R} - rR\frac{\partial H}{\partial R}\right) = 0,\end{gathered} \tag{22.4}$$

subject to the boundary conditions

$$\lim_{R\to 0} H(R,t) \text{ is finite}, \quad \lim_{R\to\infty} H(R,t) = \lim_{R\to\infty} \Lambda(R,t) = 0, \tag{22.5}$$

the final condition

$$H(R,T) = \Lambda(R,T) = \max\left(1 - \frac{R}{T}, 0\right), \tag{22.6}$$

and the conditions that

$$H(R,t) \text{ and } \frac{\partial H}{\partial R} \text{ are continuous.}$$

The condition that $H(R,t)$ is finite as $R \to 0$ implies that

$$\frac{\partial H}{\partial t} + \frac{\partial H}{\partial R} = 0 \text{ at } R = 0 \tag{22.7}$$

for the European average strike. For the American average strike we have either this condition, in the event that the finite value of $H(0,t)$ exceeds $\Lambda(0,t) = 1$, or $H(0,t) = \Lambda(0,t) = 1$. In practice, we can see easily that $H(0,t) = \Lambda(0,t)$ in all cases (see Section 11.6).

The main difficulty in solving these problems for the European and American average strike is the presence of the $\partial H/\partial R$ term in the partial differential operator. Since this term does not scale with R there are no convenient transformations that reduce the partial differential operator to a constant coefficient case. We are forced to use finite differences on the unmodified form of the partial differential operator.

At $R = 0$ the partial differential operator (22.1) reduces to the operator (22.7). That is, at $R = 0$, the operator is hyperbolic whereas for $R > 0$ (and, indeed, for $R < 0$) the operator is parabolic. This has important implications for our numerical solution strategy.

If we consider the partial differential equation

$$\frac{\partial H}{\partial t} + \frac{\partial H}{\partial R} = 0 \tag{22.8}$$

we see that the solution is of the form $H(R, t) = F(R - t)$ for some function F. Thus as t increases, information starting from $R = 0$ moves out towards greater values of R along straight lines $R = t$ + constant. The characteristics of this operator have positive slope. Since we are solving a backward problem with a final condition (the payoff), we are interested in t decreasing. In this case the information moves from $R > 0$ towards $R = 0$, back down the characteristics. In particular, as t decreases, no information from $R < 0$ can cross the line $R = 0$. This is illustrated in Figure 22.5.

Similarly, for the full equation (22.1) with t decreasing, no information from $R < 0$ can cross the line $R = 0$, which is to say that $H(R, t)$ for $R \geq 0$ cannot depend on $H(R, t)$ for $R < 0$. This is obvious from a financial point of view, since the value of the average strike for negative values of R, i.e. negative values of S, is a meaningless concept. Clearly the value of the average strike for $S \geq 0$ cannot depend on an undefined quantity. This has important consequences for the way in which we represent the various derivatives in (22.1) when we take a finite-difference approximation; if, in the usual way, we let $H_n^m = H(n\,\delta R, m\,\delta t)$, then there must be no terms with $n = -1$ in the finite-difference expression for H_0^m. If there were, then necessarily our approximation to $H(0, t)$ would depend on $H(R, t)$ for $R < 0$, which is impossible for the reasons given above.

22.4.1 Discretisation of the differential equation

As in the previous chapters, we work on a regular grid, in (R, t)-space in this case, with a constant time-step δt and a constant R-step of size δR. Since we are solving backwards in time from the payoff at

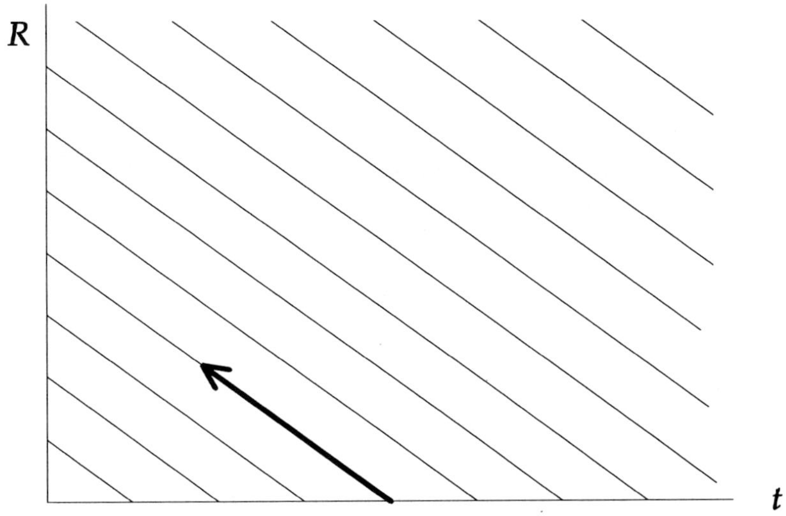

Figure 22.5: Information flow as t decreases for solutions of (22.8).

expiry, we solve for $H(R, m\,\delta t)$ in terms of values of $H(R, (m+1)\,\delta t)$. We use the standard θ-weighted finite-difference approximations

$$
\begin{aligned}
\frac{\partial H}{\partial t} &= \left(\frac{H_n^{m+1} - H_n^m}{\delta t} \right) + O(\delta t) \\
\frac{\partial^2 H}{\partial R^2} &= \theta \left(\frac{H_{n+1}^m + H_{n-1}^m - 2H_n^m}{(\delta R)^2} \right) \\
&\quad + (1-\theta) \left(\frac{H_{n+1}^{m+1} + H_{n-1}^{m+1} - 2H_n^{m+1}}{(\delta R)^2} \right) + O((\delta R)^2)
\end{aligned}
\tag{22.9}
$$

so that $\theta = 0$ leads to an explicit method (the H_n^m may be calculated explicitly if the H_n^{m+1} are known), $\theta = 1$ gives a fully implicit approximation (the H_n^m are determined implicitly in terms of the H_n^{m+1}) and $\theta = \frac{1}{2}$ gives a Crank–Nicolson approximation (which is also implicit).

Since at $n = 0$ the partial differential equation reduces to (22.7) and $H(0, t)$ does not depend on $H(R, t)$ for $R < 0$ as t decreases, we are forced to use a one-sided approximation for $\partial H/\partial R$; if we used the symmetric difference

$$\frac{\partial H}{\partial R}(0,t) = \left(\frac{H_1^m - H_{-1}^m}{2\delta R}\right) + O((\delta R)^2)$$

then $H(0,t)$ would necessarily depend on $H(-\delta R, t)$, which it cannot.

At first sight it might seem sensible to approximate $\partial H/\partial R$ by a forward difference of the form

$$\frac{\partial H}{\partial t}(n\,\delta R, m\,\delta t) = \left(\frac{H_{n+1}^m - H_n^m}{\delta R}\right) + O(\delta R)$$

since $H(0,t)$ would then depend only on $H(0, t+\delta t)$ and $H(\delta R, t+\delta t)$. Unfortunately, this approximation is only accurate to $O(\delta R)$, whereas the approximation to $\partial^2 H/\partial R^2$ is accurate to $O((\delta R)^2)$. Such a strategy would greatly reduce the accuracy of the finite-difference scheme and require very large number of R-grid points. It would also adversely affect the stability.

We look, therefore, for one-sided approximations to $\partial H/\partial R$ that are accurate to order $((\delta R)^2)$. Noting that

$$H(R+\delta R, t) = H(R,t) + \frac{\partial H}{\partial R}\delta R + \frac{\partial^2 H}{\partial R^2}\frac{(\delta R)^2}{2} + O((\delta R)^3),$$

$$H(R+2\delta R, t) = H(R,t) + 2\frac{\partial H}{\partial R}\delta R + 2\frac{\partial^2 H}{\partial R^2}(\delta R)^2 + O((\delta R)^3)$$

where the partial derivatives are evaluated at (R,t). Eliminating the terms of $O((\delta R))$, we have

$$\frac{\partial H}{\partial R}(n\,\delta R, m\,\delta t) = \frac{-H_{n+2}^m + 4H_{n+1}^m - 3H_n^m}{2\delta R} + O((\delta R)^2). \quad (22.10)$$

This is a one-sided difference approximation to $\partial H/\partial R$ which is of the same order of accuracy as the approximation for $\partial^2 H/\partial R^2$, and we use it in our finite-difference approximations (see exercise 1 in Chapter 17).

We use a θ-averaged approximation for $\partial H/\partial R$, consistent with the θ-averaged approximation for $\partial^2 H/\partial R^2$, namely

$$\begin{aligned}\frac{\partial H}{\partial R} = {} & \theta\left(\frac{4H_{n+1}^m - H_{n+2}^m - 3H_n^m}{2\delta R}\right) \\ & +(1-\theta)\left(\frac{4H_{n+1}^{m+1} - H_{n+2}^{m+1} - 3H_n^{m+1}}{2\delta R}\right) + O((\delta R)^2).\end{aligned} \quad (22.11)$$

Noting that $R = n\,\delta R$ at grid points, we find that we may approximate

$$\frac{\partial H}{\partial t} + \tfrac{1}{2}\sigma^2 R^2 \frac{\partial^2 H}{\partial R^2} + \frac{\partial H}{\partial R} - rR\frac{\partial H}{\partial R}$$

to $O(\delta t + (\delta R)^2)$ by

$$\begin{aligned}
&\frac{H_n^{m+1} - H_n^m}{\delta t} \\
&+\frac{\sigma^2 n^2}{2}\left(\theta(H_{n+1}^m - 2H_n^m + H_{n-1}^m) + \theta_1(H_{n+1}^{m+1} - 2H_n^{m+1} + H_{n-1}^{m+1})\right) \\
&+\frac{1}{2\delta R}\left(\theta(4H_{n+1}^m - H_{n+2}^m - 3H_n^m) + \theta_1(4H_{n+1}^{m+1} - H_{n+2}^{m+1} - 3H_n^{m+1})\right) \\
&-\frac{nr}{2}\left(\theta(4H_{n+1}^m - H_{n+2}^m - 3H_n^m) + \theta_1(4H_{n+1}^{m+1} - H_{n+2}^{m+1} - 3H_n^{m+1})\right),
\end{aligned} \tag{22.12}$$

where $\theta_1 = (1-\theta)$.

22.4.2 European average strikes

Rearranging (22.12) and writing h_n^m for our finite-difference approximation to $H_n^m = H(n\,\delta R, m\,\delta t)$, we obtain the finite-difference scheme

$$\begin{aligned}
&A_n h_{n-1}^m + B_n h_n^m + C_n h_{n+1}^m + D_n h_{n+2}^m \\
&\qquad = a_n h_{n-1}^{m+1} + b_n h_n^{m+1} + c_n h_{n+1}^{m+1} + d_n h_{n+2}^{m+1}
\end{aligned} \tag{22.13}$$

as an approximation to (22.1), where

$$\begin{aligned}
A_n &= -\tfrac{1}{2}\sigma^2 n^2 \theta\,\delta t, \\
B_n &= 1 + \tfrac{1}{2}\left(2\sigma^2 n^2 - 3rn + \frac{3}{\delta R}\right)\theta\,\delta t, \\
C_n &= \tfrac{1}{2}\left(-\sigma^2 n^2 + 4rn - \frac{4}{\delta R}\right)\theta\,\delta t, \\
D_n &= \tfrac{1}{2}\left(-rn + \frac{1}{\delta R}\right)\theta\,\delta t,
\end{aligned} \tag{22.14}$$

and

$$\begin{aligned} a_n &= \tfrac{1}{2}\sigma^2 n^2 (1-\theta)\,\delta t, \\ b_n &= 1 - \tfrac{1}{2}\left(2\sigma^2 n^2 - 3rn + \frac{3}{\delta R}\right)(1-\theta)\,\delta t, \\ c_n &= \tfrac{1}{2}\left(\sigma^2 n^2 - 4rn + \frac{4}{\delta R}\right)(1-\theta)\,\delta t, \\ d_n &= \tfrac{1}{2}\left(rn - \frac{1}{\delta R}\right)(1-\theta)\,\delta t. \end{aligned} \tag{22.15}$$

Note that at $n = 0$, i.e. at $R = 0$, we have

$$A_n = a_n = 0,$$

so that the finite-difference approximation becomes[1]

$$B_0 h_0^m + C_0 h_1^m + D_0 h_2^m = b_0 h_0^{m+1} + c_0 h_1^{m+1} + d_0 h_2^{m+1}$$

and h_0^m is independent of values of h_n^m with $n < 0$, as required. Also, the condition that $H(0,t)$ be finite is built into the finite-difference scheme, in the sense that with $n = 0$ the scheme reduces to the finite-difference approximation for (22.7).

If we restrict ourselves to a finite grid, and consider the equation only for $0 \le n \le N$, that is for $0 \le R \le N\delta R$, then the boundary condition that $H(R,t) \to 0$ as $R \to \infty$ can be approximated by the condition that $h_n^m = 0$ for all $n > N$. Thus we find that at $n = N-1$ we have

$$\begin{aligned} A_{N-1} h_{N-2}^m + B_{N-1} h_{N-1}^m + C_{N-1} h_N^m \\ = a_{N-1} h_{N-2}^{m+1} + b_{N-1} h_{N-1}^{m+1} + c_{N-1} h_N^{m+1}, \end{aligned}$$

and at $n = N$ the equations become

$$A_N h_{N-1}^m + B_N h_N^m = a_N h_{N-1}^{m+1} + b_N h_N^{m+1}.$$

We may therefore approximate the problem for a European average strike by the system

$$\mathbf{M}\boldsymbol{h}^m = \boldsymbol{b}^{m+1} \tag{22.16}$$

[1] Here D_0 represents D_n with $n = 0$ and *not* a constant continuous dividend yield.

where

$$\boldsymbol{h}^m = \begin{pmatrix} h_0^m \\ h_1^m \\ h_2^m \\ \vdots \\ h_{N-2}^m \\ h_{N-1}^m \\ h_N^m \end{pmatrix}, \boldsymbol{b}^m = \begin{pmatrix} b_0^m \\ b_1^m \\ b_2^m \\ \vdots \\ b_{N-2}^m \\ b_{N-1}^m \\ b_N^m \end{pmatrix}$$

and the b_n^m are determined by

$$\boldsymbol{b}^m = \begin{pmatrix} b_0 h_0^m + c_0 h_1^m + d_0 h_2^m \\ a_1 h_0^m + b_1 h_1^m + c_1 h_2^m + d_1 h_3^m \\ a_2 h_1^m + b_2 h_2^m + c_2 h_3^m + d_2 h_4^m \\ \vdots \\ a_{N-2} h_{N-3}^m + b_{N-2} h_{N-2}^m + c_{N-2} h_{N-1}^m + d_{N-2} h_N^m \\ a_{N-1} h_{N-2}^m + b_{N-1} h_{N-1}^m + c_{N-1} h_N^m \\ a_N h_{N-1}^m + b_N h_N^m \end{pmatrix}. \quad (22.17)$$

The matrix $\mathbf{M}$ is given by

$$\mathbf{M} = \begin{pmatrix} B_0 & C_0 & D_0 & 0 & 0 & \cdots & 0 \\ A_1 & B_1 & C_1 & D_1 & 0 & & 0 \\ 0 & A_2 & B_2 & C_2 & D_2 & & \vdots \\ 0 & 0 & \ddots & \ddots & \ddots & \ddots & 0 \\ \vdots & & & A_{N-2} & B_{N-2} & C_{N-2} & D_{N-2} \\ 0 & & & 0 & A_{N-1} & B_{N-1} & C_{N-1} \\ 0 & \cdots & 0 & 0 & 0 & A_N & B_N \end{pmatrix}. \quad (22.18)$$

We also have the final condition $H(R,T) = \max(1 - R/T, 0)$. Thus if $T = m\,\delta t$ we have

$$h_n^M = \max(1 - n\,\delta R/T, 0),$$

so that $\boldsymbol{h}^M$ is known. To solve the European average strike problem we have only to solve (22.16) to find $\boldsymbol{h}^{M-1}$, $\boldsymbol{h}^{M-2}$ and so on back to $\boldsymbol{h}^0$. This gives us the current value of the average strike at $n\,\delta R$ for $0 \le n \le N$.

Unless $\theta = 0$, in which case $\mathbf{M}$ reduces to the identity, (22.16) is a nontrivial linear system and we must solve it numerically. This can be done by a simple variant of the LU method described in Section 19.2.3 and in Section 19.2.4 for simple calls and puts. We write

$$\mathbf{M} = \mathbf{L}\mathbf{U}$$

where

$$\mathbf{L} = \begin{pmatrix} 1 & 0 & 0 & \cdots & 0 \\ \ell_1 & 1 & 0 & \cdots & 0 \\ 0 & \ell_2 & 1 & & \vdots \\ \vdots & 0 & \ddots & \ddots & 0 \\ 0 & \cdots & 0 & \ell_N & 1 \end{pmatrix}$$

and

$$\mathbf{U} = \begin{pmatrix} \beta_0 & \gamma_0 & \delta_0 & 0 & 0 & \cdots & 0 \\ 0 & \beta_1 & \gamma_1 & \delta_1 & 0 & & 0 \\ 0 & 0 & \beta_2 & \gamma_2 & \delta_2 & & \vdots \\ 0 & 0 & \ddots & \ddots & \ddots & \ddots & 0 \\ \vdots & & & 0 & \beta_{N-2} & \gamma_{N-2} & \delta_{N-2} \\ 0 & & & 0 & 0 & \beta_{N-1} & \gamma_{N-1} \\ 0 & \cdots & 0 & 0 & 0 & 0 & \beta_N \end{pmatrix}.$$

We find that

$$\beta_0 = B_0, \quad \gamma_0 = C_0, \quad \delta_0 = D_0, \quad \ell_1 = A_1/B_0,$$

and for $n > 0$,

$$\begin{aligned} \ell_n &= A_n/\beta_{n-1}, \\ \beta_n &= B_n - \ell_n\gamma_{n-1}, \\ \gamma_n &= C_n - \ell_n\delta_{n-1}, \\ \delta_n &= D_n. \end{aligned}$$

We first solve

$$\mathbf{L}\boldsymbol{g}^m = \boldsymbol{b}^{m+1},$$

and then we solve

$$\mathbf{U}\boldsymbol{h}^m = \boldsymbol{g}^m.$$

We find that

$$g_0^m = b_0^{m+1}, \quad g_n^m = b_n^{m+1} - A_n g_{n-1}^m/\beta_{n-1},$$

and that

$$h_N^m = g_N^m/\beta_N, \quad h_{N-1}^m = \frac{g_{N-1}^m - \gamma_{N-1}h_N^m}{\beta_{N-1}},$$

$$h_n^m = \frac{g_n^m - \gamma_n h_{n+1}^m - D_n h_{n+2}^m}{\beta_n}.$$

To solve for $\boldsymbol{h}^m$ from $\boldsymbol{h}^{m+1}$ we require $O(N)$ arithmetic operations; for $0 < \theta < 1$ we require roughly $9N$ operations (multiplications) per time-step. For $\theta < \frac{1}{2}$ there are stability restrictions. For example, if we want the scheme with $\theta = 0$ to be stable for all $n = 0, 1, 2, \ldots, N$, we require $\sigma^2 N^2 \delta t \leq 1$.

In Figure 22.6 we give numerically computed values for a European average strike with $\sigma = 0.8$, $r = 0.05$ and with three months to expiry after three months of averaging.

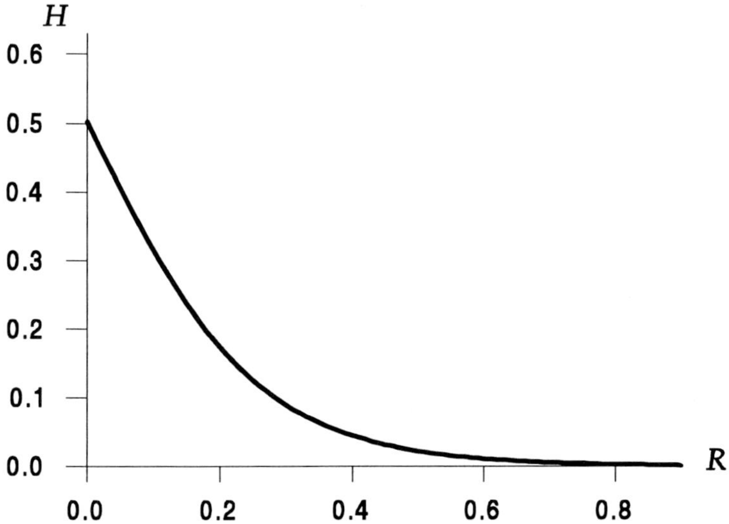

Figure 22.6: Numerically computed values of a European average strike with $\sigma = 0.8$, $r = 0.05$ with three months to expiry after three months of averaging.

22.4.3 American average strikes

We solve the American average strike problem using the discretisations described in the previous two sections and a modified form of the projected SOR algorithm described in Chapter 20.

As in the previous two sections, we work on a finite regular mesh in R,t-space with time-step δt and R-step δR. For $R > N\delta R$ we take $H(R,t) = 0$, and $m\,\delta t = T$. We use the notation h_n^m for the numerical approximation to $H(n\,\delta R, m\,\delta t)$ and Λ_n^m for

$$\Lambda_n^m = \Lambda(n\,\delta R, m\,\delta t) = \max\left(1 - \frac{n\,\delta R}{m\,\delta t}\right).$$

For $m = 0$ (i.e. $t = 0$), we take

$$\Lambda_n^0 = \begin{cases} 1 & \text{if } n = 0 \\ 0 & \text{if } n > 0. \end{cases}$$

Using the finite-difference approximations (22.9) and (22.11) and the approximation (22.12) for the partial differential operator occurring in (22.4), we find that the inequality

$$\frac{\partial H}{\partial t} + \tfrac{1}{2}\sigma^2 R^2 \frac{\partial^2 H}{\partial R^2} + \frac{\partial H}{\partial R} - rR\frac{\partial H}{\partial R} \leq 0$$

is approximated by the vector inequality

$$\mathbf{M}\boldsymbol{h}^m - \boldsymbol{b}^{m+1} \geq \mathbf{0}.$$

The vectors $\boldsymbol{h}^m$ and $\boldsymbol{b}^m$ are as given in (22.17), the matrix $\mathbf{M}$ is defined by (22.14) and (22.18), and as in Chapter 20 the notation $\boldsymbol{x} \geq \mathbf{0}$ means that $x_n \geq 0$ for each component of the vector $\boldsymbol{x}$. The condition that

$$H(R,t) \geq \Lambda(R,t)$$

is approximated by the vector inequality

$$\boldsymbol{h}^m - \Lambda^m \geq \mathbf{0}$$

where the vector Λ^m is defined by

$$\Lambda^m = \begin{pmatrix} \Lambda_0^m \\ \Lambda_1^m \\ \vdots \\ \Lambda_{N-1}^m \\ \Lambda_N^m \end{pmatrix}. \tag{22.19}$$

The condition that the product of these differences should vanish identically translates into the condition that the product of their finite-difference approximations should vanish for all $0 \le m \le M$.

The finite-difference approximation to the linear complementarity problem (22.4) can thus be written as

$$\begin{gathered}\left(\mathbf{M}\boldsymbol{h}^m - \boldsymbol{b}^{m+1}\right) \ge \mathbf{0}, \quad (\boldsymbol{h}^m - \Lambda^m) \ge \mathbf{0}, \\ \left(\mathbf{M}\boldsymbol{h}^m - \boldsymbol{b}^{m+1}\right) \cdot (\boldsymbol{h}^m - \Lambda^m) = 0.\end{gathered} \tag{22.20}$$

This approximation is only self-consistent if we choose N sufficiently large so that $\Lambda_N^m = 0$ for all $0 \le m \le M$ (otherwise we are trying to force $h_n^m \ge \Lambda_n^m$, but also forcing $h_N^m = 0 < \Lambda_N^m$). The final condition is found from the payoff function:

$$\boldsymbol{h}^M = \Lambda^M.$$

The numerical method is to solve (22.20) to find $\boldsymbol{h}^{M-1}$ from $\boldsymbol{h}^M$, then $\boldsymbol{h}^{M-2}$ from $\boldsymbol{h}^{M-1}$ and so on until we find the current value of the option from $\boldsymbol{h}^0$.

It suffices, therefore, to demonstrate how to solve the finite-difference linear complementarity problem (22.20) for a single time-step. We can do this by considering the problem

$$(\mathbf{M}\boldsymbol{h} - \boldsymbol{b}) \ge \mathbf{0}, \quad (\boldsymbol{h} - \Lambda) \ge \mathbf{0}, \quad (\mathbf{M}\boldsymbol{h} - \boldsymbol{b}) \cdot (\boldsymbol{h} - \Lambda) = 0, \tag{22.21}$$

where $\mathbf{M}$ is as given in (22.18). Since $\mathbf{M}$ is positive definite (assuming the stability of the finite-difference scheme, i.e. that the values of Λ, δt and δR lead to a stable numerical method), we may do this by projected SOR. The idea is only a minor generalisation of the algorithm given in Sections 20.3 and 21.3.

As in Sections 20.3 and 21.3, the algorithm for finding the solution is iterative. We start with an initial guess for $\boldsymbol{h}$, say $\boldsymbol{h} \approx \boldsymbol{x}^0$; the only constraint on $\boldsymbol{x}^0$ is that $\boldsymbol{x}^0 \ge \Lambda$. This constraint is necessary since the algorithm may not converge if it is not met. (In the context of time-stepping the numerical solution of the American average strike problem, a sensible initial approximation would be

$$\boldsymbol{x}^0 = \begin{pmatrix} \max(h_0^{m+1}, \Lambda_0^m) \\ \max(h_1^{m+1}, \Lambda_1^m) \\ \max(h_2^{m+1}, \Lambda_2^m) \\ \vdots \\ \max(h_N^{m+1}, \Lambda_N^m) \end{pmatrix},$$

since this guarantees that $\boldsymbol{x}^0 \geq \Lambda^m$.) During each iteration of the algorithm we form a new vector $\boldsymbol{x}^{k+1}$ from the current vector $\boldsymbol{x}^k$ by the following two-step process involving an intermediate vector $\boldsymbol{y}^{k+1}$, constructed as follows. For $n = 0$ we put

$$y_0^{k+1} = \frac{1}{B_0}\left(b_0 - C_0 x_1^k - D_0 x_2^k\right),$$

and for each $n = 1, 2, \ldots, N-2$ we put

$$y_n^{k+1} = \frac{1}{B_n}\left(b_n - A_n x_{n-1}^{k+1} - C_n x_{n+1}^k - D_n x_{n+2}^k\right),$$

while for $n = N-1$, $n = N$ we put

$$\begin{aligned} y_{N-1}^{k+1} &= \frac{1}{B_{N-1}}\left(b_{N-1} - A_{N-1} x_{N-2}^{k+1} - C_{N-1} x_N^k\right), \\ y_N^{k+1} &= \frac{1}{B_N}\left(b_N - A_n x_{N-1}^{k+1}\right). \end{aligned}$$

The values of A_n, B_n, C_n and D_n are given by (22.14). Since we use the value x_n^{k+1} in the calculation of y_{n+1}^{k+1}, we must determine it before moving on from y_n^{k+1}. We define the new x_n^{k+1} to be

$$x_n^{k+1} = \max\left(\Lambda_n, x_n^k + \omega(y_n^{k+1} - x_n^k)\right).$$

As in Chapter 20, ω is a relaxation parameter and if $0 < \omega < 2$ the method converges.

At each iteration this defines a new vector $\boldsymbol{x}^{k+1} \geq \Lambda$, and as $k \to \infty$ $\boldsymbol{x}^k \to \boldsymbol{h}$, the solution of the problem. We stop the iterations once a condition of the form

$$\left|\boldsymbol{x}^{k+1} - \boldsymbol{x}^k\right| < \epsilon$$

has been met, where $\epsilon > 0$ is some predetermined tolerance. We then take $\boldsymbol{h} = \boldsymbol{x}^{k+1}$ as the solution. Using this procedure it is simple to time-step the finite-difference approximation (22.20) and determine the current value of the American average strike.

In Figure 22.7 we give numerically computed values for an American average strike with a $\sigma = 0.8$, $r = 0.05$ and $T = 0.5$, plotted at $\frac{1}{8}$, $\frac{2}{8}$, $\frac{3}{8}$ years to expiry and at expiry.

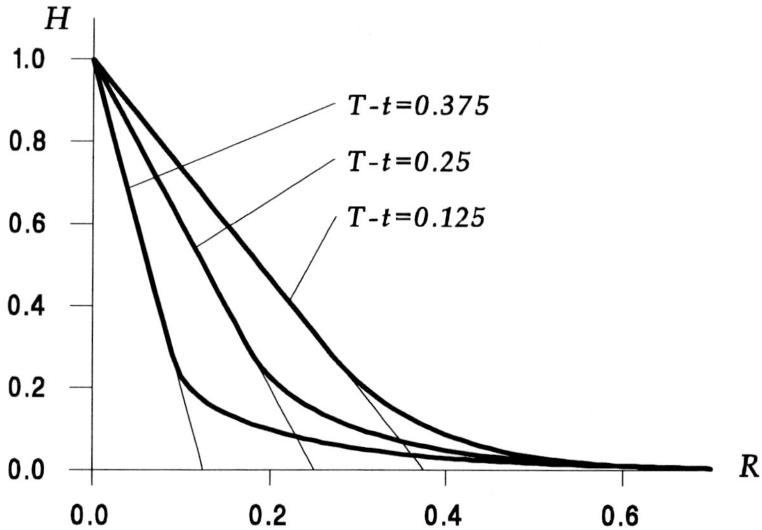

Figure 22.7: Numerically computed values of an American average strike with $\sigma = 0.8$, $r = 0.05$ and $T = 0.5$ plotted at $\frac{1}{8}$, $\frac{2}{8}$, $\frac{3}{8}$ years to expiry and at expiry.

Appendix A

The Probability Density Function

A.1 The transition density function

In the main text of this book the problems have all been deterministic: we have given a definite value for an option or a bond. In these next two appendices we discuss some probabilistic problems, beginning with the derivation of an equation for the probability density function of any random variable defined by a stochastic differential equation.

We have defined a random walk and shown how we can determine the behaviour of a function of a given random variable—this is Itô's lemma. These ideas are useful if one wants to generate realisations of the random walk. But how do we determine the behaviour of the random variable in a probabilistic sense? We discuss this question in this appendix.

So that our analysis may be as general as possible—it is not only applicable to movements of asset prices—we introduce a general[1] random variable G which satisfies the stochastic differential equation

$$dG = A(G,t)\,dX + B(G,t)\,dt, \tag{A.1}$$

where A and B are any functions of G and t.

[1]Although we are setting up the framework for any random variable, if it helps the reader can think of G as being S.

The **transition probability density function** $p(G,t;G',t')$ has the following properties: for any set $\mathcal{G}$,

- The probability that $G \in \mathcal{G}$ at t given G' at t' is

$$\int_{\mathcal{G}} p(G,t;G',t')\,dG$$

- The probability that $G' \in \mathcal{G}$ at t' given G at t is

$$\int_{\mathcal{G}} p(G,t;G',t')\,dG'.$$

For example, suppose that we know the value of G at some time t; then, unless $A = 0$, there is uncertainty in the future value of G. This future time and value of the random variable are denoted by t' and G'. Although we cannot know this future value G' for certain, we should be able to find its probability density function since, after all, (A.1) tells us everything about the movement of G. Finding this probability density function is called the **forward problem**. Conversely, if we know the value G' and t' then we can, again in principle, determine a probability density function for where G *used to be* at the earlier time t. This is called the **backward problem**. These two probability density functions are contained within the one transition density function $p(G,t;G',t')$. It turns out that this function p can be derived as the solution of partial differential equations.

We now derive the partial differential equations for each of these problems. Our derivation is not rigorous but based on a simple *trinomial* representation of the random walk (see Cox & Miller 1965). This is a discrete version of our continuous random walk for G, (A.1). In a time δt we allow the random variable G to move up or down a *fixed* amount δG or to stay where it is. (We use the notation δG, rather than dG, for the size of this jump to distinguish between the discrete and continuous walks; a similar distinction should be made between δt and dt.) It can be shown that in the limit $\delta t \to 0$ the trinomial and continuous random walks are identical.

We begin with the simpler backward problem.

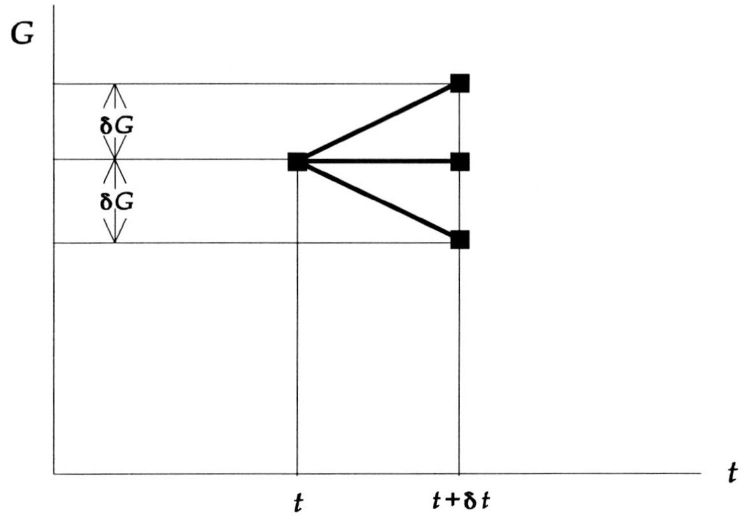

Figure A.1: The trinomial representation of the general random walk.

A.2 The backward problem

In Figure A.1 we see a schematic diagram for a general trinomial random walk in G.

At time t' our random variable takes the value G'. At an earlier time t the value of the random variable is G. In the timestep δt, the variable can either move up or down an amount δG or stay the same, with probabilities $\alpha(G,t)$, $\beta(G,t)$ and $1-\alpha(G,t)-\beta(G,t)$ respectively. Since the variable can only take one of three new values at time $t+\delta t$ it is very simple to relate the probability of being at G at time t to the probability of being at either G, $G+\delta G$ or $G-\delta G$ at the later time $t+\delta t$. In words, we have that

> The probability that we were at (G,t) is equal to the probability of going to $(G+\delta G, t+\delta t)$ multiplied by the probability of moving up, plus the probability of still being at G multiplied by the probability of not moving, plus the probability of going to $(G-\delta G, t+\delta t)$ multiplied by the probability of moving down.

Dropping the dependence of p on G' and t' for the sake of brevity,

$$\begin{aligned} p(G,t) = {} & p(G+\delta G, t+\delta t)\alpha(G,t) \\ & + p(G, t+\delta t)(1-\alpha(G,t)-\beta(G,t)) \\ & + p(G-\delta G, t+\delta t)\beta(G,t). \end{aligned} \tag{A.2}$$

For δt and δG small we can expand all of the above terms in a Taylor series about (G, t) to give

$$(\alpha-\beta)\frac{\partial p}{\partial G}\,\delta G + \tfrac{1}{2}(\alpha+\beta)\frac{\partial^2 p}{\partial G^2}\delta G^2 + \frac{\partial p}{\partial t}\,\delta t = 0. \tag{A.3}$$

We must now choose the functions α and β that give the random walk some of the same properties as equation (A.1), so that it has the same mean and variance.

The mean of the jump in G must be $B(G,t)\,\delta t$ from (A.1), and the variance of the jump must be $A^2(G,t)\,\delta t$. Our trinomial process, however, has mean jump $(\alpha-\beta)\,\delta G$ and variance $(\alpha+\beta-(\alpha-\beta)^2)\delta G^2$. A meaningful result is only possible if it has $\delta G^2/\delta t = O(1)$ so that the jumps in time and random variable scale in the way that we described in Chapter 2. We find that the choices

$$\frac{\delta G^2}{\delta t} = O(1),$$

$$\alpha(G,t) = \frac{\delta t}{2\,\delta G^2}[A^2(G,t) + B(G,t)\,\delta G]$$

and

$$\beta(G,t) = \frac{\delta t}{2\,\delta G^2}[A^2(G,t) - B(G,t)\,\delta G],$$

give the discrete and continuous random walks the same mean and variance to $O(\delta t)$. Putting these into (A.3) and dividing throughout by δt gives the backward equation

$$\tfrac{1}{2}A^2(G,t)\frac{\partial^2 p}{\partial G^2} + B(G,t)\frac{\partial p}{\partial G} + \frac{\partial p}{\partial t} = 0. \tag{A.4}$$

This is known as the **Kolmogorov equation**. It will be recognised as a backward parabolic partial differential equation.

To pose this problem fully, so that the solution for the backward problem is unique, we must impose two boundary conditions and a final condition. The boundary conditions are specific to the random variable under consideration (and whether any boundaries are special, for example they may 'absorb' the random variable so that if it hits the barrier it can never leave) and it is difficult to make a general statement of these conditions. However, the final condition is relatively straightforward.

We reintroduce the dependence on G' and t'. The final condition for the backward equation (A.4) is then

$$p(G, t'; G', t') = \delta(G - G'),$$

where $\delta(\cdot)$ is the Dirac delta function. This condition simply says that at time t' the variable G can *only* have the value G'.

A.3 The forward problem

We now come to consider the forward equation for the transition density, which tells us the probability density function for the random variable in the future, given where it is now.

The 'derivation' of the governing equation is very much as above for the backward equation. In particular we use the same trinomial walk with the same choices for the probabilities of each branch of the walk, α and β. Here, though, we relate the probability density function at G' and t' to the probability density functions at the *previous* time-step (see Figure A.2).

For brevity we drop the dependence of p on G and t. We then have

$$\begin{aligned} p(G', t') = {} & p(G' - DG, t' - \delta t)\alpha(G' - \delta G, t' - \delta t) \\ & + p(G', t' - \delta t)(1 - \alpha(G', t' - \delta t) - \beta(G', t' - \delta t)) \\ & + p(G' + \delta G, t' - \delta t)\beta(G' + \delta G, t' - \delta t). \end{aligned} \qquad \text{(A.5)}$$

This is very similar to the equivalent backward equation (A.2) above. The main difference is that the probabilities α and β are now evaluated at $G' - \delta G$ and $G' + \delta G$ as well as G' and so must also be expanded in Taylor series. The algebra is slightly more complicated than in the backward case but, in the end, we arrive at

$$\frac{1}{2}\frac{\partial^2 (A^2(G', t')p)}{\partial G'^2} - \frac{\partial (B(G', t')p)}{\partial t'} - \frac{\partial p}{\partial t'} = 0. \qquad \text{(A.6)}$$

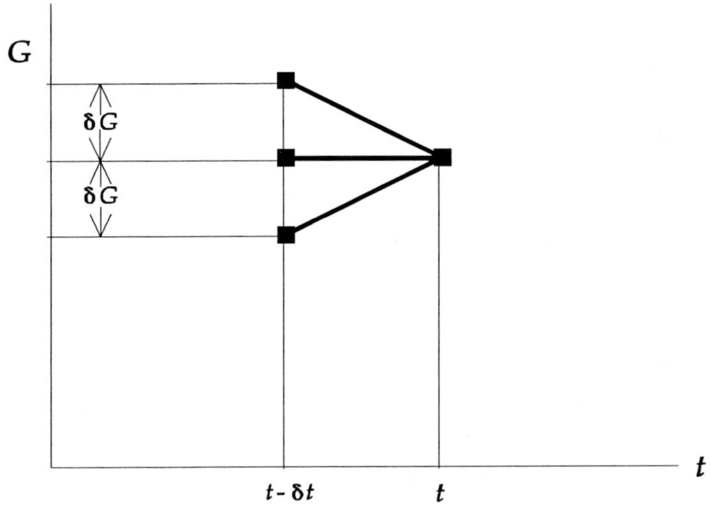

Figure A.2: The trinomial random walk for G applied to the forward problem.

This is known as the **Fokker–Planck** or **forward Kolmogorov equation**. It is a forward parabolic equation.

Reintroducing the dependence on G and t, the initial condition is

$$p(G,t;G',t)=\delta(G'-G). \tag{A.7}$$

In the next section we show how to find the boundary conditions for the forward problem in an illustrative case.

A.3.1 Boundary conditions for the forward problem

The boundary conditions for (A.6) come from looking closely at the particular random walk. Depending on the coefficients A and B, we can expect different boundary conditions. For this reason we confine this example to the random walk (2.1) for asset prices:

$$dS=\sigma S\,dX+\mu S\,dt.$$

In this case

$$\alpha(S,t)=\frac{\delta t}{2\,\delta S^2}(\sigma^2S^2+\mu S\,\delta S)$$

and

$$\beta(S,t) = \frac{\delta t}{2\,\delta S^2}(\sigma^2 S^2 - \mu S\,\delta S).$$

The forward partial differential equation becomes

$$\frac{1}{2}\frac{\partial^2(\sigma^2 S'^2 p)}{\partial S'^2} - \frac{\partial(\mu S' p)}{\partial S'} - \frac{\partial p}{\partial t'} = 0. \qquad \text{(A.8)}$$

Differentiating under the parentheses in the first term in (A.8) shows that the coefficient of the highest S' derivative is $\frac{1}{2}\sigma^2 S'^2$. This coefficient vanishes at $S' = 0$ and so the point $S' = 0$ is a singular point of the differential equation. That $S' = 0$ is somehow special can also be seen by considering the random walk (2.1). If we put $S = 0$ in (2.1) we find that $dS = 0$, therefore S remains zero: if ever S is zero it is always zero. It is therefore impossible for the asset price to become negative if it follows the random walk (2.1). Moreover, if the asset price is non-zero at some time (which is always true in a sensible problem) then it can never become zero at a later time. Another way of seeing this is by recalling the transformation $f(S) = \log S$. The random walk for f ranges over all positive and negative values of f and can never reach $-\infty$, equivalent to $S = 0$, in a finite time. We can expect that a boundary condition is to be applied at $S' = 0$. That boundary condition simply states that the probability of the asset price reaching zero is zero. Thus,

$$p(S,t;0,t') = 0. \qquad \text{(A.9)}$$

That is the first boundary condition. There is still one more to find.

There is no finite special value of S' other than zero. The remaining boundary condition is to be given at infinity. Since the probability of S reaching some large number in a finite time decreases as that number increases, the final boundary condition is simply

$$p(S,t;S',t') \to 0 \quad \text{as} \quad S' \to \infty. \qquad \text{(A.10)}$$

The technique for solving this partial differential equation has been given in Chapter 5. Here we simply quote the result. The solution of (A.8), (A.7), (A.9) and (A.10) is

$$p(S,t;S',t') = \frac{1}{\sigma S'\sqrt{2\pi(t'-t)}} e^{-\left(\log(S'/S)-(\mu-\frac{1}{2}\sigma^2)(t'-t)\right)^2/2\sigma^2(t'-t)}. \qquad \text{(A.11)}$$

This is the probability density function for a **lognormal distribution** and has the form shown in Figure 2.3. It can readily be confirmed that it satisfies the equation and conditions. For example, putting $S' = 0$ in (A.11) gives a value for p of zero. Notice that the exponent tends to minus infinity in this limit and this overwhelms the $1/S'$ in front (which also goes to infinity). As $S' \to \infty$ the exponent again goes to minus infinity.

A.4 Risk neutrality

Note that the growth rate μ does not appear in the Black–Scholes equation (3.9). Therefore although the value of an option depends on the standard deviation of the asset price, it does not depend upon its rate of growth. Indeed, different investors may have widely varying estimates of the growth rate of a share yet still agree on the value of an option. This suggests an alternative method of valuing an option by calculating the present value of its *expected* return at expiry (see Cox & Ross 1976).

To justify the following approach we must make two observations. First, in order to calculate the present value of a payoff at time T we must discount it by multiplying by $e^{-r(T-t)}$; thus, we write

$$V(S,t) = e^{-r(T-t)}U(S,t).$$

Substituting this into the Black–Scholes equation shows that U satisfies

$$\frac{\partial U}{\partial t} + \tfrac{1}{2}\sigma^2 S^2 \frac{\partial^2 U}{\partial S^2} + rS\frac{\partial U}{\partial S} = 0.$$

We now make the second observation that this equation is exactly the same as the Kolmogorov equation (A.4) derived earlier, *provided that* $\mu = r$. Thus U has an interpretation as *a* probability density function. However, this is *not* the density function for S, since that depends on μ.

In principle we know the probability density function for the share at the expiry date; this is the probability density function for a lognormal distribution and is given for the simple random walk (2.1) by (A.11). Replace μ by r in that probability density function and calculate the expected return on the option at $t' = T$. This is done as follows. The payoff function for the call option is $\max(S' - E, 0)$, which is the profit to be made at expiry and thus depends on the asset value at expiry; in our present notation this is the future value S'. Multiply the payoff function by the probability density function of the asset, *but with μ replaced by r*. Next integrate over all possible future values of the asset—S' represents the future value of S—i.e. from zero to infinity. Finally, discount to find the present value.

For a European call option this present value of the expected return can be written as

$$C(S,t) = \frac{e^{-r(T-t)}}{\sigma\sqrt{2\pi(T-t)}} \times$$
$$\int_0^\infty e^{-\left(\log(S'/S)-(r-\frac{1}{2}\sigma^2)(T-t)\right)^2/2\sigma^2(T-t)} \max(S'-E,0)\frac{dS'}{S'}.$$

This expression can be shown to satisfy equation (3.9) and can be integrated explicitly to give the Black–Scholes formula for a European call option.

It is generally the case that if a portfolio can be constructed with a derivative product and the underlying asset in such a way that the random component can be eliminated—as was the case above—then the derivative product may be valued as the 'present value of the expected return under the **risk-neutral** random walk in which μ is replaced by r'. Roughly speaking, if the risk can be hedged away then there is no reward over and above the return to be made in a risk-neutral world (Harrison & Pliska 1981).

The idea of replacing μ by r is very elegant. It does, however, have two major drawbacks. First, although it may be possible to write down 'explicit formulæ' for the price of an option, say an average rate, this is not the same as giving a value to that option. The expected return must still be calculated numerically and this requires a knowledge of the probability density function. If this is not known then it must be found numerically, often by solving a partial differential equation. It is usually quicker to solve the option pricing equation directly.

The second drawback is that risk neutrality can lead to confusion. For example it is sometimes said that

- 'It can be shown that $\mu = r$'

or that

- 'The delta of an option is the probability that it will expire in the money.'

Both of these statements are wrong. If the first statement were correct then all assets would have the same expected return as a bank deposit and no-one would invest in equities; see the Technical Point on Modern Portfolio Theory in Chapter 1. If μ were equal to r then the second statement would be correct. The probability that $S > E$ at $t = T$ can be found by calculating the expected value of $\mathcal{H}(S - E)$. This necessarily involves the parameter μ.

Further reading

- For details of valuing options under risk-neutrality see Harrison & Kreps (1979) and Hull (1992).

Exercises

1. Show that (A.11) satisfies *both* the forward (A.6) and the backward (A.4) equations.

2. Find the transition density function for the random variable that satisfies
$$dG = a\,dX + b\,dt,$$
where a and b are constants.

3. If the value of an asset S following the random walk (2.1) is $S(t)$ at time t and $S(T)$ at time $T > t$, the rate of return, η, on S over the period from t to T is defined by
$$\frac{S(T)}{S(t)} = e^{\eta(T-t)}.$$
Show that η has the normal distribution with mean $\mu - \frac{1}{2}\sigma^2$ and variance $\sigma/\sqrt{T-t}$.

Appendix B

First Exit Times

B.1 Expected first exit times

The time at which the option should be exercised, or at which the barrier is crossed, is of obvious importance to the holder of an American or a barrier option. These two problems are conceptually very similar and in this appendix we consider the probable time taken for a random walk to reach some prescribed boundary. The time at which this first happens is called a **first exit time**. In Figure B.1 we show a realisation of a random walk and the time at which the variable leaves a prescribed region, in this case the interval $0 < S < S_1$. This problem is of financial importance if, say, some action is contingent upon this region being exited. Obvious examples are the activation of the knockout boundary in a barrier option or a call feature in a convertible bond.

The simplest first exit time problem is to find the expected time at which an asset price, which we assume obeys (2.1), reaches some specified value. Suppose the asset price is S at time t. We consider the question

- How long before S reaches S_1?

Call this time $u(S)$. Because of the random nature of the asset price, we can only determine the *expected* time at which the asset price leaves the region. We now find an ordinary differential equation satisfied by $\bar{u}(\mathrm{S})$, the expected value of u. (Observe that $\bar{u}$ is independent of t because the coefficients in (2.1) are assumed constant

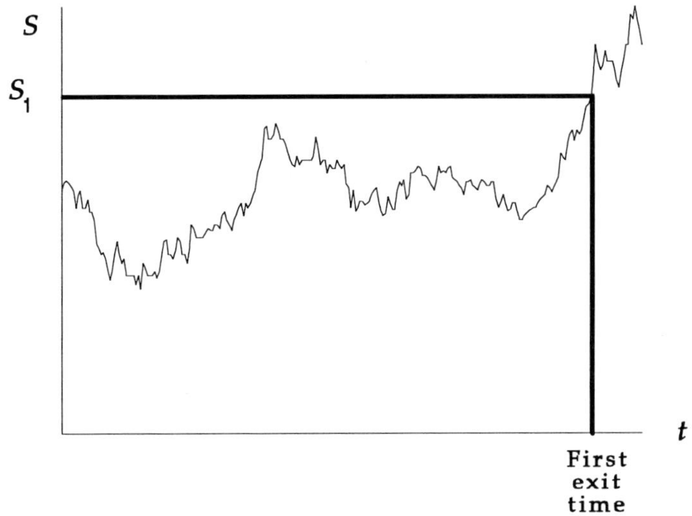

Figure B.1: A schematic diagram of the first exit time problem.

and the boundary ($S = S_1$) is independent of time.)

This is most easily accomplished by considering the trinomial discrete random walk again. The analysis of (A.2) can be repeated but with one subtle difference. First note that the expected first exit time is a duration, i.e. a length of time, and not a point in time, i.e. a date. This distinction is important here. If the date is currently t and our expected first exit time is $\bar{u}$ then the date at which S is expected to exit from the region is simply $t + \bar{u}$. Now consider the discrete trinomial random walk over the time period t to $t+\delta t$. If we do not know the outcome of this random walk, i.e. we do not know the new value of the asset price, then the expected time *at which* S reaches the boundary does not change from t to $t + \delta t$. This is because we have no new information—we do not know whether the asset price at time $t+\delta t$ has become $S+\delta S$, $S-\delta S$ or still S. Thus, by considering the three possible states for S at time $t + \delta t$ we find that

$$t + \bar{u}(S) = t + \delta t + \bar{u}(S + \delta S)\alpha(S) \\ + \bar{u}(S)(1 - \alpha(S) - \beta(S)) + \bar{u}(S - \delta S)\beta(S).$$

(Again, we have used δS to distinguish between the trinomial and continuous random walks; α and β, which were derived in the last chapter, are in this case only functions of S since the coefficients in the random walk (2.1) are independent of t.)

Expanding in a Taylor series, we find that

$$\mu S \frac{d\bar{u}}{dS} + \tfrac{1}{2}\sigma^2 S^2 \frac{d^2\bar{u}}{dS^2} = -1. \tag{B.1}$$

This is the equation for the expected first exit time.

There are three questions we can ask about the first exit time for this problem, depending on whether we are interested in upward or downward movements of S, or both. Suppose that $S_0 < S < S_1$, we can ask:

- How long before S leaves the range (S_0, S_1)?
- How long before S rises to S_1 from below? (We do not care how small it gets.)
- How long before S falls to S_0 from above? (We do not care how large it gets.)

We concentrate on the first two of these questions. The first is slightly simpler than the other two, because of the singular behaviour of (2.1) at zero and infinity.

If we are interested in when S leaves the range (S_0, S_1) then the boundary conditions are to be applied at $S = S_0$ and $S = S_1$. If the asset already has value S_0, say, then the expected exit time is clearly zero. The same applies to the boundary at S_1 and we can see that the two boundary conditions are $\bar{u}(S_0) = 0$ and $\bar{u}(S_1) = 0$. The solution, which is simple to derive, is

$$\bar{u} = \frac{1}{\frac{1}{2}\sigma^2 - \mu}\log(S/S_0) - \frac{\log(S_1/S_0)}{\frac{1}{2}\sigma^2 - \mu}\,\frac{1 - (S/S_0)^{1-\mu/\frac{1}{2}\sigma^2}}{1 - (S_1/S_0)^{1-\mu/\frac{1}{2}\sigma^2}}.$$

Now let us move on to consider the slightly more complicated case in which we do not care how small the asset gets. What are the boundary conditions? Suppose that currently $S < S_1$ and we want to know the expected time at which S reaches S_1. Since the expected exit time is zero if the asset is already at the boundary, clearly one boundary condition for (B.1) is

$$\bar{u}(S_1) = 0.$$

Before we describe the second boundary condition we write down the general solution of (B.1), something which cannot be done for a general random walk. This helps to illustrate the method for deciding on the boundary condition in more difficult cases such as the discussion of moving averages in Section B.3.

The general solution of (B.1) is

$$\bar{u} = \frac{1}{\frac{1}{2}\sigma^2 - \mu} \log S + c_1 + c_2 S^{1-\mu/\frac{1}{2}\sigma^2}, \tag{B.2}$$

where c_1 and c_2 are the two constants of integration. We can distinguish two cases, depending upon whether μ is greater or less than $\frac{1}{2}\sigma^2$. (There is also the borderline case when they are equal, but we do not consider this here.) If $\mu < \frac{1}{2}\sigma^2$ the growth of the asset is relatively weak and the dominant term in (B.2) as $S \to 0$ is the logarithm. Unfortunately, the sign of this term is negative for small S. In other words it appears that the expected first exit time is negative. This is unrealistic: it indicates that a finite, positive first exit time does not exist. The drift of S contained in (2.1) is too small for S to grow sufficiently rapidly to have a finite expected first exit time.

On the other hand, if $\mu > \frac{1}{2}\sigma^2$ the dominant term is the negative power of S. If we eliminate this term by choosing $c_2 = 0$ this gives $\bar{u}$ the weakest singularity at $S = 0$, a logarithmic singularity. This leaves us with

$$\bar{u} = \frac{1}{\frac{1}{2}\sigma^2 - \mu} \log S + c_1.$$

Applying the other boundary condition, $\bar{u}(S_1) = 0$, gives

$$\bar{u} = \frac{1}{\frac{1}{2}\sigma^2 - \mu} \log \left(\frac{S}{S_1} \right). \tag{B.3}$$

This is the expected first exit time for the second problem. This expected first exit time is important for 'up' type barrier options.

If the expected first exit time as calculated in (B.3) is less than the time left before an 'up' barrier expires then it is more likely than not that the option will trigger the barrier before expiry. Observe also that while the barrier option value is independent of the growth parameter μ, the first exit time and hence the probability of hitting the barrier are not; many properties of options *do* depend upon the growth parameter.

In the next section we show how to find the cumulative distribution function for the first exit times. This also gives us another way of finding the expected first exit time, for example when the boundary of the region is time-dependent.

B.2 Cumulative distribution functions for exit times

Let us ask the question

- What is the probability of our random variable G leaving a prescribed region Ω before time t'?

We call this probability the cumulative distribution function Q. It is a function of the current time and position (t and G) as well as the future time in question, t'; thus

$$\operatorname{Prob}(u < t' \mid G, t) = Q(G, t; t').$$

The problem is illustrated schematically in Figure B.2. We omit the details, and simply note that the use of the trinomial discretisation of the continuous random walk leads to the following partial differential equation for Q:

$$\frac{\partial Q}{\partial t} + B(G,t)\frac{\partial Q}{\partial G} + \tfrac{1}{2}A(G,t)^2\frac{\partial^2 Q}{\partial G^2} = 0. \tag{B.4}$$

The rigorous derivation of this equation, which can also be recognised as the Kolmogorov backward equation, can be found in Schuss (1980). The boundary and final conditions which must be imposed in order for Q to have a unique solution are particularly simple.

When $t = t'$ there is no time left for the random variable G to exit from the region Ω and so

$$Q(G, t'; t') = 0.$$

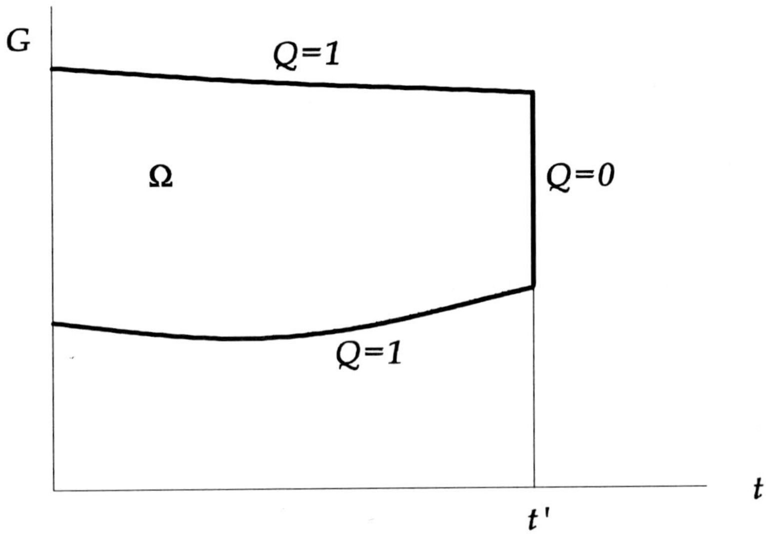

Figure B.2: The solution domain and boundary conditions for the cumulative distribution function.

On the boundary $\partial\Omega$ of Ω the probability of reaching the boundary is, of course, 1 and so

$$Q(G,t;t') = 1 \quad \text{on} \quad \partial\Omega.$$

This completes the formulation of the problem for the cumulative distribution function for exit times. It is possible to compute the solution by the finite-difference methods described earlier.

B.2.1 Relationship with the expected exit time

Before we move on to consider moving averages of asset prices we show the relationship between the cumulative distribution function for exit times and the expected exit time.

The function Q contains enough information about the exit time distribution for us to derive the problem for the *expected* first exit time. In order to make the following as general as possible we assume either that the domain is bounded by curves that are not all lines $G =$ constant, or that the stochastic differential equation for G has time-dependent coefficients. In both of these cases the expected first exit time depends on both time and position; in the previous example, the expected first exit time only satisfied an *ordinary* differential equation, since the problem was independent of the starting time.

Since $Q(G, t; t')$ is the cumulative distribution function, the probability density function for the first exit time is simply

$$\frac{\partial Q}{\partial t'}.$$

Therefore the expected first exit time is given by

$$\bar{u}(G, t) = \int_t^\infty (t' - t) \frac{\partial Q}{\partial t'}(G, t; t')\, dt'.$$

After integration by parts, this becomes

$$\int_t^\infty 1 - Q(G, t; t')\, dt'.$$

Note that as $t' \to \infty$, $Q \to 1$. Since Q satisfies (B.4), we can differentiate the expression for $\bar{u}$ to find that

$$\frac{\partial \bar{u}}{\partial t} + B \frac{\partial \bar{u}}{\partial G} + \tfrac{1}{2} A^2 \frac{\partial^2 \bar{u}}{\partial G^2} = -1.$$

The -1 on the right-hand side comes from differentiating the lower limit of integration in the expression for $\bar{u}$.

Because $Q = 1$ on the boundary $\partial\Omega$, we have

$$\bar{u} = 0 \quad \text{on} \quad \partial\Omega.$$

The final condition for this problem is more interesting. Since we are solving a backward diffusion equation we must impose a final condition and solve for times less than this. However, there is no natural time boundary on which to specify $\bar{u}$. To get round this difficulty we must solve for the expected first exit time from a region that is bounded in time; that is, the domain must be closed as in Figure B.3.

This problem reduces to the earlier ordinary differential equation when A, B and the domain are time-independent.

The estimation of expected first exit times is of obvious importance for the holders and writers of American options. We can ask the question

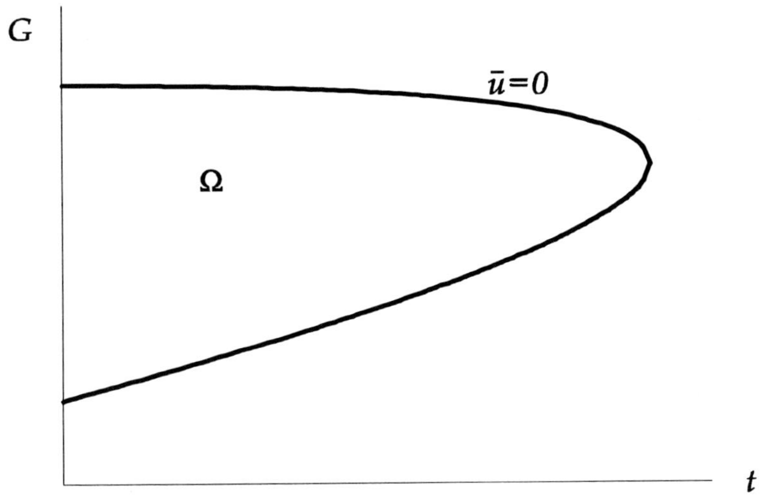

Figure B.3: The domain for the time-dependent first exit time problem.

- What is the probability of early exercise?

As with the earlier mention of first exit times in the context of barrier options the probability of early exercise *depends on* μ. One must have an estimate of μ in order to calculate first exit times but not to value the option. (This has been noted by Garman (1993) who calls the expected time to exercise the **fugit**.)

B.3 Moving averages

A significant proportion of the volume of shares, commodities etc. traded is in reaction to what are known as technical indicators. Many such indicators are proprietory, but they commonly take the form of weighted moving averages of the asset price. A trade is then triggered by, for example, the crossing of a moving average and the underlying asset. One of the ideas behind technical analysis using moving averages is that such averages can smooth out short-term fluctuations leaving behind what is hoped are the genuine underlying trends. The time-scale for this averaging is of crucial importance: too short a time-scale and the trader responds to false alarms, losing money simply through transaction costs; too long a time-scale and the trend may be over before it has been spotted. In the rest of this appendix we examine the behaviour of the average of a random quantity. In particular we consider several properties of exponentially weighted moving averages of a lognormal random walk. (For further details see Wilmott & Atkinson (1992).)

We define the **exponentially weighted moving average** to be

$$\lambda \int_{-\infty}^{t} e^{-\lambda(t-\tau)} S(\tau)\, d\tau. \tag{B.5}$$

Here λ has dimensions of inverse time; the larger λ is the more the moving average is weighted towards the present value of the asset price, $S(t)$. Note that the integral begins at minus infinity; for this integral to exist we require that S does not grow too fast as $t \to -\infty$. (In practice the error in taking the lower limit to be infinite will be negligible providing λ is not too small.)

Next we define the *scaled* moving average, M, by

$$M = \frac{\lambda}{S(t)} \int_{-\infty}^{t} e^{-\lambda(t-\tau)} S(\tau)\, d\tau, \tag{B.6}$$

which is simply the ratio of the exponentially weighted moving average (B.5) to $S(t)$. This is the variable in which we are interested. Observe that this variable is independent of the scale of S, so that if we multiply S in (B.6) by any constant then the expression for M is unchanged.

We can apply Itô's lemma to the definition of M, or, equivalently, we can consider how much M changes during a small time-step dt. In that short time M becomes $M + dM$ where

$$M + dM = \frac{\lambda}{S + dS} \int_{-\infty}^{t+dt} e^{-\lambda(t+dt-\tau)} S(\tau)\, d\tau.$$

This can be approximated for small dS and dt using Taylor's theorem to give

$$\frac{\lambda}{S}\left(1 - \frac{dS}{S} + \frac{dS^2}{S^2} + \cdots\right) \times$$
$$\left(\int_{-\infty}^{t} e^{-\lambda(t-\tau)}(1 - \lambda\, dt + \cdots) S(\tau)\, d\tau + S(t)\, dt + \cdots\right).$$

Substituting for the integral from (B.6) and for dS from (2.1), we find that dM is given by

$$dM = -\sigma M dX + (\lambda + aM)\, dt, \qquad \text{(B.7)}$$

where the constant a is given by $-\lambda + \sigma^2 - \mu$. Thus M itself follows a random walk. Observe the important point that for constant σ, λ and μ the stochastic differential equation (B.7) for M does not depend on S; other definitions for a moving average would not necessarily have this property. With this definition we can treat M without further need for the variable S.

B.4 Exit times for moving averages

One question that is asked concerning moving averages is

- How long before the asset price and its moving average meet?

This is often thought of as an important technical indicator for the end of a trend or the beginning of a new one. A lot of effort is spent on choosing the λ that gives the 'best' predictive ability. Recall that the definition of our random variable M is simply the ratio of the moving average to the asset value; thus with our notation this question becomes

- How long before M reaches the value 1?

This is a first exit time problem. If $u(M)$ is the time at which the random walk in M first crosses the boundary $M = 1$ then we consider the problem for the *expected* first exit time, $\bar{u}(M)$.

The trinomial analysis again shows that since M follows the random walk (B.7), the first exit time satisfies the ordinary differential equation

$$(\lambda + aM)\frac{d\bar{u}}{dM} + \tfrac{1}{2}\sigma^2 M^2 \frac{d^2\bar{u}}{dM^2} = -1. \qquad \text{(B.8)}$$

We first consider the case where M is initially less than 1 and we want to determine the time before it reaches 1. Later we consider the alternative case, where M is initially greater than 1.

Before finding the solution we must specify boundary conditions. Clearly, on $M = 1$ we must have $\bar{u} = 0$, since the expected time to cross the boundary $M = 1$ is zero if M is already at that boundary. The condition at $M = 0$ is not so obvious.

We can make two general observations about the expected first exit time. Firstly, $\bar{u}$ is monotonically decreasing in M since the problem is independent of time; the further that M is away from 1 the longer it takes to reach it. Secondly, when M is close to zero the dominant terms in (B.7) give $dM \sim \lambda\, dt$. This second point shows that M leaves the boundary $M = 0$ in a finite time and thus that the expected first exit time is finite at $M = 0$, i.e. $\bar{u}(0) < \infty$.

To specify the boundary condition at $M = 0$ fully we must perform a local analysis. First, introduce the variable

$$U = \frac{d\bar{u}}{dM},$$

and write (B.8) as

$$\frac{dU}{dM} = -\frac{2 + 2(\lambda + aM)U}{\sigma^2 M^2}. \tag{B.9}$$

This can be integrated explicitly, or we can perform a phase-plane analysis. These both help us to derive the correct boundary condition at $M = 0$. It is simpler, though, to perform a local analysis.

For M small we can ignore the term aM compared with λ in (B.9). Letting $U = -1/\lambda + \bar{U}$ we arrive at the approximate equation

$$\frac{d\bar{U}}{dM} \approx -\frac{2\lambda\bar{U}}{\sigma^2 M^2},$$

valid near $M = 0$. The solution of this is

$$\bar{U} = ce^{2\lambda/\sigma^2 M},$$

where c is an arbitrary constant of integration. Now remember that this still describes the local behaviour of the solution of the full equation. This is highly singular near $M = 0$ and we can conclude from this that as $M \to 0$, $\bar{u}$ becomes infinite except for the one choice of integration constant, $c = 0$; in this case $\bar{u}$ remains finite. Since we have eliminated the one remaining integration constant, we have found the unique solution to our problem; we need only insist that $\bar{u}$ is finite. If we want we can actually examine the equation further and determine the slope of $\bar{u}$ at $M = 0$. From (B.8), our second boundary condition, that $\bar{u}$ is finite, is equivalent to

$$\frac{d\bar{u}}{dM} = -\frac{1}{\lambda}.$$

We can solve for $\bar{u}$ explicitly with this boundary condition and $\bar{u}(1) = 0$, to find that

$$\bar{u} = \frac{2}{\sigma^2}\int_M^1 \int_0^{M'} \frac{1}{M''^2} e^{-\frac{2\lambda}{\sigma^2 M''} + \frac{2a}{\sigma^2}\log M'' + \frac{2\lambda}{\sigma^2 M'} - \frac{2a}{\sigma^2}\log M'} dM'' dM'. \tag{B.10}$$

This result can be extended to the alternative case where $M > 1$ and we wish to know the expected time before M decreases to 1. The ordinary differential equation and boundary condition at $M = 1$ remain unchanged but now we must consider the behaviour of $\bar{u}$ as $M \to \infty$.

First, we observe that $\bar{u}$ must be a monotonically increasing function of M; it takes longer for M to reach 1 the larger M is. Second, the first exit time must be positive. These two pieces of information are enough to determine the remaining boundary condition.

Consider M large. Then, compared with the other terms, we can ignore the term in (B.8) containing λ. The resulting equation is easily solved exactly, and we thus find that the large M behaviour of $\bar{u}$ has one of two forms. If $a/\frac{1}{2}\sigma^2 - 1 < 0$, then

$$\bar{u} \sim c_1 + c_2 M^{(\frac{1}{2}\sigma^2 - a)/\frac{1}{2}\sigma^2} + \frac{1}{\frac{1}{2}\sigma^2 - a}\log M \quad \text{as} \quad M \to \infty,$$

but if $a/\frac{1}{2}\sigma^2 - 1 > 0$, then

$$\bar{u} \sim c_1 + \frac{1}{\frac{1}{2}\sigma^2 - a}\log M \quad \text{as} \quad M \to \infty.$$

In the first case the correct choice for c_2 is zero since this gives $\bar{u}$ the weakest singularity at infinity; $\bar{u}$ behaves logarithmically for M large. In the second case the dominant term is again the logarithm but now its coefficient is negative, so that $\bar{u}$ becomes negative for M sufficiently large. We conclude that the first exit time does not exist (or rather, is infinite) for $a > \frac{1}{2}\sigma^2$ and for $a < \frac{1}{2}\sigma^2$ the boundary condition is

$$M\frac{d\bar{u}}{dM} \sim \frac{1}{\frac{1}{2}\sigma^2 - a} \quad \text{as} \quad M \to \infty.$$

B.4.1 The cumulative distribution function

We can obtain further information about first exit times by considering the cumulative distribution function. This is motivated by asking the question:

- What is the probability of M reaching 1 before time t'?

We define $Q(M,t;t')$ by

$$Q(M,t;t') = \text{Prob}(u < t' \mid M,t),$$

i.e. the probability that the random walk crosses the boundary before time t', given that its value at t is M. The differential equation for Q is

$$\frac{\partial Q}{\partial t} + (\lambda + aM)\frac{\partial Q}{\partial M} + \tfrac{1}{2}\sigma^2 M^2 \frac{\partial^2 Q}{\partial M^2} = 0, \qquad \text{(B.11)}$$

which can be recognised as the backward equation.

We begin by considering the case in which initially $M < 1$, noting that we are only interested in when the random variable M crosses an *upper* boundary.

To pose the problem fully we must impose final and boundary conditions. The final condition and one of the boundary conditions are obvious. When $t = t'$ the probability of M reaching 1 before time t' is zero, thus

$$Q(M,t';t') = 0.$$

If M is already at 1 then the probability of crossing the boundary is 1 for any time $t < t'$, thus

$$Q(1,t;t') = 1.$$

Finally, we need to impose a condition on $M = 0$. This condition comes from considering the behaviour of Q for small M. As before, the problem is highly singular at $M = 0$ and it is a sufficient boundary condition to insist that Q remains finite at $M = 0$. Equivalently, the correct boundary condition is

$$\frac{\partial Q}{\partial t} + \lambda \frac{\partial Q}{\partial M} = 0 \quad \text{on} \quad M = 0.$$

The case in which initially $M > 1$ is a trivial extension of the analysis for $M < 1$. Obviously, the governing equation is the same and the final condition is still

$$Q(M, t'; t') = 0,$$

while on $M = 1$ we have

$$Q(1, t; t') = 1.$$

Now we must apply a boundary condition as $M \to \infty$. Clearly, the probability of crossing the $M = 1$ boundary decreases to zero as M increases, and so

$$Q(M, t; t') \to 0 \quad \text{as} \quad M \to \infty.$$

B.4.2 Crossing of two moving averages

The analysis for the expected first exit time can be extended to consider another technical indicator: the crossing of two moving averages instead of the crossing of a moving average and the underlying asset. We are interested in answering the question:

- How long can I expect before the short term average crosses the long term average?

Define M_1 as M above, but with λ_1 replacing λ, and define M_2 similarly. When λ_1 and λ_2 are distinct then the two 'moving averages' have different timescales. Typical values for the parameters λ_1 and λ_2 would be 0.2 and 0.05, giving timescales of 5 and 20 days as the short and long term averages.

Observe that the two random walks for M_1 and M_2 are perfectly correlated; both have a random component proportional to dX, therefore this is still a one-factor problem. Suppose now that we are interested in finding the time at which the ratio M_1/M_2 reaches 1, from below without loss of generality. The above ideas concerning expected first exit times can be generalised to this higher dimensional problem (see Schuss 1980). We do not include the details, merely stating that the problem for the expected first exit time, $\bar{v}(M_1, M_2)$, can be written as

$$(\lambda_1 + a_1 M_1)\frac{\partial \bar{v}}{\partial M_1} + (\lambda_2 + a_2 M_2)\frac{\partial \bar{v}}{\partial M_2} + \tfrac{1}{2}\sigma^2\left(M_1^2\frac{\partial^2 \bar{v}}{\partial M_1^2} + 2M_1M_2\frac{\partial^2 \bar{v}}{\partial M_1 M_2} + M_2^2\frac{\partial^2 \bar{v}}{\partial M_2^2}\right) = -1. \tag{B.12}$$

The coefficients of the first derivative terms are the same as the coefficients of the dt terms in the stochastic differential equations for M_1 and M_2 and the coefficients of the second derivatives are the squares and the products of the coefficients of the dX terms.

We solve this equation in the region $M_1 \leq M_2$ and $M_1, M_2 \geq 0$. By considering the coefficients of the highest derivatives we find that (B.12) is a parabolic equation, since it is a one-factor problem. Thus we again need to impose final and boundary conditions. The final condition is the easiest to determine. On $M_1 = M_2$, the boundary that we are interested in crossing, we know that the expected first exit time is zero, so

$$\bar{v}(M_1, M_1) = 0.$$

The ideas of the earlier sections may be applied to determine the boundary conditions. As M_1 and M_2 tend to zero, $\bar{v}$ must be finite and so

$$\lambda_1\frac{\partial \bar{v}}{\partial M_1} + \lambda_2\frac{\partial \bar{v}}{\partial M_2} = -1 \text{ as } M_1 \text{ and } M_2 \to 0.$$

The final boundary condition is the most interesting. As M_1 and M_2 become large we can ignore the λ terms in the stochastic differential equations. It is then simple to show that

$$d(\log(M_1/M_2)) = (a_1 - a_2)dt.$$

Thus $\log(M_1/M_2)$ becomes deterministic for large M_1 and M_2, and after integration we find that

$$\frac{M_1'}{M_2'} = ce^{(a_1-a_2)(t'-t)}, \tag{B.13}$$

where c is the constant of integration and M_1' and M_2' denote the future values of the variables M_1 and M_2 at time t'; M_1 and M_2 are the values at time t, and so $c = M_1/M_2$. Our first exit time question in this deterministic limit is easily answered. The two averages cross when $M_1'/M_2' = 1$. From (B.13), we see that this happens when

$$1 = \frac{M_1}{M_2} e^{(a_1 - a_2)(t' - t)}$$

and so

$$t' - t = \frac{\log(M_2/M_1)}{a_1 - a_2}.$$

Because this problem is deterministic, $t' - t$ *is* the value of the expected first exit time; our final boundary condition is thus

$$\bar{v} \sim \frac{\log(M_2/M_1)}{a_1 - a_2} \quad \text{as} \quad M_1, M_2 \to \infty.$$

In general, the problem must be solved numerically.

Exercise

1. Find the explicit solution for the expected first exit time for the weighted moving average M when it starts at a value greater than 1.

Appendix C

Lattice Methods

C.1 The lattice structure

The lattice approach to valuing derivative securities was suggested by Cox, Ross & Rubinstein (1979). It can be used to value quite general derivative securities and also to obtain exact formulæ by taking the limit in which the lattice converges to a continuum. Cox & Rubinstein (1985) contains numerous examples and details.

Lattice methods for valuing options and other derivative securities arise from discrete random walk models of the underlying security. Thus, it is supposed that the lifetime T of the derivative security can be divided up into M discrete (equal) time-steps, $\delta t = M/T$. (Note the use of δt instead of dt to denote a small but *finite* time-step.) It is assumed that at each time-step the value of the asset can jump from its old value at the start of the time-step to a finite number N of new values at the end of the time-step. (Typically N is two or three.) The probability of the jump from the old value to each of the new values is assumed to be known. For example[1], if it is known with certainty that the underlying value is S_m at time-step $t = m\,\delta t$, then the value S_{m+1} of the underlying at time-step $t = (m+1)\,\delta t$

[1]Only in this appendix do we use the subscript to denote the time-step. Thus, for example, $V_{m,n}$ denotes the value of the option at the nth node at the mth time-step. We use this notation to avoid confusion with superscripts denoting a power.

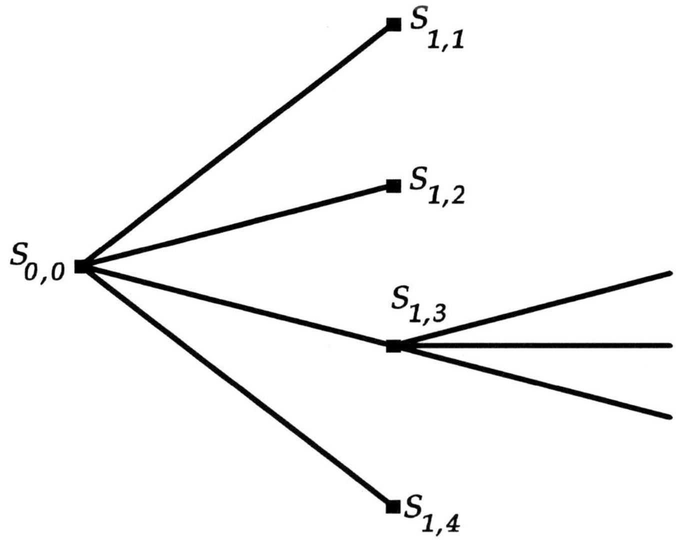

Figure C.1: Lattice for a general discrete random walk.

can be any of the values

$$S_{m+1} \in \{S_{m+1,1}, S_{m+1,2}, \dots, S_{m+1,N}\},$$

where the probability that $S_{m+1} = S_{m+1,n}$ is given by $p_{m,n}$ and

$$p_{m,1} + p_{m,2} + \cdots + p_{m,N} = 1, \quad 0 \leq p_{m,n} \leq 1, \text{ for } n = 1, 2, \dots, N.$$

This gives rise to a tree-like structure for the random walk of the asset price (see Figure C.1).

The idea is that, if we know the value of the underlying now, we can build a tree or lattice of possible values of the asset up to the expiry time. This allows us to calculate the possible values of the asset at the expiry time, and the probability of these particular values occurring.

All lattice methods assume a risk-neutral world that is, one where an investor's risk preferences are irrelevant to derivative security valuation. This assumption may be made whenever it is possible to hedge a portfolio and make it riskless (see Appendix A). Under these circumstances we may assume that investors are risk neutral (even if they are not), and that the return from the underlying is the risk-free interest rate. The μ in the stochastic differential equation $dS = \sigma S\,dX + \mu S\,dt$ is a measure of the expected growth rate of the underlying asset and, as we have seen, it does not enter into the Black–Scholes equation. Recalling the discussion of Appendix A, we choose values for probabilities to reflect a random walk with a growth rate r instead of μ.

Under the assumption of a risk-neutral world we observe that the value of the derivative security at time-step $m\,\delta t$ and asset value S_m, $V(S_m, m\,\delta t)$, must be the *expected value* of the security at time-step $(m+1)\,\delta t$ discounted by the risk-free interest rate r:

$$V_m e^{r\delta t} = \mathcal{E}\left[V_{m+1}\right] = \sum_{n=1}^{N} p_{m,n} V(S_{m+1,n}, (m+1)\,\delta t).$$

As we know all the possible values of the underlying at expiry, and their probabilities, we can calculate the possible values of the derivative security at expiry from the payoff function and their probabilities. (We are assuming here that the payoff function is determined only by the value of the underlying at expiry. This is not the case, for example, for a path-dependent option such as a lookback or an average strike.)

This procedure enables us to calculate the possible values of the security at the time-step prior to expiry, $(M-1)\,\delta t$. Hence, working back down the lattice, we calculate the possible values of the security at time-step $m\,\delta t$ given the values of security at time-step $(m+1)\,\delta t$ and the conditional probabilities of these values. This allows us to determine the value of the derivative security at the initial time. Note that 'the initial time' does not necessarily mean the start of the life of the derivative security. The above procedure works if T is interpreted as the remaining time to expiry of the security. Moreover, in order to calculate the delta for an option it is useful to use an 'initial time' prior to the start of the life of the derivative security.

The lattice method relies on building a tree of possible values of asset prices and their probabilities, given an initial asset price, then using this to determine the possible asset prices at expiry and their probabilities. The possible values of the security at expiry can be calculated, and, by working back down the tree, the security can be valued. A useful consequence is that we can quite easily deal with the possibility of early exercise and with the possibility of both continuous and discrete payment of dividends.

It is a common fallacy that lattice methods are unable to deal with path-dependent options The *standard* lattice methods are unable to deal with path-dependent options because, as noted above, in order to value a derivative security at expiry we have assumed that the payoff is uniquely determined by the value of the underlying at expiry. This is not the case for path-dependent options. Provided, however, that the history of the asset price can be encoded in the lattice, it is possible to deal with path-dependent options (or, at least, options whose values depend on the history of the price of the underlying). In particular, if the possible histories of the underlying price and the paths through the lattice are in one-to-one correspondence (see for example Figure C.2) we can find the value of a path-dependent option. This follows since we have every possible function of the asset value available for each possible history of the asset.

The number of possible asset paths grows exponentially with the number of time-steps, and it may therefore seem that the computer memory required to store such a lattice should also grow exponentially with the number of time-steps, making it impractical to implement such a method. This is not, in fact, the case since it is unnecessary to store the entire lattice. The asset prices in the tree depend only on the asset price at the previous time-step and the option values depend only on the asset price (or some function of its history which can be stored along with the asset price) and the option values at the next time-step. This means that the algorithm can be implemented recursively, and by disposing of nodes on the tree as soon as they have been used the memory required is, in fact, only a linear function of the number of time-steps. Nevertheless, the actual number of computations grows exponentially with the number of time-steps; this imposes serious limits on the number of time-steps that can be realistically used (and hence on the accuracy).

The lattice method is best illustrated by discussing a number of examples. We consider the binomial method in some detail and then go on to give a brief account of the trinomial method.

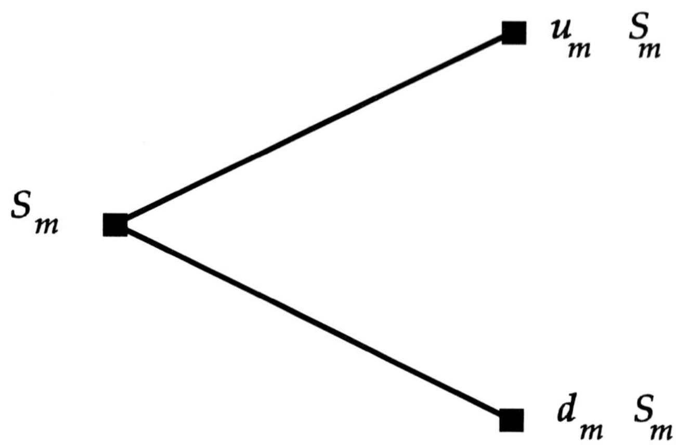

Figure C.2: The binomial model.

C.2 The binomial method

In the binomial method it is assumed that if the asset price is S_m at time-step $m\,\delta t$, then it can either jump up to a higher value $u_m S_m$ (where $u_m > 1$) or down to a lower value $d_m S_m$ (where $d_m < 1$) at time-step $(m+1)\,\delta t$. Note that u_m and d_m may depend on m, and more generally on S_m. The probability of an up-jump $S_m \to u_m S_m$ is p_m and the probability of a down-jump $S_m \to d_m S_m$ is $1 - p_m$. Thus,

$$S_{m+1} = \begin{cases} u_m S_m & \text{with probability } p_m, \\ d_m S_m & \text{with probability } 1 - p_m, \end{cases}$$

as illustrated in Figure C.2. (The lattice shown in this figure could be used to value a path-dependent option as it does not reconnect; therefore each possible asset history is represented by a unique path through the lattice.)

We assume a risk-neutral world in which the underlying random walk for S is lognormally distributed. We now approximate this continuous random walk with a discrete random walk having the same mean and variance. Thus

$$S_m e^{r\delta t} = \mathcal{E}\left[S_{m+1}\right] = S_m(p_m u_m + (1-p_m)d_m)$$

and

$$\begin{aligned}\operatorname{var}\left[S_{m+1}\right] &= \mathcal{E}\left[(S_{m+1})^2\right] - (\mathcal{E}\left[S_{m+1}\right])^2 \\ &= (S_m)^2\left(p_m(u_m)^2 + (1-p_m)(d_m)^2\right. \\ &\qquad \left. + (p_m u_m + (1-p_m)d_m)^2\right),\end{aligned}$$

where σ is the volatility. This gives us two equations for the three quantities u_m, d_m and p_m,

$$\begin{aligned} p_m u_m + (1-p_m)d_m &= e^{r\delta t}, \\ p_m(u_m)^2 + (1-p_m)(d_m)^2 &= \sigma^2\delta t + e^{2r\delta t} \end{aligned}$$

As noted, we allow the possibilities that u_m, d_m, and p_m can vary with m and with S_m. Typically, however, it is assumed that they are constants for the whole random walk, so that

$$p_m = p, \quad u_m = u, \quad d_m = d \quad \text{for all } m.$$

Assuming that the jump sizes and probabilities are constant for the entire random walk, we find that

$$\begin{aligned} pu + (1-p)d &= e^{r\delta t}, \\ pu^2 + (1-p)d^2 &= \sigma^2\delta t + e^{2r\delta t}. \end{aligned} \tag{C.1}$$

We still have only two equations for the three quantities u, d and p. Another equation that is used frequently, because it leads to a lattice with particularly useful properties, is the condition that

$$u = \frac{1}{d}. \tag{C.2}$$

Note that we could use conditions other than (C.2) if we had compelling reasons to. However, condition (C.2) leads to a balanced lattice, in that after two time-steps the asset price can return to its starting value. Other choices of u and d do not necessarily have this property.

With these conditions, (C.1) and (C.2), we can solve for u, d and p and we find that, assuming δt is small enough so that we can neglect terms of $O((\delta t)^{3/2})$ and higher,

$$\begin{aligned} p &= \tfrac{1}{2}\left(1 + \left(r - \tfrac{1}{2}\sigma^2\right)/\sigma\sqrt{\delta t} + \frac{\sigma^2}{6}\delta t + O(\delta t^{3/2})\right), \\ u &= 1 + \sigma\sqrt{\delta t} + \tfrac{1}{2}\sigma^2\delta t + O(\delta t^{3/2}) \\ d &= 1 - \sigma\sqrt{\delta t} + \tfrac{1}{2}\sigma^2\delta t + O(\delta t^{3/2}). \end{aligned} \tag{C.3}$$

These equations are, up to an error of $O(\delta t^{3/2})$, equivalent to the more familiar expressions

$$p = \frac{r\delta t - e^{-\sigma\sqrt{\delta t}}}{e^{\sigma\sqrt{\delta t}} - e^{-\sigma\sqrt{\delta t}}},$$

$$u = e^{\sigma\sqrt{\delta t}}, \quad d = e^{-\sigma\sqrt{\delta t}}.$$

We may now build up a lattice of possible asset prices. If at the current time t we know the asset price, S, then we divide the remaining life of the derivative security into M equal time-steps, $\delta t = (T-t)/M$. At the first time-step δt there are two possible asset prices, uS and $dS = S/u$. At the second time-step, $2\,\delta t$, there are three possible asset prices u^2S, $udS = duS = S$ and $d^2S = S/u^2$. At the third time-step $3\,\delta t$ there are four possible asset prices, u^3S, $u^2dS = uS$, $ud^2S = S/u$ and $d^3S = S/u^3$. In general, at the m-th time-step $m\,\delta t$ there are $m+1$ possible values of the asset price,

$$d^{m-n}u^nS = u^{2n-m}S, \quad n = 0, 1, \ldots m$$

as in Figure C.3. At the final time-step, $m\,\delta t$, we have $M+1$ possible values of the underlying asset.

Note that the lattice in Figure C.3 reconnects. This has two consequences that are of immediate interest. The first is that the history of a particular asset price is lost, as there is clearly more than one path to any given point. Thus in general path-dependent options cannot be valued using this reconnecting lattice. The second implication is that the total number of lattice points increases only quadratically with the number of time-steps. This means that a large number of time-steps can be taken.

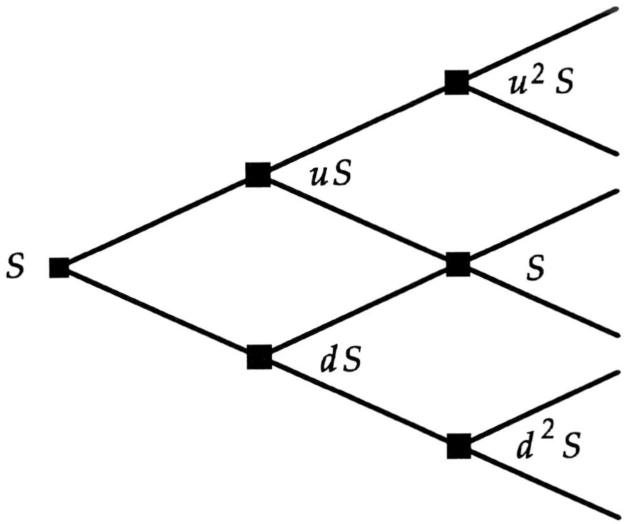

Figure C.3: Tree of asset prices for a regular binomial model.

Assuming that we know the payoff function for our derivative security and that it depends only on the values of the underlying at expiry, this enables us to value it at expiry, time-step $M\,\delta t$. If we are considering a put, for example, we find that

$$P_{M,n} = \max(E - S_{M,n}, 0), \quad n = 0, 1, \ldots, M,$$

where E is the exercise price, $P_{M,n}$ denotes the possible values of the put at time-step M and at the n-th possible asset value $S_{M,n}$. For a call, we find that

$$C_{M,n} = \max(S_{M,n} - E, 0), \quad n = 0, 1, \ldots, M,$$

where $C_{M,n}$ denotes the possible values of the call at expiry. Similarly, for a binary option, a cash or nothing call, with exercise price E and payoff

$$V(S,T) = \begin{cases} 0 & S < E, \\ B & S \geq E, \end{cases}$$

we have

$$V_{M,n} = \begin{cases} 0 & S_{M,n} < E, \\ B & S_{M,n} \geq E, \end{cases} \qquad n = 0, 1, \ldots, M.$$

We can find the expected value of the derivative security at the time-step prior to expiry, $(M - 1)\,\delta t$, and for possible asset price $S_{M-1,n}$, $n = 0, 1, \ldots M - 1$, since we know that the probability of an asset priced at $S_{M-1,n}$ moving to $S_{M,n+1}$ during a time-step is p, and the probability of it moving to $S_{M,n}$ is $(1-p)$. Using the risk-neutral argument we can calculate the value of the security at each possible asset price for time-step $(M - 1)$. Similarly this allows us to find the value of the security at time-step $(M - 2)$, and so on, back to time-step 0. This gives us the value of our security at the current time.

C.2.1 European options

Let $V_{m,n}$ denote the value of the option at time-step $m\,\delta t$ and asset price $S_{m,n}$ (where $0 \leq n \leq m$). Calculating the expected value of the put at time-step $m + 1$, given the asset price $S_{m,n}$, and discounting this for the riskless interest rate,

$$e^{r\delta t} V_{m,n} = pV_{m+1,n+1} + (1 - p)V_{m+1,n}.$$

This gives

$$V_{m,n} = e^{-r\delta t}\left(pV_{m+1,n+1} + (1 - p)V_{m+1,n}\right), \qquad n = 0, 1, \ldots, m. \tag{C.4}$$

As we know the value of $V_{M,n}$, $n = 0, 1, \ldots, M$ from the payoff function we can recursively determine the values of $V_{m,n}$ for each $n = 0, 1, \ldots, m$ for $m < M$ to arrive at the current value of the option, $V_{0,0}$.

We do not require the asset prices $S_{m,n}$ during the evaluation of the option prices, other than the $S_{M,n}$ when finding $V_{M,n}$. At each time-step we can discard the old $S_{m,n}$ as soon as we have calculated the $S_{m+1,n}$. Once the $V_{M,n}$ have been found, we can discard the $S_{M,n}$ as well. This observation leads to an extremely memory-efficient algorithm; the memory required varies linearly with the number of time-steps and the execution time varies quadratically with the number of time-steps. An example of this is given in Figure C.4.

In Figure C.5 we compare the values of a European put, calculated by a binomial method using M = 16, 32, 64, 128 and 256

```
value_euro_option( array, S0, up, down, prob, disc, M )
{
  /* build up asset prices */

  array[0]=S0;
  for(time=1; time <= M; time++) {
      for(step=time+1; step >0; --step)
          array[step]=up_jump*array[step];
      array[0]=down_jump*array[0];
  }

  /* find option value at payoff */

  for(step=0; step<=M; step++)
      array[step] = pay_off_function(array[step]);

  /* for example
           for a put    pay_off_function(S)=max(E-S,0),
           for a call   pay_off_function(S)=max(S-E,0).
  */

  /* use risk neutral argument to find option values */

  for(time=M; time>0; time--) {
      for(step=0; step<time; step++)
          array[step] = disc*( (1-p)*array[step]
                        + p*array[step+1] );

  /* present option value is in array[0] */

  }
}
```

Figure C.4: Pseudo-code for binomial model for a simple European option.

time-steps, with the Black–Scholes value.

Technical Point: variable jump sizes and probabilities. *Sometimes it is convenient to be able to vary the probabilities and jump sizes. One example arises if we insist that the possible future values of S can only take given discrete values. We can arrange this by imposing the conditions that $u_m S_m$ and $d_m S_m$ take special values. Another example is when a dividend-paying asset goes ex-dividend. This can cause the lattice to become far more complicated than it would otherwise be. By allowing variable jump sizes u_m and d_m we can prevent this.*

	Black	Binomial Method				
T	Scholes	$M = 16$	32	64	128	256
1	4.9005	4.9005	4.9005	4.9005	4.9005	4.9005
3	4.7066	4.7060	4.7062	4.7063	4.7065	4.7066
6	4.4526	4.4484	4.4523	4.4519	4.4520	4.4525
9	4.2465	4.2416	4.2475	4.2468	4.2454	4.2464
12	4.0733	4.0762	4.0700	4.0749	4.0730	4.0727

Figure C.5: Comparison of binomial and Black–Scholes values for a European put with $E = 10$, $S = 5$, $r = 0.12$, $\sigma = 0.5$. The time to expiry, T, is measured in months.

C.2.2 American options

We can easily incorporate the possibility of early exercise of an option into the binomial model. As before, we divide the time to expiry into M equal time-steps $\delta t = T/M$ and use formulæ (C.1), (C.2) and (C.3). We build our tree of possible stock prices,

$$S_{m,n} = u^{2n-m} S_{0,0}, \quad n = 0, 1, \ldots, m$$

where $S_{0,0}$ is the current value and $S_{m,n}$ is a possible value at time-step m. At time $m\,\delta t$ we can calculate the possible values of the option from the payoff function; for example, for puts, calls and binaries these are, respectively,

$$P_{M,n} = \max(E - S_{M,n}, 0), \quad C_{M,n} = \max(S_{M,n} - E, 0),$$

$$V_{M,n} = \begin{cases} 0 & S_{M,n} < E \\ B & S_{M,n} \geq E \end{cases}$$

Consider the situation at time-step m. The option can be exercised prior to expiry to yield a profit determined by the payoff function; for a puts, calls and binaries, respectively, these are

$$\max(E - S_{m,n}, 0), \quad \max(S_{m,n} - E, 0), \quad \begin{cases} 0 & S_{m,n} < E \\ B & S_{m,n} \geq E \end{cases},$$

if the stock is at price $S_{m,n}$. If the option is retained, its value $V_{m,n}$ is, as in the European case,

$$V_{m,n} = e^{-r\delta t}\left(pV_{m+1,n+1} + (1-p)V_{m+1,n}\right).$$

The value of the option is the maximum of these two possibilities. Thus for a put we have

$$P_{m,n} = \max\left(E - S_{m,n}, e^{-r\delta t}\left(pP_{m+1,n+1} + (1-p)P_{m+1,n}\right)\right)$$

and for a call

$$C_{m,n} = \max\left(S_{m,n} - E, e^{-r\delta t}\left(pC_{m+1,n+1} + (1-p)C_{m+1,n}\right)\right).$$

Implementing the scheme is almost as simple as the European case. A lattice of $S_{m,n}$ values is built first and saved. When it comes to finding $V_{m,n}$ all the possible $S_{m,n}$ are thus known. We then evaluate $V_{M,n}$ from the payoff function, and work back down the tree to find the value of the option. The only additional complication is that it is necessary to test to decide which of the two possible values (early exercise or retaining the option) is greater. In order to implement this test efficiently, we have to store the S_n^m values. This implies that the memory requirements vary quadratically with the number of time-steps, as does the execution time.

In Figure C.7 we give binomial lattice approximations to an American put with exercise price 10, current asset price 9, interest rate of $r = 0.12$, volatility of $\sigma = 0.5$, for $M = 16$, $M = 32$, $M = 64$, $M = 128$ and $M = 256$ time-steps.

```
amer_option( s, v, S0, u, d, p, disc, M, divs )
{

/* build up asset prices */

  array[0][0]=S0;
  for(time=1; time <= M; time++) {
      for(step=time+1; step > 0; --step)
          s[time][step] = u * s[time-1][step];
      s[time][0] = d * s[time-1][0];
  }

/* find option value at payoff */

  for(step=0; step<=M; step++)
      v[M][step] = pay_off(s[M][step]);

 /* use risk neutral argument to find option values */

  for(time=M-1; time >= 0; time--) {
      for(step=0; step<=time; step++) {
        hold= disc*( (1-p) * v[step-1] + p * v[step] );
        v[time][step]=max(hold,pay_off(s[time][step]));
      }

/* present option value is in v_array[0][0] */

  }
}
```

Figure C.6: Pseudo-code for binomial model for an American option.

	Binomial Method				
T	$M = 16$	32	64	128	256
1	1.1376	1.1308	1.1311	1.1317	1.1316
3	1.3815	1.3833	1.3822	1.3814	1.3805
6	1.6342	1.6191	1.6196	1.6185	1.6178
9	1.8078	1.7906	1.7814	1.7847	1.7817
12	1.9399	1.9216	1.9112	1.9106	1.9094

Figure C.7: Comparison of binomial values for an American put with $E = 10$, $S = 9$, $r = 0.12$, $\sigma = 0.5$. Time to expiry, T, is measured in months.

C.2.3 Options paying dividends

If the asset underlying an option pays a constant dividend yield rate D_0 then we can easily modify the binomial model to account for this. The effective risk-free interest rate becomes $r - D_0$ rather than r, and we replace r by $r - D_0$ in each of (C.1), (C.2) and (C.3).[2] (We are assuming that $r - D_0 > 0$ here.)

If the underlying asset pays a number of known discrete dividend yields during the lifetime of the option, the situation is not much more complicated. By a dividend yield[3] we mean that the dividend paid at asset price S is βS on the dividend date. The assumption is that the asset price then falls by an amount βS. Suppose that the asset goes ex-dividend between time-steps m and $m+1$. The effect is to discount the asset value at time-step $m+1$ by a factor of $(1-\beta)$. Thus if the value of the asset in the absence of a dividend is $\hat{S}_{m+1,n}$ then the value of the asset in the presence of a dividend yield is $S_{m+1,n} = (1-\beta)\hat{S}_{m+1,n}$. This idea is illustrated in Figure C.8.

For all times greater than the ex-dividend date, all possible values of the asset are discounted by a factor of $(1-\beta)$. Note that this does not cause the lattice to split, it merely causes a shift in the lattice points; see Figure C.8. This follows since the asset price in the absence of a dividend yield, $\hat{S}$, satisfies $\hat{S}_{m+1,n} = u\hat{S}_{m,n-1} = d\hat{S}_{m,n}$,

[2]Note that r has been replaced by $r - D_0$ but in calculating $V_{m,n}$ from $V_{m+1,n+1}$ and $V_{m+1,n}$ we still discount using r so (C.4) is still valid.

[3]In the notation of Chapter 8, $\beta = 1 - e^{-D^y_\delta}$.

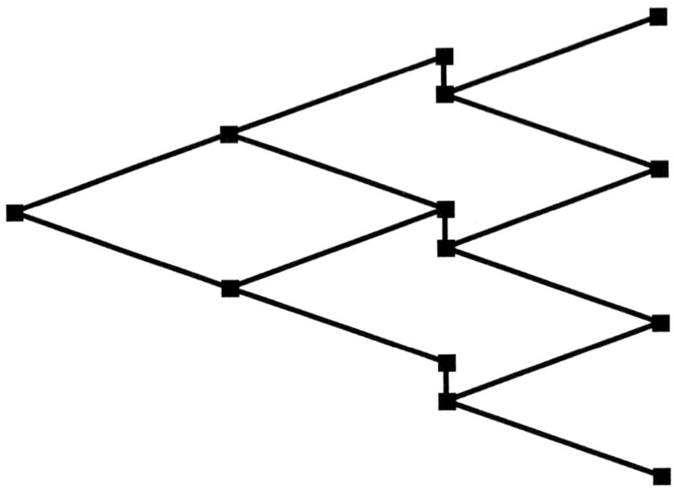

Figure C.8: The lattice for a binomial model with dividend yields.

so that in the presence of dividend yields

$$(1-\beta)\hat{S}_{m+1,n} = u(1-\beta)\hat{S}_{m,n-1} = d(1-\beta)\hat{S}_{m,n}$$

or $S_{m+1,n} = uS_{m,n-1} + dS_{m,n}$.

More generally, if there are K dividends to be paid during the lifetime of the option, and the dividend yields are known to be β_k, $k = 1, 2, \ldots, K$ then we find that the effect is to shift the lattice K times. The value of the asset at expiry of the option is seen to be

$$S_{M,n} = \hat{S}_{M,n}(1-\beta_1)(1-\beta_2)\cdots(1-\beta_K) = \hat{S}_{M,n}\prod_{k=1}^{K}(1-\beta_k),$$

where $\hat{S}_{M,n}$ is the value of the asset at expiry in the absence of dividend yields:

$$\hat{S}_{M,n} = u^{2n-M}S_{0,0}.$$

Note that the effect of the dividend yield is absorbed into the tree construction phase of the algorithm. The jump probabilities are not affected by the dividend yields and the underlying asset values have already been calculated (during the lattice construction phase) by the time it comes to valuing the option. Thus, we can find the option values (with or without early exercise) by exactly the same process as outlined in previous cases.

In Figure C.10 we show the binomial approximation to the values of an American put option on a stock that pays three dividend yields during the course of the year. The exercise price is $E = 10$, the interest rate is $r = 0.12$, the volatility $\sigma = 0.5$, and the current asset price is $S = 9$. The asset is assumed to pay dividend yields after two months, six months and ten months. The effect of these dividend yields are assumed be to reductions in the asset values by factors of $\beta_1 = 0.9$, $\beta_2 = 0.9$ and $\beta_3 = 0.8$ respectively. The ex-dividend jump in the put value is illustrated. Compare this with the dividend-free example in Figure C.7.

A slightly more complicated case arises when the discrete dividend payment is a known constant or, more generally, determined by a non-linear function of the asset price. Suppose that a dividend is paid during the lifetime of the option and that the effect on the asset price is to discount it by some known value D_m which depends on the asset price $S_{m,n}$ immediately prior to the dividend date. This poses a problem. The problem is, how should one deal with the case when D_m is greater than $S_{m,n}$? This case corresponds to a case where a company is committed to paying a dividend on each share that is greater than the value of a share—this presents arbitrage opportunities. One way to deal with this problem is to assume that the company becomes bankrupt and its shares become worthless rather than assigning to them negative values. Another possibility is to use a more realistic model for the dividend term structure—for example the company pays no dividend if its share price is very low.

Assuming a known dividend payment D_m, the effect (on an otherwise reconnecting lattice) is to split the lattice. The asset prices at time-step $m+1$ are then found to be

$$S_{m+1,n} = \hat{S}_{m+1,n} - D_m$$

where $\hat{S}_{m+1,n} = u^{2n-m-1} S_{0,0}$ is the asset price in the absence of a dividend. The splitting occurs since $\hat{S}_{m+1,n} = u\hat{S}_{m,n-1} = d\hat{S}_{m,n}$ in

```
amer_option_div(s, v, S0, u, d, p, disc, M, divs)
{
  div_day = 0;
  s[0][0]=S0;

/* build up asset prices */

  for(time=1; time <= M; time++) {
      for(step=time; step >0; --step)
          s[time][step] = u * s[time-1][step];
      s[time][0] = d*s[time-1][0];
      if ( time == divs[div_day].date ) {
          for(step = 0; step <= time; step++)
             s[time][step] *= divs[div_day].yield
          ++div_day;
      }
  }

/* find option value at payoff */

  for(step=0; step<=M; step++)
    v[M][step]=pay_off(s[M][step]);

/* use risk neutral argument to find option values */

  for(time=M-1; time >= 0; time--) {
     for(step=0; step<=time; step++) {
        hold=disc*((1-p)*v[step-1]+p*v[step]);
        v[time][step]=max(hold,pay_off(s[time][step]));
     }
/* present option value is in v_array[0][0] */
  }
}
```

Figure C.9: Pseudo-code for binomial model for an American option with dividend yields.

Expiry (Months)	Binomial Method				
	$M = 16$	32	64	128	256
1	1.1376	1.1308	1.1311	1.1317	1.1316
1.9	1.2563	1.2629	1.2583	1.2573	1.2586
2	1.8659	1.8704	1.8720	1.8727	1.8730
3	1.9659	1.9633	1.9634	1.9617	1.9620
5.9	2.1454	2.1441	2.1422	2.1403	2.1391
6	2.5304	2.5318	2.5286	2.5244	2.5256
9.9	2.7142	2.6942	2.7045	2.7021	2.7031
10	3.5146	3.5112	3.5097	3.5091	3.5088
12	3.5401	3.5574	3.5617	3.5650	3.5654

Figure C.10: Comparison of binomial values for an American put on a share that pays three dividend yields during the year, at months 2, 6 and 10. The yield factors are $\beta_1 = 0.9$, $\beta_2 = 0.9$ and $\beta_3 = 0.8$. The other option constants are $E = 10$, $S = 9$, $r = 0.12$, $\sigma = 0.5$.

the absence of dividend yields, but in the presence of dividend yields

$$\hat{S}_{m+1,n} = u\left(\hat{S}_{m,n-1} - D_m\right) \neq d\left(\hat{S}_{m,n} - D_m\right),$$

unless $D_m = 0$. See Figure C.11.

Suppose that the first dividend date occurs between times $m\,\delta t$ and $(m+1)\,\delta t$. Then at time-step $m\delta t$ the asset prices are

$$S_{m,n} = u^{2n-m} S_{0,0}, \quad n = 0, 1, \ldots, m,$$

whereas at time-step $(m+1)\,\delta t$ the asset prices are

$$(S_{m,n} - D_m)u, \quad \text{and} \quad (S_{m,n} - D_m)/u,$$

assuming that we keep $d = 1/u$. Since there are $m+1$ possible $S_{m,n}$'s, it follows that there are $2m+2$ possible $S_{m+1,n}$'s of this given form (see Figure C.11). Normally (with no dividend) there would only be $m+2$ possible values. Thus each dividend causes the tree to split and introduces m new lattice points. If there are K dividend dates, then the effect is to cause the number of lattice points to increase exponentially (as does the execution time).

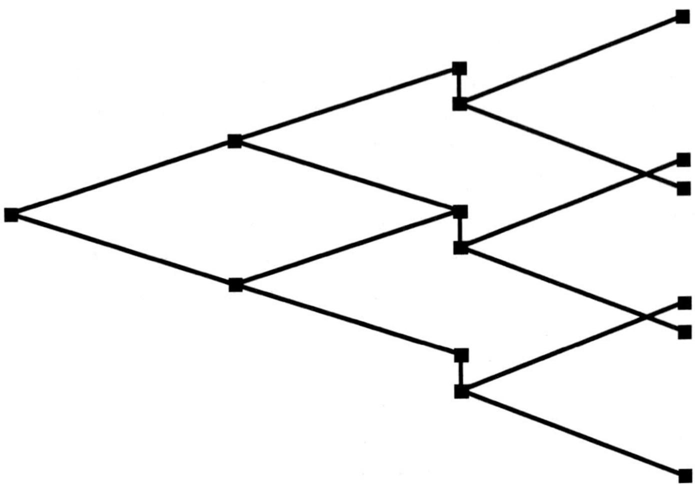

Figure C.11: Lattice splitting for a general dividend payment.

There are a number of ways of dealing with this problem. The first is to observe that it does not really make any difference to the basic algorithm at all (we can still work backwards down the tree to find the initial value of the option; the details are slightly more complicated, but the method is not), and to accept that with the computing power available these days it really does not matter whether we have to deal with $M + 1$ or $2M + 2$ terminal lattice points. Another approach is to force the lattice to reconnect, so that the number of lattice points at time m is always $m + 1$. We can do this by allowing u and d to depend on m and n (that is, on time and asset price) and choosing $u_{m,n}$ and $d_{m,n}$ so that

$$(S_{m,n} - D_n)d_{m,n} = (S_{m,n-1} - D_{n-1})u_{m,n}.$$

We must, however, then record the values of $u_{m,n}$ and $d_{m,n}$ since the jump probabilities are different at each lattice point at time $m\,\delta t$. This implies the extra complication of storing the jump probabilities so that the option value can be calculated. Another possibility is to implement the algorithm recursively (see the following section) so that although the number of computations increases dramatically (if we have many dividend dates) the memory requirements do not.

C.2.4 Path-dependent options

As an example of pricing path-dependent options by binomial methods, we consider the pricing of average strike options. The exercise price of the option is the average value of the asset over the lifetime of the option. For the case of American style options, we make the ansatz that the exercise price is the average value of the asset up until the early exercise date. Since the average value of the asset is a function of the asset price path, we cannot allow the lattice to reconnect; we must use a binary tree.

To implement our algorithm we represent each node on this binary tree by a record containing information about the current asset price, the cumulative asset price along the particular path and the time (so we can calculate the average asset value at any given node), the option value (or option values if, say, we choose to value more than one type of option at a time), and any other information that might be useful (for example, the jump probabilities and sizes if we have some reason to want these to vary as functions of asset price).

Now, given that our initial asset price and other constants such as the interest rate, volatility are known, we can implement the pricing algorithm as a recursive process. That is, we can write a general purpose routine that calls itself to value the option for the two possible cases at the next time-step (the up jump and the down jump), then uses this information to value the option for the current time-step. The basic idea is illustrated in the pseudo-code example given in Figure C.12.

The notation in Figure C.12 is as follows. `here` is a record representing the current node in the binary tree. It has components `here.asset`, the value of the asset, `here.total`, the cumulative total of asset prices along a particular branch of the tree, `here.time`, time at this node, `here.average`, the running average of the asset price and `here.option`, the value of the option at this node. Similarly, `up` and `down` are records representing the up and down nodes relative to the `here` node. They have the same components as the `here` node.

The function given in Figure C.12 is recursive in that it first creates two new nodes, an up node and a down node, for the next

```
value_option( here, time, timestep )
{
  if (time = expiry_time) {
    here.option=pay_off(here.asset,here.average);
    return
  }
  else {
    create( up );
/* value option in up node */
    up.asset = here.asset * up_jump;
    up.time  = here.time + timestep;
    up.total = here.total + up.asset;
    up.average = up.total/up.time;
    value_option(up, up.time, timestep);

    create( down );
/* value option in down node */
    down.asset = here.asset * down_jump;
    down.time  = here.time + timestep;
    down.total = here.total + down.asset;
    down.average = down.total/down.time;
    value_option(down, down.time, timestep);

    e_value=up.option*u + down.option*d;
    euro=discount*e_value;

    if (OptionType == European)
       here.option = euro;
    else if (OptionType == American)
       here.option = max(euro,
                     pay_off(here.asset,here.average));
    free(up);
    free(down);
  }
}
```

Figure C.12: Pseudo-code for the recursive implementation of a binomial model.

Expiry	European put			European call		
(Months)	$M=8$	16	24	$M=8$	16	24
1	0.304	0.305	0.306	0.354	0.355	0.356
3	0.494	0.496	0.497	0.643	0.644	0.645
6	0.655	0.656	0.657	0.949	0.950	0.951
9	0.762	0.761	0.761	1.198	1.198	1.198
12	0.841	0.838	0.838	1.416	1.414	1.414
	American put			American call		
1	0.389	0.414	0.425	0.426	0.448	0.459
3	0.650	0.694	0.713	0.758	0.796	0.815
6	0.887	0.948	0.979	1.099	1.153	1.177
9	1.056	1.133	1.169	1.373	1.437	1.465
12	1.195	1.282	1.321	1.611	1.680	1.712

Figure C.13: Comparison of binomial values for European and American average strike puts and calls, with exercise price $E = 10$ and initial share price $S = 10$, interest rate $r = 0.12$ and volatility $\sigma = 0.5$.

time-step, and then it calls itself to value each of these two new nodes. The recursion terminates because each time the function calls itself, with a new node to value, it also increases the `time` variable that it passes. Eventually the `time` variable equals the expiry time, at which point the routine invokes the `pay_off` function to value the option, and then returns without further recursive calls. Thus, the routine builds a branch of up-nodes until it reaches the expiry date. It then evaluates the option price at the end of these up-nodes, and returns to the previous level. The next step is to find the value of option at the down-node, which it does, and this allows the value of the option at the current node to be found. Since the up and down nodes are no longer useful, the function disposes of them before returning with the value of the option at the current time-step. This is then used to find the value of the option at earlier time-steps, and so on, until we return to the initial time.

Table C.13 shows results for average strike calls and puts at a variety of times to expiry. The calculations were performed using the method outlined above.

C.3 Trinomial methods

Trinomial models arise from the assumption that, given a current asset value S, the asset value after a time-step δt can take any of the three values

$$uS,\ qS,\ dS$$

where typically $0 < d < q < u$. The probability that the value of the asset at time δt is uS is p_u, the probability that it is qS is p_q and the probability that it is dS is p_d. Since there are only three possible cases we must have

$$p_u + p_q + p_d = 1, \quad 0 \le p_u \le 1, \quad 0 \le p_q \le 1, \quad 0 \le p_d \le 1.$$

Assuming a risk-neutral world in which the asset moves in a lognormally distributed manner and choosing the probabilities to reflect this, we find that we must have

$$p_u u + p_q q + p_d d = e^{r\delta t},$$

and

$$p_u u^2 + p_q q^2 + p_d d^2 = \sigma^2 \delta t - e^{2r\delta t}.$$

These are three equations for six unknowns. Even if we make the assumption that $q = 1$ (so that there is a probability that the asset price remains fixed) and $d = 1/u$, as in the binomial model, there still remain more unknowns than equations.

We can use this fact to derive a trinomial model that is, in effect, a more efficient version of the binomial model discussed in the previous section. Specifically, we notice that, in the binomial model given by (C.2), (C.3), after *two* time-steps the possible values of an asset that began with asset price S are

$$\begin{aligned} u^2 S \quad & \text{with probability } p^2, \\ S \quad & \text{with probability } 2p(1-p), \\ S/u^2 \quad & \text{with probability } (1-p)^2. \end{aligned}$$

Thus if we replace δt by $\delta t/2$ in (C.2) and in (C.3) and take

$$u = e^{2\sigma\sqrt{\delta t/2}}, \quad q = 1, \quad d = e^{-2\sigma\sqrt{\delta t/2}} \tag{C.5}$$

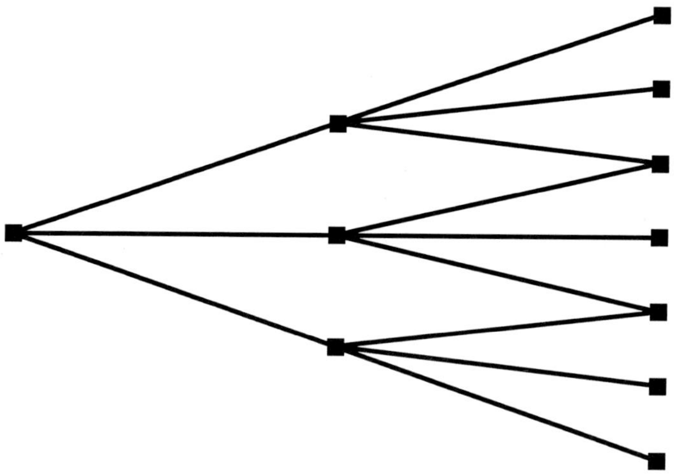

Figure C.14: Lattice generated by a trinomial model.

with

$$p = \frac{e^{r\delta t/2} - e^{-\sigma\sqrt{\delta t/2}}}{e^{\sigma\sqrt{\delta t/2}} - e^{-\sigma\sqrt{\delta t/2}}}, \quad p_u = p^2, \quad p_q = 2p(1-p), \quad p_d = (1-p)^2 \tag{C.6}$$

we see that the a single step of the resulting trinomial model is equivalent to two (half-size) steps of the binomial model. This has the important consequence that by using a trinomial model we can achieve the same accuracy with half the number of time-steps, or substantially improve the accuracy by using the same number of time-steps. The lattice generated by this scheme is illustrated in Figure C.14.

The details for valuing derivative securities using a trinomial method are nearly identical to the details for a binomial method. The only major difference is that the expected value of the security at time-step m depends on the three possible values at time-step $m+1$, and that at time-step m there are $2m+1$ possible asset and security prices rather than $m+1$. (Here we are assuming a lattice that reconnects; if we are dealing with path-dependent options then

Expiry	Trinomial Method				
(Months)	$M = 16$	32	64	128	256
1	1.1299	1.1307	1.1314	1.1315	1.1316
3	1.3807	1.3810	1.3809	1.3803	1.3799
6	1.6151	1.6176	1.6175	1.6173	1.6169
9	1.7870	1.7795	1.7831	1.7810	1.7818
12	1.9177	1.9085	1.9088	1.9087	1.9084

Figure C.15: Comparison of trinomial values for an American put with $E = 10$, $S = 9$, $r = 0.12$, $\sigma = 0.5$.

the trinomial method gives rises to ternary tree rather than a binary tree.) The formula for finding the expected value of a security at time-step m from time-step $m+1$ is

$$\mathcal{E}\left[V_{m+1}\right] = \left(p_u V_{m+1,n+1} + p_q V_{m+1,n} + p_d V_{m+1,n-1}\right),$$

and for a European derivative security this gives

$$V_{m,n} = e^{-r\delta t}\left(p_u V_{m+1,n+1} + p_q V_{m+1,n} + p_d V_{m+1,n-1}\right).$$

This has the same form as the finite-difference equations that result from discretizing the continuous Black–Scholes equation.

In Figure C.15 we give trinomial lattice approximations to the same American put problem considered in Figure C.7. The convergence is more rapid than in the binomial case.

Further reading

- For details of the binomial method as a model of asset prices see Cox & Rubinstein (1985) and Hull (1993).

Exercises

1. Assume a binomial method where the up jump u and the down jump d are constant and $u = 1/d$. Show that at time-step m there are $m+1$ possible values of the underlying. If at time-step m we denote the underlying prices in the tree by $S_{m,n}$ where $n = 0, 1, \dots, m$ show that

$$S_{m,n} = u^{2n-m} S_{0,0},$$

where $S_{0,0}$ is the known starting price. Deduce that

$$S_{m,0} = u^{-m} S_{0,0}$$

is the lowest possible price at time-step $m\,\delta t$ and

$$S_{m,m} = u^{m} S_{0,0}$$

is the highest. Consider the implications for the binomial valuation of a call option that is very well in the money.

2. Show that the memory required to value a European option by the binomial model varies linearly with the number of time-steps, and that the execution time varies quadratically with the number of time-steps.

3. Consider the case of a down-and-out barrier option, that is, a binary option that becomes worthless if the asset price ever falls below a barrier X. How could you modify the binomial and trinomial methods described above to deal with such an option?

4. What changes to the algorithm for valuing an average strike (given above) would be necessary in order to value a lookback put (where the exercise price is the highest value achieved by the asset during the lifetime of the option) or a lookback call (where the exercise price is the lowest value achieved by the asset during the lifetime of the option)?

5. Generalize the recursive algorithm for valuing average strikes to a recursive trinomial algorithm.

Appendix D

Finite-element Methods

D.1 Introduction

In this appendix we briefly discuss the finite-element method for solving free boundary partial differential equations. This method is particularly well-suited to the solution of free boundary problems in variational inequality forms. Since, however, it usually leads to exactly the same numerical problem as the finite-difference form of the linear complementarity problem, we only discuss it briefly.

In the first sections we consider the finite-element formulation for the obstacle problem, and then go on to consider the finite-element problem for American style options. Again the method is much easier to understand in the context of the simpler obstacle problem.

D.2 Finite elements and the obstacle problem

Recall from Chapter 7 that the variational inequality form of the obstacle problem, which may be derived from the linear complementarity form (20.1), is to find a $u(x) \in \mathcal{K}$ such that

$$\int_{-1}^{1} u'(\phi - u)'\, dx \geq 0 \tag{D.1}$$

for *every* $\phi \in \mathcal{K}$, where $\mathcal{K}$ is the set of all test functions $\phi(x)$ such that

- $\phi(-1) = 0$ and $\phi(1) = 0$,
- $\phi(x) \geq f(x)$ for $-1 \leq x \leq 1$,

- $\phi(x)$ is continuous,
- $\phi'(x)$ is piecewise continuous.

D.2.1 Finite-element formulation

In order to solve the variational inequality formulation (D.1) we introduce the **finite-element** method. Instead of using finite differences to approximate the derivatives occurring in (D.1), we approximate the integrals. This is done by approximating the space of test functions $\mathcal{K}$ by a smaller set of test functions, $\mathcal{K}_n$. Specifically, we choose a set of n independent functions called **basis functions** or **shape functions**,

$$\{\psi_1(x), \psi_2(x), \ldots, \psi_n(x)\},$$

and restrict our attention to those test functions that can be written as linear combinations of the basis functions. That is, we restrict our attention to test functions of the form

$$\phi(x) = \sum_{i=1}^{n} \phi_i \psi_i(x) = \phi_1 \psi_1(x) + \phi_2 \psi_2(x) + \cdots + \phi_n \psi_n(x),$$

where the constants ϕ_i are such that the condition $\phi(x) \geq f(x)$ holds, but are otherwise arbitrary. We call this set of restricted test functions $\mathcal{K}_n$. We also assume that the solution $u(x)$ of the variational inequality is itself a member of $\mathcal{K}_n$, so that

$$u(x) = \sum_{i=1}^{n} u_i \psi_i(x) = u_1 \psi_1(x) + u_2 \psi_2(x) + \cdots + u_n \psi_n(x).$$

The only restrictions, at this point, on the constants u_i are that they must be such that $u(x) \geq f(x)$, so that $u \in \mathcal{K}_n$. (Note that $\mathcal{K}_n$ is not necessarily a subset of $\mathcal{K}$, since if $u(x) \in \mathcal{K}_n$, $f(x)$ may rise above $u(x)$ in between mesh points.)

With this restriction on the class of test functions, we find that the integral in (D.1) can be written as

$$\begin{aligned}\int_{-1}^{1} u'(v-u)'\,dx &= \int_{-1}^{1} \left(\sum_{i=1}^{n} u_i \psi_i'(x) \right) \left(\sum_{j=1}^{n} (\phi_j - u_j) \psi_j'(x) \right) dx \\ &= \sum_{i=1}^{n} \sum_{j=1}^{n} u_i (\phi_j - u_j) \left(\int_{-1}^{1} \psi_i'(x) \psi_j'(x)\,dx \right).\end{aligned}$$

If we introduce the notation

$$A_{ij} = \int_{-1}^{1} \psi_i'(x)\psi_j'(x)\,dx, \tag{D.2}$$

we then have

$$\int_{-1}^{1} u'(\phi - u)'\,dx = \sum_{i=1}^{n}\sum_{j=1}^{n} A_{ij}u_i(\phi_j - u_j).$$

Thus we have a finite system of linear inequalities that is an approximation to the variational inequality (D.1), namely

$$\sum_{i=1}^{n}\sum_{j=1}^{n} A_{ij}u_i(\phi_j - u_j) \geq 0, \quad \text{for all} \quad \phi_j$$

subject to the constraint that the u_n and ϕ_n are such that $u \geq f$ and $\phi \geq f$.

The finite-element formulation of the variational inequality is the problem of finding constants u_i such that

$$u(x) = u_1\psi_1(x) + u_2\psi_2(x) + \cdots + u_n\psi_n(x) \geq f(x) \tag{D.3}$$

for all $-1 < x < 1$, and

$$\sum_{i=1}^{n}\sum_{j=1}^{n} A_{ij}u_i(\phi_j - u_j) \geq 0 \tag{D.4}$$

for all constants ϕ_j consistent with the condition that

$$\phi_1\psi_1(x) + \phi_2\psi_2(x) + \cdots + \phi_n\psi_n(x) \geq f(x) \tag{D.5}$$

for all $-1 < x < 1$.

We can regard the quantities A_{ij} defined by (D.2) as elements of a matrix $\mathbf{A} = (A_{ij})$. We have $A_{ij} = A_{ji}$, since (D.2) is evidently unchanged if we swap i and j, so that the matrix $\mathbf{A}$ is symmetric. Introducing the notation $\boldsymbol{u} = (u_1, u_2, \ldots, u_n)$ and $\boldsymbol{\phi} = (\phi_1, \phi_2, \ldots, \phi_n)$, we can rewrite equation (D.4) in matrix form,

$$\boldsymbol{u} \cdot \mathbf{A}(\boldsymbol{\phi} - \boldsymbol{u}) \geq 0. \tag{D.6}$$

The problem is to find a $\boldsymbol{u}$, consistent with condition (D.3), such that (D.6) is satisfied for *all* $\boldsymbol{\phi}$ consistent with (D.5).

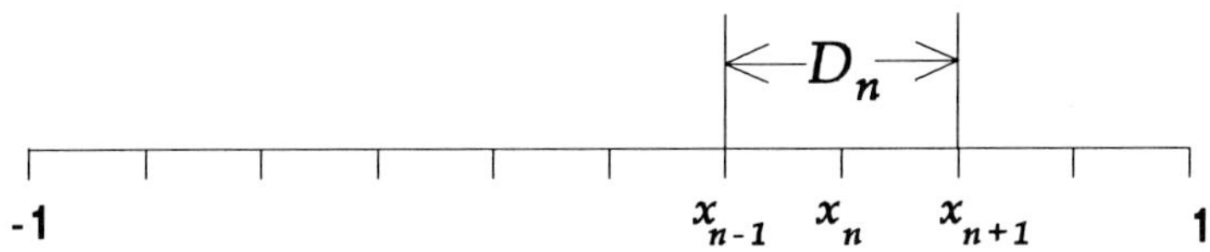

Figure D.1: The interval $-1 < x < 1$ divided into finite elements.

D.2.2 Implementing the finite-element method

Up to this point we have not been specific about our basis or shape functions $\psi_i(x)$. In the finite-element method (in its simplest form) we choose these shape functions so that they vanish outside a (small) finite element, are piecewise linear, and piecewise continuously differentiable on the element.

For simplicity, wc exploit the symmetry to write $n = 2N+1$, following which we construct our elements by partitioning the interval $-1 < x < 1$ into $2N$ equally spaced sub-intervals of length $\delta x = 1/N$, as shown in Figure D.1. Let the ends of these sub-intervals be denoted by $x_i = i\,\delta x$ where $i = -N, -N+1, \dots, -1, 0, 1, \dots N-1, N$, so that $x_{-N} = -1$, $x_0 = 0$, $x_N = 1$, as shown in Figure D.1. An **element** is two consecutive sub-intervals, as shown in Figure D.1. Note that most sub-intervals belong to two different elements, the exceptions being the sub-intervals at the two ends of the interval. Each element contains three consecutive x_i's, called the **nodes** of the element. We number our elements from $-N+1$ to $N-1$, and use the notation D_i to denote the i-th element. Thus, $D_{-N+1} = [-1, x_{-N+2}]$, $D_0 = [-x_{-1}, x_1]$ and, in general, $D_i = [x_{i-1}, x_{i+1}]$. Notice that we always have $x_i \in D_i$ and, since we have chosen the x_i's equally spaced, x_i is at the centre of the finite element D_i; see Figure D.1.

We define our basis functions $\psi_i(x)$ by following properties (see Figure D.2):

- $\psi_i(x)$ is zero for x not in D_i, i.e. $\psi_i(x) = 0$ for $x < x_{i-1}$ and for $x > x_{i+1}$;

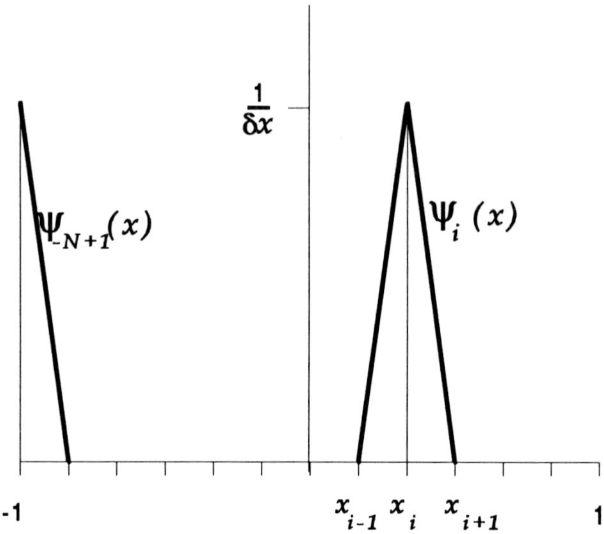

Figure D.2: Typical basis functions for the finite-element method.

- $\psi_i(x)$ is zero at the ends of D_i, i.e. $\psi_i(x_{i-1}) = \psi_i(x_{i+1}) = 0$;
- $\psi_i(x)$ is unity at the mid point of D_i, i.e. $\psi_i(x_i) = 1$;
- $\psi_i(x)$ is a linear function on $[x_{i-1}, x_i]$ and on $[x_i, x_{i+1}]$.
- $\psi_i(x)$ is continuous for all $-1 \le x \le 1$.

In Figure D.2 we illustrate typical basis functions. An exact formula for the basis function $\psi_i(x)$ is

$$\psi_i(x) = \frac{1}{\delta x}\begin{cases} 0 & x < x_{i-1} \\ (x - x_{i-1}) & x_{i-1} < x < x_i \\ (x_i - x) & x_i < x < x_{i+1} \\ 0 & x > x_{i+1} \end{cases}$$

although this is not especially helpful. It suffices to make two observations.

Firstly, note that for $\phi(x) \in \mathcal{K}_n$

$$\phi(x) = \sum_j \phi_j \psi_j(x) \quad \text{is equivalent to} \quad \phi(x_i) = \phi_i$$

since $\psi_j(x_i) = 0$ for $i \neq j$ and $\psi_i(x_i) = 1$. Therefore by approximating

$$f(x) = \sum_j f_j \psi_j(x) \quad \Leftrightarrow \quad f_i = f(x_i),$$

the conditions (D.3), that $u(x) \geq f(x)$, and (D.5), $\phi(x) \geq f(x)$, are reduced to the conditions

$$u_i \geq f_i, \quad \phi_i \geq f_i.$$

If we introduce the vector $\boldsymbol{f} = (f_1, f_2, \ldots, f_n)$, then we can write conditions (D.3), (D.5) as

$$\boldsymbol{u} \geq \boldsymbol{f}, \quad \boldsymbol{\phi} \geq \boldsymbol{f}.$$

Secondly, we note that

$$\psi'(x) = \frac{1}{\delta x} \begin{cases} 0 & x < x_{i-1} \\ 1 & x_{i-1} < x < x_i \\ -1 & x_i < x < x_{i+1} \\ 0 & x > x_{i+1} \end{cases}$$

where δx is the constant distance between the nodes (or half the length of an element D_i). This result is important, since it implies that

$$A_{ij} = \int_{-1}^{1} \psi_i'(x)\psi_j'(x)\, dx = \frac{1}{\delta x} \begin{cases} 2 & j = i \\ -1 & j = i \pm 1 \\ 0 & j \neq i, i \pm 1 \end{cases}$$

The consequence is that the matrix $\mathbf{A}$ in (D.6) can be written as $\mathbf{A} = (\delta x)^{-1}\mathbf{B}$, where $\mathbf{B}$ is the matrix

$$\mathbf{B} = \begin{pmatrix} 2 & -1 & 0 & \cdots & 0 \\ -1 & 2 & -1 & & \vdots \\ 0 & -1 & 2 & \ddots & 0 \\ \vdots & & \ddots & \ddots & -1 \\ 0 & \cdots & 0 & -1 & 2 \end{pmatrix}, \tag{D.7}$$

defined in (20.4).

With this notation, our finite-element approximation to the variational inequality problem (D.1) is to find a vector $\boldsymbol{u}$ such that

$$\boldsymbol{u} \geq \boldsymbol{f}, \quad \boldsymbol{u} \cdot \mathbf{B}(\boldsymbol{\phi} - \boldsymbol{u}) \geq 0 \quad \text{for all } \boldsymbol{\phi} \geq \boldsymbol{f}. \tag{D.8}$$

The $1/\delta x$ makes no difference to the inequality, and has been removed.

D.2.3 Solving the finite-element equations

We now show that problem (D.8) is, in fact, equivalent to the finite-difference problem, (20.3). This means that we solve the finite-element equations by exactly the same process we use to solve the finite-difference equations. First we show that (D.8) implies (20.3) and then the converse.

From (D.8) we note that $\boldsymbol{u} - \boldsymbol{f} \geq 0$ automatically.

Next, since $\mathbf{B}$ is symmetric,

$$\boldsymbol{a} \cdot \mathbf{B}\boldsymbol{b} = \boldsymbol{b} \cdot \mathbf{B}\boldsymbol{a},$$

and thus we can write the inequality in (D.8) as

$$(\boldsymbol{\phi} - \boldsymbol{u}) \cdot \mathbf{B}\boldsymbol{u} \geq 0. \tag{D.9}$$

We rewrite (D.9) in the form

$$\boldsymbol{\phi} \cdot \mathbf{B}\boldsymbol{u} \geq \boldsymbol{u} \cdot \mathbf{B}\boldsymbol{u},$$

for all $\boldsymbol{\phi} \geq \boldsymbol{f}$. We now observe that $\mathbf{B}$ is positive definite, i.e.

$$\boldsymbol{u} \cdot \mathbf{B}\boldsymbol{u} > 0 \quad \text{for} \quad \boldsymbol{u} \neq \mathbf{0}.$$

This implies that every component of $\mathbf{B}\boldsymbol{u}$ must be positive, that is $\mathbf{B}\boldsymbol{u} \geq \mathbf{0}$.

(If this were not the case, we could find some $\boldsymbol{\phi} \geq \boldsymbol{f}$ such that $\boldsymbol{\phi} \cdot \mathbf{B}\boldsymbol{u} < 0$ as the following argument shows. Suppose that the i-th component of $\mathbf{B}\boldsymbol{u}$ is negative. Choose all of the components of $\boldsymbol{\phi}$, except the i-th one, to be as small (but positive) as the condition $\boldsymbol{\phi} \geq \boldsymbol{f}$ will permit. Now choose the i-th component of $\boldsymbol{\phi}$ to be arbitrarily large, so that the product of the i-th components of $\boldsymbol{\phi}$ and $\mathbf{B}\boldsymbol{u}$ is arbitrarily large and negative. By choosing the i-th component of $\boldsymbol{\phi}$ large enough, we must be able to make $\boldsymbol{\phi} \cdot \mathbf{B}\boldsymbol{u} < 0$. But this is inconsistent with $\boldsymbol{u} \cdot \mathbf{B}\boldsymbol{u} > 0$. Therefore, $\mathbf{B}\boldsymbol{u} \geq \mathbf{0}$.)

It only remains to show that $(\boldsymbol{u} - \boldsymbol{f}) \cdot \mathbf{B}\boldsymbol{u} = 0$. This follows because $\mathbf{B}\boldsymbol{u} \geq \mathbf{0}$, $\boldsymbol{u} - \boldsymbol{f} \geq 0$ and therefore we must have

$$(\boldsymbol{u} - \boldsymbol{f}) \cdot \mathbf{B}\boldsymbol{u} \geq 0.$$

We now use the fact that $\boldsymbol{f} \geq \boldsymbol{f}$, so (D.9) must hold with $\boldsymbol{\phi} = \boldsymbol{f}$, showing that

$$(\boldsymbol{f} - \boldsymbol{u}) \cdot \mathbf{B}\boldsymbol{u} \geq 0.$$

The only possibility is that

$$(\boldsymbol{u} - \boldsymbol{f}) \cdot \mathbf{B}\boldsymbol{u} = 0.$$

Thus we have shown that (D.8) implies that $\boldsymbol{u}$ satisfies

$$(\boldsymbol{u} - \boldsymbol{f}) \cdot \mathbf{B}\boldsymbol{u} = 0, \quad \mathbf{B}\boldsymbol{u} \geq 0, \quad (\boldsymbol{u} - \boldsymbol{f}) \geq 0. \tag{D.10}$$

This is identical to (20.3).

We now show that the finite-difference problem, (20.3) or (D.10), for the linear complementarity problem implies the finite-element problem (D.8) for the variational inequality.

Assume that $\boldsymbol{\phi}$ is any vector satisfying $\boldsymbol{\phi} \geq \boldsymbol{f}$. From (D.10) we have $\mathbf{B}\boldsymbol{u} \geq \mathbf{0}$, so that we must also have

$$(\boldsymbol{\phi} - \boldsymbol{f}) \cdot \mathbf{B}\boldsymbol{u} \geq 0.$$

Since (20.3) has $(\boldsymbol{u} - \boldsymbol{f}) \cdot \mathbf{B}\boldsymbol{u} = 0$ we find, by subtraction, that

$$\begin{aligned}(\boldsymbol{\phi} - \boldsymbol{u}) \cdot \mathbf{B}\boldsymbol{u} &= [(\boldsymbol{\phi} - \boldsymbol{f}) - (\boldsymbol{u} - \boldsymbol{f})] \cdot \mathbf{B}\boldsymbol{u} \\ &= (\boldsymbol{\phi} - \boldsymbol{f}) \cdot \mathbf{B}\boldsymbol{u} - (\boldsymbol{u} - \boldsymbol{f}) \cdot \mathbf{B}\boldsymbol{u} \\ &= (\boldsymbol{\phi} - \boldsymbol{f}) \cdot \mathbf{B}\boldsymbol{u} \\ &\geq 0.\end{aligned}$$

Together with the symmetry of $\mathbf{B}$, this implies that

$$\boldsymbol{u} \cdot \mathbf{B}(\boldsymbol{\phi} - \boldsymbol{u}) = (\boldsymbol{\phi} - \boldsymbol{u}) \cdot \mathbf{B}\boldsymbol{u} \geq 0, \quad \text{for any } \boldsymbol{\phi} \geq \boldsymbol{f}.$$

Since (20.3), (D.10) also asserts that $\boldsymbol{u} \geq \boldsymbol{f}$, we see that problem (20.3), (D.10) implies that

$$\boldsymbol{u} \geq \boldsymbol{f}, \quad \boldsymbol{u} \cdot \mathbf{B}(\boldsymbol{\phi} - \boldsymbol{u}) \geq 0, \quad \text{for all } \boldsymbol{\phi} \geq \boldsymbol{f},$$

which is, of course, problem (D.8). Thus the finite-difference discretisation (20.3) and (D.10) of the linear complementarity problem (20.1) and (20.2), and the finite-element approximation (D.8) of the variational inequality (D.1) are equivalent.

Therefore, the finite-difference solution of the linear complementarity problem (20.1), (20.2) and the finite-element solution of the variational inequality (D.1) lead to exactly the same numerical problem. We have already shown in Chapter 20 how to solve it. The importance of the finite-element approach is that it allows rigorous error estimates to be obtained for the numerical solution. That is, the proof of the convergence of the projected SOR scheme is most easily given in terms of the finite-element solution for the variational inequality, rather than the finite-difference solution of the linear complementarity problem. The details of the convergence proofs may be found in Elliott & Ockendon (1982).

Note that the equivalence of the numerical methods for the linear complementarity problem and the variational inequality can be used (subject to a proof of the convergence) to infer the equivalence of the two formulations of the obstacle problem.

D.3 American options

D.3.1 Variational inequality formulation

As in Chapter 7, we can write an American option problem problem in the variational inequality form

Find $u \in \mathcal{K}$ such that

$$\int_{-x^-}^{x^+} \frac{\partial u}{\partial \tau}(\phi - u) + \frac{\partial u}{\partial x}\left(\frac{\partial \phi}{\partial x} - \frac{\partial u}{\partial x}\right) dx \geq 0 \qquad \text{(D.11)}$$

for all $\phi \in \mathcal{K}$ and for all $0 \leq \tau \leq \frac{1}{2}\sigma^2 T$. Here ϕ is a test function, and the space of test functions, $\mathcal{K}$ is defined as follows; $\phi(x,\tau)$ is a test function (i.e. $\phi(x,\tau) \in \mathcal{K}$) if and only if

- $\phi(x,\tau)$ and $\partial\phi/\partial\tau$ are both continuous and $\partial\phi/\partial x$ is piecewise continuous;
- $\phi(x,\tau) \geq g(x,\tau)$ for all x and τ;
- $\phi(x^+,\tau) = g(x^+,\tau)$ and $\phi(-x^-,\tau) = g(-x^-,\tau)$;

- $\phi(0,x) = g(0,x)$.

Here $g(x,\tau)$ is the transformed payoff function, which for the put is

$$g(x,\tau) = e^{\frac{1}{4}((k_2-1)^2+4k_1)\tau} \max\left(e^{\frac{1}{2}(k_2-1)x} - e^{\frac{1}{2}(k_2+1)x}, 0\right),$$

for the call is

$$g(x,\tau) = e^{\frac{1}{4}((k_2-1)^2+4k_1)\tau} \max\left(e^{\frac{1}{2}(k_2+1)x} - e^{\frac{1}{2}(k_2-1)x}, 0\right),$$

and for the cash-or-nothing binary call is

$$g(x,\tau) = e^{\frac{1}{4}((k_2-1)^2+4k_1)\tau} \begin{cases} 0 & x < 0 \\ be^{\frac{1}{2}(k_2-1)x} & x \geq 0 \end{cases}$$

(see Section 17.1). It follows that $u(x,\tau)$ is itself an element of $\mathcal{K}$, $u \in \mathcal{K}$.

D.3.2 Finite-element formulation

We now consider the finite-element solution to the variational inequality form, (D.11), of the American option problem. By analogy with the corresponding formulation of the obstacle problem, (D.1), we obtain a numerical solution to (D.11) by restricting the class of test functions in (D.11). Following the example of the variational inequality for the obstacle problem (D.1), we choose a finite set of *time-independent* basis functions

$$\{\psi_1(x), \psi_2(x), \ldots, \psi_n(x)\},$$

and assume that our solution $u(x,\tau)$ and test functions $\phi(x)$ can be expressed in the form

$$\begin{aligned} u(x,\tau) &= \sum_{i=1}^{n} u_i(\tau)\psi_i(x), \\ \phi(x,\tau) &= \sum_{i=1}^{n} \phi_i(\tau)\psi_i(x). \end{aligned} \qquad \text{(D.12)}$$

The only important difference between the approach to the obstacle problem and the American put problem is that, since the latter is a time-dependent problem, the coefficients of the basis functions are time-dependent.

The condition that u and all test functions ϕ should be greater than or equal to the payoff g imply the conditions

$$\sum_{i=1}^{n} u_i(\tau)\psi_i(x) \geq g(x,\tau), \quad \sum_{i=1}^{n} \phi_i(\tau)\psi_i(x) \geq g(x,\tau), \tag{D.13}$$

on the test function coefficients $u_i(\tau)$ and $\phi_i(\tau)$.

If we substitute expressions (D.12) into the variational inequality (D.11) and introduce the notation

$$M_{ij} = \int_{-x^-}^{x^+} \psi_i(x)\psi_j(x)\,dx, \quad K_{ij} = \int_{-x^-}^{x^+} \psi_i'(x)\psi_j'(x)\,dx, \tag{D.14}$$

the resulting problem can be written in the form

$$\sum_{i=1}^{n}\sum_{j=1}^{n} M_{ij}\frac{du_i}{d\tau}(\phi_j - u_j) + K_{ij}u_i(\phi_j - u_j) \geq 0$$

for all admissible functions $\phi_i(\tau)$.

We introduce the matrices $\mathbf{M}$ and $\mathbf{K}$, whose elements are M_{ij} and K_{ij} respectively, and the vectors $\boldsymbol{u} = (u_1, u_2, \ldots, u_n)$, $\boldsymbol{\phi} = (\phi_1, \phi_2, \ldots, \phi_n)$. We can then write the system of equations above in the matrix form

$$(\boldsymbol{\phi} - \boldsymbol{u}) \cdot \left(\mathbf{M}\frac{d\boldsymbol{u}}{d\tau} + \mathbf{K}\boldsymbol{u}\right) \geq 0. \tag{D.15}$$

We split our τ interval into a finite number of steps of length $\delta\tau$ and make the difference approximation

$$\frac{d\boldsymbol{u}}{d\tau} \approx \frac{\boldsymbol{u}(\tau + \delta\tau) - \boldsymbol{u}(\tau)}{\delta\tau}.$$

or, with $\boldsymbol{u}^m = \boldsymbol{u}(m\,\delta\tau)$,

$$\frac{d\boldsymbol{u}}{d\tau} = \left(\frac{\boldsymbol{u}^{m+1} - \boldsymbol{u}^m}{\delta\tau}\right) + O(\delta\tau).$$

We make an average θ-approximation (as in the finite-difference method)

$$\mathbf{K}\boldsymbol{u} = \theta\mathbf{K}\boldsymbol{u}^{m+1} + (1-\theta)\mathbf{K}\boldsymbol{u}^m,$$

and write (D.15) in the discretised form

$$(\boldsymbol{\phi}^{m+1} - \boldsymbol{u}^{m+1}) \cdot \left(\mathbf{M}(\boldsymbol{u}^{m+1} - \boldsymbol{u}^m) + \delta\tau\,\mathbf{K}(\theta\boldsymbol{u}^{m+1} + (1-\theta)\boldsymbol{u}^m)\right) \geq 0. \tag{D.16}$$

D.3.3 Finite-element discretisation

We divide the interval $[-x^-, x^+]$ into n equally spaced nodes, $x_i = -x^- + i\,\delta x$, so $x_0 = -x^-$, $x_n = x^+$. As for the obstacle problem, we introduce the basis functions $\psi_i(x)$ given by

$$\psi_i(x) = \frac{1}{\delta x}\begin{cases} 0 & x < x_{i-1} \\ (x - x_{i-1}) & x_{i-1} \leq x < x_i \\ (x_i - x) & x_i \leq x < x_{i+1} \\ 0 & x > x_{i+1} \end{cases}$$

Then we find that, as in the obstacle problem, we have

$$u_i(\tau) = u(x_i, \tau), \quad \phi_i(\tau) = \phi(x_i, \tau),$$

and writing

$$g_i(\tau) = g(x_i, \tau)$$

we find that the constraints (D.13) reduce to

$$\boldsymbol{u}^m \geq \boldsymbol{g}^m, \quad \boldsymbol{\phi}^m \geq \boldsymbol{g}^m, \tag{D.17}$$

where $\boldsymbol{g}^m = (g_1(m\,\delta\tau), \ldots, g_n(m\,\delta\tau))$. The initial conditions reduce to

$$\boldsymbol{u}^0 = \boldsymbol{g}^0. \tag{D.18}$$

With this choice of basis functions $\psi_i(x)$, we have

$$M_{ij} = K_{ij} = 0 \quad \text{unless} \quad i = j \text{ or } i = j \pm 1.$$

We can simplify the problem even further by using the 'lumped mass' integration rule (frequently used in finite elements; see for example Elliott & Ockendon (1982) or Crank (1984)) for the M_{ij} terms to reduce the matrix $\mathbf{M}$ to a diagonal matrix (if we use the same technique as we did in the previous section, $\mathbf{M}$ would be tridiagonal). Specifically, we use the rule that

$$M_{ij} = \int_{-x^-}^{x^+} \psi_i(x)\psi_j(x)\,dx \approx 2\delta x \sum_{k=1}^{n} \psi_i(x_k)\psi_j(x_k),$$

then we find that $M_{ij} = 0$ if $i \neq j$ and $M_{ij} = \delta x$ if $i = j$. Thus we can rewrite (D.16) as

$$\left(\boldsymbol{\phi}^{m+1} - \boldsymbol{u}^{m+1}\right)\cdot\left(\boldsymbol{u}^{m+1} + \frac{\delta\tau}{\delta x}\theta\mathbf{K}\boldsymbol{u}^{m+1} - \boldsymbol{u}^m + \frac{\delta\tau}{\delta x}(1-\theta)\mathbf{K}\boldsymbol{u}^m\right) \geq \mathbf{0}. \tag{D.19}$$

With this choice of basis functions,

$$K_{ij} = \frac{1}{\delta x}\begin{cases} 2 & i = j \\ -1 & i = j \pm 1 \\ 0 & i \neq j, j \pm 1 \end{cases}$$

Thus, we can put $\mathbf{K} = \mathbf{B}/\delta x$ where $\mathbf{B}$ is the tridiagonal matrix with diagonal elements 2 and off-diagonal elements -1, given in (D.7).

Introducing the familiar

$$\alpha = \frac{\delta\tau}{(\delta x)^2},$$

we see that (D.19) can be rearranged to give

$$\left(\boldsymbol{\phi}^{m+1} - \boldsymbol{u}^{m+1}\right) \cdot \left((\mathbf{I} + \alpha\theta\mathbf{B})\boldsymbol{u}^{m+1} - (\mathbf{I} - \alpha(1-\theta)\mathbf{B})\boldsymbol{u}^{m}\right) \geq 0,$$

where $\mathbf{I}$ is the identity matrix. Observe that $\mathbf{I} + \alpha\theta\mathbf{B}$ is equal to the matrix $\mathbf{C}$ defined in (21.17) and used in the finite-difference approximation to the linear complementarity form of the American put problem, (21.18). We also note, after inspection of equations (21.14), (21.15), that the term

$$(\mathbf{I} - \alpha(1-\theta)\mathbf{B})\boldsymbol{u}^{m}$$

is, effectively, the same quantity as the vector $\boldsymbol{b}^m$ arising in (21.18). If we therefore define $\boldsymbol{b}^m$ here to be

$$\boldsymbol{b}^m = \boldsymbol{u}^m - \alpha(1-\theta)\mathbf{B}\boldsymbol{u}^m, \qquad \text{(D.20)}$$

or, in component form, define b_n^m by

$$b_n^m = V_n^m + \alpha(1-\theta)(V_{n+1}^m - 2V_n^m + V_{n-1}^m),$$

then we can rewrite (D.19) in the form

$$\left(\boldsymbol{\phi}^{m+1} - \boldsymbol{u}^{m+1}\right) \cdot \left(\mathbf{C}\boldsymbol{u}^{m+1} - \boldsymbol{b}^m\right) \geq 0. \qquad \text{(D.21)}$$

Thus, in total, our finite-element approximation of the variational inequality (D.11) is to solve problem (D.21) for all test vectors $\boldsymbol{\phi}^m$ that satisfy condition (D.17), subject to the initial condition (D.18) and where the vector $\boldsymbol{b}^m$ is calculated from $\boldsymbol{u}^m$ using (D.20).

D.4 Solution of the finite-element problem

We now show that the finite-element problem (D.17), (D.18), (D.20), (D.21) for the variational inequality (D.11) is identical to the finite-difference problem (21.18) for the linear complementarity problem (21.5).

We first show that (21.18) implies (D.21). If $\boldsymbol{u}^{m+1}$ is a solution of (21.18) then we have

$$\begin{aligned}&(\boldsymbol{\phi}^{m+1} - \boldsymbol{u}^{m+1}) \cdot (\mathbf{C}\boldsymbol{u}^{m+1} - \boldsymbol{b}^m) = \\ &(\boldsymbol{\phi}^{m+1} - \boldsymbol{g}^{m+1}) \cdot (\mathbf{C}\boldsymbol{u}^{m+1} - \boldsymbol{b}^m) - (\boldsymbol{u}^{m+1} - \boldsymbol{g}^{m+1}) \cdot (\mathbf{C}\boldsymbol{u}^{m+1} - \boldsymbol{b}^m).\end{aligned}$$

Equation (21.18) asserts that

$$\mathbf{C}\boldsymbol{u}^{m+1} - \boldsymbol{b}^m \geq 0,$$

and that

$$(\boldsymbol{u}^{m+1} - \boldsymbol{g}^{m+1}) \cdot (\mathbf{C}\boldsymbol{u}^{m+1} - \boldsymbol{b}^m) = 0,$$

so it follows that

$$\begin{aligned}(\boldsymbol{\phi}^{m+1} - \boldsymbol{u}^{m+1}) \cdot (\mathbf{C}\boldsymbol{u}^{m+1} - \boldsymbol{b}^m) &= (\boldsymbol{\phi}^{m+1} - \boldsymbol{g}^{m+1}) \cdot (\mathbf{C}\boldsymbol{u}^{m+1} - \boldsymbol{b}^m) \\ &\geq 0,\end{aligned}$$

as $\boldsymbol{\phi}^m \geq \boldsymbol{g}^m$, and this is true for all test function vectors $\boldsymbol{\phi}^m$. Thus we have (D.21).

Starting now with (D.21), (D.17) and (D.18), we derive (21.18). We write (D.21) in the form

$$\boldsymbol{\phi}^{m+1} \cdot (\mathbf{C}\boldsymbol{u}^{m+1} - \boldsymbol{b}^m) \geq \boldsymbol{u}^{m+1} \cdot (\mathbf{C}\boldsymbol{u}^{m+1} - \boldsymbol{b}^m).$$

For fixed $\mathbf{C}^{m+1}$ and $\boldsymbol{b}^m$, the right-hand side of this equation is clearly a bounded constant. If, however, any component of $(\mathbf{C}\boldsymbol{u}^{m+1} - \boldsymbol{b}^m)$ is negative, then by choosing the corresponding component of $\boldsymbol{\phi}^{m+1}$ to be arbitrarily large (which is certainly consistent with the constraint the $\boldsymbol{\phi}^m \geq \boldsymbol{g}^m$) then we can make the left-hand side as large and negative as we please. This is inconsistent with the inequality, and therefore we must have

$$(\mathbf{C}\boldsymbol{u}^{m+1} - \boldsymbol{b}^m) \geq \mathbf{0}.$$

We also know from (D.17) that $\boldsymbol{u}^{m+1} - \boldsymbol{g}^{m+1} \geq \mathbf{0}$, and consequently we must have

$$(\boldsymbol{u}^{m+1} - \boldsymbol{g}^{m+1}) \cdot (\mathbf{C}\boldsymbol{u}^{m+1} - \boldsymbol{b}^{m}) \geq 0.$$

From equation (D.21), however, we see that on putting $\boldsymbol{\phi}^{m+1} = \boldsymbol{g}^{m+1}$ we have

$$(\boldsymbol{u}^{m+1} - \boldsymbol{g}^{m+1}) \cdot (\mathbf{C}\boldsymbol{u}^{m+1} - \boldsymbol{b}^{m}) \leq 0,$$

and so we must have

$$(\boldsymbol{u}^{m+1} - \boldsymbol{g}^{m+1}) \cdot (\mathbf{C}\boldsymbol{u}^{m+1} - \boldsymbol{b}^{m}) = 0.$$

We have therefore derived (21.18) from the finite-element formulation of the variational inequality.

Thus the numerical solution of the American option problem by either finite-difference methods applied to the linear complementarity formulation or by finite-element methods applied to the variational inequality is the same.

Further reading

- See Davies (1980) and and Strang & Fix (1973) for more about the finite-element method in general.

- See Elliott & Ockendon (1982) and Crank (1984) for more about the use of the finite-element method for free boundary problems.

Appendix E

Summary of Differential Equations

To conclude the book we bring together many of the partial differential equation models for option prices and their boundary and final conditions. Details of these options and their modelling may be found in the text, as can the differences in final and boundary conditions for call and put versions, effects of dividends, time-dependent parameters, etc.

E.1 Vanilla options

The Black–Scholes model for a European call

The original Black–Scholes equation is

$$\frac{\partial V}{\partial t} + \tfrac{1}{2}\sigma^2 S^2 \frac{\partial^2 V}{\partial S^2} + rS\frac{\partial V}{\partial S} - rV = 0,$$

with final condition

$$V(S,T) = \max(S - E, 0),$$

and boundary conditions

$$V(0,t) = 0$$

and

$$V(S,t) \sim S \quad \text{as} \quad S \to \infty.$$

There is an explicit solution.

The Black–Scholes model for a European put

The equation is still

$$\frac{\partial V}{\partial t} + \tfrac{1}{2}\sigma^2 S^2 \frac{\partial^2 V}{\partial S^2} + rS\frac{\partial V}{\partial S} - rV = 0,$$

but with final condition

$$V(S,T) = \max(E - S, 0)$$

and boundary conditions

$$V(0,t) = Ee^{-r(T-t)}$$

and

$$V(S,t) \to 0 \quad \text{as} \quad S \to \infty.$$

There is an explicit solution.

The European call with constant and continuous dividend yield

$$\frac{\partial V}{\partial t} + \tfrac{1}{2}\sigma^2 S^2 \frac{\partial^2 V}{\partial S^2} + (r - D_0)S\frac{\partial V}{\partial S} - rV = 0.$$

The final condition is still

$$V(S,T) = \max(S - E, 0)$$

and one boundary condition is still

$$V(0,t) = 0;$$

the other boundary condition is

$$V(S,t) \sim Se^{-D_0(T-t)} \quad \text{as} \quad S \to \infty.$$

There is an explicit solution.

The American call with constant and continuous dividend yield

The equation is

$$\frac{\partial V}{\partial t} + \tfrac{1}{2}\sigma^2 S^2 \frac{\partial^2 V}{\partial S^2} + (r - D_0) S \frac{\partial V}{\partial S} - rV = 0.$$

with final condition

$$V(S,T) = \max(S - E, 0)$$

and a boundary condition

$$V(0,t) = 0.$$

On the free boundary $S = S_f(t)$ we have

$$V(S_f(t),t) = \max(S_f(t) - E, 0)$$

and

$$\frac{\partial V}{\partial S}(S_f(t),t) = 1.$$

We require

$$V(S,t) \geq \max(S - E, 0)$$

everywhere.

E.2 Path-dependent options

Path-dependent options: general

We define

$$I(t) = \int_0^t f(S(\tau),\tau)\, d\tau.$$

Then an option whose payoff $\Lambda(S,I)$ depends on $I(T)$ satisfies

$$\frac{\partial V}{\partial t} + f(S,t)\frac{\partial V}{\partial I} + \tfrac{1}{2}\sigma^2 S^2 \frac{\partial^2 V}{\partial S^2} + (rS - D(S,t))\frac{\partial V}{\partial S} - rV = 0.$$

The final condition is

$$V(S,I,T) = \Lambda(S,I);$$

we do not give a general description of the boundary conditions here, but refer to the text and the following examples.

Barrier options

We must solve the basic Black–Scholes equation

$$\frac{\partial V}{\partial t} + \tfrac{1}{2}\sigma^2 S^2 \frac{\partial^2 V}{\partial S^2} + (rS - D(S,t))\frac{\partial V}{\partial S} - rV = 0.$$

subject to suitable final and boundary conditions. For an 'out' call option we have

$$V(S,T) = \max(S-E, 0),$$

with

$$V(X,t) = 0$$

(or equal to the rebate, Z) on the barrier $S = X$. The other boundary condition is the same as the vanilla option. For an 'in' call option we have

$$V(S,T) = 0$$

with

$$V(X,t) = C(X,t)$$

and

$$V(S,t) \to 0$$

away from the barrier. C is the value of a vanilla call option.

Arithmetic average strike call options

If the average is measured continuously, the option is a function of I where

$$I = \int_0^t S(\tau)\,d\tau,$$

and the differential equation is

$$\frac{\partial V}{\partial t} + S\frac{\partial V}{\partial I} + \tfrac{1}{2}\sigma^2 S^2 \frac{\partial^2 V}{\partial S^2} + (rS - D(S,t))\frac{\partial V}{\partial S} - rV = 0.$$

The final condition is

$$V(S,I,T) = \max(S - I/T, 0).$$

The boundary conditions are

$$V(S,I,t) \sim S \quad \text{as} \quad S \to \infty$$

and

$$V(0, I, t) = 0.$$

If the average is measured discretely then the basic Black–Scholes equation must be solved but with the jump condition

$$V(S, I, t_i^-) = V(S, I + S, t_i^+).$$

There are similarity solutions of the form

$$V(S, I, t) = SH(I/S, t).$$

Geometric average strike call options

If the average is measured continuously then the option depends on

$$I = \int_0^t \log S(\tau)\, d\tau,$$

and the differential equation is

$$\frac{\partial V}{\partial t} + \log S \frac{\partial V}{\partial I} + \tfrac{1}{2}\sigma^2 S^2 \frac{\partial^2 V}{\partial S^2} + (rS - D(S,t))\frac{\partial V}{\partial S} - rV = 0.$$

The final condition is

$$V(S, I, T) = \max(S - e^{I/T}, 0).$$

The boundary conditions are

$$V(S, I, t) \sim S \quad \text{as} \quad S \to \infty$$

and

$$V(0, I, t) = 0.$$

If the average is measured discretely then the basic Black–Scholes must be solved but with the jump condition

$$V(S, I, t_i^-) = V(S, I + \log S, t_i^+).$$

Average strike foreign exchange options

With

$$R = \frac{1}{S}\int_0^t S\,d\tau,$$

and r_f the foreign interest rate, we have

$$\frac{\partial V}{\partial t} + \tfrac{1}{2}\sigma^2 R^2 \frac{\partial^2 V}{\partial R^2} + \frac{\partial V}{\partial R} + (\sigma^2 - r + r_f)R\frac{\partial V}{\partial R} - rV = 0,$$

with final condition

$$V(R,T) = \max\left(1 - R/T, 0\right),$$

and boundary conditions

$$\frac{\partial V}{\partial t} + \frac{\partial V}{\partial R} - rV = 0 \quad \text{on} \quad R = 0$$

and

$$V(R,t) \to 0 \quad \text{as} \quad R \to \infty.$$

American average strike foreign exchange options

The equation is still

$$\frac{\partial V}{\partial t} + \tfrac{1}{2}\sigma^2 R^2 \frac{\partial^2 V}{\partial R^2} + \frac{\partial V}{\partial R} + (\sigma^2 - r + r_f)R\frac{\partial V}{\partial R} - rV = 0,$$

with final condition

$$V(R,T) = \max\left(1 - R/T, 0\right),$$

and boundary condition

$$V(R,t) \to 0 \quad \text{as} \quad R \to \infty;$$

now

$$V(R,t) \geq \max\left(1 - \frac{R}{t}, 0\right),$$

with the free boundary conditions on $R = R_f(t)$

$$V = \max(1 - R/t, 0)$$

and

$$\frac{\partial V}{\partial R} = -\frac{1}{t}.$$

Lookbacks

With the definition

$$J = \max_{0<\tau<t} S(\tau),$$

we have the Black–Scholes equation

$$\frac{\partial V}{\partial t} + \tfrac{1}{2}\sigma^2 S^2 \frac{\partial^2 V}{\partial S^2} + rS\frac{\partial V}{\partial S} - rV = 0,$$

with final condition

$$V(S, J, T) = J - S$$

and boundary conditions

$$V(0, J, t) = 0$$

and

$$\frac{\partial V}{\partial J}(J, J, t) = 0.$$

If the maximum is measured discretely then we must solve the basic Black–Scholes equation together with the jump condition

$$V(S, J, t_i^-) = V(S, \max(S, J), t_i^+).$$

E.3 Bond pricing

Convertible bonds with known interest rate

We must solve

$$\frac{\partial V}{\partial t} + \tfrac{1}{2}\sigma^2 S^2 \frac{\partial^2 V}{\partial S^2} + (rS - D)\frac{\partial V}{\partial S} - rV + K = 0,$$

where K is the coupon, with

$$V(S,T)=\max(nS,Z),$$

$$V(0,t)=Ze^{-r(T-t)}$$

and

$$V(S,t)\to nS \quad \text{as} \quad S\to\infty$$

subject to

$$V\geq nS.$$

Bonds with stochastic interest rates

With interest rates governed by

$$dr=w(r,t)\,dX+u(r,t)\,dt$$

the equation to be solved is

$$\frac{\partial V}{\partial t}+\tfrac{1}{2}w^2\frac{\partial^2 V}{\partial r^2}+(u-\lambda w)\frac{\partial V}{\partial r}-rV+K=0$$

with

$$V(r,T)=1$$

and

$$V(r,t)\to 0 \quad \text{as} \quad r\to\infty.$$

The remaining boundary condition depends upon the form of u and w but is equivalent to insisting that V remain finite.

Convertible bonds with stochastic interest rates

With S governed by

$$dS=\sigma S\,dX_1+\mu S\,dt$$

and

$$dr=w\,dX_2+u\,dt$$

the equation to be solved is

$$\frac{\partial V}{\partial t} + \tfrac{1}{2}\sigma^2 S^2 \frac{\partial^2 V}{\partial S^2} + \rho\sigma w S \frac{\partial^2 V}{\partial S \partial r} + \tfrac{1}{2} w^2 \frac{\partial^2 V}{\partial r^2} + (rS - D)\frac{\partial V}{\partial S} + (u - \lambda w)\frac{\partial V}{\partial r} - rV + K = 0,$$

with

$$V(S, r, T) = \max(nS, Z).$$

Boundary conditions are

$$V(0, r, t) = Ze^{-r(T-t)},$$

$$V(S, r, t) \sim nS \quad \text{as} \quad S \to \infty,$$

and

$$V(S, r, t) \to 0 \quad \text{as} \quad r \to \infty,$$

with the constraint

$$V(S, r, t) \geq nS.$$

The remaining boundary condition depends upon the form of u and w but is equivalent to insisting that V remain finite.

Appendix F

Bibliography

Baker, C.T.H. (1977) *The Numerical Treatment of Integral Equations*, Clarendon Press, Oxford.

Barone-Adesi, G. & Whaley, R.E. (1987) Efficient analytic approximation of American option values. J. Fin. **42** 301–320.

Barrett, J.W., Moore, G. & Wilmott, P. (1992) Inelegant efficiency. *Risk* Magazine, **9** (5) 82–84.

Black, F., Derman, E. & Toy, W. (1990) A one-factor model of interest rates and its application to Treasury bond options. Finan. Analysts J. **46** 33–9.

Black, F. & Scholes, M. (1973) The pricing of options and corporate liabilities. J. Pol. Econ. **81** 637–659.

Blank, S.C., Carter, C.A. & Schmiesing, B.H. (1991) *Futures and Options Markets*, Prentice-Hall.

Boyle, P.P. (1977) Options: a Monte Carlo approach. J. Finan. Econ. **4** 323–338.

Boyle, P.P. (1991) Multi-asset path-dependent options. FORC Conf., Warwick.

Boyle, P.P. & Emanuel, D. (1980) Discretely adjusted option hedges. J. Finan. Econ. **8** 259–282.

Brealey, R.A. (1983) *An Introduction to Risk and Return from Common Stock*, MIT Press, Cambridge, Mass.

Brennan, M. & Schwartz, E. (1977) Convertible bonds: valuation and optimal strategies for call and conversion. J. Fin. **32** 1699–1715.

Brennan, M. & Schwartz, E. (1978) Finite-difference methods and jump processes arising in the pricing of contingent claims: a synthesis. J. Finan. Quant. An. **13** 462–474

Carslaw, H.S. & Jaeger, J.C. (1989) *Conduction of Heat in Solids*, Oxford University Press.

Conze, A. & Viswanathan (1991) Path-dependent options—the case of lookback options. J. Fin. **46** 1893–1907.

Copeland, T., Koller, T. & Murrin, J. (1990) *Valuation: measuring and managing the value of companies*, Wiley.

Cox, D.R. & Miller, H.D. (1965) *The Theory of Stochastic Processes*, Chapman & Hall.

Cox, J.C., Ingersoll, J. & Ross, S. (1981) The relationship between forward prices and futures prices. J. Fin. Econ. **9** 321–346.

Cox, J.C., Ingersoll, J. & Ross, S. (1985) A theory of the term structure of interest rates. Econometrica **53** 385–467.

Cox, J.C. & Ross, S.A. (1976) The valuation of options for alternative stochastic processes. J. Fin. Econ. **3** 145–166.

Cox, J.C., Ross, S.A. & Rubinstein, M. (1979) Option pricing: a simplified approach, J. Fin. Econ., **7** 229–263.

Cox, J.C. & Rubinstein, M. (1985) *Options Markets*, Prentice Hall.

Crank, J., (1984) *Free and Moving Boundary Problems*, Oxford University Press.

Crank, J. (1989) *Mathematics of Diffusion*, Oxford University Press.

Cryer, C.W. (1971) The solution of a quadratic programming problem using systematic overrelaxation, SIAM J. Control **9** 385–392.

Davies, A.J. (1980) *The Finite Element Method: A first approach*, Oxford University Press.

Davis, M.H.A. & Norman, A.R. (1990) Portfolio selection with transaction costs. Math. Oper. Res. **15** 676–713.

Dewynne, J.N. & Wilmott, P. (1993 a) Partial to the exotic. *Risk* Magazine **6** (3) 38–46.

Dewynne, J.N. & Wilmott, P. (1993 b) Lookback options. OCIAM working paper, Mathematical Institute, Oxford University.

Dewynne, J.N. & Wilmott, P. (1993 c) Average rate options with discrete fixing. OCIAM working paper, Mathematical Institute, Oxford University.

Dewynne, J.N. & Wilmott, P. (1993 d) Average strike options—European and American. OCIAM working paper, Mathematical Institute, Oxford University.

Dothan, M.U. (1978) On the term structure of interest rates. J. Finan. Econ. **6** 59–69.

Duffie, D. (1992) *Dynamic Asset Pricing Theory*, Princeton.

Duffie, J.D. & Harrison, J.M. (1992) Arbitrage pricing of Russian options and perpetual lookback options. Working paper.

Elliott, C.M. & Ockendon, J.R. (1982) *Weak and Variational Methods for Free and Moving Boundary Problems*, Pitman.

Fama, E. (1965) The behaviour of stock prices. J. Bus. **38** 34–105.

Fitt, A.D., Dewynne, J.N. & Wilmott, P. (1993) An integral equation for the value of a stop-loss option. OCIAM working paper, Mathematical Institute, Oxford University.

Friedman, A. (1988) *Variational Principles and Free Boundary Problems*, Robert E. Krieger Publishing.

Garman, M. (1993) Recollections in tranquility, in *From Black-Scholes to Black Holes*, *Risk* magazine and Finex.

Garman, M. (1993) *Semper tempus fugit*, in *From Black-Scholes to Black Holes*, *Risk* magazine and Finex.

Geman, H. & Yor, M. (1992) Bessel processes, Asian options and perpetuities. FORC Conf., Warwick.

Gemmill, G. (1992) *Options Pricing*, McGraw-Hill.

Geske, R. (1978) Pricing of options with stochastic dividend yield. J. Fin. **33** 617–25.

Geske, R. (1979) The valuation of compound options. J. Finan. Econ. **7** 63–81.

Geske, R. & Shastri, K. (1985) Valuation by approximation: a comparison of alternative option valuation techniques, J. Fin. & Quant. Anal. **20**, 45–71.

Goldman, M.B., Sozin, H.B. & Gatto, M.A. (1979) Path dependent options: buy at the low, sell at the high. J. Fin. **34** 1111–1128.

Hammersley, J.M. & Handscomb, D.C. (1992) *Monte Carlo Methods*, Chapman and Hall.

Harper, J. (1993) Reducing parabolic partial differential equations to canonical form. To appear in Europ. J. Appl. Maths.

Harrison, J.M. & Kreps, D. (1979) Martingales and arbitrage in multiperiod securities markets. J. Econ. Theory **20** 381–408.

Harrison, J.M. & Pliska, S.R. (1981) Martingales and stochastic integrals in the theory of continuous trading. Stoch. Proc. Appl. **11** 261–271.

Hill, J.M. & Dewynne, J.N. (1990) *Heat Conduction*, CRC Press.

Ho, T. & Lee, S. (1986) Term structure movements and pricing interest rate contingent claims. J. Fin. **42** 1129–1142.

Hodges, S. & Neuberger, A. (1989) Optimal replication of contingent claims under transaction costs. Working paper, FORC, Warwick.

Hoggard, T., Whalley, A.E. & Wilmott, P. (1993) Hedging option portfolios in the presence of transaction costs. Adv. Fut. Opt. Res., forthcoming.

Hull, J. (1993) *Options, Futures and Other Derivative Securities*, second edition, Prentice-Hall.

Hull, J. & White, A. (1987) The pricing of options on assets with stochastic volatilities. J. Fin. **42** 281–300.

Hull, J. & White, A. (1990) Pricing interest rate derivative securities. Rev. Fin. Stud. **3** 573–92.

Ingersoll, J.E. (1987) *Theory of Financial Decision Making*, Rowman & Littlefield.

Jarrow, R.A. & Rudd, A. (1983) *Option Pricing*, Irwin.

Johnson, H.E. (1983) An analytical approximation to the American put price. J. Finan. Quant. An. **18** 141–148.

Johnson, L.W. & Riess, R.D. (1982) *Numerical Analysis* (2nd edition), Addison-Wesley.

Keener, J. (1988) *Principles of Applied Mathematics*, Addison-Wesley.

Kemna, A.G.Z. & Vorst, A.C.F. (1990) A pricing method for options based upon average asset values. J. Bank. Fin. March 113–129.

Kevorkian, J. (1990) *Partial Differential Equations: Analytical solution techniques*, Wadsworth and Brooks/Cole, Belmont, Calif.

Kinderlehrer, D. & Stampacchia, G. (1980) *An Introduction to Variational Inequalities and their Applications*, Academic Press.

Klemkosky, R.C. & Resnick, B.G. (1979) Put-call parity and market efficiency. J. Fin. **34** 1141–1155.

Klugman, R. (1992) Interest rate modelling, OCIAM working paper, Mathematical Institute, Oxford University.

Klugman, R. & Wilmott, P. (1993) A four parameter model for interest rates. OCIAM working paper, Mathematical Institute, Oxford University.

Leland, H.E. (1985) Option pricing and replication with transaction costs. J. Fin. **40** 1283–1301.

Leong, K. (1993) Estimates, guesstimates and rules of thumb, in *From Black-Scholes to Black Holes*, *Risk* magazine and Finex.

Levy, E. (1990) Asian arithmetic. *Risk* magazine May 7–8.

MacBeth, J.D. & Merville, L.J. (1979) An empirical examination of the Black-Scholes call option pricing model. J. Fin. **34** 1173–1186.

MacMillan, L.G. (1980) *Options as a Strategic Investment*, New York Inst. Fin., NY.

Mandelbrot, B. (1963) The variation of certain speculative prices. J. Bus. **36** 394–419.

Markowitz, H.M. (1991) Foundations of portfolio theory. J.Fin. **46** 469–477

McHattie, A. (1992) *The Investor's Guide to Warrants*, Pitman, London.

Merton, R.C. (1973) Theory of rational option pricing. Bell J. Econ. Manag. Sci. **4** 141–83.

Merton, R.C. (1976) Option pricing when underlying stock returns are discontinuous. J. Finan. Econ. **3** 125–144.

Merton, R.C. (1990) *Continuous Time Finance*, Blackwell.

Pearson, N. & Sun, T-S. (1989) A test of the Cox, Ingersoll, Ross model of the term structure of interest rates using the method of moments. Sloan School of Management, MIT.

Richards, J.I. & Youn, H.K (1990) *Theory of Distributions*, Cambridge University Press.

Richtmyer, R.D. & Morton, K.W. (1967) *Difference Methods for Initial-value Problems*, Wiley Interscience.

Risk Magazine (1993) *From Black-Scholes to Black Holes*, *Risk* Magazine and Finex.

Roll, R. (1977) An analytical formula for unprotected American call options on stocks with known dividends. J. Finan. Econ. **5** 251–258.

Rubinstein, M. (1992) Exotic options. FORC Conf., Warwick.

Schuss, Z. (1980) *Theory and Applications of Stochastic Differential Equations*, Wiley.

Sharpe, W.F. (1985) *Investments*, Prentice-Hall

Smith, G.D. (1985) *Numerical Solution of Partial Differential Equations: Finite Difference Methods* (3rd edition), Oxford University Press.

Spiegel, M. (1980) *Probability and Statistics*, McGraw-Hill.

Stephenson, G. (1980) *Partial Differential Equations for Scientists and Engineers*, Longman.

Stoer, J. & Bulirsch, R. (1993) *Introduction to Numerical Analysis*, second edition, Springer.

Strang, G. (1986) *Introduction to Applied Mathematics*, Wellesley-Cambridge Press.

Strang, G. & Fix, G.J. (1973) *An Analysis of the Finite Element Method*, Prentice-Hall.

Stulz, R.M. (1982) Options on the minimum or maximum of two risky assets. J. Finan. Econ. **10** 161–185.

Vasicek, O.A. (1977) An equilibrium characterization of the term structure. J. Fin. Econ. **5** 177–188.

Whaley, R. (1981) On the valuation of American call options on stocks with known dividends. J. Finan. Econ. **9** 207–211.

Whalley, A.E. & Wilmott, P. (1993) A hedging strategy and option valuation model with transaction costs. OCIAM working paper, Mathematical Institute, Oxford University.

Williams, W.E. (1980) *Partial Differential Equations*, Oxford University Press.

Wilmott, P. & Atkinson, C. (1992) Properties of random walk moving averages. IMA J. Math. Appl. Bus. Ind., forthcoming.

Index